Intersectional Encounters in the
Nineteenth-Century Archive

New Directions in Social and Cultural History

Series Editors: Sasha Handley (University of Manchester, UK), Rohan McWilliam (Anglia Ruskin University, UK) and Lucy Noakes (University of Brighton, UK)

Editorial Board:
Robert Aldrich, University of Sydney, Australia
James W. Cook, University of Michigan, USA
John H. Arnold, University of Cambridge, UK
Alison Rowlands, University of Essex, UK
Penny Summerfield, University of Manchester, UK
Mrinalini Sinha, University of Michigan, USA

The *New Directions in Social and Cultural History* series brings together the leading research in social and cultural history, one of the most exciting and current areas for history teaching and research, contributing innovative new perspectives to a range of historical events and issues. Books in the series engage with developments in the field since the post-cultural turn, showing how new theoretical approaches have impacted on research within both history and other related disciplines. Each volume will cover both theoretical and methodological developments on the particular topic, as well as combine this with an analysis of primary source materials.

Published:
New Directions in Social and Cultural History, ed. Sasha Handley,
Rohan McWilliam and Lucy Noakes (2018)
Art, Propaganda and Aerial Warfare in Britain during the Second World War,
Rebecca Searle (2020)
Welfare State Generation: Women, Agency and Class in Britain since 1945,
Eve Worth (2022)
Family History, Historical Consciousness and Citizenship: A New Social History,
Tanya Evans (2022)

Forthcoming:
Capital Labour in Victorian England: Manufacturing Consensus, Donna Loftus
British Humour and the Second World War: 'Keep Smiling Through',
edited by Juliette Pattinson and Lindsey Robb
Captive Fathers, Captive Children: Legacies of the War in the Far East,
Terry Smyth

Intersectional Encounters in the Nineteenth-Century Archive

New Essays on Power and Discourse

Edited by
Rachel Bryant Davies and Erin Johnson-Williams

BLOOMSBURY ACADEMIC
LONDON • NEW YORK • OXFORD • NEW DELHI • SYDNEY

BLOOMSBURY ACADEMIC
Bloomsbury Publishing Plc
50 Bedford Square, London, WC1B 3DP, UK
1385 Broadway, New York, NY 10018, USA
29 Earlsfort Terrace, Dublin 2, Ireland

BLOOMSBURY, BLOOMSBURY ACADEMIC and the Diana logo are trademarks of Bloomsbury Publishing Plc

First published in Great Britain 2023
This paperback edition published 2024

Copyright © Rachel Bryant Davies and Erin Johnson-Williams, 2023

Rachel Bryant Davies and Erin Johnson-Williams have asserted their right under the Copyright, Designs and Patents Act, 1988, to be identified as Authors of this work.

For legal purposes the Acknowledgements on pp. x–xi constitute an extension of this copyright page.

Series design by Liron Gilenberg | www.ironicitalics.com
Cover images © clockwise from top left: Many file folders, Nikada/Getty. Antique wooden storage boxes in an archive, Nikada/Getty. Many file folders blue toned, Nikada/Getty. Filing cabinets housing historical photographs from the Bettmann photographic collection, kept 220ft underground in temperature controlled facility within a limestone mine. Photo by Bob Ahern/Epics/Getty Images.

All rights reserved. No part of this publication may be reproduced or transmitted in any form or by any means, electronic or mechanical, including photocopying, recording, or any information storage or retrieval system, without prior permission in writing from the publishers.

Bloomsbury Publishing Plc does not have any control over, or responsibility for, any third-party websites referred to or in this book. All internet addresses given in this book were correct at the time of going to press. The author and publisher regret any inconvenience caused if addresses have changed or sites have ceased to exist, but can accept no responsibility for any such changes.

A catalogue record for this book is available from the British Library.

A catalog record for this book is available from the Library of Congress.

ISBN: HB: 978-1-3502-0033-3
PB: 978-1-3502-0034-0
ePDF: 978-1-3502-0035-7
eBook: 978-1-3502-0036-4

Series: New Directions in Social and Cultural History

Typeset by Integra Software Services Pvt. Ltd.

To find out more about our authors and books visit www.bloomsbury.com and sign up for our newsletters.

Contents

List of figures	vii
List of tables	ix
Acknowledgements	x
Notes on contributors	xii

1 Introduction: Encountering the intersectional archive
  Rachel Bryant Davies and Erin Johnson-Williams — 1

Part 1 Archival ownership

2 'Found in store': Working with source communities and difficult objects at Durham University's Oriental Museum *Rachel Barclay, Lauren Barnes, Gillian Ramsay, Craig Barclay and Helen Armstrong* — 31

3 Transforming the archive of slavery at the Tropenmuseum
  Adiva Lawrence — 51

4 Maqdala and the South Kensington Museum: 150 years later
  Alexandra Watson Jones — 71

Part 2 Colonial power

5 Encountering 'colonial science' in the visual archive: The natural history paintings of Raja Serfoji II of Tanjore (1777–1832) *David Lowther* — 91

6 Enclosing archival sound: Colonial singing as discipline and resistance
  Erin Johnson-Williams — 115

7 The infantilization of Indigeneity in colonial Australia *Roisín Laing* — 137

8 'Some nameless, dreadful wrong': Reading the silencing of police rape in the Indian colonial archive *Deana Heath* — 157

Part 3 Biographical silences

9 Completing the mosaic: Sara Baartman and the archive
  Tiziana Morosetti — 171

10 Mercury, sulphur baths and fine art: Censorship and the sexual health of John and Joséphine Bowes, founders of The Bowes Museum *Judith Phillips* — 187

11 Empowering the invisible: The archival legacy of Christian Cole
    Philip Burnett — 203

Part 4 Layered archives

12 The power of invisibility: Nursing nuns and archival gatekeeping
    Jemima Short — 221
13 The instability and ideology of the archive: Archival evidence and nineteenth-century British theatre *Jim Davis* — 239
14 'Our mind strives to restore the mutilated forms': Nineteenth-century virtual museum tours in children's periodicals *Rachel Bryant Davies* — 255
15 Afterword: Intersectional Albertopolis *Tim Barringer* — 281

Index — 302

Table

11.1 Pamphlets authored by Christian Cole and their present locations
(researched and prepared by Philip Burnett) 208

Acknowledgements

So many wonderful people have contributed to the creation of this book. Through navigating the precarities of being early career scholars, and the challenges of trying to write about, not to mention actually undertake, historical archival work during a global pandemic, the fact that we have only become even closer friends through the course of working on this volume is a testament to the extraordinary community of scholars who have supported us in this endeavour.

Thank you to Abigail Lane, Lucy Noakes, Sasha Handley and Rohan McWilliam at Bloomsbury for all of your support and guidance. Thank you as well to our anonymous reviewer for your encouragement of the project as a whole. To all of the authors in this book – Rachel Barclay, Lauren Barnes, Gillian Ramsay, Craig Barclay, Helen Armstrong, Adiva Lawrence, Alexandra Watson Jones, David Lowther, Roisín Laing, Deana Heath, Tiziana Morosetti, Judith Phillips, Philip Burnett, Jemima Short, Jim Davis and Tim Barringer – you have all generously contributed so much truly interdisciplinary work, and it has been such a pleasure working with each and every one of you. A special thanks go to Tim Barringer for coalescing so many of the intersectional themes together in the Afterword, for reading several drafts of the manuscript while it was in progress, and for delivering the keynote lecture for our initial workshop. Bennett Zon also read several of our own chapter drafts and has been unfailingly supportive both professionally and personally: thank you.

The wider community of the Centre for Nineteenth-Century Studies (CNCS) gave birth to this project and continues to be an incredible supportive network. We first met through a CNCS meeting in Durham in 2017, and were inspired and supported by CNCS Director Bennett Zon to develop a two-day interdisciplinary workshop, 'The Nineteenth-Century Archive as a Discourse of Power', which took place 8–9 February 2019 at Durham University's St Aidan's and Hatfield Colleges, and which was funded by the CNCS, the British Association for Victorian Studies, the Royal Historical Society, the Durham Centre for Classical Reception Studies and the Durham University Music Department. Many of the authors in this book participated, which led us to pursue the idea of the nineteenth-century archive as being *necessarily* intersectional across academic disciplines and museum sectors. Particular thanks go to Lindsay Macnaughton for chairing the postgraduate roundtable on historical archival work, which included Sarah Budasz, Thomas Couldridge, Carrie Long, Hannah Martin and Jemima Short. Rachel Barclay, Helen Armstrong and Craig Barclay provided a Handling Session at Durham's Oriental Museum on the first evening of the workshop, which was a turning point for many of our attendees in terms of bringing their disciplinary expertise into dialogue with sensitive issues around race, representation and ownership in material objects. Thank you also to the Oriental Museum for hosting Tim Barringer's keynote address. We would also like to thank Diane Tisdall, Angus

Patterson, Sadiah Qureshi, Joan Allen, Helen Roche, Laura O'Brien, Kate Newey, Jennifer Ingleheart and Bennett Zon for their workshop contributions, which were instrumental in helping to shape the future directions of this book. Rosemary Mitchell, who passed away in 2021, and who is so much missed, chaired the workshop's final roundtable. Her memory is very much with us, and her generosity and encouragement are felt throughout the pages of this book.

Finally, thank you to Robin and to Ed – for being there.

We are extremely grateful for the community of people that came together to make this volume possible. It is our hope that its publication is only the start of future intersectional conversations about archival meaning, past and present.

Notes on contributors

Helen Armstrong is the collections manager for Libraries and Collections at Durham University, UK. She started her career at the National Waterways Museum, worked at the V&A and has now been in Durham for fifteen years. Her area of specialist interest is terminology control and thesauri.

Craig Barclay is Head of Museums, Galleries and Exhibitions at Durham University, UK. He is responsible for the oversight of world-class collections (including two ACE Designated Collections) of art and archaeology, as well as the development and delivery of teaching across multiple courses. Internationally, Craig has contributed to the planning of major museum development projects in West Asia and museums capacity building initiatives in SE Asia, as well as collaborating with the Durham University's UNESCO Chair on multiple research-led projects in Nepal, Sri Lanka, Myanmar and East Asia.

Rachel Barclay is Curator of the Oriental Museum at Durham University, UK. Rachel trained as an Egyptologist at Oxford University, participating in Cambridge University excavations in Egypt. After working in international marketing across Southern Europe, North Africa and China she returned to the museum sector to join Oxford's Pitt Rivers Museum. Since moving to Durham Rachel has led the redisplay of the Oriental Museum's permanent galleries and an active programme of temporary exhibitions and installations. Rachel is heavily involved in university teaching across academic departments. Internationally, Rachel has worked on research projects and partnerships in China, Japan, Malaysia, Nepal, Sri Lanka, Taiwan and Vietnam.

Tim Barringer is Paul Mellon Professor of the History of Art at Yale University, USA. His books include *Men at Work: Art and Labour in Victorian England* and *Reading the Pre-Raphaelites*. He co-edited *Colonialism and the Object*, *Victorian Jamaica*, and *Art and the British Empire*.

Lauren Barnes is Lim Ai Fang Fellow at The University Gallery, Northumbria University, UK. In this role her responsibilities include collections management, curatorial and engagement projects, and collections research. Lauren is also undertaking a PhD at The University of Manchester, UK, where she is analysing the development of Korean collections in UK museums. She is a committee member of The British Korean Society and a member of both the International Research Centre for the History and Culture of Nanzhao and Dali Kingdoms at Northumbria University, and the University of Manchester's Digital Futures Research Network.

Rachel Bryant Davies is a Lecturer in Comparative Literature at Queen Mary, University of London, UK. Her research focuses on popular, playful and pedagogic adaptations of Greco-Roman antiquity. She is author of *Troy, Carthage and the Victorians: The Drama of Classical Ruins in the Nineteenth-Century Imagination* (CUP, 2018), *Victorian Epic Burlesques* (Bloomsbury, 2018) and with Barbara Gribling co-edited *Childhood Encounters with History in British Culture, 1750–1914* (Manchester University Press, 2020). Her current monograph project is *Classics at Play: Greco-Roman Antiquity in British Children's Culture, c. 1750–1914*.

Philip Burnett is Assistant Librarian at University College, Oxford, UK. His doctorate from the University of Bristol was titled 'Music and Mission: A Case Study of the Anglican-Xhosa Missions of the Eastern Cape, 1854–1880'. His current research focusses on the music of British overseas missions in the nineteenth century.

Jim Davis is Professor of Theatre Studies at the University of Warwick, UK. His most recent books are *Comic Acting and Portraiture in Late-Georgian and Regency England* (Cambridge, 2015), *Theatre & Entertainment* (2016) and *Dickens Dramatized* Volume II (Oxford, 2017). He is also joint-author of *Reflecting the Audience: London Theatregoing 1840–1880* (2001) and has edited a book on Victorian pantomime (2010). He has published many book chapters and articles on nineteenth-century theatre. He is an editor of the refereed journal *Nineteenth-Century Theatre and Film*.

Deana Heath is a Reader in Indian and Colonial History at the University of Liverpool, UK. Her research interests focus on colonial violence, particularly torture and sexual and gendered violence, as well as on colonial sovereignties and governmentalities. Her most recent books are *Colonial Terror: Torture and State Violence in Colonial India* (Oxford, 2021) and *South Asian Governmentalities: Michel Foucault and the Question of Postcolonial Orderings* (Cambridge, 2018), co-edited with Stephen Legg.

Erin Johnson-Williams is a Leverhulme Early Career fellow in the Department of Music at Durham University, UK. Her research focuses on decolonization, the imperial legacies of music education and soundscapes of colonial violence. Her current Leverhulme project examines the role of singing, religious experience and trauma in spaces of colonial incarceration, with particular focus on the concentration camps of the South African War.

Roisín Laing is a Leverhulme Early Career Fellow with the English Studies department and the Centre for Nineteenth-Century Studies at Durham University, UK. She finished her PhD at Durham in 2016, after which she undertook a Visiting Research Fellowship at the University of Sydney. She returned to Durham in 2017 to take up her current post, researching the intersection of nineteenth-century ideas about childhood, race and evolution.

Adiva Lawrence is a PhD candidate at the Wilberforce Institute for the Study of Slavery and Emancipation at the University of Hull, UK. She works on the representation of transatlantic slavery in museums and contemporary art from a transnational perspective and has written about art in Brazil and women artists. She is a 2019 Junior Research Fellow at the Research Center for Material Culture in Leiden.

David Lowther is Assistant Principal at University College, Durham University, UK. In his previous role as Leverhulme Early Career Fellow, his research focused on networks of scientific and artistic exchange, and the role of visual culture in the creation and codification of natural history knowledge in late eighteenth and early nineteenth-century India. His doctoral thesis (Newcastle, 2016) examined the scientific culture of late-Georgian and early-Victorian Britain, with a particular emphasis on Quinarian taxonomy and its impact on the development of zoology.

Tiziana Morosetti is an Associate Lecturer in Theatre and Performance at Goldsmiths, University of London, UK, and an associate with the African Studies Centre, Oxford, UK. Her research focuses on postcolonial and African theatre, and on representations of race, diversity and Blackness on the nineteenth-century and contemporary British stage. Her recent publications include the edited collections *Africa on the Contemporary London Stage* (Palgrave 2018) and (with Osita Okagbue) *The Palgrave Handbook of Theatre and Race* (2021). She is the General Secretary of the African Theatre Association (AfTA) and the co-founder and deputy director of the journal *Quaderni del '900*.

Judith Phillips is the Honorary Archivist at The Bowes Museum in Barnard Castle, County Durham, UK. She has over thirty years' experience as an archivist in local government and other record repositories. Since 2009 she has been engaged in cataloguing the archives held in the museum and supervising the archive service there for staff and members of the public. In 2020 she was awarded a doctorate by Teesside University for her dissertation 'National Identity, Gender, Social Status and Cultural Aspirations in Mid-Nineteenth Century England and France: Joséphine Bowes (1825–74), Collector and Museum Creator'.

Gillian Ramsay MA (Hons), MSc, MLitt is the Assistant Curator of the Oriental Museum at Durham University, UK. With a background in Near Eastern and Mediterranean archaeology, she started her career in commercial archaeology before moving into the museum sector, working in a range of organizations including the National Trust for Scotland and National Museums Scotland. Since joining the Oriental Museum she has been involved in undergraduate and postgraduate teaching across Durham University, supported a number of international partnerships and is active in developing the collections, with a particular focus on contemporary collecting.

Jemima Short is an Early Career Researcher who currently holds the post of Lecturer in French at Newcastle University, UK. Her interests include the intersections between gender, labour, politics and care with a particular focus on France in the long nineteenth century. Her book manuscript – based on a PhD funded by the AHRC and provisionally titled *An Invisible Workforce: Nursing Nuns in France (1830–1905)* – is forthcoming with Liverpool University Press.

Alexandra Watson Jones is a PhD Student at the University of St Andrews, UK. Her PhD research, a collaborative project with National Museums Scotland, explores British Collecting in Ethiopia from 1790 to 1960. She curated *Maqdala 1868* while working as the V&A's Assistant Curator of Metalwork from 2017 to 2019.

1

Introduction: Encountering the intersectional archive

Rachel Bryant Davies and Erin Johnson-Williams

Dust is the opposite thing to Waste, or at least, the opposite principle to Waste. It is about circularity, the impossibility of things disappearing, or going away, or being gone. Nothing *can be* destroyed. The fundamental lessons of [nineteenth-century] physiology, of cell-theory, and of neurology were to go with this ceaseless making and unmaking, the movement and transmutation of one thing to another. Nothing goes away.[1]

What does it mean, today, to encounter the nineteenth-century archive? What legacies of power and understanding – racial, institutional, ideological – inform the ways in which archives are curated and read? As Carolyn Steedman evocatively describes in her book *Dust: The Archive and Cultural History*, the nineteenth century was a time when the idea of material 'debris' became reified, codified and, out of compulsion, sometimes hidden.[2] In the epigraph above, Steedman relates the growth of the nineteenth-century archive to an impulse of 'ordering' the scientific (and also very imperial) western understandings of the world, where natural matter comprises a circular archive where 'nothing *can be* destroyed', and 'nothing goes away'.[3] When the researcher enters the dusty archive, Steedman, drawing on Derrida's construction of the Freudian 'death drive' in his essay 'Archive Fever',[4] describes how the historical researcher literally breathes in the airborne remnants of dead bodies once lived; the dust, emanating from 'official' archival documents, revealing its own story about what has been silenced. If nothing *can* go away because silenced 'waste' turns into particles that can never truly disappear, then the experience – both real and metaphorical – of breathing in archival dust is also an inherently physical, embodied inhalation of untold stories.[5] As explored vividly by scholars such as Nicola Abram, Christina Sharpe, Imtiaz Habib, Saidiya Hartman and Sadiah Qureshi, new archival narratives can, indeed, emerge from intersectional enquiries, through asking critical questions and adopting new forms of observing and understanding.[6]

At a time when mortality rates in many countries across the globe are rising, and the lack of access to institutional archives for researchers has coincided with a fresh veneration for what we might call the 'everyday ephemeral archive' – pictures of rainbows by children, photos of chalk drawings, collections of diaries in community deposits for Covid-19 archives – it feels timely to be asking questions about what the (hidden) 'dust' of the nineteenth-century record can tell us about today's world.[7] The context of the ongoing UK Covid-19 lockdowns of 2020–21, during which we drafted this Introduction, might on the surface have appeared to alleviate the historical researcher from the burden of breathing in too much unwarranted, distracting or uncomfortable archival dust. At the same time, the drive to 'know' the archive, even via digital, remote outlets, has perhaps only intensified academic fevers about the 'archival time' that Derrida once connected to being under 'house arrest',[8] as in reality we find ourselves enmeshed in a germ-conscious research ecosystem despite our disconnect from many material sources.[9]

This context of being 'away' from the institutional archive, and yet still under archival 'house arrest', offers a particularly crucial moment to examine how legacies of the past have shaped how we read, experience and critically listen to the 'debris' of history. If 'dust' is at the core of a relational archive – where material records are bound up with legacies of power and cultural memory – then an interdisciplinary discussion about how history has shaped our perceptions of archival value and access is not only timely, but also vital to understanding the archival ecosystems around us today. From the threat of viral germs, to climate-conscious academics deciding not to travel by air for conferences or research, we face a future where what constitutes an 'archive' *must* be intersectional.

The context of Covid-19 lockdowns has therefore created a unique environment for new political discussions about power, historiography and de/colonial value. Amidst the global rise of the Black Lives Matter protests in the summer of 2020, and ongoing calls for decolonization across academic and museum sectors, there has been a growth of conversations that explicitly link institutional power today to histories of nineteenth-century imperialism and bureaucratic control. Indeed, between an initial interdisciplinary workshop on the 'Nineteenth-Century Archive as a Discourse of Power' that we organized at Durham University through the Centre for Nineteenth-Century Studies (CNCS) in February 2019,[10] and the publication of this book, public conversations about institutions, ownership and access have reflected a rising sense of urgency around sensitively addressing ethical representation within archival holdings.[11] Collaborating on this project between the disciplines of Classics and musicology – in which we as editors were respectively trained – we found that the commonalities between our work lay in how nineteenth-century attempts at 'archiving' simultaneously curated and silenced new forms of historical power, whether through modes of pedagogy, canon formation, historical writing or performance. On a deeper structural level, we also found through our own experiences that many archival institutions today are endlessly grappling with their own legacies of how nineteenth-century structures of power – imperial, religious, capitalist – have shaped both their foundation and their legacies.

Such institutional and cultural reassessments have now brought academic discourses about the archive to a pivotal juncture. To a certain extent, the experience of compiling this collection of essays during a pandemic, combined with an increasing recognition of the urgent need to decolonize nineteenth-century history, provided us with an opportunity to examine our archival biases while being *away* from the archive – at least physically. On the one hand, spatial distance from 'The Archive' as a physical structure (i.e. as 'an institution') has inspired us to embrace a critical (re)assessment of the reification of archival authority as funnelled through a physical establishment. On the other hand, this enforced spatial distance has, to some extent, reinforced a fetishization of the physical archive, as many researchers now long for an archival experience outside of their homes, and may now view archival institutions through increasingly nostalgic lenses.[12] Furthermore, despite many utopian claims about open-access online sources, the reality is that researchers still often need logins from elite institutions to access material behind paywalls, therefore rendering those without institutional affiliations or the financial means to fully access digital information powerless.[13] Archival inequalities endure through new technologies – but the inequalities themselves are not new.

Intersectional methodologies

The cover design for this book is intentionally abstract. To a certain extent, the diverse images are (like the nineteenth-century archive itself), fantasies that invite readers to engage with their own preconceptions about the authority and permanence of the archive, as well as their attendant presumptions about access, and who the archive is really for.[14] Our cover does not point to any particular institutions because fantasies of the nineteenth-century archive, of course, do not 'look like' a homogenous entity: whether researchers imagine the archive to consist of wooden cabinets, shelves of boxed documents, glass cases, long corridors lined with books or even no physical institution at all, depends on cultural conditioning. Moreover, many researchers are taught, often within inherently hierarchical systems of learning, that crossing the threshold of a prestigious institutional archive is a measure either of our own professional success – or of social, racial or gendered privilege.[15]

The fetishization of 'accessing' the archive as the pinnacle of 'classified order' has been inherited from the nineteenth century, a time when archival institutions (which had, of course, existed for centuries) were expanded, systematized and reified in unprecedented ways.[16] The standardization and categorization of the material world – and its peoples – through the rise of newly regularized establishments such as prisons, schools, workhouses, museums, libraries, entertainment venues and universities, all came about through a substantial growth of bureaucratic forms of taxonomic systems that reified new hierarchies of classificatory power.[17] As the essays in this volume explore, however, the nineteenth-century archive existed both within and beyond physical institutions, reflecting a range of overlapping intersectional negotiations of power through attempts at ordering, classifying and narrating. Since most historical researchers today have, however, inherited many utopian fantasies about what an archive looks like (permanent, authoritative, categorical, 'clean', yet also 'dusty'), it is increasingly imperative to untangle many of our ingrained assumptions about the archive as a space of relational encounter – past and/or present, physical and/or virtual.

These tensions are strongly indicative of what we call here a 'new archival turn' for the early 2020s: a time when the nineteenth-century archive is increasingly understood to replicate western institutional hierarchies (imperial, settler colonial, religious or nationalist). The 'new archival turn', as embodied by the essays in this volume, envisions the historical archive as a relational site of discourse that is in constant tension with how nineteenth-century legacies are re-presented, fetishized and challenged in the present day.

The 'archive' more broadly is increasingly receiving critical scholarly attention. After Thomas Richards set the scene with publication of *The Imperial Archive* in 1993, more recent interdisciplinary research by scholars including Kirsty Reid and Fiona Paisley, Ann Laura Stoler, Antoinette Burton and Tony Ballantyne has engaged with such themes as postcolonialism and the construction of colonial archives as forms of power, which in turn have profound implications for nineteenth-century scholarship.[18] Building on research across the humanities on the 'archival turn' as a way to critique how archives have shaped the writing of history,[19] we propose that the intersectional connections across our chapters demonstrate how a 'new archival turn' is explicitly – and inescapably – in dialogue with the conversations around decolonization and institutionalized power that are happening in the present day. As we explore, a 'new archival turn' is as much about how the historical archive shapes our understanding of present-day power structures (archival or otherwise), as it is a study of the past. We therefore intend *Intersectional Encounters* to open possibilities for collaborative engagement with the nineteenth-century archive in all its various manifestations, examining, through specific case studies, how snapshots of different sorts of archival production and interpretation influence institutional discourses today. Our chapters broach critical and topical questions about how the complex discourses of power involved in creating nineteenth-century archives have impacted, and continue to influence, constructions of knowledge across disciplinary boundaries – and beyond the confines of academia.

Drawing upon disciplinary fields including – but not limited to, and frequently speaking across – literature, classical reception, musicology, museum studies, biography, visual culture and colonial history, this volume challenges the power structures that have framed, and continue to inform, the nineteenth-century archive. Written from this wide range of interdisciplinary perspectives, our authors grapple with urgent problems, including how to deal with potentially sensitive nineteenth-century archival items, both within academic scholarship and in present-day public-facing institutions, which often reflect colonial and imperial, racist, sexist, violent or elitist ideologies and taboos. The interdisciplinary and intersectional connections between the chapters here demonstrate how the legacies of the nineteenth-century archive resonate across contexts both past and present, and are in dialogue with notions of archival authority that are being challenged (and yet, sometimes reinforced) in the present day.

The 'meeting place' of the nineteenth-century archive serves as an intersectional focal point across all fifteen chapters. Coming from multiple disciplinary backgrounds in museum curatorship and academia – many of which were established during the period under discussion[20] – our authors consider the nineteenth-century archive to be a site of entrenched *systemic* ways of ordering the world. We suggest, moreover, that the force of the nineteenth-century archive, both then and now, was inherently interdisciplinary and intersectional, and that nineteenth-century archival legacies can be understood most constructively through dialogues across and between different forms of media.

In initiating this interdisciplinary conversation, our questions were: What is a nineteenth-century archive, broadly defined? Do archival holdings today still run the risk of perpetuating the ideological frameworks within which they were created? What are the discourses that lie behind the institutional collection, preservation, exhibition of and access to, such material – and what are the ethical implications for the researcher, curator and public historian? And finally, as we 're-encounter' the physical archive through the lifting of Covid lockdown restrictions, will we critique, reify or re-appreciate material holdings in productive ways? In developing our intersectional approaches, we suggest that the points of connection between these essays fit into the four categories of 'Archival ownership', 'Colonial power', 'Biographical silences' and 'Layered archives'. Each of these sections explores how the nineteenth-century archive created and reinforced both explicit and implicit forms of power. We also highlight particular strands that emerge across each section, such as material which illuminates issues of gender, religion, state power, the metropole versus the provincial and children's culture. Together, our authors suggest how such intersectional approaches to archival interpretation are necessary for engagement with the archive, both within and beyond the university and the museum.

Jennifer C. Nash has defined intersectionality as the 'notion that subjectivity is constituted by mutually reinforcing vectors of race, gender, class, and sexuality'.[21] For more than twenty years, scholars, activists, educators and lawyers have employed the concept of intersectionality both to describe problems of inequality and to fashion concrete solutions. In particular, as the *Washington Post* reported in 2015, 'the term has been used by social activists as both a rallying cry for more expansive progressive movements and a chastisement for their limitations'.[22] Drawing on Black feminist and critical legal theory, Kimberlé Crenshaw first coined the concept of intersectionality as a term to reflect the multiple social forces, social identities and ideological instruments through which power and disadvantage are expressed and legitimized.[23] As Crenshaw argues, an intersectional approach to history can also help to reveal that archival omissions are as powerful as their inclusions:

> Black women are sometimes excluded from feminist theory and antiracist policy discourse because both are predicated on a discrete set of experiences that often does not accurately reflect the interaction of race and gender. These problems of exclusion cannot be solved simply by including Black women within an already established analytical structure. Because the intersectional experience is greater than the sum of racism and sexism, any analysis that does not take intersectionality into account cannot sufficiently address the particular manner in which Black women are subordinated.[24]

Crenshaw's idea of intersectionality has been enormously influential across the academic humanities.[25] The 2019 edited volume *Intersectionality and Higher Education* has further shown how an intersectional framework can forge new understandings of the structures of power, race and inequality within the higher education sector.[26]

Increasingly, intersectionality has been incorporated as a framework for discussions on gender and decolonization,[27] and as a tool for examining the historical archive.[28]

This volume offers a sustained examination of how intersectional approaches to the nineteenth-century archive can reveal a more nuanced understanding of what the archive has been – and can be. If the nineteenth-century archive is an inherently relational space, where exhibition and concealment are two sides of the same coin, we consequently hold that it is also an intrinsically intersectional site of encounter. The chapters in this volume therefore comprise complementary approaches to archival subjectivity, revealing the strength and limitations of the archive for historical understanding – as well as a redefinition of what the archive is, whether as a physical document, a visual image or even a fragmented memory of a song once sung. From the chapters that engage with race and colonization (Lawrence; Heath; Laing; Johnson-Williams, Morosetti; Lowther), to biographical and communal censorship (Phillips; Burnett; Davis; Short; Laing), to how curating the past was itself an archival curation for the future (Short; Barringer; Bryant Davies), our essays encompass vastly different archival genres and medias. For this reason, we chose not to focus on only one empire: British, Dutch and French cultures of imperialism are discussed, and chapter case studies touch upon Britain, The Netherlands, South Africa, Canada, India and Australia. We encompass both specific museums, with chapters on the Oriental Museum (Barclay et al.), the Tropenmuseum (Lawrence), The Bowes Museum (Phillips) and the V&A (Watson Jones; Barringer), as well as the more abstract idea of the archive as a form of literature (Laing), visual culture (Lowther; Barringer), music (Johnson-Williams), theatre history (Davis) and biography (Morosetti; Phillips; Burnett).

Our primary intersectional meeting point, therefore, is the broader growth, across western Europe and the post/colonial world, of an intersectional nineteenth-century archive, where issues of race, representation, colonialism, gender and scientific categorization are all relevant. These themes, moreover, speak to the sedimentation of – and resistance to – enduring classifications of gender, race, science, class and highbrow versus lowbrow art, which (as is seen in Barringer's vivid image of 'Albertopolis') became deeply institutionalized during the long nineteenth century. We ultimately hold that the nineteenth-century archive was a location of persistent value systems that, in and of themselves, systematically omit and censure marginalized voices. As such, we propose that a 'new archival turn', as a form of archival 'encountering', is an indispensable tool for bringing the silences of history into dialogue with the conversations about equality and repatriation that are happening in the present. We therefore suggest that a critical engagement with nineteenth-century historiographical legacies, today, can be a form of archival activism. In this framework, interdisciplinary and intersectional encounters with a range of sources *as* 'performances' of a historical archival imaginary can reimagine and resituate the nineteenth century as a site where that which was once deemed ephemeral, or that which was once silenced, ultimately becomes as (or more) powerful than a written record.[29]

A useful perspective for approaching the idea of an archive as a discourse of power has long been Michel Foucault's notion of the 'archaeology' of knowledge, which enables the historian to describe the discourses of meanings within institutional structures, including archival formations.[30] Further, as explored in Johnson-Williams' discussion of colonial incarceration, Foucault's construction of biopower in *The History of Sexuality* as a political rationality concerned with the administration of living bodies is a powerful metaphor for the institutional compulsion to order and categorize.[31] As Foucault maintained, the nineteenth century was an era in which administration, examination, imprisonment and institutional archiving became systematized in unprecedented ways. Yet Foucault does not write about race and colonial contexts, and much of his work, as argued by Alison Howell and Melanie Richter-Montpetit, rests on an unspecified concept of 'the human', which does not account for how nineteenth-century notions of humanity were 'constituted through the savage and slave other'.[32] In approaching the archive with an intersectional mindset, we acknowledge Foucault's influence but also recognize that concepts of power, discourse and control need to be brought into a decolonial dialogue about community, identity and shared collective memory.

Moving on from strictly Foucauldian and/or Derridean discourses about archives as a form of power and discourse, interdisciplinary conversations over the last several decades have embraced the possibilities of using postcolonial and decolonial approaches to study how social practice, language and performance have shaped historical narratives. Motivated by Gayatri Chakravorty Spivak's landmark question, 'Can the Subaltern Speak?',[33] studies in agency and decolonization have explored questions of narrativity and resistance.[34] Understanding the archive, echoing Steedman, as a 'relational' entity creates space for examining how nineteenth-century archives were fundamentally shaped by the mobility of global travel and encounter, rather than simply through the establishment of static institutions. Mary Louise Pratt's concept of the 'contact zone' is useful, here, as a metaphor for the archive as a location of intersectional encountering: Pratt articulates the colonial contact zone as a space where relations between the colonizer and colonized are improvised, co-present, interactive and interlocking 'within radically asymmetrical relations of power'.[35]

We argue that the various disciplines represented in this volume have significant potential for reframing the archive as a relational, performative and 'live' site of encounter that is not tied to a specific institution, geographical remit or canon alone. The challenge, of course, is that nineteenth-century reifications of power through classification and canonization have created deep-seated legacies of 'ordering', which carry contingent value systems. Drawing on our backgrounds in Classics and musicology, we found that the nineteenth century was a time when the content considered 'worthy' of preservation for future generations became 'set' and canonized according to newly entrenched elite-versus-popular value judgements. It is, therefore, the critical attention to archival ephemera, archival silences and the various overlapping meanings facilitated in an intersectional archive that will enable more flexible, antiracist and critical narratives to emerge in the future.

There have been various attempts in recent years, within our own respective disciplines, towards re-envisioning a critical approach to the archive. In musicology, a forthcoming special issue of *Postcolonial Studies* on 'Music, Empire, Colonialism: Sounding Out the Archives' examines how music and sound were in dialogue with the formation of colonial archival power and authority.[36] While these articles are limited to the British imperial context, this work draws on attempts in musicology over the last couple of decades to relocate empire as an influential part of nineteenth-century music history, in terms of canon formation, reception and value.[37] There has also been a recent upsurge of publications on music, empire and colonialism outside of the British empire, although not much specifically on the 'archive' and nineteenth-century history.[38] Overall, the relative reticence in much 'mainstream' historical musicology to engage with the archive might be explained by Kofi Agawu's comment that 'unlike political history, with its kingdoms and wars, migrations and inventions, music – an art of sound and a performing art in an oral culture – leaves different, more complex and elusive traces on the historical record'.[39] Notably, where music studies *has* recently turned its attention to the archive, this has often been with regard to ethnomusicological fieldwork,[40] or contexts of digital record-keeping.[41] Exceptions that do integrate historical questions with the idea of musical archiving include, but are not limited to, Annegret Fauser's reflection on historical archives as 'sites of listening' to histories of violence, Antti-Ville Kärjä's consideration of historiography and the role of the archive for the preservation of popular music heritage and Lizabé Lambrechts's exploration of the relation between institutional musical archives, decolonization and curricular reform.[42] What will be useful, for our purposes, will be to bring these conversations about musical ephemera, constructed communities and archival 'belonging' into dialogue with nineteenth-century historical memory, asking how a more intersectional approach to archiving can initiate a broader understanding of the past.

In Classics, the prevalence of classical allusions and imagery in nineteenth-century elite and popular culture is beginning to be explored in more depth, drawing on many nineteenth-century archives which had fallen through disciplinary gaps.[43] Since the establishment of the now-burgeoning field of classical reception, controversy has raged over the selection of material to be included in reception histories of Greco-Roman antiquity.[44] The role of Classics as a subject within the British Empire and its colonies has been examined,[45] and the collections, display and accessibility at institutions such as the British Museum, Crystal Palace and Berlin's Pergamonmuseum have also been studied, as has the reconstruction of ancient artefacts in museum displays considered as a nineteenth-century colonial enterprise.[46] The role of archaeology, as it became highly visible in museums, newspapers and popular culture[47] – against the wider backdrop of privileged educational curricula and institutions,[48] and the recent focus on uncovering non-elite, middle-class and working-class sources,[49] as well as those which illumine women's[50] and children's[51] encounters with Greco-Roman antiquity – demonstrate the increasing variety of the archives used to reconceptualize the field. Within Classics and classical reception, more broadly, an emphasis on 'ethical, diverse, intersectional, and especially feminist' Classics has also been found in digital spaces, such as the online journal *Eidolon* (2015–20),[52] as well as in printed monographs,[53] a new series on 'Intersectionality in Classical Antiquity' from Edinburgh University Press and a renewed surge of studies on Black and decolonizing Classics.[54] Across the growing interdisciplinary tendency to draw on a wide range of archives and theorize in different ways, it will be interesting to see how these trends continue to merge from and merge with nineteenth-century classical reception.

Towards a 'new archival turn': Embedded archival activism

We propose that a 'new archival turn' envisions the historical archive as a relational site of discourse that is in constant dialogue with how nineteenth-century legacies are played out in the present day. Our essays encompass a variety of understandings of intersectionality to illustrate such a 'new archival turn', and to broaden interpretations of 'archives' to uncover a range of power dynamics and (im)balances. Our scope deliberately emphasizes the people, communities and relationships inherent in the formation and usage of archives, promoting a human, relational dimension to a concept that can appear impersonal or individual. Shared concerns, across all the essays, are communities of people, constructed and understood in very different ways, and whose relationships to the archives vary: stakeholders, readerships, visitors, viewers listeners/singers/performers, creators and participants, researchers and archivists/curators, historical figures and biographical subjects. Each essay grapples with the issue of archival gaps and silences, and the subjective metaphorical possibilities of experience. Another commonality is the analysis of challenging case studies which reshape 'the archive' and reflect on different expressions of power and discourse in archival formation.

The essays are arranged in roughly chronological order within four complementary sections: 'Archival ownership', 'Colonial power', 'Biographical silences' and 'Layered archives'. The essays also intersect across these categories (as spelled out below), but this structure enables exploration of some key shared concerns, as well as contrasting different disciplinary approaches.

The collection opens with three essays on 'Archival ownership', which explore some of the most visible, familiar examples of nineteenth-century archives: museum displays. Such outward-facing archives are frequently in the public eye as controversies over repatriation continue to rage, with increased focus on provenance, display narratives and community engagement. These essays explore specific displays, which all sought community input into arrangement and labelling, across different institutions with significant nineteenth-century collections: a University teaching and research collection from the North East of England (the Oriental Museum), Amsterdam's Tropenmuseum, a major 'museum of world cultures' and London's Victoria and Albert Museum (V&A). Collections and displays are a constant feature of the book: we return to County Durham, to The Bowes Museum, in Chapter 10, and to the V&A in the Afterword (Chapter 15), while Chapter 14 discusses nineteenth-century perceptions of the British Museum's displays. This section, however, shares a focus on the relationships between individual institutions *as* institutions – their mission statements, their formation and their collections and displays – and stakeholders: visitors, community focus groups, donors (whether modern and willing or historically forced), curators and researchers.

We begin with '"Found in Store": Working with source communities and difficult objects at Durham University's Oriental Museum', written collaboratively by a team of curators: Rachel Barclay, Lauren Barnes, Gillian Ramsay, Craig Barclay and Helen Armstrong. Two case studies drawn from the internationally outstanding collections, which have their origins firmly rooted in the colonial era despite the Museum's 1960s foundation, examine the processes of co-development and co-curation on different scales: an individual object, and an entire gallery. The creation of a permanent gallery for Himalayas, South Asia and Southeast Asia (2013–15), and the deaccession of an individual object following student-led research into its provenance (2017–21) centre upon stakeholders, engage with colonial legacies, and deal with the issue of repatriation. The issues of curatorial decisions, stakeholder feedback, community participation and sensitivities surrounding repatriation and provenance introduced here are the focus of the following two chapters.

Adiva Lawrence, in her essay on 'Transforming the archive of slavery at the tropenmuseum', examines 'Afterlives of Slavery', a semi-permanent exhibition (2017–21) exploring the legacies of transatlantic slavery in contemporary Dutch society. The Tropenmuseum was founded in 1864 as a colonial ethnographic museum, and is now part of the Dutch National Museums of World Cultures. Expanding on Foucauldian metaphors of the archival ordering, Lawrence explains how its innovative curatorial choices aimed at changing the narrative about the impact of slavery on Dutch history. In assessing this attempt to promote new, radical approaches to slavery, she argues for the adoption of methodologies aiming at effectively disrupting the colonial archive from within.

Just as these two studies reflect on curatorial decisions and co-curation with community participants including artists, so the final essay of this section considers the role of contemporary museum practice in both challenging and reinforcing the legacies of colonialism through the example of the V&A's Ethiopian collections. In 'Maqdala and the South Kensington Museum: 150 years later', Alexandra Watson Jones reflects on the 'Maqdala 1868' anniversary display of around twenty objects connected to the British Expedition to Abyssinia in 1868. The display, which she developed in consultation with the Ethiopian embassy in London and advisory community groups, considered the role of the objects as witnesses to a significant period in Ethiopian and British history, and addressed the ongoing conversations surrounding looted objects in UK museums.

The problematic role of imperial and military power in acquiring loot by force, and in shaping contentious discourses surrounding the ongoing holding and display of these items, is further illuminated by the volume's second section, which focuses on the role of 'Colonial power' in shaping nineteenth-century archival encounters. Four interdisciplinary essays explore how political and ideological power shaped colonial archives in arenas ranging from scientific artwork, coercive music-making, the rhetoric of children's literature and the codification of police records.

David Lowther's essay, 'Encountering colonial science in the visual archive: The natural history paintings of Raja Serfoji II of Tanjore (1777–1832)' highlights a collection of paintings depicting southern Indian wildlife which merge South Asian and European practices of knowledge creation. Held for many years in the archives of the East India Company, the paintings are now in the British Library (London). Setting these paintings within the context of the colonial scientific networks in which visual culture played a prominent role, Lowther analyses these paintings as fundamentally distinct from, although drawing upon, contemporary colonial methods and preoccupations.

Moving from visual art to music, and from colonial scientific networks to missionary imperialism, Erin Johnson-Williams examines the role of hymn singing within institutions of biopolitical 'enclosure' in colonial Canada and post/colonial South Africa, in her essay 'Enclosing archival sound: Colonial singing as discipline and resistance'. Given that acts of coercive music-making are often absent from official institutional archives, Johnson-Williams challenges Foucauldian discourses of institutional power by exploring how singing in spaces of colonial incarceration both reinforced and resisted imperial narratives of disciplinary containment. She proposes that, while the hymn may have been largely silenced by the archive of empire, its archival traces confirm the potential of singing as a way to negotiate a more resistive sonic 're-archiving' of imperial violence.

Our next essay also juxtaposes canonical genres of colonization and education (moving here from hymns to children's books) within coercive, supposedly educational, contexts. In 'The infantilization of indigeneity in colonial Australia', Roisín Laing analyses the rhetorical devices through which a supposedly canonical text, Jeannie Gunn's *The Little Black Princess* (1905), idealizes a parent-child model of settler-Indigenous relations. Its rhetoric – and particularly the child reader it implies – obscure some of this text's racism. By contrast, many archived texts – those kept behind physical or, increasingly, digital, walls – articulate quite explicitly both the ideology underlying infantilization, and its colonial functions. A comparative analysis of these readings demonstrates that infantilization is consonant with the ideological construction of a white Australia, and therefore with historical acts of genocide associated with this ideology. Laing then draws on writing by Indigenous authors, systematically neglected in the historiography of colonialism, to complicate the vision of white Australia perpetuated in white archives and literary canons.

Deana Heath's contribution, '"Some Nameless, Dreadful Wrong": Reading the silencing of police rape in the Indian colonial archive', similarly examines ways of drawing out and making visible acts of violence in historical sources. Heath investigates how acts of rape committed by the Indian police have been coded in the colonial archive. Focusing on the rape of a subaltern mother and daughter, which culminated in their suicide and the conviction of their rapists – all members of the Indian police – for wrongful confinement rather than rape, she interrogates how the process of making sexual violence visible reveals the limits of such visibility: subaltern women and girls could only enter the colonial archive as a victim of their own act of self-destruction, in light of the colonial state's need to hide the sexually predatory nature of its violence workers.

The prevalence of silences in the colonial archive, and the taboos surrounding sexual health, leads us on to our third section, 'Biographical silences'. Zooming in on three individual case studies whose biographies are conditioned by imperialism (from both ends of privilege and exploitation), we see the challenges of constructing individual experiences in the face of archival gaps and silences – and how such intersections play out – when the privileged spaces of nineteenth-century Britain came into contact with various facets of empire, whether this be through theatrical exhibitions or education. Arranged chronologically, these chapters consider subjects ranging from an exhibited person, as seen through the eyes of London's spectators, including theatrical stars such as Kemble; a marriage between aristocratic landowner and a French actress; and a Black student at Oxford University.

In 'Completing the mosaic: Sara Baartman and the archive', Tiziana Morosetti examines scholarly approaches since the 1980s to the colonial material on Sara Baartman (c. 1789–1815), who was exhibited in London as the 'Hottentot Venus' from 1810. Morosetti argues that, in pursuing present-day political agendas, scholarship on Baartman has re-inscribed the 'text' of her life with *expectations* of what primary sources should contain: employing absolute notions of whiteness and Europeanness have supported the symbolism of Baartman's Blackness in contemporary debates, while ventriloquizing for Baartman has masked the absence of her voice from the archive. Morosetti's essay suggests the inescapability of archival evidence and a need to respect the silences of both Baartman and the archive in assessing her significance and legacy.

Whereas Morosetti surveys the absence of an exhibited person's own voice from the archive, our next essay examines how some personal aspects of collectors' lives, which can be pieced together from archival evidence and which influenced the formation of the collection, have not been included in the narrative of their legacy museum. Judith Phillips, in 'Mercury, sulphur baths, and fine art: Censorship and the sexual health of John and Joséphine Bowes, founders of the Bowes Museum', explains how discussions of the sexual health of John (1811–1885) and his wife Joséphine (1825–1874) are notably missing from displays relating to the museum's narrative despite archival evidence that was suppressed (sub)consciously in the past. Phillips considers the Bowes' sexual health within the context of censorship and 'hidden' stories found in the shadows of the archives. Their childlessness, moreover, potentially contributed to the decision to collect fine and decorative art and found a public museum. Reasons for their childlessness are largely absent from the museum's public narrative, raising questions over how, or even whether, to balance the privacy of the founders' personal lives with a fuller archival narrative and the market imperative to offer a family-friendly visitor experience.

Continuing the exploration of disconnects between public and private, Philip Burnett's essay, 'Empowering the invisible: The archival legacy of Christian Cole', explores how the life of Christian Frederick Cole (1851/2–1885) is documented. Recognized as the first Black African to be awarded a BA from the University of Oxford, and to practise law in the English Courts, Cole was educated by Anglican missionaries in Sierra Leone and published seven pamphlets. Burnett examines the disconnect between the institutional recognition of Cole's achievements and his material obscurity, compounded by the scattering of scant information about him in archival repositories around the world. He suggests that focusing on the networks and spaces Cole inhabited is essential to the historiography of his biography, and to understanding broader struggles for the shifting identities of the Black intelligentsia in the nineteenth century.

The shared concern of these three essays with archival, biographical absences, which also highlight tensions between the taboo topics of archival fetishization and censorship, is continued in our fourth and final section, 'Layered archives'. Jemima Short explores the archival practices of three religious congregations founded in mid-nineteenth-century France in 'The power of invisibility: Nursing nuns and archival gatekeeping'. Catholic women in these congregations cared for the poor and socially marginalized. Despite the scale and importance of their work, the invisibility of nursing nuns in the historical archive of medicine and welfare, and in historical scholarship, is a widely recognized issue. Short highlights how congregations perpetuate their own invisibility by restricting access to their records, thereby limiting the possibility for histories of their patients to be written. She explores the negotiations between researchers and congregations and the ethical challenges which must be addressed when writing congregational histories.

Jim Davis, in 'instability and ideology of the archive: Archival evidence and nineteenth-century British theatre audiences, also focuses on the instability of archival evidence available for research in nineteenth-century British theatre audiences. Drawing on memoranda, letters, police reports and other theatre-related documents preserved in the Lord Chamberlain's Papers in the Public Record Office, Davis considers the value and limitations of this evidence in relation to the social, political and cultural factors impacting government oversight of British theatre. In considering the origins of British theatrical collections, and the ways in which content and preservation choices have been determined (including through digital resourcing), he also explores the archive as a source for creativity and performance, contextualized within the broader discourses pertaining to contemporary notions of the archive.

The challenges of excavating archival evidence for spectatorship are taken up by Rachel Bryant Davies in her essay '"Our Mind Strives to Restore the Mutilated Forms": Layered archives of virtual museum tours in nineteenth-century children's periodicals'. Concentrating on another ephemeral popular medium, children's magazines, she proposes that virtual tours of museum displays represent a crucial resource for understanding how nineteenth-century child consumers were acculturated into idealized interactions with the 'classical' past through museum displays and cheap print. Bryant Davies argues that this multi-layered archive of museum curation and spectating formed mediated 'meta-archives' which illumine how imaginatively restored sculptural fragments facilitated acculturation into gatekeeping of museum displays, and how debates surrounding the acquisition, significance and repatriation of ancient artefacts were communicated. Her essay demonstrates that informally didactic explanations of the notoriously controversial display of the Parthenon Sculptures in the British Museum's Elgin room epitomizes wider intersections between preservation, collection, display and public engagement.

Together, these instances of archival silence and invisibility demonstrate how nineteenth-century hierarchies of power persist into the present. These themes are further explored by Tim Barringer in his concluding essay, 'Intersectional Albertopolis'. Barringer draws together themes from across the essays as a way of re-examining the institutions at South Kensington, from the Crystal Palace and the South Kensington Museum to the Albert Hall and the Royal College of Music. This cultural state machinery formed a fulcrum for the processes of liberal governmentality in Victorian Britain. The institutions aimed to bring together art, industry, science, horticulture, music, natural history and imperial commercial knowledge under the patronage of the Crown, a spectacular display of power over objects and ideas, and the very essence of the imperial nineteenth-century archive.

Summary of themes

As indicated above, the chapters here overlap in different ways across and within their intersectional themes. While all the essays are in dialogue with intersectionality in their approach to the archive, the four sections emphasize their most constructive congruences. Overall, our authors interrogate key points of contention across the broad themes of: archival silences (Johnson-Williams; Heath), visibility and invisibility (Phillips, Burnett; Short), archival gatekeeping (Barclay et al.; Watson Jones; Burnett; Short; Davis; Bryant Davies), decolonial challenges to Foucauldian power systems (Lawrence; Heath; Johnson-Williams), biography as archive (Laing; Morosetti; Phillips; Burnett), archival fragments and ephemera (Lowther; Bryant Davies; Laing), communal memory and education (Burnett; Johnson-Williams), censorship (Davis; Short; Phillips; Heath), racial voyeurism (Morosetti; Lawrence; Watson Jones), religion and control (Johnson-William; Short), children's literature as archive (Laing; Bryant Davies), visual culture as archive (Lowther; Bryant Davies; Barringer) and the institutionalization of museums as a metaphor for an archive of empire (Barringer). The chapters focusing on specific museums, moreover, suggest and exemplify strategies for institutions to drive practical change, to incorporate a more diverse and decolonial range of voices and to engage new audiences.

The 'new archival turn' as we understand it is therefore necessarily, and vitally, intersectional, and will help to pave connections between academic research and decolonial conversations happening more broadly in popular media and education sectors. During our compilation of this volume, we have tracked a marked increase in press conversations about archival repatriation, where words such as 'looted' – to refer to the bringing of material objects from the rest of the world to Britain, for example – are becoming more common.[55] On 7 May 2021, for example, an article by Dan Hicks in *The Guardian* argued strongly in favour of repatriating material objects from museums, concluding that decolonial actions of returning stolen objects to the cultures that they were taken from 'are overdue measures to keep Britain's global museums in step with an ever-changing world'.[56] A month later, another *Guardian* article described protests over the reopening of the Museum of the Home as part of a 'growing row around controversial statues across the country – including the decision of Oriel College at the University of Oxford to keep a statue of British imperialist Cecil Rhodes, despite an independent commission backing its removal'.[57] The questions then remain: if we view contemporary engagements with the nineteenth-century archive as necessarily intersectional, can conversations about repatriation be extended beyond material objects, to traditions of artistic expression (like music, visual art, theatre, curatorship and literature), and to how the writing and teaching of history, both past and present, persistently constitutes new archival orderings?

The prevalence of conversations about repatriation in the press is a telling reminder that this is, indeed, the start of a potentially very exciting new decade, particularly given enormous upheavals in not only the practicalities of, but also the ideologies informing, how we approach constructions of historical knowledge. What, then, will the remainder of the decade of the 2020s hold for how the nineteenth-century archive is stored, framed, (re)used and (re)imagined in a digital (post/lockdown) era? With ever-expanding digital resources, will our archival work necessarily rely less on the idea of a permanent, physical structure, and instead embrace a more utopian fantasy of 'open access'? Or will the increase of researchers working from home reinforce a nostalgic fetishization of the institutional archive, further complicated by the wealth of nineteenth-century material currently flooding the digital humanities, which has pre-empted a revolution in the ways that academics – and public historians – access, understand, define and negotiate the archival experience?

The saturation of information that accompanies the digitization of the nineteenth-century archive – sparking many instances of Derridean archival 'fever' in the present day – ultimately returns us, full circle, to the permeation and circulation of archival dust as laid out by Steedman. For the 'circularity' of dust that infuses the archive, as she maintains, is about 'the impossibility of things disappearing … Nothing goes away'.[58] In an age of digital saturation we are, indeed, attuned to the bittersweet possibility that, on the internet, 'nothing goes away', while admitting that much can be silenced by corporate decisions. In this way, the utility of an intersectional encounter with the constantly shifting archive of information around us does stretch usefully – and necessarily – beyond a nineteenth-century frame. In its most productive formulations, then, intersectional openness to the relational possibilities of the archive will help to create sustainable decolonial, equitable and critical conversations about historiography, ownership and access for a creative future.

Notes

1. Carolyn Steedman, *Dust: The Archive and Cultural History* (Manchester: Manchester University Press, 2001), p. 164. Emphasis original.
2. Ibid., pp. 116–28. See also Carolyn Steedman, 'Something She Called a Fever: Michelet, Derrida, and Dust', *The American Historical Review* 106. 4 (2001): 1159–80; and Matthew Harle, *Afterlives of Abandoned Work: Creative Debris in the Archive* (London: Bloomsbury Academic, 2019).
3. Steedman, *Dust*, p. 164.
4. See Jacques Derrida, *Archive Fever: A Freudian Impression*, translated by Eric Prenowitz (Chicago: University of Chicago Press, 1995).
5. On breathing in the dust of the dead, see Steedman, *Dust*, pp. 38, 117, 160.
6. See Saidiya Hartman, *Lose Your Mother: A Journey Along the Atlantic Slave Route* (New York: Farrar, Straus and Giroux, 2007); *Scenes of Subjection: Terror, Slavery, and Self-Making in Nineteenth-Century America* (New York and Oxford: Oxford University Press, 1997); and 'Venus in Two Acts', *Small Axe* 26 (2008): 1–14; Christina Sharpe, *In the Wake: On Blackness and Being* (Durham: Duke University Press, 2016); Imtiaz Habib, *Black Lives in the English Archives, 1500–1677* (London: Routledge, 2008); Nicola Abram, *Black British Women's Theatre: Intersectionality, Archives, Aesthetics* (Cham: Palgrave Macmillan, 2020). See also the essays in David Thomas, Simon Fowler, and Valerie Johnson (eds), *The Silence of the Archive* (Chicago: Neal-Schuman, 2017); and Sadiah Qureshi, *Peoples on Parade: Exhibitions, Empire, and Anthropology in Nineteenth-Century Britain* (Chicago and London: The University of Chicago Press, 2011).

7   On the 'new' kinds of archives that have arisen as a result of the Covid-19 lockdowns, see: Laura Spinney, 'What Are COVID Archivists Keeping for Tomorrow's Historians?', *Nature* (17 December 2020): https://www.nature.com/articles/d41586-020-03554-0, accessed 2 December 2021; Tim Galsworthy, 'Archival Research in a Time of Coronavirus', https://www.blogs.hss.ed.ac.uk/pubs-and-publications/2020/05/10/archival-research-coronavirus/, accessed 2 December 2021; Paul Tully and Neil Carr, 'Obstacles and Possibilities in Archival Research: Archives as a Data Source for Leisure Scholars in Lockdown', *Leisure Studies* 40. 6 (2021): 888–94; Esyllt W. Jones, Shelley Sweeney, Ian Milligan, Greg Bak, and Jo-Anne McCutcheon, 'Remembering Is a Form of Honouring: Preserving the Covid-19 Archival Record', *Facets* 6 (2021): https://doi.org/10.1139/facets-2020-0115; and Shai M. Dromi, 'Archival Research during COVID-19', *Footnotes* 48. 3 (2020): 6–8.
8   For a helpful discussion of Derrida's 'Archive Fever', see Steedman, *Dust*, p. 11.
9   See, for further reading, Michael J. Paulus, 'Reconceptualizing Academic Libraries and Archives in the Digital Age', *Libraries and the Academy*, 11. 4 (2011): 939–52.
10 The workshop was entitled 'The Nineteenth-Century Archive as a Discourse of Power', organized by Rachel Bryant Davies and Erin Johnson-Williams (Durham University, 8–9 February 2019), hosted by the Centre for Nineteenth-Century Studies and with financial support from the British Association for Victorian Studies, the Royal Historical Society, and the Durham Centre for Classical Reception Studies.
11 A rich example of such an initiative to decolonize the historical archive in the pursuit of a 'Pan-African' archive that works to find healing through changing historical narratives can be found at: Decolonising the Archive, https://www.decolonisingthearchive.com/, accessed 2 December 2021.
12 The outpouring of sympathy expressed internationally following the tragic fire that destroyed the collections in the J. W. Jagger Library at the University of Cape Town in April 2021 speaks to an ongoing sense of loss about physical archival access and postcolonial archival ownership. See, for example, Christina Goldbaum and Kimon de Greef, 'Wildfire Deals Hard Blow to South Africa's Archives' (19 April 2021), https://www.nytimes.com/2021/04/19/world/africa/cape-town-table-mountain-fire.html, accessed 2 December 2021; and Shannon Morreira, 'Significant Archives are Under Threat in Cape Town's Fire. Why They Matter So Much', *The Conversation* (19 April 2021), https://theconversation.com/significant-archives-are-under-threat-in-cape-towns-fire-why-they-matter-so-much-159299, accessed 2 December 2021.
13 On the global complexities and inequalities of archival 'access' and open academic publishing, see Márton Demeter and Ronina Istratii, 'Scrutinising What Open Access Journals Mean for Global Inequities', *Publishing Research Quarterly* 36 (2020): 505–22.
14 The use of the word 'fantasy' here is a play on the title of Thomas Richards, *The Imperial Archive: Knowledge and the Fantasy of Empire* (London: Verso, 1993), where he makes the argument that the nineteenth-century imperial archive was a fantasy, both about the ordering of knowledge and the project of western imperialism.
15 See, for further reading, Arlette Farge, *The Allure of the Archives*, translated by Thomas Scott-Railton (New Haven: Yale University Press, 2013); and Kate Dorney, 'The Ordering of Things: Allure, Access, and Archives', *Shakespeare Bulletin* 28. 1 (2010): 19–36.
16 Indeed, the lack of attention to the history of archival institutions prior to the nineteenth century is partly a result of the nineteenth-century reification of, and control over, the archive itself: see Alexandra Walsham, 'The Social History of the Archive: Record-Keeping in Early Modern Europe', *Past & Present* 230. 11 (2016): 9–48.

17 See Joan M. Schwartz and Terry Cook, 'Archives, Records, and Power: The Making of Modern Memory', *Archival Science* 2 (2002): 1–19; and Richards, *Imperial Archive*.
18 See Antoinette Burton, 'Introduction: Archive Fever, Archive Stories', in Antionette Burton (ed.), *Archive Stories: Facts, Fictions, and the Writing of History* (Durham: Duke University Press, 2006), pp. 1–24; Tony Ballantyne, *Entanglements of Empire: Missionaries, Maori, and the Question of the Body* (Auckland: Auckland University Press, 2015); Kirsty Reid and Fiona Paisley, *Sources and Methods in Histories of Colonialism: Approaching the Imperial Archive* (London: Routledge, 2017); Ricardo Roque and Kim A. Wagner (eds), *Engaging Colonial Knowledge: Reading European Archives in World History* (Houndmills, Basingstoke: Palgrave Macmillan, 2012); Ann Laura Stoler, *Along the Archival Grain: Epistemic Anxieties and Colonial Common Sense* (Princeton: Princeton University Press, 2009); and Ann Laura Stoler, *Imperial Debris: On Ruins and Ruination* (Durham: Duke University Press, 2013). For further reading on the archive, accessibility and public history, see Paul Griffin, 'Making Usable Pasts: Collaboration, Labour and Activism in the Archive', *Area* 50. 4 (2018): 501–8; Victoria Hoyle, 'Editorial: Archives and Public History', *Archives and Records* 38. 1 (2017): 1–4; and Peter J. Wosh, 'Reflections on Public History and Archives Education', *Journal of Archival Organization* 15. 3 (2018): 95–9.
19 On the 'archival turn', see Burton, 'Introduction: Archive Fever', pp. 1–24; Ariel Martino, 'Revisioning the Archival Turn', *Criticism* 62. 4 (2020): 629–33; Kate Eichhorn, *The Archival Turn in Feminism: Outrage and Order* (Philadelphia: Temple University Press, 2013); Naomi Milthorpe, 'Archives, Authority, Aura: Modernism's Archival Turn', *Papers on Language and Literature* 55. 1 (2019): 3–14; Charles E. Morris, 'The Archival Turn in Rhetorical Studies; Or, the Archives Rhetorical (Re)turn', *Rhetoric & Public Affairs* 9. 1 (2006): 113–15; Paul Herman, 'The Heroic Study of Records: The Contested Persona of the Archival Historian', *History of the Human Sciences* 26. 4 (2013): 67–83; Cheryl Simon, 'Introduction: Following the Archival Turn', *Visual Resources* 18. 2 (2002): 101–7; Randolph Starn, 'Truths in the Archives', *Common Knowledge* 8. 2 (2002): 387–401; Carolyn Steedman, 'After the Archive', *Comparative Critical Studies* 8. 2–3 (2011): 321–40; and Elizabeth Yale, 'The History of Archives: The State of the Discipline', *Book History* 18 (2015): 332–59.
20 See Bernard Lightman and Bennett Zon (eds), *Victorian Culture and the Origin of Disciplines* (New York: Routledge, 2020).
21 Jennifer C. Nash, 'Re-Thinking Intersectionality', *Feminist Review* 89 (2008): 2.
22 Christine Emba, 'Opinion: Intersectionality', *The Washington Post* (21 September 2015), https://www.washingtonpost.com/news/in-theory/wp/2015/09/21/intersectionality-a-primer/, accessed 29 August 2021.
23 Crenshaw has been so influential as to receive coverage about the impact of the term 'intersectionality' in the non-academic press. See, for example, Katy Steinmetz, 'She Coined the Term "Intersectionality" Over 30 Years Ago. Here's What It Means to Her Today', *TIME* (20 February 2020), https://time.com/5786710/kimberle-crenshaw-intersectionality/, accessed 29 August 2021.
24 Kimberlé Crenshaw, 'Demarginalizing the Intersection of Race and Sex: A Black Feminist Critique of Antidiscrimination Doctrine, Feminist Theory and Antiracist Politics', *University of Chicago Legal Forum* 31 (1989): 140. See also Jane Coaston, 'The Intersectionality Wars', *Vox* (28 May 2019), https://www.vox.com/the-highlight/2019/5/20/18542843/intersectionality-conservatism-law-race-gender-

discrimination, accessed 17 May 2021. We also look forward to the forthcoming publication: Kimblerlé Crenshaw, *On Intersectionality: Essential Writings* (New York: New Press, 2022).

25   A field of 'intersectionality studies' has been proposed by Sumi Cho, Kimberlé Williams Crenshaw, and Leslie McCall, 'Towards a Field of Intersectionality Studies: Theory, Application, and Praxis', *Signs: Journal of Women in Culture and Society* 38. 4 (2013): 785–810.

26   See, for example, W. Carson Byrd, Rachelle J. Brunn-Bevel, and Sarah M. Ovink (eds), *Intersectionality and Higher Education: Identity and Inequality on College Campuses* (New Brunswick: Rutgers University Press, 2019).

27   On gender and intersectionality, see Helma Lutz, Maria Vivar and Linda Supik (eds), *Framing Intersectionality: Debates on a Multi-faceted Concept in Gender Studies* (London: Routledge, 2016). On decolonization and intersectionality see Heidi Safia Mirza, 'Decolonizing Higher Education: Black Feminism and the Intersectionality of Race and Gender', *Journal of Feminist Scholarship* 7. 7 (2014–15): 1–12.

28   See Verne Harris, *Ghosts of Archive: Deconstructive Intersectionality and Praxis* (London: Routledge, 2020); and Jennifer C. Nash, 'Intersectionality and Its Discontents', *American Quarterly* 69. 1 (2017): 117–29.

29   We use the term 'archival activism' here in relation to the term 'curatorial activism' as used by Maura Reilly, *Curatorial Activism: Towards an Ethics of Curating* (London: Thames & Hudson, 2018). See also Griffin, 'Making Usable Pasts', pp. 501–8.

30   Michel Foucault, *The Archaeology of Knowledge* (London: Tavistock, 1972). For more on Foucault, Derrida and the archive see Marlene Manoff, 'Theories of the Archive from Across the Disciplines', *Libraries and the Academy* 4. 1 (2004): 9–25.

31   Michel Foucault, *The History of Sexuality: An Introduction*, Vol. 1, translated by R. Hurley (New York: Random House, 1978), p. 138.

32   Alison Howell and Melanie Richter-Montpetit, 'Racism in Foucauldian Security Studies: Biopolitics, Liberal War, and the Whitewashing of Colonial and Racial Violence', *International Political Sociology* 13 (2019): 2. See also the essays in Stephen Legg and Deana Heath (eds), *South Asian Governmentalities: Michel Foucault and the Question of Postcolonial Orderings* (Cambridge: Cambridge University Press, 2018).

33   See Gayatri Chakravorty Spivak, 'Can the Subaltern Speak? Speculations on Widow Sacrifice', in Patrick Williams and Laura Chrisman (eds), *Colonial Discourse and Post-Colonial Theory: A Reader* (London: Routledge, 1993), pp. 66–111.

34   See, for example, Linda Tuhiwai Smith, *Decolonizing Methodologies: Research and Indigenous Peoples* (London: Zed Books, 2012).

35   See Mary Louise Pratt, *Imperial Eyes: Travel Writing and Transculturation* (London: Routledge, 2008), p. 8.

36   Special Issue of *Postcolonial Studies*, 'Music, Empire, Colonialism: Sounding Out the Archives', edited by Philip Burnett, Erin Johnson-Williams, and Yvonne Liao (forthcoming, 2022).

37   See, for example, Jeffrey Richards, *Imperialism and Music: Britain, 1876–1953* (Manchester: Manchester University Press, 2001); and Bennett Zon, *Representing Non-Western Music in Nineteenth-Century Britain* (Rochester: University of Rochester Press, 2007).

38   See Geoffrey Baker, *Imposing Harmony: Music and Society in Colonial Cuzco* (Durham: Duke University Press, 2008); and David Irving, *Colonial Counterpoint: Music in Early Modern Manila* (Oxford: Oxford University Press, 2010).

39 Kofi Agawu, *Representing African Music: Postcolonial Notes, Queries, Positions* (New York and London: Routledge, 2003), p. 2.
40 See Eva-Maria, Alexandra van Straaten, 'The *White* Ethnomusicologist's Burden: *White* Innocence and the Archive in Music Studies', *The World of Music* 10. 1 (2021): 131–67; Svanibor Pettan and Jeff Todd Titon (eds), *Public Ethnomusicology, Education, Archives, & Commerce* (Oxford: Oxford University Press, 2019); Carolyn Landau and Janet Topp Fargion, 'We're All Archivists Now: Towards a More Equitable Ethnomusicology', *Ethnomusicology Forum* 21. 2 (2012): 125–40; and John Vallier, 'Preserving the Past, Activating the Future: Collaborative Archiving in Ethnomusicology', in Jennifer C. Post (ed.), *Ethnomusicology: A Contemporary Reader* (New York: Routledge: 2017), pp. 307–17.
41 See, for example, Peter Beate, 'Negotiating the Co-Curation of an Online Community Popular Music Archive', *Popular Music History* 13. 1–2 (2020): 58–76; Sarah Cuk, 'Do-It-Yourself Music Archives: A Response and Alternative to Mainstream Exclusivity', *The Serials Librarian* (2021): https://doi.org/10.1080/03615 26X.2021.1910614; and Erin Johnson-Williams, 'Online EDI Resources: Towards a Reflexive Archive', *Royal Musical Association Research Chronicle* (2021): https://doi.org/10.1017/rrc.2021.3.
42 See Annegret Fauser, 'Sound, Music, War and Violence: Listening from the Archive', *Transposition* 2 (2020): https://doi.org/10.4000/transposition.4310; Antti-Ville Kärjä, 'Historiography and the Role of the Archive', in Sarah Baker, Catherine Strong, Lauren Istvandity, and Zelmarie Cantillon (eds), *The Routledge Companion to Popular Music History and Heritage* (London and New York: Routledge, 2018), pp. 108–18; and Lizabé Lambrechts, 'The Becoming of An Archive: Perspectives on a Music Archive and the Limits of Institutionality', *Social Dynamics: A Journal of African Studies* 46. 2 (2020): 310–22.
43 The foundational works on classical reception and the nineteenth century – even though these sources do not locate 'the archive' as their primary focus – include: Richard Jenkyns, *The Victorians and Ancient Greece* (Oxford: Blackwell, 1980); Frank M. Turner, *The Greek Heritage in Victorian Britain* (New Haven: Yale University Press, 1981); Norman Vance, *The Victorians and Ancient Rome* (Oxford: Blackwell Publishers, 1997); and Simon Goldhill, *Victorian Culture and Classical Antiquity: Art, Opera, Fiction, and the Proclamation of Modernity* (Princeton: Princeton University Press, 2011).
44 See Charles Martindale, *Redeeming the Text: Latin Poetry and the Hermeneutics of Reception* (Cambridge: Cambridge University Press, 1993); Lorna Hardwick and Christopher Stray (eds), *A Companion to Classical Receptions* (Oxford: Wiley-Blackwell, 2011); Lorna Hardwick and Stephen Harrison (eds), *Classics in the Modern World: A Democratic Turn?* (Oxford: Oxford University Press, 2013); and David Rijser, Maarten De Pourcq, and Nathalie De Haan (eds), *Framing Classical Reception Studies: Different Perspectives on a Developing Field* (Leiden and Boston: Brill, 2020).
45 See Mark Bradley, *Classics and Imperialism in the British Empire* (Oxford: Oxford University Press, 2010); and Phiroze Vasunia, *The Classics and Colonial India* (Oxford: Oxford University Press, 2013).
46 See Viccy Coltman, *Classical Sculpture and the Culture of Collecting in Britain Since 1760* (Oxford: Oxford University Press, 2009); Can Bilsel, *Antiquity on Display: Regimes of the Authentic in Berlin's Pergamon Museum* (Oxford: Oxford University Press, 2012); and Kate Nichols, *Greece and Rome at the Crystal Palace: Classical Sculpture and Modern Britain, 1854–1936* (Oxford: Oxford University Press, 2015).

47 See Noah Heringman, *Sciences of Antiquity: Romantic Antiquarianism, Natural History and Knowledge Work* (Oxford: Oxford University Press, 2013); David Gange, *Dialogues with the Dead: Egyptology in British Culture and Religion, 1822–1922* (Oxford: Oxford University Press, 2013); Rachel Bryant Davies, *Troy, Carthage and the Victorians: The Drama of Classical Ruins in the Nineteenth-Century Imagination* (Cambridge: Cambridge University Press, 2018); and Edmund Richardson, *Alexandria: The Quest for the Lost City* (London: Bloomsbury 2021).

48 See Christopher Stray, *Classics Transformed: Schools, Universities, and Society in England, 1830–1960* (Oxford: Clarendon Press, 1998); Christopher Stray, *Classics in Britain: Scholarship, Education, and Publishing 1800–2000* (Oxford: Oxford University Press, 2018); and Edmund Richardson, *Classical Victorians: Scholars, Scoundrels and Generals in Pursuit of Antiquity* (Cambridge: Cambridge University Press, 2013).

49 See Edith Hall and Henry Stead (eds), *Greek and Roman Classics in the British Struggle for Social Reform* (London: Bloomsbury, 2015); Laura Monrós-Gaspar, *Victorian Classical Burlesques: A Critical Anthology* (London: Bloomsbury, 2015); Rachel Bryant Davies, *Victorian Epic Burlesques: A Critical Anthology of Nineteenth-Century Theatrical Entertainments After Homer* (London: Bloomsbury, 2018); and Edith Hall and Henry Stead, *A People's History of Classics: Class and Greco-Roman Antiquity in Britain and Ireland 1689 to 1939* (New York: Routledge, 2020).

50 See Isobel Hurst, *Victorian Women Writers and the Classics: The Feminine of Homer* (Oxford: Oxford University Press, 2008); Rosie Wyles and Edith Hall (eds), *Women Classical Scholars: Unsealing the Fountain from the Renaissance to Jacqueline de Romilly* (Oxford: Oxford University Press, 2016); and Yopie Prins, *Ladies' Greek: Victorian Translations of Tragedy* (Princeton: Princeton University Press, 2017).

51 See Lisa Maurice (ed.), *The Reception of Ancient Greece and Rome in Children's Literature: Heroes and Eagles* (Leiden: Brill, 2015); Katarzyna Marciniak, *Our Mythical Childhood: The Classics and Literature for Children and Young Adults* (Leiden: Brill, 2016); Sheila Murnaghan and Deborah H. Roberts, *Childhood and the Classics: Britain and America, 1850–1965* (Oxford: Oxford University Press, 2018); Owen Hodkinson and Helen Lovatt (eds), *Classical Reception and Children's Literature: Greece, Rome and Childhood* (London and New York: I.B. Tauris, 2018); Claudia Nelson and Anne Morey, *Topologies of the Classical World in Children's Fiction: Palimpsests, Maps, and Fractals* (Oxford: Oxford University Press, 2020); Rachel Bryant Davies and Barbara Gribling (eds), *Pasts at Play: Childhood Encounters with History in British Culture, 1750–1914* (Manchester: Manchester University Press, 2020); and Rachel Bryant Davies, *Greco-Roman Antiquity in British Children's Culture* (Oxford: forthcoming, Oxford University Press).

52 See, for example, Donna Zuckerberg, 'My Classics Will Be Intersectional, Or …', *Eidolon* (4 December 2020), https://eidolon.pub/my-classics-will-be-intersectional-or-14ed6e0bcd1c, accessed 29 August 2021.

53 See Donna Zuckerberg, *Not All Dead White Men: Classics and Misogyny in the Digital Age* (Cambridge and London: Harvard University Press 2018); and Helen Morales, *Antigone Rising: The Subversive Power of the Ancient Myths* (New York: Bold Type Books, 2020).

54 Zuckerberg, 'My Classics Will Be Intersectional'. See also Adam Lecznar, Heidi Morse, Ian S. Moyer (eds), *Classicisms in the Black Atlantic* (Oxford: Oxford University Press, 2020); and Jonathan Cahana-Blum, Karmen MacKendrick (eds), *We and They: Decolonizing Greco-Roman and Biblical Antiquities* (Aarhus: Aarhus University Press, 2019).

55 The word 'looted' is used, for example, in Ben Quinn, 'Calls for Full Inventory of World Artefacts Held by Church of England', *The Guardian* (9 April 2021), https://www.theguardian.com/world/2021/apr/09/calls-for-full-inventory-of-world-artefacts-held-by-church-of-england-benin-bronzes, accessed 29 August 2021. Similar repatriative acts have also happened from the United States; see, for example, BBC News, 'US Returns Ancient Stone Carvings to Thailand', *BBC News* (28 May 2021), https://www.bbc.co.uk/news/world-us-canada-57286063, accessed 29 August 2021.
56 Dan Hicks, 'Decolonising Museums Isn't Part of a "Culture War". It's about Keeping Them Relevant', *The Guardian* (7 May 2021), https://www.theguardian.com/commentisfree/2021/may/07/decolonising-museums-isnt-part-of-a-culture-war-its-about-keeping-them-relevant, accessed 29 August 2021.
57 Miranda Bryant, 'Museum of the Home Reopens to Protests Over Statue of Slave Ship Owner', *The Guardian* (12 June 2021), https://www.theguardian.com/culture/2021/jun/12/museum-of-the-home-reopens-to-protests-over-statue-of-slave-ship-owner, accessed 29 August 2021.
58 Steedman, *Dust*, p. 164.

Bibliography

Abram, Nicola. *Black British Women's Theatre: Intersectionality, Archives, Aesthetics*. Cham: Palgrave Macmillan, 2020.

Agawu, Kofi. *Representing African Music: Postcolonial Notes, Queries, Positions*. New York and London: Routledge, 2003.

Baker, Geoffrey. *Imposing Harmony: Music and Society in Colonial Cuzco*. Durham: Duke University Press, 2008.

Ballantyne, Tony. *Entanglements of Empire: Missionaries, Maori, and the Question of the Body*. Auckland: Auckland University Press, 2015.

BBC News. 'US Returns Ancient Stone Carvings to Thailand'. *BBC News* (28 May 2021). https://www.bbc.co.uk/news/world-us-canada-57286063. Accessed 29 August 2021.

Beate, Peter. 'Negotiation the Co-Curation of an Online Community Popular Music Archive'. *Popular Music History* 13, no. 1–2 (2020): 58–76.

Bilsel, Can. *Antiquity on Display: Regimes of the Authentic in Berlin's Pergamon Museum*. Oxford: Oxford University Press, 2012.

Bradley, Mark. *Classics and Imperialism in the British Empire*. Oxford: Oxford University Press, 2010.

Bryant, Miranda. 'Museum of the Home Reopens to Protests over Statue of Slave Ship Owner'. *The Guardian* (12 June 2021). https://www.theguardian.com/culture/2021/jun/12/museum-of-the-home-reopens-to-protests-over-statue-of-slave-ship-owner. Accessed 29 August 2021.

Bryant Davies, Rachel. *Troy, Carthage and the Victorians: The Drama of Classical Ruins in the Nineteenth-Century Imagination*. Cambridge: Cambridge University Press, 2018.

Bryant Davies, Rachel. *Victorian Epic Burlesques: A Critical Anthology of Nineteenth-Century Theatrical Entertainments after Homer*. London: Bloomsbury, 2018.

Bryant Davies, Rachel. *Greco-Roman Antiquity in British Children's Culture* (forthcoming, Oxford: Oxford University Press).

Bryant Davies, Rachel, and Barbara Gribling (eds). *Pasts at Play: Childhood Encounters with History in British Culture, 1750–1914*. Manchester: Manchester University Press, 2020.

Burnett, Philip, Erin Johnson-Williams, and Yvonne Liao. 'Music, Empire, Colonialism: Sounding Out the Archives'. Special Issue of *Postcolonial Studies*, edited by Philip Burnett, Erin Johnson-Williams, and Yvonne Liao (forthcoming, 2022).

Burton, Antoinette. 'Introduction: Archive Fever, Archive Stories'. In *Archive Stories: Facts, Fictions, and the Writing of History*, edited by Antionette Burton, 1–24. Durham: Duke University Press, 2006.

Byrd, W. Carson, Rachelle J. Brunn-Bevel, and Sarah M. Ovink (eds). *Intersectionality and Higher Education: Identity and Inequality on College Campuses*. New Brunswick: Rutgers University Press, 2019.

Cahana-Blum, Jonathan, and Karmen MacKendrick (eds). *We and They: Decolonizing Greco-Roman and Biblical Antiquities*. Aarhus: Aarhus University Press, 2019.

Cho, Sumi, Kimberlé Williams Crenshaw, and Leslie McCall. 'Towards a Field of Intersectionality Studies: Theory, Application, and Praxis'. *Signs: Journal of Women in Culture and Society* 38, no. 4 (2013): 785–810.

Coaston, Jane. 'The Intersectionality Wars'. *Vox* (28 May 2019). https://www.vox.com/the-highlight/2019/5/20/18542843/intersectionality-conservatism-law-race-gender-discrimination. Accessed 17 May 2021.

Coltman, Viccy. *Classical Sculpture and the Culture of Collecting in Britain since 1760*. Oxford: Oxford University Press, 2009.

Crenshaw, Kimberlé. 'Demarginalizing the Intersection of Race and Sex: A Black Feminist Critique of Antidiscrimination Doctrine, Feminist Theory and Antiracist Politics'. *University of Chicago Legal Forum* 31 (1989): 139–67.

Crenshaw, Kimberlé. *On Intersectionality: Essential Writings*. New York: New Press, 2022.

Cuk, Sarah. 'Do-It-Yourself Music Archives: A Response and Alternative to Mainstream Exclusivity'. *The Serials Librarian* (2021): https://doi.org/10.1080/0361526X.2021.1910614.

Decolonising the Archive. https://www.decolonisingthearchive.com/. Accessed 2 December 2021.

Demeter, Márton, and Ronina Istratii. 'Scrutinising What Open Access Journals Mean for Global Inequities'. *Publishing Research Quarterly* 36 (2020): 505–22.

Derrida, Jacques. *Archive Fever: A Freudian Impression*, translated by Eric Prenowitz. Chicago: University of Chicago Press, 1995.

Dorney, Kate. 'The Ordering of Things: Allure, Access, and Archives'. *Shakespeare Bulletin* 28, no. 1 (2010): 19–36.

Dromi, Shai M. 'Archival Research during COVID-19'. *Footnotes* 48, no. 3 (2020): 6–8.

Eichhorn, Kate. *The Archival Turn in Feminism: Outrage and Order*. Philadelphia: Temple University Press, 2013.

Emba, Christine. 'Opinion: Intersectionality'. *The Washington Post* (21 September 2015). https://www.washingtonpost.com/news/in-theory/wp/2015/09/21/intersectionality-a-primer/. Accessed 29 August 2021.

Farge, Arlette. *The Allure of the Archives*, translated by Thomas Scott-Railton. New Haven: Yale University Press, 2013.

Fauser, Annegret. 'Sound, Music, War and Violence: Listening from the Archive'. *Transposition* 2 (2020). https://doi.org/10.4000/transposition.4310.

Foucault, Michel. *The Archaeology of Knowledge*. London: Tavistock, 1972.

Foucault, Michel. *The History of Sexuality: An Introduction*, Vol. 1, translated by R. Hurley. New York: Random House, 1978.
Galsworthy, Tim. 'Archival Research in a Time of Coronavirus'. https://www.blogs.hss.ed.ac.uk/pubs-and-publications/2020/05/10/archival-research-coronavirus/. Accessed 2 December 2021.
Gange, David. *Dialogues with the Dead: Egyptology in British Culture and Religion, 1822-1922*. Oxford: Oxford University Press, 2013.
Goldbaum, Christina, and Kimon de Greef. 'Wildfire Deals Hard Blow to South Africa's Archives' (19 April 2021). https://www.nytimes.com/2021/04/19/world/africa/cape-town-table-mountain-fire.html. Accessed 2 December 2021.
Goldhill, Simon. *Victorian Culture and Classical Antiquity: Art, Opera, Fiction, and the Proclamation of Modernity*. Princeton: Princeton University Press, 2011.
Griffin, Paul. 'Making Usable Pasts: Collaboration, Labour and Activism in the Archive'. *Area* 50, no. 4 (2018): 501–8.
Hall, Edith and Henry Stead (eds). *Greek and Roman Classics in the British Struggle for Social Reform*. London: Bloomsbury, 2015.
Hall, Edith and Henry Stead. *A People's History of Classics: Class and Greco-Roman Antiquity in Britain and Ireland 1689 to 1939*. New York: Routledge, 2020.
Hardwick, Lorna, and Christopher Stray (eds). *A Companion to Classical Receptions*. Oxford: Wiley-Blackwell, 2011.
Hardwick, Lorna, and Christopher Stray (eds). *Classics in the Modern World: A Democratic Turn?* Oxford: Oxford University Press, 2013.
Harle, Matthew. *Afterlives of Abandoned Work: Creative Debris in the Archive*. London: Bloomsbury Academic, 2019.
Harris, Verne. *Ghosts of Archive: Deconstructive Intersectionality and Praxis*. London: Routledge, 2020.
Hartman, Saidiya. *Scenes of Subjection: Terror, Slavery, and Self-Making in Nineteenth-Century America*. New York and Oxford: Oxford University Press, 1997.
Hartman, Saidiya. *Lose Your Mother: A Journey along the Atlantic Slave Route*. New York: Farrar, Straus and Giroux, 2007.
Hartman, Saidiya. 'Venus in Two Acts'. *Small Axe* 26 (2008): 1–14.
Heringman, Noah. *Sciences of Antiquity: Romantic Antiquarianism, Natural History and Knowledge Work*. Oxford: Oxford University Press, 2013.
Herman, Paul. 'The Heroic Study of Records: The Contested Persona of the Archival Historian'. *History of the Human Sciences* 26, no. 4 (2013): 67–83.
Hicks, Dan. 'Decolonising Museums Isn't Part of a "Culture War". It's about Keeping Them Relevant'. *The Guardian* (7 May 2021). https://www.theguardian.com/commentisfree/2021/may/07/decolonising-museums-isnt-part-of-a-culture-war-its-about-keeping-them-relevant. Accessed 29 August 2021.
Hodkinson, Owen, and Helen Lovatt (eds). *Classical Reception and Children's Literature: Greece, Rome and Childhood*. London and New York: I.B. Tauris, 2018.
Howell, Alison, and Melanie Richter-Montpetit. 'Racism in Foucauldian Security Studies: Biopolitics, Liberal War, and the Whitewashing of Colonial and Racial Violence'. *International Political Sociology* 13 (2019): 2–19.
Hoyle, Victoria. 'Editorial: Archives and Public History'. *Archives and Records* 38, no. 1 (2017): 1–4.
Hurst, Isobel. *Victorian Women Writers and the Classics: The Feminine of Homer*. Oxford: Oxford University Press, 2008.

Irving, David. *Colonial Counterpoint: Music in Early Modern Manila*. Oxford: Oxford University Press, 2010.
Jenkyns, Richard. *The Victorians and Ancient Greece*. Oxford: Blackwell, 1980.
Johnson-Williams, Erin. 'Online EDI Resources: Towards a Reflexive Archive'. *Royal Musical Association Research Chronicle* (2021). https://doi.org/10.1017/rrc.2021.3.
Jones, Esyllt W., Shelley Sweeney, Ian Milligan, Greg Bak, and Jo-Anne McCutcheon. 'Remembering is a Form of Honouring: Preserving the Covid-19 Archival Record'. *Facets* 6 (2021): https://doi.org/10.1139/facets-2020-0115.
Kärjä, Antti-Ville. 'Historiography and the Role of the Archive'. In *The Routledge Companion to Popular Music History and Heritage*, edited by Sarah Baker, Catherine Strong, Lauren Istvandity, and Zelmarie Cantillon, 108–18. London and New York: Routledge, 2018.
Lambrechts, Lizabé. 'The Becoming of an Archive: Perspectives on a Music Archive and the Limits of Institutionality'. *Social Dynamics* 46, no. 2 (2020): 310–22.
Landau, Carolyn, and Janet Topp Fargion. 'We're All Archivists Now: Towards a More Equitable Ethnomusicology'. *Ethnomusicology Forum* 21, no. 2 (2012): 125–40.
Lecznar, Adam, Heidi Morse, and Ian S. Moyer (eds). *Classicisms in the Black Atlantic*. Oxford: Oxford University Press, 2020.
Legg, Stephen, and Deana Heath (eds). *South Asian Governmentalities: Michel Foucault and the Question of Postcolonial Orderings*. Cambridge: Cambridge University Press, 2018.
Lightman, Bernard, and Bennett Zon (eds). *Victorian Culture and the Origin of Disciplines*. New York: Routledge, 2020.
Lutz, Helma, Maria Vivar, and Linda Supik (eds). *Framing Intersectionality: Debates on a Multi-faceted Concept in Gender Studies*. London: Routledge, 2016.
Manoff, Marlene. 'Theories of the Archive from across the Disciplines'. *Libraries and the Academy* 4, no. 1 (2004): 9–25.
Marciniak, Katarzyna. *Our Mythical Childhood: The Classics and Literature for Children and Young Adults*. Leiden: Brill, 2016.
Martindale, Charles. *Redeeming the Text: Latin Poetry and the Hermeneutics of Reception*. Cambridge: Cambridge University Press, 1993.
Martino, Ariel. 'Revisioning the Archival Turn'. *Criticism* 62, no. 4 (2020): 629–33.
Maurice, Lisa (ed.). *The Reception of Ancient Greece and Rome in Children's Literature: Heroes and Eagles*. Leiden: Brill, 2015.
Morreira, Shannon. 'Significant Archives Are Under Threat in Cape Town's Fire. Why They Matter So Much'. *The Conversation* (19 April 2021). https://theconversation.com/significant-archives-are-under-threat-in-cape-towns-fire-why-they-matter-so-much-159299. Accessed 2 December 2021.
Murnaghan, Sheila, and Deborah H. Roberts. *Childhood and the Classics: Britain and America, 1850–1965*. Oxford: Oxford University Press, 2018.
Milthorpe, Naomi. 'Archives, Authority, Aura: Modernism's Archival Turn'. *Papers on Language and Literature* 55, no. 1 (2019): 3–14.
Mirza, Heidi Safia. 'Decolonizing Higher Education: Black Feminism and the Intersectionality of Race and Gender'. *Journal of Feminist Scholarship* 7, no. 7 (2014–15): 1–12.
Monrós-Gaspar, Laura. *Victorian Classical Burlesques: A Critical Anthology*. London: Bloomsbury, 2015.

Morales, Helen. *Antigone Rising: The Subversive Power of the Ancient Myths*. New York: Bold Type Books, 2020.
Morris, Charles E. 'The Archival Turn in Rhetorical Studies; Or, the Archives Rhetorical (Re)turn'. *Rhetoric & Public Affairs* 9, no. 1 (2006): 113–15.
Nash, Jennifer C. 'Re-Thinking Intersectionality'. *Feminist Review* 89 (2008): 1–15.
Nash, Jennifer C. 'Intersectionality and Its Discontents'. *American Quarterly* 69, no. 1 (2017): 117–29.
Nelson, Claudia, and Anne Morey. *Topologies of the Classical World in Children's Fiction: Palimpsests, Maps, and Fractals*. Oxford: Oxford University Press, 2020.
Nichols, Kate. *Greece and Rome at the Crystal Palace: Classical Sculpture and Modern Britain, 1854–1936*. Oxford: Oxford University Press, 2015.
Paulus, Michael J. 'Reconceptualizing Academic Libraries and Archives in the Digital Age'. *Libraries and the Academy* 11, no. 4 (2011): 939–52.
Pettan, Svanibor, and Jeff Todd Titon (eds). *Public Ethnomusicology, Education, Archives, & Commerce*. Oxford: Oxford University Press, 2019.
Pratt, Mary Louise. *Imperial Eyes: Travel Writing and Transculturation*. London: Routledge, 2008.
Prins, Yopie. *Ladies' Greek: Victorian Translations of Tragedy*. Princeton: Princeton University Press, 2017.
Quinn, Ben. 'Calls for Full Inventory of World Artefacts Held by Church of England'. *The Guardian* (9 April 2021). https://www.theguardian.com/world/2021/apr/09/calls-for-full-inventory-of-world-artefacts-held-by-church-of-england-benin-bronzes. Accessed 29 August 2021.
Qureshi, Sadiah. *Peoples on Parade: Exhibitions, Empire, and Anthropology in Nineteenth-Century Britain*. Chicago and London: The University of Chicago Press, 2011.
Reid, Kirsty, and Fiona Paisley. *Sources and Methods in Histories of Colonialism: Approaching the Imperial Archive*. London: Routledge, 2017.
Reilly, Maura. *Curatorial Activism: Towards an Ethics of Curating*. London: Thames & Hudson, 2018.
Richards, Jeffrey. *Imperialism and Music: Britain, 1876–1953*. Manchester: Manchester University Press, 2017.
Richards, Thomas. *The Imperial Archive: Knowledge and the Fantasy of Empire*. London: Verso, 1993.
Richardson, Edmund. *Classical Victorians: Scholars, Scoundrels and Generals in Pursuit of Antiquity*. Cambridge: Cambridge University Press, 2013.
Richardson, Edmund. *Alexandria: The Quest for the Lost City*. London: Bloomsbury, 2021.
Rijser, David, Maarten De Pourcq, and Nathalie De Haan (eds). *Framing Classical Reception Studies: Different Perspectives on a Developing Field*. Leiden and Boston: Brill, 2020.
Roque Ricardo, and Kim A. Wagner (eds). *Engaging Colonial Knowledge: Reading European Archives in World History*. Houndmills, Basingstoke: Palgrave Macmillan, 2012.
Schwartz Joan M., and Terry Cook. 'Archives, Records, and Power: The Making of Modern Memory'. *Archival Science* 2 (2002): 1–19.
Sharpe, Christina. *In the Wake: On Blackness and Being*. Durham: Duke University Press, 2016.

Simon, Cheryl. 'Introduction: Following the Archival Turn'. *Visual Resources* 18, no. 2 (2002): 101–7.

Smith, Linda Tuhiwai. *Decolonizing Methodologies: Research and Indigenous Peoples*. London: Zed Books, 2012.

Spinney, Laura. 'What Are COVID Archivists Keeping for Tomorrow's Historians?'. *Nature* (17 December 2020). https://www.nature.com/articles/d41586-020-03554-0. Accessed 2 December 2021.

Spivak, Gayatri Chakravorty. 'Can the Subaltern Speak? Speculations on Widow Sacrifice'. In *Colonial Discourse and Post-Colonial Theory: A Reader*, edited by Patrick Williams and Laura Chrisman, 66–111. London: Routledge, 1993.

Starn, Randolph. 'Truths in the Archives'. *Common Knowledge* 8, no. 2 (2002): 387–401.

Steedman, Carolyn. *Dust: The Archive and Cultural History*. Manchester: Manchester University Press, 2001.

Steedman, Carolyn. 'After the Archive'. *Comparative Critical Studies* 8, no. 2–3 (2011): 321–40.

Steedman, Carolyn. 'Something She Called a Fever: Michelet, Derrida, and Dust'. *The American Historical Review* 106, no. 4 (2001): 1159–80.

Steinmetz, Katy. 'She Coined the Term "Intersectionality" over 30 Years Ago. Here's What It Means to Her Today'. *TIME* (20 February 2020). https://time.com/5786710/kimberle-crenshaw-intersectionality/. Accessed 29 August 2021.

Stoler, Ann Laura. *Along the Archival Grain: Epistemic Anxieties and Colonial Common Sense*. Princeton: Princeton University Press, 2009.

Stoler, Ann Laura. *Imperial Debris: On Ruins and Ruination*. Durham: Duke University Press, 2013.

van Straaten, Eva-Maria Alexandra. 'The *White* Ethnomusicologist's Burden: *White* Innocence and the Archive in Music Studies'. *The World of Music* 10, no. 1 (2021): 131–67.

Stray, Christopher. *Classics Transformed: Schools, Universities, and Society in England, 1830–1960*. Oxford: Clarendon Press, 1998.

Stray, Christopher. *Classics in Britain: Scholarship, Education, and Publishing 1800–2000*. Oxford: Oxford University Press, 2018.

Thomas, David, Simon Fowler, and Valerie Johnson (eds). *The Silence of the Archive*. Chicago: Neal-Schuman, 2017.

Tully, Paul, and Neil Carr. 'Obstacles and Possibilities in Archival Research: Archives as a Data Source for Leisure Scholars in Lockdown'. *Leisure Studies* 40, no. 6 (2021): 888–94.

Turner, Frank M. *The Greek Heritage in Victorian Britain*. New Haven: Yale University Press, 1981.

Vallier, John. 'Preserving the Past, Activating the Future: Collaborative Archiving in Ethnomusicology'. In *Ethnomusicology: A Contemporary Reader*, edited by Jennifer C. Post, 307–17. New York: Routledge: 2017.

Vance, Norman. *The Victorians and Ancient Rome*. Oxford: Blackwell Publishers, 1997.

Vasunia, Phiroze. *The Classics and Colonial India*. Oxford: Oxford University Press, 2013.

Walsham, Alexandra. 'The Social History of the Archive: Record-Keeping in Early Modern Europe'. *Past & Present* 230, no. 11 (2016): 9–48.

Wosh, Peter J. 'Reflections on Public History and Archives Education'. *Journal of Archival Organization* 15, no. 3 (2018): 95–9.

Wyles, Rosie, and Edith Hall (eds). *Women Classical Scholars: Unsealing the Fountain from the Renaissance to Jacqueline de Romilly*. Oxford: Oxford University Press, 2016.

Yale, Elizabeth. 'The History of Archives: The State of the Discipline'. *Book History* 18 (2015): 332–59.

Zon, Bennett. *Representing Non-Western Music in Nineteenth-Century Britain*. Rochester: University of Rochester Press, 2007.

Zuckerberg, Donna. *Not All Dead White Men: Classics and Misogyny in the Digital Age*. Cambridge and London: Harvard University Press 2018.

Zuckerberg, Donna. 'My Classics Will Be Intersectional, Or … '. *Eidolon* (4 December 2020). https://eidolon.pub/my-classics-will-be-intersectional-or-14ed6e0bcd1c. Accessed 29 August 2021.

Part One

Archival ownership

2

'Found in store': Working with source communities and difficult objects at Durham University's Oriental Museum

Rachel Barclay, Lauren Barnes, Gillian Ramsay, Craig Barclay and Helen Armstrong

Introduction

Durham University's Oriental Museum is often described as a 'hidden gem'. Opened in 1960, today it is home to world-class collections of more than 35,000 objects from across North Africa and Asia. Originally envisioned as a teaching and research resource for the university's School of Oriental Studies, the museum now combines its academic role with a commitment to making its collections accessible to local, national and international communities.

The Museum's mid-twentieth-century origins do not mean that its collections have escaped the influence of Empire and colonialism. This should come as no surprise, as many of the objects held by the museum were collected either during the nineteenth century or the early years of the twentieth century. Moreover, the men and women whose collections are today housed within the museum were very often products – if not active agents – of the British Empire, and their collections inevitably reflect the established colonial norms and mindsets of an Empire that lasted well into the last century.

The opening sections of this chapter address some of the broad issues raised across this volume. Questions addressed relate to origins and roles of museums as institutions such as who are, and who can and should be, a museum's stakeholders? Online access to collections, acquisition, storage and disposal of collections, and approaches to display are also discussed.

Following this are two focused case studies, one at gallery level (2013–15), and one at the level of an individual object (2017–21). Both examples centre upon stakeholders, different categories of knowledge and the purpose of collections, but with very different outcomes. The first emphasizes the challenges and mutual benefits of actively engaging with a range of stakeholder communities in the process of developing a new gallery.[1] The second explores how museum objects can serve as a valuable resource to support research and international engagement, showcasing how a student-led research project contributed to the deaccessioning and return of a challenging object.

Origins and role of the Oriental Museum

The study of the languages and literature of the ancient Near East formed part of the theology curriculum of Durham University from its foundation in 1832. In the 1920s teaching expanded to include courses in both classical and modern Arabic. Following the conclusion of the Second World War, the Scarborough Commission recommended that Durham University be selected as one of five UK universities in which special facilities should be developed for the teaching of the Near and Far Eastern languages.[2] As a result, a new School of Oriental Studies was established in Durham in 1951, with Professor Thomas W. Thacker as its director.

From the outset, Thacker was keen that an understanding of material culture must support the teaching of languages, arguing that 'An Oriental School which aims to teach the cultural background of the oriental peoples must have a museum at its disposal'.[3] Not only was there no such museum in Durham but, in Thacker's opinion, there were no adequate collections anywhere in the North East of England. He therefore set out to create his own museum which, from its inception, was intended to be firmly embedded within the university's teaching environment.

Plans drawn up for Durham by Thacker were heavily influenced by H. N. Spalding, the Oxford-based scholar and philanthropist. Spalding believed that future global conflict could only be avoided by nurturing understanding between, and study of, the world's great faiths, including their literature, art, architecture and music. Spalding's proposals to establish an 'Asia House' at the University of Oxford, incorporating library, seminar and study spaces alongside museum displays, never came to fruition.[4] However, they are strongly reflected in the plans drawn up for a Durham by Thacker.

The museum still exists to support learning focused on the cultures of North Africa and Asia, but over time its wider remit has increased significantly. Today, staff seek to address formal and informal learning across a range of communities. Widening participation in Higher Education (hereafter HE), raising aspirations among deprived communities in the North East of England, tackling racism and contributing to community cohesion are as important as ensuring that families and tourists visiting Durham have an enjoyable afternoon out. At times this has put the curatorial team in conflict with senior managers solely focused upon the research priorities of Durham University. However, as the museum today receives only around a third of its annual funding directly from the university, the priorities of other funders and stakeholders – as well as the university's developing interest in community engagement – must also be addressed.

Space, storage and collecting

To meet his aspirations, Thacker embarked upon ambitious programmes of fundraising and collecting during the late 1940s and 1950s. Many of the collections that he sought to acquire had roots firmly in nineteenth-century collecting practices and philosophies, and the UK's colonial past.

A museum building was required to house these collections, and between 1957 and 1960 a grant of £60,000 from the Calouste Gulbenkian Foundation funded the construction of what was planned to be the first phase of an ambitious construction project. The aim was to display the whole collection in a manner suitable for use in HE teaching, and so the new museum building was constructed without any dedicated storage spaces. Two further phases, to allow for the expansion of the collections, and to provide a home for all the supporting infrastructure facilities needed, were planned but never built.

Within a very short time, the ambition to merge teaching, library and gallery spaces was lost. Today, every available space within the museum has been turned to public display, and a converted service space beneath the building serves as the museum's main object store. Since opening, the museum's collection has more than tripled in size, from fewer than 10,000 objects in 1960 to more than 35,000 today. This means that the entire collection can no longer be displayed. Currently only around 5 per cent of the collection is on display, a situation not uncommon in many museums worldwide.

This does not mean that the stored collections are not in use. Quite the opposite: these collections sit at the heart of the museum's hands-on teaching. Up to 2,000 objects a year are used for object-based learning sessions with students from Durham University and other regional institutions. Similar numbers of objects are retrieved for study by researchers from around the globe.

Despite limitations on space the Oriental Museum continues actively to collect. Research and teaching at Durham University are constantly evolving and, as such, the museum must respond. A museum which ceases to collect risks becoming an artefact in itself. For example, until 2008 the Oriental Museum's Chinese collections were effectively terminated at the end of the Imperial Era, with twentieth-century material being almost absent. Today there are growing collections relating to recent Chinese history, which are now used to support teaching on a range of undergraduate courses.

In common with most museums, the Oriental Museum has very limited funds for new acquisitions. Staff undertake targeted acquisitions to meet specific needs for teaching, display or engagement. Beyond this, the museum is heavily reliant on the generosity of donors. There is a symbiotic relationship between institutions and the collectors who make donations. Many donors are emotionally invested in their collections and see them as their legacy. Even after a donor has died, their descendants often take an active interest in their collections and seek to maintain a relationship with the curators and the institution. Curators at the Oriental Museum are in regular communication with the family of donors whose collections are rooted in nineteenth-century British colonialism. Families do not always wish for stories to be told if they feel the stories may cast their forbearers in a negative light. These issues need to be handled with care and understanding.

Almost all museums are short of physical space, and the deaccessioning of inappropriate and unwanted collections has become an important topic of discussion within the sector in recent years. Space limitations create major challenges for institutions like the Oriental Museum, which follows a policy of active collecting. The approach of the Oriental Museum to the question of deaccessioning material has been one of considerable caution. Over the last fifty years there have been many changes in fashion with regard to teaching and research. Collections which might have been regarded as unnecessary twenty or thirty years ago are now in high demand by the international research community. Where deaccessioning is appropriate, transfer to another, Accredited museum must always be the preference.[5] Up to this point however, the Oriental Museum has generally preferred to look for other solutions, such as more efficient storage.

Deaccessioning must not be confused or compared with repatriation. Like all forms of engagement with communities, repatriation at its best can be a positive and beneficial experience for all involved. It takes time and care and the building of relationships based on trust and understanding, as addressed in the second case study.

Displays

Whilst the Oriental Museum's academic and pedagogical functions remain, it has also developed into an outward-facing public museum, with strong commitments to widening participation, inclusive engagement, schools and community learning, international partnership working and co-curation.

Despite these changes, until the early 2000s the museum's displays were still laid out in a very academic style with dense displays, detailed academic labelling and little in the way of interactivity, seating or activities for children (Figure 2.1). In 2008 however, the museum embarked upon a major redevelopment programme which has resulted in the complete regeneration of all the museum's permanent galleries to better reflect contemporary use of the galleries and changing curatorial practices (Figure 2.2). At

Figure 2.1 The Oriental Museum in 2009 before the redisplay project began. Courtesy of Oriental Museum, Durham University.

Figure 2.2 The Oriental Museum in 2021 after the completion of the new gallery of the Himalayas, South Asia and Southeast Asia. Courtesy of Oriental Museum, Durham University.

this juncture, a completely new interpretative approach was needed. The curatorial and learning teams worked together to agree on a set of working principles and practices. With very rare exceptions, no museum has the depth and breadth of collections to approach all time periods or topics equally. Display is always a compromise between the desire to include a topic and the reality of the contents of the collection, taking into account the ways in which the space will be used, and by whom.

After considering a range of theoretical approaches, consulting with stakeholders and undertaking front-end evaluation with users, the decision was made to lay out the galleries on a geographical basis. In order to help visitors understand the differences and points of connection between the cultures represented, a set of recurring themes – designed to play to the strengths of the collection – were developed within an overarching interpretation strategy. These themes were allied to a target audience strategy, which reflected the core priorities of the museum's key funders and stakeholders. The redisplay project team allocated gallery space based upon the relative size of each collection and level and type of use by target audiences.

Who are our stakeholders?

Within a postcolonial context, the debate on who has the right to interpret or respond to objects from a particular culture has grown in the museum world in recent years.[6] As discussed by Adiva Lawrence and Alexandra Watson Jones elsewhere in this volume, new voices beyond that of the 'authoritative curator' have been introduced. Today, decolonization sits at the heart of museum practice and it is expected that museums will consult with, and reflect the views of, their local and source communities.[7] Particular emphasis has been placed on working with ethnic minority stakeholder communities by funders such as the Arts Council England and the National Lottery Heritage Fund.

This is a very laudable sentiment, but not all of England is ethnically diverse. Census data from 2011 shows that 95.3 per cent of the population of the North East of England identify as white. This rises to 98.2 per cent for County Durham. Case study 1 in this chapter focuses on South and Southeast Asia. South Asian communities represent just 1.8 per cent of the North East population, falling to only 0.4 per cent in County Durham.[8]

Each museum must develop a strategy that meets the requirements of its own unique situation, and the physical location of the museum can have as much impact on who constitutes a stakeholder as its curatorial philosophy or the contents of its collection. If the Oriental Museum was located in a major multicultural conurbation such as London or Birmingham, it would undoubtedly need to adopt different approaches to engagement. At the Oriental Museum, the approach has been adopted that the collections are housed and cared for in a museum in the North East of England and, as such, are an integral part of the history and culture of that region as well their countries of origin.

Lack of knowledge and understanding of ethnic and faith minority communities – sometimes manifesting as overt racism – are major issues within our broader community.[9] As such, in all of our projects, the museum actively seeks to engage with a range of groups, including not only relevant ethnic and faith communities, but also those who are not of Asian or North African ethnicity and lacking in any particular prior interest in the cultures of the region. These groups include local schools, students, artists and groups living with a variety of mental and physical health conditions. Working with as broad a range of local people as possible provides opportunities for preconceptions to be broken down and for building new understanding and appreciation.

At the same time, the museum continues to sit at the heart of an international research community. Our philosophy is that all of these local and international voices have an equal right to be heard. Curators should be able to listen and learn with humility and then apply what they have learnt to their work using their own knowledge and expertise.

Collections online

At Durham University the development of a combined museum, library and archive online discovery system has been delivered in parallel with the physical redisplay project.[10] This makes the whole collection accessible in digital form to audiences around the globe. The sharing of collections information online is particularly relevant to the wider research community. In the first year after the database went online in

2015, the museum saw a five-fold increase in the annual number of research enquires. In 2018–19 (the last complete year before the Covid-19 pandemic) around 60 per cent of academic research enquiries were dealt with entirely online via the sharing of data, images and curatorial expertise. Only 40 per cent of researchers visited the museum physically to undertake their research.

Whilst massively increasing the 'reach' of the museum's collections, the nature of online catalogues is that the records may be incomplete or contain errors, including misidentifications. They may also contain terminology and language that might be considered outdated or offensive.

The curatorial team have consciously decided not to remove such language from the records. Instead, the guide to using the online database contains the following information for users:

> It is important to understand how objects were viewed in the past. As such, we use our database to preserve all information ever recorded about our collections. This means that historic or outdated terms may be included in some database entries, and some of these terms may be offensive or discriminatory.[11]

Academic researchers and community participants are encouraged to share feedback, corrections and insights, and the database is updated accordingly. Contributions are attributed to a named individual or group whenever possible so that the process of knowledge creation relating to each object is explicit.

'Permanent' galleries and small museums

The average life cycle of a permanent gallery in UK museums today is ten to twenty years. If a museum is to be responsive, it is critical that its 'permanent' galleries are anything but permanent. Rather, they need to be capable of being updated regularly in order to respond to visitor, community and staff feedback, reflect developing research and scholarship, and address the conservation needs of delicate objects.

Today's widespread preference for designer-led galleries – built around custom-made cases, bespoke mounts and externally produced graphics and labels – makes it difficult, if not impossible, for curators to respond to the need for change in a permanent display. In contrast to this approach, all gallery development at the Oriental Museum has been collections-focused and curatorially led, with subject specialists working in close collaboration with the learning and engagement professionals. This has allowed staff to keep users at the heart of the design and allow for maximum flexibility.

All displays are designed to be easily adaptable, and object labels are removable and can be updated quickly and cheaply using templates created in-house. A small museum working with off-the-shelf display materials on a tight budget is more likely to retain the advantage of flexibility. If, a week after opening, you realize an object is in the wrong place to work well for teaching, you can move it, try it out somewhere else and keep tweaking until you get it right.

Case study 1: New permanent gallery for Himalayas, South Asia and Southeast Asia

The Roberts Gallery, which showcases the cultures of South Asia, Southeast Asia and the Himalayas was opened in 2015.[12] The introductory panel for the completed gallery begins with the quotation:

> South Asian history has no one beginning, no one chronology, no single plot or narrative. It is not a singular history but rather many histories with indefinite, contested origins and with countless separate trajectories that multiply as we learn more about the past.[13]

This sums up the challenge the team faced in creating this gallery. An initial review of the collections revealed that 2,420 objects and more than 4,000 uncatalogued photographs from nineteen modern states needed to be assessed for potential inclusion in the gallery.[14] Many objects in the South Asian collection were acquired during the 1950s and 1960s, when the School of Oriental Studies planned to teach the languages and cultures of India. These plans did not come to fruition, and the collections remained largely unstudied and unused. As a result, the cataloguing for many objects remained basic.

The very richness and diversity of South and Southeast Asian history and culture is one of the things that makes it so fascinating and exciting, but it is also the enemy of the non-specialist embarking upon their research. The museum team found it very difficult to source reliable, up-to-date reference texts that were accessible to a non-specialist. Many general introductions reflected outdated and often western-centric views of history and cultural achievement. The current academic climate in the UK does not encourage writing books for non-specialist audiences and, faced with the daunting scale of such a task, few have risen to the challenge in recent years, particularly in regard to material culture. Moreover, there is no Subject Specialist Network (SSN) for South or Southeast Asian curators, and so this route was not available as a way of contacting experts for advice.[15]

All curators use other museums as a source of inspiration and ideas, but even in this case it was noticeable that despite Britain's long and close connection with the region, few museums have large galleries dedicated to South Asia and even fewer to Southeast Asia. Moreover, even where such galleries existed, more often than not their displays have not recently been updated. There are a wider range of specialist galleries in the United States. The South Asian catalogues of museums such as Dallas Museum of Art and Virginia Museum of Fine Arts provided not only detailed information on collection highlights but also useful introductory essays.[16] In addition, freely available online educational resources created by museums such as the Metropolitan Museum of Art provided much needed inspiration.[17] For smaller museums and those without subject-specialist expertise, the publications and online resources of these large, well-funded US museums serve as an invaluable and accessible source of expertise.

Ideally, the Himalayan, South Asian and Southeast Asian collections would each have been assigned its own gallery. Restrictions in terms of space, and the relative size and level of use of the collections, drove the decision to instead create a single combined gallery. The aim of the project team was to turn this potential negative into a positive by emphasizing the connections between, as well as the diversity of, the cultures of the region.

The project was designed from the outset around active engagement with community partners. Given the paucity of academic sources, the insights into the collections gained from community stakeholders took on even greater significance. In line with our approach to stakeholders outlined above, the museum actively engaged with a range of groups. This included those from South and Southeast Asian communities, as well as others who were not of Asian ethnicity and who did not have prior expertise in these cultures.

Sharing knowledge

When engaging with members of ethnic minority communities in a museum setting, there can be an underlying assumption on the part of western curators that the members of those communities must be in possession of privileged knowledge relating to a wide range of historical and cultural artefacts that were created and used in their ancestral homelands. This is not, however, always the case, and such assumptions can place undue pressure upon community members and stifle discussion.

As a result of previous work with other stakeholder communities, this project sought to relieve such preconceptions. In a series of community engagement sessions, the Access Officer instead explicitly stated that there was no expectation of prior knowledge, and that there were no 'right' or 'wrong' interpretations of the objects. This served to nurture a productive environment that encouraged wide-ranging conversation and idea-sharing. More specific information was also sought from members of the local Hindu and Sikh faith groups, who were able to use their deep knowledge of their faiths to input into and shape gallery text, education sessions and team training.

The project engaged with stakeholders from Durham, Newcastle-upon-Tyne, Sunderland and Middlesbrough representing a range of ethnic and faith groups.[18] Feedback gained from these sessions included information such as 'we used this broom for many different uses, this is how we hold it',[19] or 'this script is from the South, I can't read it all but some of it talks about the story of the Ramayana'.[20] This type of response formed the basis for constructive collaborations where further questions were asked about specific objects, and the community's knowledge and experience were used both to enhance database entries and to inform display plans. Information of this type was most readily obtained when the objects discussed related to people's faiths and everyday lives.

Participants often displayed a deep and profound knowledge about the culture of their own local area, but the team also received comments such as 'I don't recognise it so it's not from my country'.[21] Indeed, many community members themselves noted the numerous regional differences between north and south India and the only commonality that some participants could identify was the shared language of English. This feedback confirmed the project team's pre-existing concerns that the permanent gallery could not hope to equally and fairly represent all of the region's diverse cultural groups. We decided that the gallery had to play to the strengths of the collection and that the introductory text should make clear that we are very well aware of the inadequacy of the space and collections to tell 'the whole story' of the region.

Colonial legacies

During the course of the gallery development process, museum staff were questioned by many participants about the acquisition of objects and, in particular, any links between objects, collectors and the British colonial era in India. Anger at the injustices of the colonial era was strongly felt by many members of the community across age groups, ethnicities and faiths.

The project team therefore agreed that the 'British in India' should be one of the themes to be critically addressed in the gallery. This decision was reinforced by changes to the National Curriculum from September 2014, and which placed greater emphasis on the role of imperial conquest, with 'the development of the British Empire with a depth study (for example, of India)' being identified as a specific study topic at Key Stage 3.[22]

Many of the objects initially identified as possessing potential for inclusion in this section were regarded as unhelpful by participants. In particular, sets of figures and paintings depicting 'typical' trades or costumes of different groups were seen as having the potential to perpetuate stereotypes.[23] Staff worked with community members to choose objects that told the story of the British in India in a different way. In response to the wishes of community members, key objects in the finished display relate to British aggression and violence and to the struggle for Indian Independence.

Faith

South Asia is the birthplace of four of the world's major religions and is an important centre for several others. One of the major aims of the redevelopment programme has been to increase the resources for teaching world religions. However, faith is a very personal and highly contentious issue. Gaining access to – and building trust with – stakeholder communities, especially with regard to religious knowledge, is widely recognized as being a difficult and time-consuming endeavour. Developing trust through long-term engagement is difficult in today's funding environment, which is often premised on short-term project funding and a demand for quick results. It soon became apparent that this would be the most difficult aspect of the gallery to manage sensitively.

Early discussions emphasized the need to give equal space to each faith, but also the need to separate the representation of some faiths from others. For example, members of the Sikh community looked at the old displays before they were de-installed and found the association of Sikh and Mughal pieces in the same case (albeit on different shelves) highly problematic and expressed their uneasiness to museum staff.[24] There were clear curatorial reasons behind this display – all of the objects came from northern India and from the same time period. Moreover, they were all examples of skilled artistry and spoke of links between Sikh and Mughal craftsmanship. For the Sikh community members, many of whom had left South Asia as a result of Partition, the long-standing enmity between the two communities nevertheless made it impossible for them to accept these justifications.

In the late 1980s the Oriental Museum received a large donation of weapons which, in 2015, represented a significantly under-researched and under-utilized resource. After discussions with the local Sikh group, it was established that traditional weaponry is an area of interest for some individuals of the Sikh community and so a project was created with the aim of identifying any weapons from the Oriental Museum's collection that might be Sikh in origin.

This symbiotic, collaborative project created tangible benefits both for the museum and the community. The initial audit gave these community members access to all of the museum's South Asian weapons. During this process, they identified several important weapons, one of which was a rare eighteenth-century Sikh *Khanda* sword – a weapon of immense spiritual significance.[25] The project raised awareness of the important collections at the Oriental Museum among the whole community. Museum staff were able to receive advice on the preferred storage of sacred objects and were also able to take pieces from the museum to the *gurdwara* in Newcastle to be shared at a summer school for children in the community. It was our intention that the aims of the museum and the aims of the community would become linked and mutually beneficial.

From the focus on weapons, members of the Sikh community went on to identify other objects relating to Sikhism suitable for display in the new gallery. In addition, gaps in the Oriental Museum's collection relating to Sikhism were identified and many of these were filled via long-term loans made by community members. The result is a completely community-curated and researched case in the permanent gallery (Figure 2.3). This key display output reflected not only the commitment of the Sikh community to the project, but also the relaxed environment in which it was nurtured and developed.

The process of co-developing a range of small, manageable and mutually beneficial projects with different communities supported the development of strong bonds of mutual trust and respect that have outlasted the initial project. This case study highlights the ways in which the building of these relationships blurs boundaries between collectors, donors, curators, researchers and community stakeholders. In this case, and others, the Oriental Museum team have found that working with communities has led to both individuals and groups becoming donors, researchers and curators themselves. These stakeholders have become as invested in the success of the aims of the museum as its staff.

Figure 2.3 One result of mutually beneficial stakeholder working: members of the Sikh community curating a display relating to their faith in the new gallery. Courtesy of Oriental Museum, Durham University.

Case study 2: The Japanese 'Good Luck' Flag

Many western museums house artefacts or collections that were looted during the course, or in the wake, of conflict or conquest. In recent years, debates around how to manage such collections have become increasingly vocal, both within the museum profession and the wider community.[26]

The Japanese Good Luck Flag or *yosegaki hinomaru*,[27] was traditionally presented to Japanese servicemen prior to their departure for military service. Taking the form of a silk or cotton Japanese flag (known as the *hinomaru*, or circular sun), the *yosegaki hinomaru* was decorated with good-luck and patriotic messages by the soldier's family and friends and served as a reminder to its owner not only of his family and home, but also of his duties to the army and Empire.

Reportedly first produced in the late nineteenth century, *yosegaki hinomaru* could vary considerably in size but most were small enough to be folded and stored inside a soldier's helmet or uniform. This seems to have been a common practice, as many of the flags in museum collections today are stained with blood, indicating they were on the person's body at the time of their death.

During the Second World War flags became a popular morbid memento among allied soldiers fighting in the Pacific. In Eugene Sledge's book *With the Old Breed*, he recalls that 'The men gloated over, compared, and often swapped their prizes. It was a brutal, ghastly ritual the likes of which have occurred since ancient times on battlefields where antagonists have possessed a profound mutual hatred'.[28] While *katanas* and other weapons were highly prized as trophies, they were difficult to transport while fighting was ongoing and were likely to be confiscated by commanding officers or stolen by other soldiers. The compact and lightweight flags could however readily be stowed inside a soldier's uniform or pack. Many flags made their way to Europe and North America with returning allied servicemen. Over time, having been stored, and sometimes placed on show, within private settings, many have found their way into museum collections and have been displayed in public institutions.

The acquisition and display of these flags, by both private individuals and museums, raise a number of ethical and moral issues. In Japan many families never received the remains of their fallen loved ones following the end of the War. The return of their flags, frequently bloodstained and imbued with the spirit or *kami* of the soldier as a consequence of having been on their body at the time of their passing, represents the closest thing that the family of a casualty will have to finally laying their relative to rest. In recent years there has understandably been a growing call for *yosegaki hinomaru* to be repatriated.

One such *yosegaki hinomaru* flag was, until recently, in the collections of the Oriental Museum (Figure 2.4). How it came into the collection is unknown. There is no information in the museum archive and it was assigned a 'GQ number'[29] which was often used to catalogue objects of unknown origin 'found in store', perhaps reflecting a pre-existing unease relating to the object and a desire by previous custodians to place it 'out of sight and out of mind'. Museum staff were acutely aware of the difficult nature of the object, which had been used as a case study during an international workshop on Japanese nationalism hosted by Durham University in March 2017.[30] At the workshop, dialogue between western curators and academics and their colleagues from East Asia had identified the emotive and contentious issue of artefacts of this type and highlighted their unsuitability as objects for public display. The workshop also underlined the need for this object to be subjected to in-depth study and, in 2018, it was selected by an undergraduate student to be the subject of a research project.[31]

The student began her research by translating the calligraphy on the flag. As the student did not speak or read Japanese, she turned to the online Reddit community for help. Once images of the flag had been posted, the student received a number of responses from people identifying temple stamps, translating the names of those who

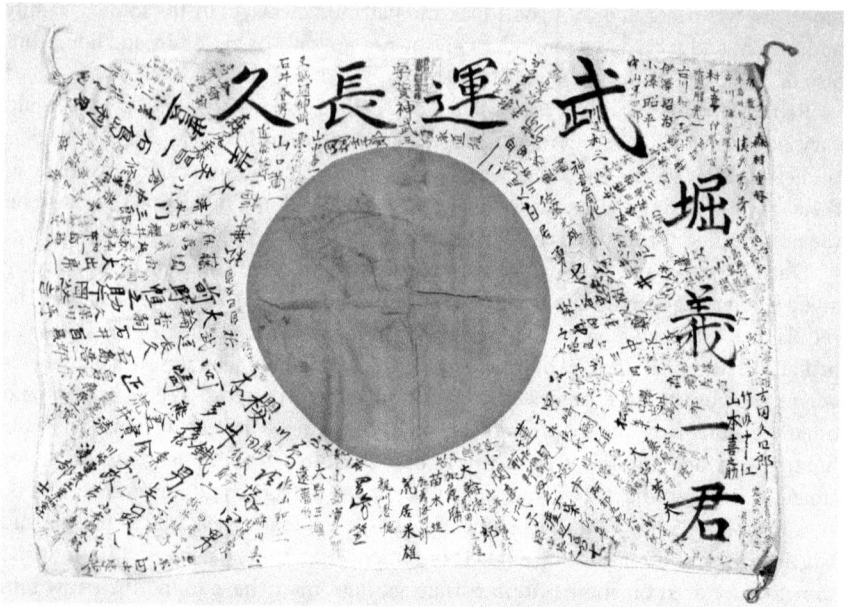

Figure 2.4 Japanese *yosegaki hinomaru* flag, DUROM.Gq100. Courtesy of Oriental Museum, Durham University.

signed the flag and, most important of all, the name of the Japanese soldier for whom the *yosegaki hinomaru* had been created.

Once the student had this vital information, she was encouraged by museum staff to contact the OBON Society, a non-profit organization with the mission to return 'good luck flags' to their families in Japan.[32] The student was able to acquire more information on the history of the flags and their importance to the families of the fallen soldiers. In light of this research the museum took the decision actively to attempt to repatriate the flag to the soldier's family. Phillida Purvis MBE, the Director of Links Japan,[33] introduced the museum to the Ministry of Health, Labour and Welfare of Japan and in September 2019 curators submitted a formal Application for Research on Lost Artefacts. The Ministry assigned a team to research the flag and attempt to track down the soldier's remaining family members. Just over a year later, in December 2020, the museum received confirmation from the Planning Division of Recovery of the Remains of War Dead that the surviving family of the soldier had been located and had requested the return of their ancestor's flag.

As anyone working in an accredited museum will attest, deaccessioning an object from a collection is no simple task. All due diligence must be taken and the process fully recorded. In January 2021 a paper was taken to the university's Acquisitions and Disposals Panel requesting formal permission to deaccession and return the remains of the soldier to his family in Japan. The panel unanimously supported the request, which was passed to the Durham University Library and Collections Steering Group for final sign-off. The final step in the flag's journey was completed in May 2021, when it was returned to the soldier's family. It is to be hoped that the return of his *kami* has brought the surviving family the peace and comfort they had been denied for over eighty years.

Conclusions and future directions

Although a small specialist museum founded in the mid-twentieth century, the entrenched legacies of British colonialism have until recently underpinned many of the Oriental Museum's public displays and engagement activities. Since 2008, however, significant proactive steps have been taken to address these issues, in a process that has been facilitated to no small degree by the modest size (and associated relatively simple decision-making processes) of the museum and its location at the heart of an internationally renowned research university. Today communities are routinely involved in the development and interpretation of the galleries which showcase their arts and cultures.[34] This approach is not without its problems and challenges. Conversations with community representatives have on occasion raised difficult issues and it must be borne in mind that engagement with faith and ethnic minority communities is not a panacea which cures all ills.

As Jemima Short discusses elsewhere in this volume, communities can be protective of their heritage and gaining access to – and building trust with – stakeholder communities, especially with regard to religious knowledge, is a difficult and time-consuming endeavour. Developing trust through long-term engagement can also be undermined by today's funding environment, which is often premised on short-term project funding and a demand for quick and quantifiable results. It is increasingly difficult to secure funding for a two- or three-year project without needing to demonstrate the delivery of outcomes as milestones much earlier in the project. Despite these challenges the team has been able, through the application of learning gleaned over a period of years, to create a process of co-developing and co-curating exhibitions and engagement programmes which has become part of the museum's normal way of working.

Building on the examples given in the case studies, recent co-curated projects have actively sought to address imperial and colonial narratives. These have included co-developing a successful bilingual touring exhibition telling the story of the Chinese volunteers who served alongside the British Army in the First World War[35] and the co-development and co-delivery of an annual programme of faith events in collaboration with South, East and Southeast Asian university students and local community members.

Guidance received from representatives of multiple stakeholder communities has helped to shape current collecting priorities. Recent examples include Bangladeshi students guiding and supporting the collection of material from their homeland which had previously been under-represented within the collection; students from a partner Japanese university advising on the development of collections focusing on Japanese youth culture; and members of the Hong Kong Chinese community contributing material relating to the recent political protests in the former British colony.

Moving forward, 2021 has seen the opening of not only a new *Silk Roads Gallery* reflecting the experiences of multiple national and faith communities, but also fully refurbished storage and research facilities that will both allow the reserve collections to become accessible to new audiences and enable our active collecting programme to continue. Most recently, the Covid-19 pandemic has driven the development of online engagement – and international reach – in ways that would have seemed unthinkable only eighteen months ago. This has created opportunities for new types of digital co-curation and, during 2021, Durham-based curators and academics worked with colleagues in Pakistan to co-develop a project that used the Oriental Museum's collection of colonial-era photographs of South Asian archaeological sites to underpin a bilingual online exhibition focused upon the preservation and interpretation of the UNESCO World Heritage Site of Taxila in Pakistan.[36] Ironically, a pandemic that has stranded millions of people for months within the confines of their own homes has also created opportunities for a small university museum and its world-class collections to engage with a global audience.

Notes

1. Cf. Chapter 4 on the role of community consultation at the V&A.
2. Benjamin Ifor Evans, *Commission for Enquiry into the Facilities for Oriental, Slavonic, East European and African Studies* (University of London: SOAS Archives, 1943–1945), ref. GB 102 MS 380612.
3. Thomas W. Thacker, *Memorandum on the General Background and Development of the Durham School of Oriental Studies* (Durham University: Oriental Museum Archive, 1960), p. 5.
4. E. Hulmes, *The Spalding Trust and the Union for the Study of Great Religions: H N Spalding's Pioneering Vision* (Spennymoor: The Memoir Club, 2002), pp. 128–33.
5. Accredited museums meet industry standards established for the sector by Arts Council England.
6. See for example Alison K. Brown and Laura Peers. (eds), *Museums and Source Communities: A Routledge Reader* (London: Routledge, 2003); and Museums Association, *Supporting Decolonisation in Museums* (2021), https://ma-production.ams3.digitaloceanspaces.com/app/uploads/2021/11/07135807/Supporting-decolonisation-in-museums-final-version.pdf, accessed 21 December 2021.
7. See for example Fisun Güner, 'Why Decolonising Museums Is Not Enough', *Elephant* 10 December 2020, https://elephant.art/why-decolonising-museums-is-not-enough-10122020/, accessed 21 December 2021; and Elisa Shoenberger, 'What Does It Mean to Decolonize a Museum?', *Museums Next* 11 May 2021, https://www.museumnext.com/article/what-does-it-mean-to-decolonize-a-museum/, accessed 21 December 2021.
8. Office for National Statistics; National Records of Scotland; Northern Ireland Statistics and Research Agency, 'Table LC2101EW: Ethnic Group by Sex and Age', *2011 Census Aggregate Data* (2016), http://www.nomisweb.co.uk/census/2011/lc2101ew, accessed 20 February 2021.

9   Based on verbal feedback received from community project participants and members of Durham University Learning and Engagement Team.
10 See https://www.dur.ac.uk/oriental.museum/whatshere/discover/, accessed 20 February 2021.
11 See Durham University website: https://durham-uk.libguides.com/mge/search-our-collections, accessed 16 July 2021.
12 The gallery is named after two generous supporters of the Oriental Museum: Dr J. T. and Mrs D. W. Roberts. The project was supported by the Arts Council England, DCMS/Wolfson Gallery Improvement Fund and the Dr and Mrs Roberts Fund.
13 David Ludden, *India and South Asia: A Short History* (London: Oneworld Publications, 2014), p. 9.
14 During the course of the project, new donations and purchases, as well as partial cataloguing of the Marshall archive of photography, meant that the number of database records for these countries had risen to 6,348 by February 2015.
15 Arts Council England (ACE) supports the development of knowledge and expertise associated with specialist collections via Subject Specialist Networks (SSNs). See https://www.artscouncil.org.uk/supporting-collections-and-cultural-property/subject-specialist-networks, accessed 20 February 2021.
16 Anne R. Bromberg, *The Arts of India, Southeast Asia, and the Himalayas at the Dallas Museum of Art* (New Haven and London: Yale University Press, 2013); and Joseph M. Dye III, *The Arts of India: Virginia Museum of Fine Arts* (London: Virginia Museum of Fine Arts in association with Philip Wilson Publishers, 2001).
17 Steven M. Kossak and Edith W. Watts, *The Art of South and Southeast Asia: A Resource for Educators* (New York: Metropolitan Museum of Art, 2001). See https://www.metmuseum.org/-/media/files/learn/for-educators/publications-for-educators/sseasia.pdf, accessed 20 February 2021.
18 The participant feedback included in this case study was shared by participants with the curatorial team during a series of outreach sessions relating to exhibition development. The feedback was then verbally shared with the wider project team when this related to object display, and was recorded in the 'Notes' field of object database entries when comments pertained to specific objects.
19 Feedback from Participant 1, 29 May 2014.
20 Feedback from Participant 2, 29 May 2014.
21 Ibid.
22 Department for Education, *National Curriculum in England, History Programmes of Study: Key Stage 3* (September 2013), p. 4. See https://assets.publishing.service.gov.uk/government/uploads/system/uploads/attachment_data/file/239075/SECONDARY_national_curriculum_-_History.pdf, accessed 20 July 2021.
23 For an example, see a set of 36 paintings of Indian costumes: Accession numbers DUROM.1962.163–198.
24 Feedback from Participant 1, 30 August 2014.
25 Accession number DUROM.O167. For an exploration of the religious and cultural significances of objects and sites in Sikhism, see: Ann Murphy, *The Materiality of the Past: History and Representation in the Sikh Tradition* (New York: Oxford University Press, 2012).
26 See for example Richard Curt Kraus, 'The Repatriation of Plundered Chinese Art', *The China Quarterly* 199 (2009), pp. 837–42; and Dan Hicks, *The Brutish Museums: The Benin Bronzes, Colonial Violence and Cultural Restitution* (London: Pluto

Press, 2020); and 'Decolonising Museums isn't Part of a "Culture War". It's About Keeping them Relevant', *The Guardian* (7 May 2021), https://www.theguardian.com/commentisfree/2021/may/07/decolonising-museums-isnt-part-of-a-culture-war-its-about-keeping-them-relevant, accessed 21 December 2021.
27   Loosely translated as 'collection of writing around the red sun'.
28   Eugene B. Sledge, *With the Old Breed in Peleliu and Okinawa* (Oxford: Oxford University Press, 1992), p. 120.
29   Accession number DUROM.Gq100.
30   'Critical Nationalism Studies Workshop: National Imaginaries and Beyond', School of Government and International Affairs, Durham University, 14–15 September 2017.
31   Anonymous student, Durham University School of Education module 'Objects of Desire: Oriental Art and its Histories', 2018.
32   See https://obonsociety.org/eng/, accessed 20 February 2021.
33   Links Japan was founded in 1998 with the objective of promoting civil society understanding between the United Kingdom and Japan, through sharing good practice, effective strategy and innovation and facilitating joint research and long-term links, including partnerships with developing countries. See http://www.linksjapan.org/, accessed 20 February 2021.
34   See for example Karen Exell, 'Community Consultation and the Redevelopment of Manchester Museum's Ancient Egypt Galleries', in V. Golding and W. Modest (eds), *Museums and Communities: Curators, Collections and Collaboration* (London: Bloomsbury Academic, 2013), pp. 130–42.
35   Anna Chen, 'First Ever UK exhibition on the Great War's Chinese Labour Corps: Durham University 7th April to 24th September', *Madam Miaow Blogspot* 13 April 2017, https://madammiaow.blogspot.com/2017/04/chinese-labour-corps-world-war-1-exhibition-durham-university.html, accessed 4 January 2022.
36   See https://stories.durham.ac.uk/TaxilaInFocus-Urdu/, and https://stories.durham.ac.uk/Marshall100-Urdu/, accessed 4 January 2022.

Bibliography

Arts Council England. https://www.artscouncil.org.uk/supporting-collections-and-cultural-property/subject-specialist-networks. Accessed 20 February 2021.

Bromberg, Anne R. *The Arts of India, Southeast Asia, and the Himalayas at the Dallas Museum of Art*. New Haven and London: Yale University Press, 2013.

Brown, Alison K. and Peers, Laura (eds). *Museums and Source Communities: A Routledge Reader*. London: Routledge, 2003.

Chen, Anna. 'First Ever UK exhibition on the Great War's Chinese Labour Corps: Durham University 7th April to 24th September', *Madam Miaow Blogspot* (13 April 2017), https://madammiaow.blogspot.com/2017/04/chinese-labour-corps-world-war-1-exhibition-durham-university.html. Accessed 4 January 2022.

Department for Education. *National Curriculum in England*, History *Programmes of Study: Key* Stage 3. https://assets.publishing.service.gov.uk/government/uploads/system/uploads/attachment_data/file/239075/SECONDARY_national_curriculum_-_History.pdf. Accessed 20 July 2021.

Durham University. https://www.dur.ac.uk/oriental.museum/whatshere/discover/. Accessed 20 February 2021.

Durham University. https://durham-uk.libguides.com/mge/search-our-collections. Accessed 16 July 2021.

Durham University. https://stories.durham.ac.uk/TaxilaInFocus-Urdu/. Accessed 4 January 2022.

Durham University. https://stories.durham.ac.uk/Marshall100-Urdu/. Accessed 4 January 2022.

Dye, Joseph M. III. *The Arts of India: Virginia Museum of Fine Arts*. London: Virginia Museum of Fine Arts in Association with Philip Wilson Publishers, 2001.

Evans, Benjamin Ifor. *Commission for Enquiry into the Facilities for Oriental, Slavonic, East European and African Studies*. SOAS University of London, SOAS Archives, 1943–1945, Item reference: GB 102 MS 380612.

Exell, Karen. 'Community Consultation and the Redevelopment of Manchester Museum's Ancient Egypt Galleries'. In Museums and Communities: *Curators, Collections and Collaboration*, edited by V. Golding and W. Modest, 130–42. London: Bloomsbury Academic, 2013.

Güner, Fisun. 'Why Decolonising Museums Is Not Enough', *Elephant* (10 December 2020). https://elephant.art/why-decolonising-museums-is-not-enough-10122020/. Accessed 21 December 2021.

Hicks, Dan. *The Brutish Museums: The Benin Bronzes, Colonial Violence and Cultural Restitution*. London: Pluto Press, 2020.

Hicks, Dan. 'Decolonising Museums Isn't Part of a "Culture War". It's about Keeping Them Relevant'. *The Guardian* (7 May 2021). https://www.theguardian.com/commentisfree/2021/may/07/decolonising-museums-isnt-part-of-a-culture-war-its-about-keeping-them-relevant. Accessed 21 December 2021.

Hulmes, E. *The Spalding Trust and the Union for the Study of Great Religions: H N Spalding's Pioneering Vision*. Spennymoor: The Memoir Club, 2002.

Kossak, Steven M., and Edith W. Watts. *The Art of South and Southeast Asia: A Resource for Educators*. New York: Metropolitan Museum of Art, 2001.

Kraus, Richard Curt. 'The Repatriation of Plundered Chinese Art', *The China Quarterly* 199 (September 2009): 837–42.

Links Japan. http://www.linksjapan.org/. Accessed 20 February 2021.

Ludden, David. *India and South Asia: A Short History*. London: Oneworld Publications, 2014.

Metropolitan Museum of Art. https://www.metmuseum.org/-/media/files/learn/for-educators/publications-for-educators/sseasia.pdf. Accessed 20 February 2021.

Murphy, Ann. *The Materiality of the Past: History and Representation in the Sikh Tradition*. New York: Oxford University Press, 2012.

Museums Association. *Supporting Decolonisation in Museums*. 2021. https://ma-production.ams3.digitaloceanspaces.com/app/uploads/2021/11/07135807/Supporting-decolonisation-in-museums-final-version.pdf. Accessed 21 December 2021.

Obon Society. https://obonsociety.org/eng/. Accessed 20 February 2021.

Office for National Statistics, National Records of Scotland, Northern Ireland Statistics and Research Agency. 'Table LC2101EW: Ethnic Group by Sex and Age'. *2011 Census Aggregate Data* (2016). http://www.nomisweb.co.uk/census/2011/lc2101ew. Accessed 20 February 2021.

Shoenberger, Elisa. 'What Does It Mean to Decolonize a Museum?' *Museums Next* (11 May 2021). https://www.museumnext.com/article/what-does-it-mean-to-decolonize-a-museum/. Accessed 21 December 2021.

Sledge, Eugene B. *With the Old Breed in Peleliu and Okinawa*. Oxford: Oxford University Press, 1992.

Thacker, Thomas W. *Memorandum on the General Background and Development of the Durham School of Oriental Studies*. Durham University, Oriental Museum Archive, 1960, Item location: Museum History File 1960.

3

Transforming the archive of slavery at the Tropenmuseum

Adiva Lawrence

This chapter examines some of the strategies put in place by a museum founded at the height of Dutch colonialism in order to redefine its identity in a postcolonial world. As its starting-point, it examines the exhibition 'Afterlives of Slavery', which was held between November 2017 and May 2021 at the Tropenmuseum, Amsterdam (part of the Dutch National Museum of World Cultures). 'Afterlives of Slavery' invited visitors to explore Dutch involvement in the institution of Atlantic slavery through the lenses of the present, in order to draw attention to the fact that racism and racial inequality in the Netherlands today directly result from this history. Many museums in the west are currently debating over whether museums should and can be decolonized,[1] and the Dutch National Museum of World Cultures has itself engaged with this question on several occasions. This will not be the subject of this essay, which proposes instead to develop an analytical framework in order to assess how initiatives like the 'Afterlives of Slavery' exhibition may contribute to transforming what is said about slavery. Therefore, rather than ask if 'Afterlives of Slavery' contributes to a decolonizing agenda, it reflects on how mobilizing 'the colonial' in the exhibition challenges a traditionally accepted understanding of slavery in relation to Dutch national identity, and asks what such reformulations can tell us about current structures of power.

According to the sociologist Melissa Weiner, 'Most white Dutch attribute "Dutchness", and thus membership in the national community, to White Europeans born in the Netherlands'.[2] This categorization is made manifest in the widespread use of the terms *autochtonen* (referring to people of European Dutch background), and *allochtonen* (to refer to Dutch people with an immigrant background),[3] even though these terms have not been used in administrative procedures and communications since 2016.[4] Dutch Antilleans, Surinamese, Turks and Moroccans constitute the four largest non-European minorities in the Netherlands today.[5] Dutch Antilleans and Surinamese citizens are descendants of formerly enslaved populations in Dutch colonies.

The Dutch were involved in the slave trade and slavery from the early sixteenth century and slavery was abolished in their colonies in 1863. According to data available on the platform *Slave Voyages*, they transported about half a million people from Africa to the New World.⁶ They established colonies in Brazil, Suriname and the Antilles, and subsequently in Indonesia from 1800 to 1945. However, the importance of the West Indies in the constitution of the modern state of the Netherlands is a contested subject, which was for a long time downplayed on various accounts. Rik van Welie notes in a 2018 study that, for a long time, the subject of slavery in the Netherlands had received little scholarly attention by historians.⁷ This silence contrasts with the central role slavery played in the construction and wealth of the Dutch nation, as historians such as Karwan Fatah-Black, Mathias Van Rossum and Pepijn Brandon have argued.⁸

Initially founded in 1867, since 2014 the Tropenmuseum and three other ethnographic museums in the country have formed the Nationaal Museum van Wereldculturen (National Museum of World Cultures) or NMW. Home to 450,000 objects, 260,000 photographs and 350,000 items of documentary film material,⁹ the NMW was also endowed with a new research centre, the Research Center for Material Culture (RCMC) in 2014. Writing in 2016, Wayne Modest and Anouk de Koning have referred to the period as a moment of 'anxious politics',¹⁰ highlighting issues centring around multiculturalism and how to deal with legacies of colonial histories in contemporary society.¹¹ In recent years, it appears that Dutch museums have increasingly been looking to build a new paradigm; moving away from their role as keepers of the material culture amassed by private or public bodies, to institutions with a mission to intervene in societal debates. These changes were brought about, in part, in response to calls that museums recognize their lack of inclusivity and their failure to deal with their colonial legacies.

My research objective was to understand how 'colonial' logics are mobilized in the exhibition, and in specifically grasping the significance of instances where they are actively challenged and reconfigured. Here, I test the benefits of applying archaeological methodologies to study the remains of the nineteenth-century colonial archive rooted in Michel Foucault's understanding of archaeology as the study of discursive formations. This analytical frame is motivated, in the first instance, by the conceptual framework on which 'Afterlives of Slavery' is built. The title of the exhibition is inspired by a powerful expression in African American writer Saidiya Hartman's memoir-essay *Lose Your Mother*.¹² Hartman's concept of the 'afterlife of slavery' as the precarious position that Black people inhabit in the world as a result of the institution of transatlantic slavery shapes the exhibition's focus on how the slavery of the past still inhabits the present. As Hartman writes:

> If slavery persists as an issue in the political life of black America, it is not because of an antiquarian obsession with bygone days or the burden of a too-long memory, but because black lives are still imperilled and devalued by a racial calculus and a political arithmetic that were entrenched centuries ago. This is the afterlife of slavery – skewed life chances, limited access to health and education, premature death, incarceration, and impoverishment.¹³

Drawing on Hartman's notion of 'racial calculus', the exhibition's premise is that colonialism and slavery shaped and still condition the lives of Dutch citizens today. In *Lose your Mother*, Hartman's reflections are rooted in an intimate reading of historical archives related to the history of slavery, which is understood as unfinished. Seen as such, what constitutes the archive of slavery is still in the making. How does the exhibition support this approach?

The term 'archive' is generally defined as both a 'collection of historical documents or records providing information about a place, institution, or group of people' and 'The place where historical documents or records are kept'.[14] In the *Archaeology of Knowledge* (1968), however, Foucault defines the archive as 'the first law of what can be said'; that is, as the processes that regulate all discourse and knowledge production: the ensemble of statements, which though they may pertain to different fields of knowledge, function according to similar rules. In a section of the *Archaeology of Knowledge*, dedicated to what he calls a 'surface of emergence', Foucault also lays out a reflection between 'saying and seeing', which sheds light on the role the museum may play with regard to the archive.[15] Kevin Hetherington argues that a 'surface of emergence' is, for Foucault, a space where 'otherwise diverse things become apparent and visible as a common set of discursive objects'.[16] Hetherington contends that the museum constitutes 'a surface of emergence', and can be analysed as a place where archival discourses are made apparent, or 'positive'.

According to Carole Blair, this framework allows for distinct discursive formations to be isolated so as to seize information about the 'epistemological structures, systems of power and specific articulations of the human as an ethical actor' that transpire through them, as well as to 'locate points of transformation and change from one discursive formation to the other'.[17] Therefore, Foucault was interested in the historical conditions that led to the emergence of discursive formations, and in the apparatuses that enable them to be operative, the 'external conditions of existence'.[18]

In this essay I treat the exhibition 'Afterlives of Slavery' as a 'positive' place of archival discourse emerging out of an epistemological structure and system of power, and the Tropenmuseum as the 'surface of emergence' where exterior discursive formations can be apprehended as they transform and emerge. The exhibition team identified issues with the way slavery was dealt with in the Netherlands and in museums in general, and developed an exhibition that aimed at challenging those ways through the 'Afterlives of Slavery' project. My analysis seeks to understand what those issues are, as well as what kinds of political rationalities are made readable in – and what conceptions of social political change can be extracted from – the rectifications proposed in the exhibition.

The research for this chapter was conducted primarily between April and June 2019. I drew on material produced by the museum, and on interviews with the curatorial team and other museum staff members: these interviews have been anonymised and are used with participants' consent. My aim is to explore the potential and limitations of these re-negotiations of the museum's colonial heritage through interventions in the nineteenth-century museum archive. I focus on their political significance, as museums claim a more active position in societal movements aiming at fostering more social justice.

I provide an analysis here of the arguments developed in the exhibition, and how they are supported by curatorial strategies. I will argue that the exhibition constitutes an attempt to transform the museum into a new form of civic space through the subversion of elements of its colonial foundations: the ways in which objects associated with slavery are deployed in the 'new museum' effectively repurposes the Tropenmuseum as a site to foster social change. However, when the political scientist Catherine Lu assessed the recent changes that took place at the Tropenmuseum,[19] she suggested that it might be too early to consider the ethnographic era ended, and that the colonial epistemology which created ethnographic museums has not yet disappeared. According to her view, the museum constitutes more than a vessel, encapsulating a set of methodologies that emerged out of a modern colonial worldview, and that are emblematic of a specific organization of power and domination. This is why I set out to apply an archival analytical frame that allows me to approach the exhibition as a place where the liberal rationality that gave it shape could be read and analysed. I interrogate some of the ramifications attached to the recourse to the register of the personal, drawing on writings by Black feminist thinkers, and in the concluding part of my case-study analysis, I argue that the transformation of the slavery archive can additionally be found in collective praxis, by turning the museum into a place where new alliances can be formed.

A colonial site

In 1864, a colonial museum was founded in Haarlem, with the task of researching natural products and raw materials from the Dutch-colonized regions. Following the establishment in 1910 of a Colonial Institute in Amsterdam at Mauritskade in the South-Eastern side of Amsterdam, the museum collection was transferred to the Institute's premises in 1913. The Institute was intended to showcase Dutch colonial achievements. It largely focused on the Dutch East India Company's commercial successes, and was also involved in monitoring colonial rule abroad. The museum officially opened its doors within the Institute in 1926.[20]

The museum went on to redefine its identity on several occasions, following historical developments. After Indonesia gained independence in 1945 and the Netherlands officially recognized it in 1949, the Colonial Institute decided to shift its focus from Indonesia to the broader 'tropical regions of the world'[21] and was renamed the Koninklijk Instituut voor de Tropen (KIT), or Royal Tropical Institute. The Colonial Museum it hosted became the Tropical Museum, or Tropenmuseum. From 1952, they were funded by the Ministry of Foreign Affairs (formerly known as 'Colonial Affairs'). According to David Hildering, Wayne Modest and Warda Aztouti, the institution started focusing on Suriname, the Dutch Antilles and Dutch New Guinea, which remained overseas territories.[22] Development progressively became a growing matter of interest for the Dutch government in the 1960s, and in 1966, the KIT became endowed with a developmental mission focused on the Third World. A focus on 'living conditions' shifted to emphasize culture in the 1980s and 1990s.

The first decade of the twenty-first century was marked by a growing awareness of previous shortcomings and limitations on the part of the museum's staff.[23]

Despite constant attempts to reinvent itself, at the turn of the 2010s the museum found its survival threatened again and its importance questioned. In a context of economic austerity imposed by the government, State Secretary for Foreign Affairs Ben Knapen announced that along with countless other museums in the country, all its funding would be cut by the end of 2012.[24] After months of negotiations, it was decided that it would merge with two other museums, making half of its staff redundant.

The Tropenmuseum is now part of the Nationaal Museum van Werelculturen, or National Museum of World Cultures. The NWM was founded in 2014, by merging of the Tropenmuseum with two other ethnographic museums: the Volkenkunde in Leiden and the Africa Museum in Berg-en-Dal. The Werelmuseum of Rotterdam is also affiliated. Despite their differing trajectories, all three museums are steeped in colonial history. The establishment of a new organization allowed for the creation of a fully fledged research department: the Research Centre for Material Culture (RCMC).

On its website, the Tropenmuseum is no longer presented as an ethnographic museum but as a museum of world cultures:

> People all over the world face the same questions of life. The answers that they give differ and are often culturally determined. What unites us are universal human emotions. The objects from our collection are a testament to this. They all tell a human story ... In the Tropenmuseum you discover that, apart from the differences, we are the same: people.[25]

Wayne Modest, a renowned museum curator and scholar, who was head of the curatorial department at the Tropenmuseum from 2010 to 2014, is the founding director of the Research Centre for Material Culture. In 2014, Modest was responsible for defining the RCMC's mission, which he calls the 'critical hub' of the museum group.[26] The centre officially opened in 2015 and constitutes a distinct department within the museum. On its website, the RCMC is said to 'foster interdisciplinary research' to shed new lights on societal questions around issues of heritage, cultural identity and belonging that these objects raise.[27] The programmes and collaborations that the RCMC develop revolve around an evolving set of research themes, which elaborate on issues raised by the objects stored in the organization's collections. The RCMC is involved in a wide range of activities such as events and public lectures, workshops, as well as publications, research fellowships and artistic residencies. The RCMC staff also act as consultants on certain exhibition projects.

From 2015, as the organization vowed to rethink its treatment of the colonial past, the RCMC began to run a series of events focusing on the role of ethnographic museums in western histories of colonialism, including a symposium entitled 'A Shared History – Conversations on the Slavery Past in the Present',[28] where interrogations about the 'afterlives of slavery' were introduced. A larger permanent exhibition entitled 'Our Inheritance', exploring the history and legacies of Dutch colonialism across the world, is due to open in June 2022.

'Afterlives of Slavery' as an unravelling of the slavery archive

'Afterlives of Slavery' was designed as a semi-permanent exhibition. As I will argue, the exhibition, through its critical approach to curating, illustrates the influence the RCMC has had on the museum group's programming. This impact was also manifested in the composition of the curatorial team which, in addition to the customary museum curator and exhibition designer, included an RCMC researcher. It was one of three exhibitions located on the second floor of the museum, between permanent displays on Indonesia, and on the other side, Oceania. A rather small exhibition, it occupied one main room and two smaller ones. It presented as an ensemble of colourful thematic booths where objects and texts are arranged on a structure of wire mesh. An important part of the exhibition-making process was its consultation with interlocutors the team referred to as 'experts'. Those were selected by Wayne Modest, and approached by the museum group to take part in focus groups (approximately five all-day sessions) aimed at giving feedback on the work of curators, as well as to give suggestions based on their own practices.[29] The focus group participants came from antiracist activist and academic circles, active in public and academic debates currently taking place on the subject of race in the Netherlands. Some of the 'experts' had collaborated with Wayne Modest or the museum in the past. Simone Zeefuik, for example, who was affiliated with the collective Decolonize the Museum,[30] had been invited in 2015 by the museum to write new labels – aimed at casting more attention to the violent processes involved in collecting objects from the colonial era – for the permanent displays of Indonesian arts and culture (which stood next door to the 'Afterlives of Slavery' exhibition and will be replaced by the 'Our Inheritance' exhibition in 2022).[31]

The 'Afterlives of Slavery' exhibition made a number of bold curatorial and narrative choices. On exhibition's webpage, it was presented as an exhibition aimed at initiating a necessary 'dialogue':

> The exhibition places the enslaved and their descendants centre stage. To initiate a sometimes difficult but productive dialogue, the Tropenmuseum has sought out personal stories from past and present that bring the history of slavery and its current-day legacies up close.[32]

This focus on personal stories was also partly explained by the fact the collection of slavery-related items was rather limited, and the curators felt that it was, as is the case with most ethnographic collections in the west, illustrative of a very Eurocentric perspective on this history. The collection of Caribbean artefacts makes up less than 1 per cent of the total organization, and they tend to reflect a very partial view on the history of slavery. Therefore, their stated intention to place the experience of the enslaved and their descendants at the heart of the exhibition meant not taking the collection as the primary starting point. As a result, the scenographic dimension of the exhibition became an important feature of the exhibition-making process. The design of the exhibition consists of large rectangular free-standing panels made of wire grids that the text panels are woven into aimed at illustrating the idea of an 'entangled history'. Themes and narratives guided the selection of objects mostly from the organization's collection, but some of them were loaned from external organizations such as the Black Archives. The Black Archives, a regular interlocutor of the RCMC, is a grassroots archives centre founded by activists Jessica de Abreu and Mitchell Esajas (who was also consulted as an expert in the development of the exhibition), and located minutes from the Tropenmuseum, in the east of Amsterdam.

'Afterlives of Slavery' was relatively cautious with its use of images and objects, displaying careful arrangements of a small number of items. It focused instead on a number of themes and personal trajectories that the objects come to support. This is explained by the fact that the curators were strongly urged by focus groups and advisors to avoid reproducing some of the shortcomings or tropes that other exhibitions had committed in the past, such as allocating a large proportion of exhibition space to objects of torture or stereotypical depictions of Black suffering.[33] The literary scholar and artist scholar Marcus Wood, who wrote extensively about representations of slavery in the western imaginary, asks what is actually understood from seeing an original instrument of torture beyond voyeurism.[34] This stems from a consideration of the positionality of viewers: who is Black suffering exposed to?[35] Indeed, one can wonder if it primarily triggers empathy and if it does not mostly replicate the very limited lens through which Black people have been viewed for centuries in the west.[36] Engraving and painting were some of the 'privileged' ways in which representations of the Black body circulated, and contributed to manufacture a visual rhetoric about slavery and Blackness.[37] It is precisely these processes of manufacturing that the exhibition attempts to capture, through, for example, the examination of ethnographic exhibitions in the nineteenth century.

An example of this is the reframing of a drum acquired by the museum as a 'colonial prop' to recreate exotic sceneries of the colonies in the Amsterdam International Colonial and Export Exhibition of 1883. The drum is displayed next to a photograph depicting a young Surinamese boy named Johannes Kodjo, who was known to have been paraded at one of these exhibitions. As the exhibition curator explained, it was important for objects not to be shown as simply ethnographic artefacts. Drums, for example, are often presented in exhibitions about slavery as pieces of evidence for an alleged retained 'Africanity' of enslaved people, a query that has been the topic of a lot of ethnographic studies.[38] The refusal to present the drums as such was meant to circumvent falling into the trap of attempting to communicate ideas about alleged immutable and essentialized conceptualizations of identity and tradition.

Curating from the point of view of the enslaved also meant reconfiguring the colonial gaze and its manifestations in museum settings. It thus entailed making the conscious effort to write from a 'Black' perspective.[39] One comment made by an invited advisor during a feedback session is illustrative of the issues the curators had to grapple with when devising the exhibition texts. They remarked that preliminary exhibition texts described Dutch efforts to take control over maroon territories using the word 'conquer', submitting that this language, whilst appearing neutral, actually reveals an order of value which privileges the perspective of Dutch colonizers over those of the enslaved.[40] The term 'maroons' refers to enslaved people who ran away from slavery and went on to set up independent settlements in various parts of the Caribbean and South America. The Tropenmuseum's feedback process for its 'Afterlives of Slavery' exhibition therefore demonstrates a willingness to tackle the coloniality of museums by going at the heart of the processes through which positions of power operate, and through which racism is produced.

The curators made the conscious choice of tackling the issue of racism in the Netherlands and its manifestations in exhibition culture, by highlighting the ways in which certain scientific disciplines such as biology and religion were instrumental in propagating racist views of Black people.[41] The most explicit way in which this is done is through the affirmation of a clear political position on the condemnation of the tradition of 'Zwarte Piet' ('Black Pete'), a highly politicized and divisive issue in Dutch society. In Dutch Christmas celebrations, referred to as 'Sinterklaas', 'Zwarte Piets' are Santa Claus's blackfaced helpers, who roam the streets running after and offering candy to children.

This stance is supported by material from The Black Archives. A connection is proposed in the panels between Maroon resistance to enslavement and the contemporary resistance to racist stigmatization by contemporary activists from Black Dutch communities. For decades now, activists such as the artist Quinsy Gario have demanded that this tradition be stopped, calling attention to the roots of the character in transatlantic slavery. However, a significant portion of the white Dutch population reject these accusations, and feel they are unfairly asked to let go of an important part of their identity, as they consider the tradition to be an essential part of their heritage.[42] The anthropologist Gloria Wekker has termed the reluctance to recognize the harmful character of this tradition as a manifestation of 'white innocence'.[43] As a result, some local visitors to the exhibition might have felt a sense of defensiveness when confronted by this particular display.

Addressing this issue thus constitutes a curatorial choice that attests to the political stance the curatorial team sought to convey. Moreover, the display dedicated to Zwarte Piet and Black activism also brings visibility to the figure of Anton de Kom, a Surinamese anti-colonialist writer.[44] The aim was, it seems, to not only help visitors to make sense of the material and visual culture associated with slavery and Blackness in the Netherlands, but also to invite visitors to see, in line with the exhibition's premise inspired by Saidiya Hartman, that the history of slavery is still active in struggles for equality in the contemporary world, and that it continues to produce material culture.

Finally, two rooms were almost exclusively dedicated to performances by artists of Surinamese descent, commissioned by the museum. The two performances, by Surinamese-Dutch spoken-word artists Dorothy Blokland and Onias Landsveld, were filmed within the museum by the exhibition's project team. The artists both adapted previously created work specifically for this commission. In both performances, the artists interrogate the aspects of their identities that they see as inherited from slavery. Dorothy Blokland's performance reflects on the name Blokland, imposed on her ancestors by Dutch bureaucracy, while Onias Landsveld dwells on the meaning of the term 'slave', which he perceives as an unwanted inheritance, and myth of origins.

I have sought to demonstrate how a deployment of critical curatorial methodologies can facilitate the reconfiguration of interpretations of colonial collections in order to express progressive political ideas, not by erasing the colonial archive, but by repurposing it. In 'Afterlives of Slavery' this investment was made manifest through its attempt to contest registers of visuality, language and use of sources perceived as stemming from colonial epistemology. The exhibition's material attempted to make clear that the topic of slavery is not confined to the past of the nation, but that it is still present through legacies of racism and cultural markers such as names – as explored in the performances. The curatorial process also sought to distance itself from methodologies rooted in colonial racism and to denounce them: this is visible, for instance, in the described section about the drum.

In a similar way to efforts at reconfiguring the gaze, the exhibition's investment in personal narratives, too, seems to be a way to dismantle the authoritative and neutral tone the colonial ethnographic museum has traditionally adopted to speak about non-western people. It was done by asking direct questions in panels such as, 'What is our shared history of slavery?', and also inviting participants to respond by writing their answers on pieces of paper that could then be added onto the metal grid structure as part of the display. This approach indicated a focus on instigating a sense of responsibility by inviting people to feel like they are part of the recounted history. The comments made by visitors on pieces of paper have been compiled by the RCMC team, and are likely to inform the development of the larger exhibition in 2022.[45]

Similar initiatives can be found in museums in the Netherlands and in the rest of Europe (see also, for example, Chapter 2 in this volume for community input into display labels at the V&A's Maqdala 1868 display in London, and galleries at the Oriental Museum, Durham). One interesting example is that of the exhibition entitled 'Shifting Image: In Search of Johan Maurits',[46] held at The Hague's Mauritshuis museum. Johann Maurits, Count of Nassau-Siegen, was governor of the Dutch possessions in Brazil between 1637 and 1643. The exhibition aimed at addressing the complex history of the Dutch involvement in colonization and enslavement in Brazil, as well as that of the figure of Johan Maurits. Each painting and object displayed were accompanied by labels written by several authors from various fields of expertise, in order to emphasize the partiality of any given text, and to allow for multiple levels of interpretation to be communicated to the public.

In this understanding of the critical curating, the exhibition space is understood as a field of negotiation of the terms through which history is communicated, but also, by positioning itself as a place of dialogue, it posits an ambition to extend the scope of what exhibitions can do.

The exhibition as archival impasse?

'Afterlives of Slavery' demonstrates an ambition to use the contemporary European museum as a vessel for devising less harmful articulations of historical narratives, by proposing it as the very site of subversion of its own foundations through the exhibition medium. One central strategy of 'Afterlives of Slavery' is its investment in the personal as a way to oppose the identified false neutrality of the western colonial archive. By positioning itself in opposition to modern colonial standards of storytelling, 'Afterlives of Slavery' reveals much about how the harmful character of colonial legacies is perceived today. But an archival analysis of the exhibition as a surface of emergence also encapsulates what exhibition-making today shares with colonial epistemic foundations, begging the question of the extent to which changes to external conditions can be enacted through it.

From the late-eighteenth century onwards, as Carol Duncan has shown in her book *Civilising Rituals*, new forms of public museums came to replace the princely galleries in Europe and were endowed with a mission to educate a broader public.[47] She notes that, in a context of transition towards more liberal regimes, the 'direct' mode of communication that the museum is able to offer becomes perceived as an ability to inform citizens about new conceptions of truth and high values. Foucault's concept of 'biopolitics' as a process of subjectivation and state formation is useful here in that it helps to conceive of the exhibition as a technology of power whose form is rooted in a particular epistemic formation identified as liberalism that emerged in the nineteenth century in the west. Foucault had looked at liberalism as a specific 'art of governing', characterized by a focus on processes of subjectivation and state formation.[48] He was concerned with how certain rationalities develop rules to organize power relations through internal regulation aimed at guaranteeing the exercise of freedom, making use of institutional apparatuses to do so. Thomas Lemke explains:

> Foucault sees the distinctiveness of liberal forms of government in the fact that they replace an external regulation by an internal production. Liberalism is not limited to providing a simple guarantee of liberties (freedom of the market, of private property, of speech, and so on) that exist independently of governmental practice. Quite on the contrary: liberalism organizes the conditions under which individuals could and should exercise these liberties.[49]

Treating the nineteenth-century exhibition as a surface of emergence of liberal rationality, as suggested by Hetherington, allows us to bring attention to how these ideas of the subject were shaped by the historical and political context of the time. This was identified by Kevin Hetherington, who has qualified the type of engagement favoured by nineteenth-century technologies of spectacles as 'distracted', and as constituting a paradigmatic feature of the modern subject's relationship to the world.[50] This points to a type of engagement that is turned inwards, whereby the modern western subject defines itself through displays of things and people external to them. Hetherington writes:

> It might be described as an important surface of emergence (Foucault, 1974) in which the modern discourse of "the problem of experience" is enunciated through the narrative orderings of material culture, most notably through discourses of civilization, progress, evolution and place.[51]

It is indeed significant that the emergence of the 'distracted' mode of engagement identified as pertaining to the museum exhibition took place in the west in a context of rapid industrialization and accumulation enabled by colonization and imperialism. Partly inspired by Foucault, Tony Bennett argues that the formation of 'new understandings of the person as an archaeologically layered entity and its role in contemporary debates concerning the ambiguous role of habit in the mechanisms of progress' was an important concern for West European governments in the eighteenth and nineteenth centuries.[52] These ideas about the 'progress of man' were highly racialized, and depended on hierarchizations that museums supported through scientific language.

As Lemke further explains, asymmetrical power relations can solidify into states of domination.[53] Museum exhibitions in the context of European colonialism in the nineteenth century contributed to the stabilization of unequal hierarchies between people and places, and to the primacy of the white western subject-viewer. Initiatives such as 'Afterlives of Slavery' challenge these hierarchies, and therefore constitute efforts to disrupt the stability of associated categories of thought that perpetuate inequality and racism. As addressed in the previous part of this essay, one way in which that was done was through the inclusion of works by Dutch artists of African descent, for example, constituting an incursion into the museum archive of a register of recognition of a different nature from that of a purely factual historical approach, one granting legitimacy to the experiences of the enslaved and their descendants, whilst encouraging a position of identification and empathy in the visitor. It appears to promote an engagement of visitors at the 'individual level' with the subject-matter of slavery, in line with the Tropenmuseum's ambition to be a museum about universally shared 'human experiences'.[54]

This can be taken as a transgression to the normative language of exhibitions, and therefore as a form of political action. The political potential of personal stories was identified and popularized by second-wave feminist writers around the slogan 'the personal is political'.[55] These authors paid attention to the structural ramifications of the personal situations of oppression women found themselves in, and challenged the divide between the personal and the public at the heart of the liberal project.[56] A large body of work has explored the potentialities offered by the recognition of the relevance of women's personal struggles, but also the possible traps and dead ends it can lead to. Black feminist thinker bell hooks cautions for example that the ability to describe one's personal reality should only be the starting point of a broader examination of and investment in global revolutionary politics,[57] or it would run the risk of limiting the reach of such actions failing to lead to political unity. Similar concerns can be raised with regard to the incursion of the personal in a slavery exhibition. Viewed in this light, attempts to reconfigure the discourse of slavery through an investment in the personal, if not done as part as a broader collective political endeavour, may run the risk of simply acting as a manifestation of symbolic inclusion into an otherwise unchanged ensemble. In other words, transforming the contents of an exhibition is likely not enough from an archival point of view, as the processes determining the conditions in which subjects receive the information remain the same, re-inscribing the primacy of the 'distracted' subject as recipient of personal stories external to them.

Beyond the personal

Patricia Hill Collins, in a text about the development of Black feminist thought, shows that the power of the alternative narratives produced by Black women lies in their ability to transform the epistemic formations that had until now rendered them unintelligible:

> Alternative knowledge claims, in and of themselves, are rarely threatening to conventional knowledge. Such claims are routinely ignored, discredited, or simply absorbed and marginalized in existing paradigms. Much more threatening is the challenge that alternative epistemologies offer to the basic process used by the powerful to legitimate their knowledge claims. If the epistemology used to validate knowledge comes into question, then all prior knowledge claims validated under the dominant model become suspect. An alternative epistemology challenges all certified knowledge and opens up the question of whether what has been taken to be true can stand the test of alternative ways of validating truth.[58]

While changing what is said and shown about slavery may appear necessary in the first instance in order to gain recognition within the dominant epistemological system, Hill Collins also suggests that the mere presence of an alternative narrative is cause for invalidation of that same system. Therefore, when considering the alternative narratives of slavery presented in 'Afterlives of Slavery', it can be deduced that attempts by the curators to undo some of the harm museum methodologies have caused could equally lead to the unravelling of the museum's epistemic foundations. The urgency for those wanting the archive of slavery to follow other epistemic routes then becomes to create other forms of reception and validation. And this is, I argue, what is currently happening behind the scenes in the background of the 'Afterlives of Slavery' exhibition.

By engaging in attempts at transforming of the colonial archive, museum workers and participants to initiatives like 'Afterlives of Slavery' invest political meaning into the work they undertake to address issues of injustice. Anti-Black racism and exclusion continue to be extremely pervasive and manifest in various areas of Dutch public life.[59] Recently, the responses of the current government's leaders to subjects such as Zwarte Piet demonstrate an unwillingness to condemn the practice; moreover, local iterations of Black Lives Matter, such as calls to replace statues, have also been met with uneasiness. It is worth noting that the context of emergence of the new National Museum of World Cultures in 2014 was one of budgetary cuts to the field of culture and of growing polarization around the status of non-White Dutch populations in the country, illustrated by the rise of far-right populist parties throughout the 2010s.[60] Politically engaged museum workers activate the spaces located in the interstices of the limited spaces of action that the Dutch postcolonial state reserves for them, repurposing the tools that are made available to them. While it appears that the colonial structures of the western museum exhibition have formed a model that is hard to shift, the RCMC director suggests that the exhibition is only one piece of a broader curatorial ensemble.[61] The RCMC is developing an approach which could be termed 'bigger than the exhibition curating', aimed at finding ways to enter complex and divisive questions into public dialogue. Other 2019 projects by the RCMC are aimed at engaging communities, like 'Mijn Rituel' ('My Ritual'),[62] developed by RCMC member and curator Amal Alhaag and guest curator Liza Swaving, which resulted in an exhibition that opened in May 2019 in a small gallery space not far from the Tropenmuseum. The aim of this project was to create a more active dialogue between the museum and its surroundings, a very diverse area of Amsterdam, which is said to be disconnected from the museum and its resources. The aim, therefore, became to find ways to share these resources.

In addition, the RCMC publishes a number of tools and reports. One of them is *Words Matter*, a free publication directed at museum institutions in the Netherlands and beyond, featuring research and critical reflections on 'potentially sensitive' language commonly found in museums, as well as insights regarding how to ensure better practice.[63] These activities contribute to an ongoing project of repurposing museums beyond the exhibition. Importantly, the conferences and conversations that the RCMC hosts with local and global participants on a regular basis may be seen to be functioning as a political platform, exceeding the realms of traditional museum work. Some of these discussions were direct continuations of the conversations ignited by the 'Afterlives of Slavery' exhibition. Examples of such discussions include 'Slavery, Colonialism and Global Inequality' (27 June 2019) and 'Afterlives: Slavery and Contemporary Global Inequalities' (2 October 2019).[64] Both of these events formed part of the broader research programme initiated by the RCMC on the materialities of slavery, in partnership with the Center for Slavery and Justice at Brown University (US), the Smithsonian Museum for African American History and Culture (US), the Iziko Slave Lodge Museum (South Africa), the Royal Museum of Central Africa Tervuren (Belgium) and the International Slavery Museum in Liverpool (UK). All of these institutions are developing their own programmes of exhibition, conversations and publications, and ideas circulate amongst them. The museum becomes a place where alliances are formed between interested subjects who get involved in a praxis focused on articulating new languages to speak about the colonialism of slavery, and in building platforms of organization around collective causes. Seen within this broader ensemble, the new articulations of slavery history may be seen as effectively 're-archiving' slavery according to a new archival trajectory, in a way comparable to the possibilities of resistance identified by Erin Johnson-Williams in this volume in relation to re-appropriated carceral hymns in Canada and South Africa.

I have shown that the Tropenmuseum exhibition 'Afterlives of Slavery' constitutes an effort to correct some of the harmful ways in which slavery and race are talked about in the Netherlands, and to interrogate the role of the museum institution in propagating these views. This chapter offers a compelling use of personal narratives in order to do so. But I argue that what matters even more is that the exhibition forms part of a broader initiative aiming at opening up the museum, and at repurposing the resources it offers. This commitment to re-examining the histories and legacies of slavery may be seen as operating within a praxis of 'thick' transitional justice,[65] that is, as defined by Sarah Maddison and Laura Shepherd, able to revisit the long ago in order to circumvent short-term solutions 'forged against the backdrop of historical injustices' that avoid substantial transformations and society.⁶⁶ The curatorial praxis developed at the RCMC is demonstrative of the urgent need for museums to renew their efforts to find ways to go beyond instigating awareness in individuals, by developing activities that support the construction of collective ideals, as well as the strategies to implement them, keeping in mind the necessity identified by Catherine Lu to 'redress structural injustices', not only through acts of recognition but also through active efforts to identify and alter current manifestations of ongoing injustices and inequalities.⁶⁷

Notes

1. See Media Diversified, 'The Museum Will Not Be Decolonised', https://mediadiversified.org/2017/11/15/the-museum-will-not-be-decolonised/, accessed 22 August 2021; Eliza Schoenberger, 'What Does It Mean to Decolonize a Museum?', https://www.museumnext.com/article/what-does-it-mean-to-decolonize-a-museum/, accessed 22 August 2021; and Sharon Heal, 'Who's Afraid of Decolonisation?', https://www.museumsassociation.org/museums-journal/opinion/2019/07/03072019-whos-afraid-of-decolonisation-policy-column/, accessed 22 August 2021.
2. Melissa F. Weiner, 'The Ideologically Colonized Metropole: Dutch Racism and Racist Denial', *Sociology Compass* 8. 6 (2014): 731–44.
3. Ibid.
4. See DutchNews.nl, 'Government Agencies to Stop Using "Allochtoon" to Describe Immigrants', https://www.dutchnews.nl/news/2016/11/government-agencies-to-ditch-allochtoon-to-describe-immigrants/, accessed 22 August 2021.
5. Weiner, 'The Ideologically Colonized Metropole', pp. 731–44.
6. Rik Van Welie, 'Slave Trading and Slavery in the Dutch Colonial Empire: A Global Comparison', *New West Indian Guide / Nieuwe West-Indische Gids* 82. 1–2 (2018): 47–96.
7. Ibid.
8. John Donoghue and Evelyn P. Jennings, 'Building the Atlantic Empires: Unfree Labor and Imperial States in the Political Economy of Capitalism, ca. 1500–1914', in John Donoghue and Evelyn P. Jennings (eds), *Building the Atlantic Empires: Unfree Labor and Imperial States in the Political Economy of Capitalism, ca. 1500–1914* (Leiden: Brill, 2015), pp. 69–73.
9. See Tropenmuseum, 'Collection', https://www.tropenmuseum.nl/en/themes/collection, accessed 22 August 2021.
10. Wayne Modest and Anouk de Koning, 'Anxious Politics in the European City: An Introduction', *Patterns of Prejudice* 50. 2 (2016): 97–108.
11. Ibid.
12. Saidiya Hartman, *Lose Your Mother: A Journey along the Atlantic Slave Route* (New York: Farrar, Straus and Giroux, 2007).
13. Ibid.
14. See Oxford Learner's Dictionaries, 'Archive', https://www.oxfordlearnersdictionaries.com/definition/english/archive_1#:~:text=%2F%CB%88%C9%91%CB%90rka%C9%AAv%2F,where%20these%20records%20are%20stored, accessed 22 August 2021.
15. Michel Foucault, *Archaeology of Knowledge* (London: Routledge, 2013).

16 Kevin Hetherington, 'Foucault and the Museum', in Sharon Macdonald and Helen Rees Leady (eds), *The International Handbooks of Museum Studies, Vol. 1: Museum Theory* (Chichester: Wiley Blackwell, 2015), pp. 21–40.
17 Ibid.
18 Carole Blair, 'The Statement: Foundation of Foucault's Historical Criticism', *Western Journal of Speech Communication* 51. 4 (1987): 364–83.
19 Catherine Lu, 'Redressing Colonial Alienation', Paper Presentation at the Tropenmuseum, Amsterdam (June 2019).
20 Daan van Dartel, 'The Tropenmuseum and Trade: Products and Sources', *Journal of Museum Ethnography* 20 (2008): 82–93.
21 David Hildering, Wayne Modest, and Warda Aztouti, 'Visualizing Development: The Tropenmuseum and International Development Aid', in Paul Basu and Wayne Modest (eds), *Museums, Heritage and International Development* (New York: Routledge, 2015), pp. 310–32.
22 Ibid., 32.
23 Alex van Stipriaan, 'Dutch Dealings with the Slavery Past: Contexts of an Exhibition', in Carla von Boxtel, Maria Grever and Stephan Klein (eds), *Sensitive Pasts: Questioning Heritage in Education* (New York and Oxford: Berghahn 2019), pp. 92–107; Mirjam Shatanawi, 'Contemporary Art in Ethnographic Museums', in Hans Belting and Andrea Buddensieg (eds), *The Global Art World: Audiences, Markets and Museums* (Ostfildern: Hatje Cantz, 2009), pp. 368–85; and Mary Bouquet, 'Reactivating the Colonial Collection: Exhibition-Making as Creative Process at the Tropenmuseum, Amsterdam', in Annie E. Coombes and Ruth B. Phillips (eds), *The International Handbooks of Museum Studies: Vol. 4, Museum Transformations* (Chichester: Wiley Blackwell, 2015), pp. 133–55.
24 See Dutch Amsterdam, 'Survival of Amsterdam's Tropenmuseum Uncertain after Subsidy Stop', https://www.dutchamsterdam.nl/2075-subsidy-stop-tropenmuseum-amsterdam, accessed 22 August 2021.
25 See Tropenmuseum, 'About Tropenmuseum', https://www.tropenmuseum.nl/en/about-tropenmuseum, accessed 22 August 2021.
26 Wayne Modest, Personal Communication [Interviewed by the author], May 2019, Amsterdam.
27 See Research Center for Material Culture, 'About', https://www.materialculture.nl/en/about, accessed 22 August 2021.
28 See Research Center for Material Culture, 'A Shared History: Conversations on the Slavery Past in the Present', https://www.materialculture.nl/en/events/shared-history-conversations-on-slavery-past-present, accessed 22 August 2021.
29 Curatorial team, Personal Communications [Interviewed by the author], May 2019, Tropenmuseum, Amsterdam.
30 See Hodan Warsame, 'Decolonize the Museum', https://hodanwarsame.com/decolonize-the-museum/, accessed 19 August 2021.
31 Iris van Huis, 'Contesting Cultural Heritage: Decolonizing the Tropenmuseum as an Intervention in the Dutch/European Memory Complex', in T. Lähdesmäki, L. Passerini, S. Kaasik-Krogerus and I. van Huis (eds), *Dissonant Heritages and Memories in Contemporary Europe* (Cham: Palgrave Macmillan, 2019), pp. 215–49.
32 See Tropenmuseum, 'Afterlives of Slavery', https://www.tropenmuseum.nl/en/whats-on/exhibitions/afterlives-slavery?_ga=2.174265445.673765982.1530528895-942435970.1530528895, accessed 19 August 2021.

33 Curatorial team, Personal Communication [Interviewed by the author], May 2019, Tropenmuseum, Amsterdam.
34 Marcus Wood, *Blind Memory: Visual Representations of Slavery in England and America* (Manchester: Manchester University Press, 2000).
35 This is also an issue that Saidiya Hartman addresses in her first book, *Scenes of Subjection: Terror, Slavery, and Self-Making in Nineteenth-Century America* (New York and Oxford: Oxford University Press, 1997).
36 For further reading, see Yasmin Ibrahim, 'The Dying Black Body in Repeat Mode: The Black "Horrific" on a Loop', *Identities* (2021): 1–19.
37 Ibid.
38 Robin D. G. Kelley and Tiffany Ruby Patterson describe an early twentieth-century African diaspora scholarship that focused on African cultural retentions in the New World. See Tiffany Ruby Patterson and Robin D. G. Kelley, 'Unfinished Migrations: Reflections on the African Diaspora and the Making of the Modern World', *African Studies Review* 43. 1 (2000): 11–45.
39 Curatorial team, Personal Communication [Interviewed by the author], May 2019, Tropenmuseum, Amsterdam.
40 Ibid.
41 Colin Kidd, *The Forging of Races: Race and Scripture in the Protestant Atlantic World, 1600–2000* (Cambridge: Cambridge University Press, 2006).
42 Jeroen Rodenberg and Pieter Wagenaar, 'Essentializing "Black Pete": Competing Narratives Surrounding the Sinterklaas Tradition in the Netherlands', *International Journal of Heritage Studies* 22. 9 (2016): 716–28.
43 Gloria Wekker, *White Innocence: Paradoxes of Colonialism and Race* (Durham: Duke University Press, 2016).
44 Anton de Kom is the author of the book *We Slaves of Surinam* (London: Pluto Press, 2016).
45 Curatorial team, Personal Communication [Interviewed by the author], May 2019, Tropenmuseum, Amsterdam.
46 See https://www.mauritshuis.nl/en/discover/exhibitions/shifting-image/ (accessed 20 August 2021).
47 Carol Duncan, *Civilizing Rituals: Inside Public Art Museums* (London: Routledge, 2005).
48 Thomas Lemke, *Foucault, Governmentality, and Critique* (London and New York: Routledge, 2015), pp. 18–19.
49 Ibid., p. 45.
50 Kevin Hetherington, 'Kevin Hetherington', *Society* (1999): 597–603.
51 Ibid.
52 Tony Bennett, *Pasts Beyond Memory: Evolution, Museums, Colonialism* (London: Routledge, 2004).
53 Lemke, *Foucault*, pp. 24–7.
54 See https://www.tropenmuseum.nl/en/about-tropenmuseum, accessed 22 August 2021.
55 See Carol Hanisch, 'The Personal Is Political' (1969), in Barbara A. Crow (eds), *Radical Feminism: A Documentary Reader* (New York: New York University Press, 2000), pp. 113–16.
56 See Theresa Man Ling Lee, 'Rethinking the Personal and the Political: Feminist Activism and Civic Engagement', *Hypatia* 22. 4 (2007): 163–79.
57 bell hooks, *Feminist Theory: From Margin to Center* (London: Pluto Press, 2000).

58 Patricia Hill Collins, 'The Social Construction of Black Feminist Thought', *Signs: Journal of Women in Culture and Society* 14. 4 (1989): 745–73.
59 Weiner, 'The Ideologically Colonized Metropole', pp. 731–44.
60 Guno Jones, 'What Is New about Dutch Populism? Dutch Colonialism, Hierarchical Citizenship and Contemporary Populist Debates and Policies in the Netherlands', *Journal of Intercultural Studies* 37. 6 (2016): 605–20.
61 Wayne Modest, Personal Communication [Interviewed by the author], May 2019, Amsterdam.
62 See Tropenmuseum, 'Buurtsalon: Mijn Ritueel', https://www.tropenmuseum.nl/nl/zien-en-doen/tentoonstellingen/buurtsalon-mijn-ritueel, accessed 22 August 2021.
63 See Tropenmuseum, *Words Matter*, https://issuu.com/tropenmuseum/docs/wordsmatter_english, accessed 22 August 2021.
64 See Research Center for Material Culture, 'Events', https://www.materialculture.nl/en/events, accessed 10 January 2022.
65 See for example Buckley-Zistel, Susanne, Teresa Koloma Beck, Christian Braun, and Friederike Miet (eds), *Transitional Justice Theories* (London: Routledge, 2013).
66 Sarah Maddison and Laura J. Shepherd, 'Peacebuilding and the Postcolonial Politics of Transitional Justice'. *Peacebuilding* 2. 3 (2014): 253–26.
67 Lu, 'Redressing Colonial Alienation'.

Bibliography

Andermann, Jens, and Silke Arnold-de Simine. 'Introduction: Memory, Community and the New Museum'. *Theory, Culture and Society* 29, no. 1 (2012): 3–13.

Bennett, Tony. *Pasts Beyond Memory: Evolution, Museums, Colonialism*. London: Routledge, 2004.

Blair, Carole. 'The Statement: Foundation of Foucault's Historical Criticism'. *Western Journal of Speech Communication* 51, no. 4 (1987): 364–83.

Bouquet, Mary. 'Reactivating the Colonial Collection: Exhibition-Making as Creative Process at the Tropenmuseum, Amsterdam'. In *The International Handbooks of Museum Studies: Vol. 4, Museum Transformations*, edited by Annie E. Coombes and Ruth B. Phillips, 133–55. Chichester: Wiley Blackwell, 2015.

Buckley-Zistel, Susanne, Teresa Koloma Beck, Christian Braun, and Friederike Miet (eds). *Transitional Justice Theories*. London: Routledge, 2013.

Chouliaraki, Lilie. '"Improper Distance": Towards a Critical Account of Solidarity as Irony'. *International Journal of Cultural Studies* 14, no. 4 (2011): 363–81.

Collins, Patricia Hill. 'The Social Construction of Black Feminist Thought'. *Signs: Journal of Women in Culture and Society* 14, no. 4 (1989): 745–73.

Donoghue, John, and Evelyn P. Jennings. 'Building the Atlantic Empires: Unfree Labor and Imperial States in the Political Economy of Capitalism, ca. 1500–1914'. In *Building the Atlantic Empires: Unfree Labor and Imperial States in the Political Economy of Capitalism, ca. 1500–1914*, edited by John Donoghue and Evelyn P. Jennings, 69–73. Leiden: Brill, 2015.

van Dartel, Daan. 'The Tropenmuseum and Trade: Products and Sources'. *Journal of Museum Ethnography* 20 (2008): 82–93.

Duncan, Carol. *Civilizing Rituals: Inside Public Art Museums*. London: Routledge, 2005.

Dutch Amsterdam. 'Survival of Amsterdam's Tropenmuseum Uncertain after Subsidy Stop'. https://www.dutchamsterdam.nl/2075-subsidy-stop-tropenmuseum-amsterdam. Accessed 22 August 2021.

DutchNews.nl. 'Government Agencies to Stop Using "Allochtoon" to Describe Immigrants'. https://www.dutchnews.nl/news/2016/11/government-agencies-to-ditch-allochtoon-to-describe-immigrants/. Accessed 22 August 2021.

DutchNews.nl. 'No Apology for Slavery, Says Dutch PM in Bad-Tempered Debate about Racism'. https://www.dutchnews.nl/news/2020/07/no-apology-for-slavery-says-dutch-pm-in-bad-tempered-debate-about-racism/. Accessed 19 August 2021.

Foucault, Michel. *Archaeology of Knowledge*. London: Routledge, 2013.

Gario, Quinsy. 'Zwarte Piet Is Racisme'. https://www.visibleproject.org/blog/project/zwarte-piet-is-racisme/. Accessed 19 August 2021.

Hanisch, Carol. 'The Personal Is Political' (1969). In *Radical Feminism: A Documentary Reader*, edited by Barbara A. Crow, 113–16. New York: New York University Press, 2000.

Hartman, Saidiya. *Scenes of Subjection: Terror, Slavery, and Self-Making in Nineteenth-Century America*. New York and Oxford: Oxford University Press, 1997.

Hartman, Saidiya. *Lose Your Mother: A Journey Along the Atlantic Slave Route*. New York: Farrar, Straus and Giroux, 2007.

Heal, Sharon. 'Who's Afraid of Decolonisation?' https://www.museumsassociation.org/museums-journal/opinion/2019/07/03072019-whos-afraid-of-decolonisation-policy-column/. Accessed 22 August 2021.

Hetherington, Kevin. 'Kevin Hetherington', *Society* 23, no. 2–3 (1999): 597–603.

Hetherington, Kevin. 'Foucault and the Museum'. In *The International Handbooks of Museum Studies, Vol. 1: Museum Theory*, edited by Sharon Macdonald and Helen Rees Leady, 21–40. Chichester: Wiley Blackwell, 2015.

Hicks, Dan. *The Brutish Museums: The Benin Bronzes, Colonial Violence and Cultural Restitution*. London: Pluto Press, 2020.

Hildering, David, Wayne Modest, and Warda Aztouti. 'Visualizing Development: The Tropenmuseum and International Development Aid'. In *Museums, Heritage and International Development*, edited by Paul Basu and Wayne Modest, 310–32. New York: Routledge, 2015.

hooks, bell. *Feminist Theory: From Margin to Center*. London: Pluto Press, 2000.

van Huis, Iris. 'Contesting Cultural Heritage: Decolonizing the Tropenmuseum as an Intervention in the Dutch/European Memory Complex'. In *Dissonant Heritages and Memories in Contemporary Europe*, edited by T. Lähdesmäki, L. Passerini, S. Kaasik-Krogerus and I. van Huis, 215–49. Cham: Palgrave Macmillan, 2019.

Ibrahim, Yasmin. 'The Dying Black Body in Repeat Mode: The Black "Horrific" on a Loop'. *Identities* (2021): 1–19.

Jones, Guno. 'What Is New about Dutch Populism? Dutch Colonialism, Hierarchical Citizenship and Contemporary Populist Debates and Policies in the Netherlands'. *Journal of Intercultural Studies* 37, no. 6 (2016): 605–20.

Kidd, Colin. *The Forging of Races: Race and Scripture in the Protestant Atlantic World, 1600–2000*. Cambridge: Cambridge University Press, 2006.

de Kom, Anton. *We Slaves of Surinam*. London: Pluto Press, 2016.

Lee, Theresa Man Ling. 'Rethinking the Personal and the Political: Feminist Activism and Civic Engagement'. *Hypatia* 22, no. 4 (2007): 163–79.

Lemke, Thomas. *Foucault, Governmentality, and Critique*. London and New York: Routledge, 2015.

Lu, Catherine. 'Redressing Colonial Alienation'. Paper Presentation at the Tropenmuseum, Amsterdam, June 2019.
Maddison, Sarah, and Laura J. Shepherd. 'Peacebuilding and the Postcolonial Politics of Transitional Justice'. *Peacebuilding* 2, no. 3 (2014): 253–69.
Media Diversified. 'The Museum Will Not Be Decolonised'. https://mediadiversified.org/2017/11/15/the-museum-will-not-be-decolonised/. Accessed 22 August 2021.
Message, Kylie. 'The New Museum'. *Theory, Culture & Society* 23, no. 2–3 (2006): 603–6.
Modest, Wayne, and Anouk de Koning. 'Anxious Politics in the European City: An Introduction'. *Patterns of Prejudice* 50, no. 2 (2016): 97–108.
Munley, Mary Ellen. 'Evaluating Public Value: Strategy and Practice'. In *Museums and Public Value: Creating Sustainable Futures*, edited by Carol A. Scott, 45–63. Farnham, Ashgate, 2016.
Oksala, Johanna. *Foucault, Politics, and Violence*. Evanston: Northwestern University Press, 2012.
Oxford Learner's Dictionaries. 'Archive'. https://www.oxfordlearnersdictionaries.com/definition/english/archive_1#:~:text=%2F%CB%88%C9%91%CB%90rka%C9%AAv%2F,where%20these%20records%20are%20stored. Accessed 22 August 2021.
Patterson, Tiffany Ruby and Robin D. G. Kelley. 'Unfinished Migrations: Reflections on the African Diaspora and the Making of the Modern World'. *African Studies Review* 43, no. 1 (2000): 11–45.
Research Center for Material Culture. 'About'. https://www.materialculture.nl/en/about. Accessed 22 August 2021.
Research Center for Material Culture. 'A Shared History: Conversations on the Slavery Past in the Present'. https://www.materialculture.nl/en/events/shared-history-conversations-on-slavery-past-present. Accessed 22 August 2021.
Research Center for Material Culture. 'Events'. https://www.materialculture.nl/en/events. Accessed 10 January 2022.
Rodenberg, Jeroen, and Pieter Wagenaar. 'Essentializing "Black Pete": Competing Narratives Surrounding the Sinterklaas Tradition in the Netherlands'. *International Journal of Heritage Studies* 22, no. 9 (2016): 716–28.
Schoenberger, Eliza. 'What Does It Mean to Decolonize a Museum?' https://www.museumnext.com/article/what-does-it-mean-to-decolonize-a-museum/. Accessed 22 August 2021.
Shatanawi, Mirjam. 'Contemporary Art in Ethnographic Museums'. In *The Global Art World: Audiences, Markets and Museums*, edited by Hans Belting and Andrea Buddensieg, 368–85. Ostfildern: Hatje Cantz, 2009.
van Stipriaan, Alex. 'Dutch Dealings with the Slavery Past: Contexts of an Exhibition'. In *Sensitive Pasts: Questioning Heritage in Education*, edited by Carla von Boxtel, Maria Grever and Stephan Klein, 92–107. New York and Oxford: Berghahn 2019.
Tropenmuseum. 'About Tropenmuseum'. https://www.tropenmuseum.nl/en/about-tropenmuseum. Accessed 22 August 2021.
Tropenmuseum. 'Afterlives of Slavery'. https://www.tropenmuseum.nl/en/whats-on/exhibitions/afterlives-slavery?_ga=2.174265445.673765982.1530528895-942435970.1530528895. Accessed 19 August 2021.
Tropenmuseum. 'Buurtsalon: Mijn Ritueel'. https://www.tropenmuseum.nl/nl/zien-en-doen/tentoonstellingen/buurtsalon-mijn-ritueel. Accessed 22 August 2021.
Tropenmuseum. 'Collection'. https://www.tropenmuseum.nl/en/themes/collection. Accessed 22 August 2021.

Tropenmuseum. *Words Matter*. https://issuu.com/tropenmuseum/docs/wordsmatter_english. Accessed 22 August 2021.
Warsame, Hodan. 'Decolonize the Museum'. https://hodanwarsame.com/decolonize-the-museum/. Accessed 19 August 2021.
Weiner, Melissa F. 'The Ideologically Colonized Metropole: Dutch Racism and Racist Denial'. *Sociology Compass* 8, no. 6 (2014): 731–44.
Wekker, Gloria. *White Innocence: Paradoxes of Colonialism and Race*. Durham: Duke University Press, 2016.
Welie, Rik Van. 'Slave Trading and Slavery in the Dutch Colonial Empire: A Global Comparison'. *New West Indian Guide/Nieuwe West-Indische Gids* 82, no. 1–2 (2018): 47–96.
Wood, Marcus. *Blind Memory: Visual Representations of Slavery in England and America*. Manchester: Manchester University Press, 2000.
Wood, Marcus. 'Slavery, Empathy and Pornography'. *Textual Practice* 3, no. 17 (2002): 582–7.

4

Maqdala and the South Kensington Museum

150 years later

Alexandra Watson Jones

The display *Maqdala 1868* at London's Victoria and Albert Museum (V&A), which ran from 5 April 2018 to 30 June 2019, told the story of the 1867–68 British Expedition to Abyssinia (as Ethiopia was then known in Britain), and highlighted objects whose presence in the Museum's collection has been the subject of intense debate ever since they were first brought to the UK over 150 years ago. This project formed part of the V&A's continued efforts, along with other UK museums and heritage organizations, to confront and interrogate the colonial histories of their collections. As Ann Laura Stoler has written, 'ethnography in and of the colonial archives attends to processes of production, relations of power in which archives are created, sequestered, and rearranged'.[1] Museums are no exception: their nineteenth-century collections, the displays created with those objects and the documentation surrounding them are all part of the colonial archive, and have the potential to embody what Hannah Turner, in her analysis of the documentary practices of ethnographic museums, has termed 'legacies of colonialism'.[2] Similarly, Sarah Longair has defined a 'colonial moment' in the biographies of objects: 'the period when an object's trajectory is influenced by the forces of imperialism'.[3] As this chapter will demonstrate, the V&A's Ethiopian collections are undisputedly part of the archive of colonialism.

The V&A's presentation of its Ethiopian collections, and our collective understanding of their significance, have been continually revised and redefined throughout history, and must be considered, as Nicholas Thomas puts it in his analysis of object exchanges in the Pacific, as 'not what they were made to be but what they have become'.[4] This chapter will explore how the display *Maqdala 1868* fits into the broader history of the V&A's Ethiopian collections and displays, and will consider how those displays have contributed, over time, to Britain's understanding of Ethiopia. As the curator of *Maqdala 1868* and a researcher on the histories of Ethiopian museum collections, I will reflect on the lessons that can be learned from such projects about knowledge production in museums, ideas of expertise and authority in a museum context, and how museum practices today can both challenge and reinforce historic and ongoing instances of colonial violence. Drawing on Thomas Osborne's assertion that 'the person who speaks from the archive is the person who mediates between the secrets or obscurities of the archive and some or other kind of public',[5] I will also consider the roles of myself and other museum professionals as mediators of the information contained within the museum stores, and how we as individuals play our own roles in continuing to enforce the 'legacies of colonialism' today.

The 1867–8 British expedition to Abyssinia

Helen Mears and Wayne Modest, who have explored the history of the V&A's African collections in detail, stress the importance of recognizing that African collections in UK museums 'did not come about spontaneously or independently' but as a result of 'the significant social, political, cultural and economic changes brought to that continent by the experience of colonialism'.[6] The events that led to the V&A and other UK institutions acquiring vast quantities of Ethiopian material culture represent a brief but significant chapter in British and Ethiopian history, which saw Ethiopia – the only African country never to have been colonized by a European power – subject to the forces of colonialism in the form of a large-scale British military expedition.[7] These objects are therefore imbued with a 'colonial moment' within their histories, even as they originate from an uncolonized country.[8]

At the centre of this story is Emperor Tewodros II, who became Emperor of Ethiopia in 1855. Ethiopia is one of the world's oldest Christian countries, and Tewodros was keen to forge alliances with other Christian nations. He therefore wrote letters to Queen Victoria in 1857 and 1862 to request military assistance and weapons that would help him secure his position in Ethiopia. In 1863, when he had received no reply, he took hostage around thirty European diplomats and missionaries who were living in Ethiopia at the time.[9] After failed diplomatic efforts to secure the release of Tewodros's captives, in 1867 the British Army launched a large-scale military expedition to Ethiopia from Bombay, comprising around 12,000 British and Indian troops. While this expedition was ostensibly a rescue mission to bring home the British hostages, a communication from General Robert Napier written shortly after the climax of the expedition demonstrates its punitive nature, with Napier stating that defeating Tewodros was 'essential for the vindication of our national honour'.[10] The British Army was equipped with enormous firepower which allowed them to quickly overwhelm Tewodros's troops in a brutal battle at his fortress at Maqdala on 13 April 1868. Tewodros killed himself as the fortress was captured, using a gun that had previously been sent to him as a diplomatic gift from Queen Victoria.

Napier's troops ransacked Tewodros's library and treasury as well as churches and other buildings in the surrounding area, an act of looting which was, at the time, framed as an opportunity to find 'articles of worth' for Britain's museum collections, and to raise funds for the army's Prize Fund.[11] The fortress was evacuated and then burned to the ground. The loot taken from Maqdala was said to have required 15 elephants and almost 200 mules to carry it away to the Dalanta Plain, where items were auctioned off.[12] Tewodros's orphaned seven-year-old son Prince Alemayehu was also brought to England, where the British government assumed responsibility for him.

Material culture from Maqdala

Today, objects looted from Maqdala can be found in museums, libraries and private collections all over the world. They include textiles, jewellery, weapons, manuscripts and sacred metalwork. The Association for the Return of the Maqdala Ethiopian Treasures (AFROMET), founded in 1999 by the late Richard and Rita Pankhurst, has dedicated its efforts to locating objects from Maqdala across the world and campaigning for their return to Ethiopia. An eighteenth-century gold sacerdotal crown and chalice, thought to have once been royal gifts to a church in Gondar,[13] are two of the most significant, famous and controversial items looted from Tewodros's treasury at Maqdala (Figure 4.1). These are now in the V&A collection, and there have been calls for their return to Ethiopia ever since they were brought to Britain. They were the subject of a formal restitution request by the Ethiopian government in 2008, when several other UK institutions were also approached with similar requests. None of these requests were granted.

History of Ethiopian displays at the V&A

While many of the objects displayed in *Maqdala 1868* have spent most of their time at the museum in storage, other objects – especially the famous crown and chalice – are thought to have been on display ever since their arrival in the museum.[14] Soon after the

Figure 4.1 Gold Crown and Chalice probably made in Gondar, Ethiopia, around 1740. © Victoria and Albert Museum, London.

1868 expedition, objects looted from Maqdala were presented in a display of 'trophies' at the South Kensington Museum (as the V&A was then known) which, as Tim Barringer notes, 'made no contribution to the museum's original mission in relation to design and social reform but rather offered the Victorian public the spectacle of the remains of a defeated enemy whose perceived status as a racial and cultural inferior was implicit in the mode of display'.[15] A report on these the displays by the *Gentleman's Magazine* noted the inclusion of a sketch, made shortly after Tewodros's suicide, of the deceased Emperor's head.[16] The inclusion of this sketch makes clear the violent and triumphalist nature of the museum's earliest Ethiopian displays, and recalls Annie Coombes's important exploration of the 'role of "spectacle" in the constituting of racial difference' in the collecting and display of African material culture by museums.[17]

The V&A's Ethiopian collections therefore cannot be separated from their violent provenance, or from the racism and colonial power-structures which surrounded their initial acquisition and display by the museum. As Constance Classen and David Howes have observed, in their study of historic western attitudes to so-called indigenous material culture, 'collecting is a form of conquest and collected artifacts are material signs of victory over their former owners and places of origin'.[18] The objects that the museum selected for acquisition, the modes of display that incorporated these objects and the written texts that accompanied them, are therefore all part of the nineteenth-century archive of colonialism, and have played a role in shaping Britain's knowledge of Ethiopia and its people. Collections and archives are not simply repositories of objects, but 'full-fledged historical actors' and 'technologies of imperial power, conquest and hegemony', as asserted by Antoinette Burton.[19] However, objects in museum collections can also be used to explore 'other, divergent histories'.[20] This was the aim of *Exploring Hidden Histories*, a 2012 V&A display which presented around 100 African objects from the museum's collections, and featured one case dedicated entirely to Ethiopian material culture. The interpretive text for the display recounted the 'violent event' at Maqdala and told the stories of Tewodros and Alemayehu, through 'the personal and public narratives of conflict' inherent in the biographies of the objects.[21]

The museum's permanent galleries had, meanwhile, come to entirely omit the Maqdala provenance of its Ethiopian collections in their interpretive texts. From 2005, the famous gold crown and chalice were on display in the museum's Sacred Silver and Stained Glass galleries, where they were presented in a case entitled 'The Eastern Churches', alongside objects from other Orthodox Christian Churches. The accompanying labels made no reference to the Maqdala provenance of the objects, instead focusing solely on their role and significance in the Ethiopian Orthodox Church. As Sarah Longair and John McAleer have observed, 'objects and the changing interpretations they have been subject to over the intervening period clearly illustrate how the meanings of objects are modified and altered in response to external influences and changing political priorities'.[22] The V&A's Ethiopian collections, once clear trophies of colonial violence, had thus come to be presented in an entirely different context, with no acknowledgement of their controversial history.[23] Longair observed a similar process of decontextualization at work in the British Museum's display of the chair of Witu Sultan: once presented as a seized object and an item of propaganda, the chair is now displayed in the museum as an interesting example of Swahili culture and design.[24]

150 years later

2018 marked 150 years since the events at Maqdala. In mid-2017, significant discussions took place between the museum and the Ethiopian Embassy in London, in which it was decided that the museum should present a new display of its Ethiopian collections to mark the anniversary. This display – as later explained by V&A Director Tristram Hunt in a public blog post – would 'celebrate the beauty of [the objects'] craftsmanship, shine a light on their cultural and religious significance and reflect on their living meaning, while being open about how they came to Britain'.[25] This project came at a time when museums were finding themselves subjected to increasing media attention and pressure from the public to confront their colonial histories and respond to calls for the repatriation of looted African objects, in part due to French President Emmanuel Macron's commissioning of a 2018 report by Bénédicte Savoy and Felwine Sarr which recommended the restitution of stolen African works of art from French museums.

Curating *Maqdala 1868*

As an Assistant Curator in the V&A's Metalwork section, I was given the task of curating the display. Janet Browne, the V&A's Programme Manager for African Heritage and Culture, convened a focus group that brought together Ethiopian and Rastafarian community leaders, historians and activists. The challenges and shortcomings of

Figure 4.2 *Maqdala 1868* at the V&A, 5 April 2018 to 30 June 2019. © Victoria and Albert Museum, London.

convening community focus groups for museum projects have been explored at length by Eithne Nightingale and Chandan Mahal, who highlight the tendency for such groups to hinge on relationships forged by individual staff members.[26] *Maqdala 1868*'s focus group was only made possible by Janet's existing links with individual community members and organizations that had been forged as a result of earlier V&A projects. It is also important to note that a focus group that brings together the views of individuals – in this case all individuals living in London – can never be assumed to represent the views of a global community, as is also emphasized in the case studies from Durham University's Oriental Museum in Chapter 2 of this volume. This focus group, nonetheless, played a pivotal role in shaping the purpose and messaging of the display.[27] The group met in January 2018, and the biggest takeaway from this meeting was that participants wanted to see the provenance of the objects presented openly and honestly. Members of the group stressed that it would be disappointing if the museum was seen to be 'shying away' from controversy.

The focus group participants expressed some disappointment when shown the planned location for the display: a single large glass case in the V&A's Silver Galleries (Figure 4.2). The V&A does not currently have any galleries dedicated to African material culture, and the location in the Silver Galleries was chosen as the best option from a limited number of available temporary display spaces in the museum. The case in the Silver Galleries was large and adaptable enough to incorporate a wide range of objects, and it also occupied a high-traffic area due to its proximity to the museum's main Lecture Theatre, ensuring it would be seen by many visitors. However, being situated in the middle of a gallery filled with displays of British and European silver, and being partially obstructed by a large, immovable electrotype wine-cooler installed directly in front of the case, the focus group raised some concerns about whether this was an appropriate location for such an important display. In Chapter 3 of this volume, Adiva Lawrence has stressed the importance of the 'scenographic' element of the Tropenmuseum's 'Afterlives of Slavery' exhibition. Similarly, it was essential for the V&A's Design team to find ways to make *Maqdala 1868* stand out from the rest of the Silver Galleries, marking it out as an important display and ensuring that it would be easy for visitors to find, while also remaining sensitive to the sacred objects and to the subject matter.

Maqdala 1868 incorporated objects from across the museum's collections including textiles, manuscripts and photography, normally stored in separate areas of the museum and cared for by different collections departments. This inclusion of objects from across multiple departments was somewhat unusual for a temporary display in one of the museum's material-focused galleries. The selection of objects also highlighted the many different ways in which objects associated with the 1867–8 expedition subsequently found their way into the museum. While the crown and chalice – the centrepieces of the display – are unquestionably war loot, other objects included in the display (Figure 4.3) have a more 'ambiguous status',[28] such as clothing and jewellery belonging to Tewodros's wife Queen Terunesh, which were sent to London after her death from lung disease, a month after her husband's suicide. These objects are thus 'not technically war booty, but clearly in the possession of the British as a result of military action'.[29] The same can be said of an Ethiopian priest's cross purchased from a church in Chelicut by the war artist William Simpson, who accompanied the expedition to provide sketches for the *Illustrated London News*.[30] The display also included photographs taken by the British Army's Corps of Royal Engineers, in one of the earliest examples of a British military campaign being documented by official photographic records.[31] The display therefore showed the many different ways in which objects can be connected to the same story of colonialist violence.

One of the biggest challenges in curating the display was to produce interpretive text which could fulfil multiple roles. The display needed to tell the Maqdala story and discuss the controversies surrounding the objects, while also highlighting that the objects have a historic and contemporary significance that goes beyond their status as loot and trophies from Maqdala. The museum's Interpretation and Design teams worked closely to come up with an approach to the display's labelling which could incorporate all of these elements without overwhelming the case with swathes of text. Two large introductory text panels, along with a simple timeline, gave a brief synopsis of the historic events, while a multi-layered approach was adopted in the labels for individual objects. This labelling scheme incorporated not only traditional 'museum' labels (researched and written by me), but also included short commentaries on each object written by members of the focus group, and direct quotes from historic British and Ethiopian sources. This resulted in some objects having two or three labels attached to them, thus beginning to challenge the assumption that a single museum label can ever contain all of the complex layers of history and meaning inherent in one object.

The historic quotes used in the display included excerpts from letters written by Emperor Tewodros and General Napier, a passage from the Ethiopian Royal Chronicles translated into English, and accounts by British eye-witnesses to the events. A crucial part of the display's overall messaging was encapsulated in the inclusion of an extract from an 1871 Parliamentary debate by British Prime Minister William Gladstone, in which he expressed regret that the crown and chalice had ever been taken from Ethiopia:

> He (Mr Gladstone) deeply regretted that those articles were ever brought from Abyssinia, and could not conceive why they were so brought. They were never at war with the people or the churches of Abyssinia. They were at war with Theodore [Tewodros], who personally had inflicted on them an outrage and a wrong; and he deeply lamented, for the sake of the country, and for the sake of all concerned, that those articles, to us insignificant, though probably to the Abyssinians sacred and imposing symbols … were thought fit to be brought away by a British Army.[32]

By including this regretful statement from Gladstone, the display challenged the assumption that debates about the provenance of objects are solely a modern concern, and showed that the removal of these objects from Ethiopia has been controversial ever since they were brought to Britain.

Members of the focus group who contributed their own object labels were encouraged to respond to the objects however they wished. Some chose to share personal reflections or anecdotes, while others shared historic details that they felt were particularly interesting or noteworthy. The labels were printed at the same size and in the same typeface as the more 'traditional' museum labels, and all labels were placed side by side in the case, distinguished only by different background colours. The display thus attempted to avoid the implication of any kind of hierarchy of knowledge, indicating that the information presented in each label was of equal relevance. However, it must be recognized that visitors will come to a display such as this with their own assumptions about the authority and expertise that can be ascribed to such texts, and the subtle ways in which such ideas may be reinforced.

While the focus group's labels included a credit line attributing them to each individual author, the museum labels had no such attribution. Particularly in a large museum like the V&A, such texts have often passed through multiple departments and have gone through many rounds of edits, so that the resulting labels are not merely the work of one author, but the product of a rigorous process which ensures that the final text fits with the museum's broader interpretation strategy.[33] *Maqdala 1868* was anticipated to be a high-profile display that would likely attract a great deal of scrutiny, so the texts for this project were given even more attention than typical for a temporary display of this size, and the labels were reviewed and edited by senior curators, the Interpretation and Press teams, and the museum's Director. Each reviewer approached these texts with different priorities, tensions and concerns regarding the display and its messaging, all of which needed to be balanced and taken into consideration before the final labels could be presented as the work of 'the museum'.

Osborne draws a distinction between 'keepers' and 'interpreters' of archival information and compares this to the distinction often drawn between 'primary' and secondary' sources in historiography. In the context of a museum display, this perceived hierarchy of expertise can also be applied to the labels that accompany objects, and the public's perception of the legitimacy of different forms of knowledge. As Karen Exell has explored in her analysis of a 'community consultation' project in Manchester, visitors tend to look to museum labels for 'basic information' about objects such as 'the age of something, what it is made of, its understood function, and where exactly ... it came from', and will see the museum's declarations on this to be authoritative and factual.[34] By presenting certain labels in *Maqdala 1868* as the work of 'the museum', while attributing others to named authors, visitors who would tend to view 'the museum' as a knowledgeable, trustworthy and unbiased source of expertise may therefore still have perceived the museum labels to be the primary source of information on the objects.

Conversely, because the labels written by the focus group were not subjected to the same rigorous approval process as the museum labels, they were able to speak much more frankly and openly than the museum's internal tensions would permit. These labels received no copy-editing by V&A staff, and this authorial freedom is the reason that a label written for the gold chalice by Samuel Berhanu, a London-based artist and member of the Ethiopian Orthodox Church, contained the only usage of the word 'loot' in the display – a word that several parties had been reluctant to use in the museum's own labelling for fear of inflammatory connotations:

> The inscription highlights the devotion and connection of the Ethiopian Orthodox Church to the country's royal family. Bittersweet, as I can't help

thinking about the Maqdala loot – how many masterpieces alike have been auctioned off, undocumented and without trace?³⁵

However, it must be noted that since *Maqdala 1868*, the V&A has become less reluctant to use such language. The 2019 display *Asante Goldweights*, for example, explicitly mentioned 'looting' in its labels, and a 2019 intervention in the museum's Rosalinde and Arthur Gilbert Galleries even had the word 'looting' in its title: *Concealed Histories: Uncovering the Story of Nazi Looting.*

While Berhanu's label made a powerful statement in the display, it also raises questions about whether the museum should be relying on marginalized voices to raise the most pertinent points, instead of being more frank and open in its own interpretive text, and where the burden of education is placed when inviting external stakeholders to contribute to a project.³⁶ Most members of the *Maqdala 1868* focus group were paid a small honorarium from museum funds for their time, but it also nevertheless remains the case that some of the most meaningful and impactful elements of the display were provided by individuals not on the museum's payroll. As Exell has noted, it is difficult to integrate 'communities' into projects in a meaningful way if those communities are not at all represented in the museum's own staff.³⁷

Responses to *Maqdala 1868*

Maqdala 1868 began to receive considerable attention in the UK press in the weeks leading up to its opening. Much of the initial coverage focused on the looted objects and the calls for their return to Ethiopia. The *Daily Telegraph*'s announcement of the display ran under the headline 'For the V&A's latest show … shamelessly looted treasure', anticipating that the display would 'reviv[e] a diplomatic row over a controversial episode in Britain's military history'.³⁸ The *Socialist Worker* suggested that the display would 'glorify murder and plunder' and 'celebrate Britain's murderous past in Africa'.³⁹ A statement from the V&A that it would be open to a 'long term loan' of the objects to Ethiopia was also highlighted by many outlets.⁴⁰

Maqdala 1868 opened on 5 April 2018 with a reception that included speeches from the Ethiopian Ambassador to the UK, Dr Hailemichael Aberra Afework and poet Lemn Sissay, OBE. Afework stated in his speech that the display was a 'significant first step towards the eventual return of these treasures home' and thanked the V&A 'for their supreme efforts in bringing together this fascinating exhibition which, we hope, will bring about greater understanding of our cultural heritage and greater cooperation going forward'.⁴¹ Sissay agreed that the display was 'opening us up to debate, and that's a wonderful thing', but also emphasized the 'live' nature of the subject matter.⁴²

Many visitors responded positively to the display, with the V&A's front-of-house team informing me that members of the public often expressed their excitement at seeing Ethiopian objects given such prominence in a V&A gallery, and that visitors from London's Ethiopian community had brought their children to see the objects and to learn about Emperor Tewodros. Some visitors were pleased to see the museum speaking more openly about the history of the collection and acknowledging the controversy around it. However, visitors also regularly asked questions about the provenance of the objects and expressed that they wanted to see firmer plans made for their return to Ethiopia. With all the press attention that the display had received, where many articles had referred to an 'exhibition' of Ethiopian treasures, many visitors also arrived at the museum expecting a much larger show, and were sometimes disappointed to find that the 'exhibition' was only a single display case.

In a review for *Shades of Noir*, writer Kerian Magloire observed that 'the launch attracted a range of people from different backgrounds and ages; including members of the Ethiopian community whose historical narratives are rarely represented in the west'.[43] Magloire also praised the display for 'bring[ing] forth the issues that face encyclopaedic museums of the twenty first century – questions of ownership, cultural property, and the way communities are engaged through exhibitions'.[44] This positive response was echoed in a review of the display by Museum Studies researcher Anna Tulliach, who felt that it 'productively tackled the issue on how to better display a collection's complex history by explaining what happened in the past and by putting the objects again in context'.[45] Anthropologist Charlotte Joy praised the inclusion of Prince Alemayehu's story, which made the display 'one of the few in the UK to describe the fate of people linked to the historical violence'. However, Joy also noted that Alemayehu's fate is 'documented in a museum-ready way' due to his links with Queen Victoria, and that 'the voices of other victims of colonial violence are much harder to recover and therefore usually silenced'.[46]

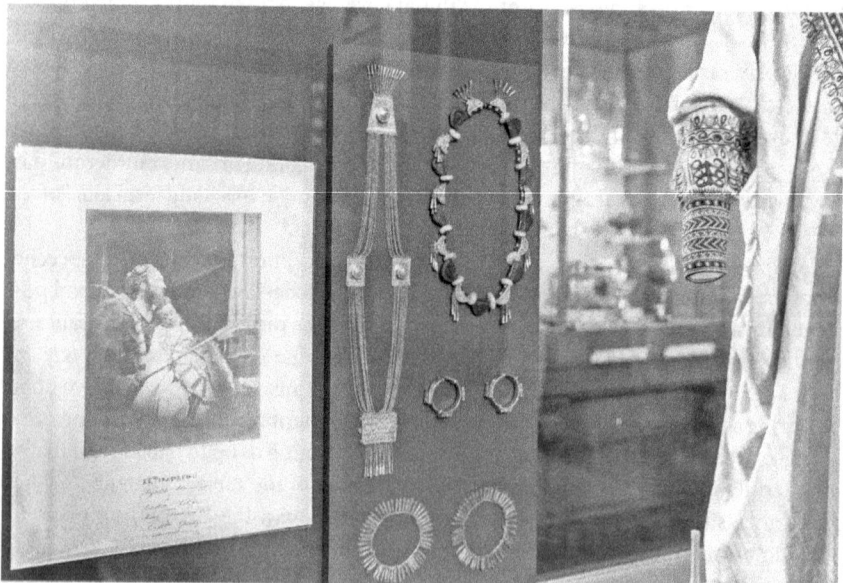

Figure 4.3 Photograph of Prince Alemayehu with Captain Tristram Speedy by Julia Margaret Cameron, displayed alongside items of jewellery belonging to Alemayehu's mother Queen Terunesh. © Victoria and Albert Museum, London.

The display's multi-layered labelling was also well-received. Author Rachel Morris on Twitter described the display as 'a showcase full of voices' and called it 'genuinely touching',[47] while Tulliach felt that the labels were 'one of the strengths of this exhibition' in that they 'challenged existing accounts on the exhibited objects, and gave an advanced understanding of the collection's significance thanks to their individual narratives'.[48] Writer Chris Hayes noted that the labels were an attempt to 'balance the institutional voice with the perspective of people with a direct link to Ethiopia', highlighting my lack of any personal connection to Ethiopia as the curator of the display.[49]

Maqdala 1868 also received criticism, much of which expressed that the display was not explicit enough in confronting the question of repatriation. Tulliach suggested that the 'theme of the debate on the legitimacy of the V&A's ownership was told merely between the lines', contrasting this with text panels at the British Museum which acknowledge the restitution debate surrounding the Parthenon marbles.[50] The interpretive texts were critiqued by artist and curator Shaheen Kasmani, an attendee at the display's opening reception, who questioned on Twitter the imprecise and indirect language used to describe how objects were acquired, posting a series of close-up photographs of the display labels to highlight the use of ambiguous terms such as 'collected' and 'taken'.[51]

Post-deinstallation: The legacy of *Maqdala 1868*

Mears and Modest have observed that museum projects which prioritize 'hidden histories' are 'rarely given the opportunity to move into, or fundamentally unsettle, the mainstream'.[52] *Maqdala 1868*, however, has had a small but lasting impact on the museum's permanent displays. After the display closed on 30 June 2019, most of the objects were returned to the museum's stores, but the crown and chalice were returned to the Sacred Silver gallery. Rather than being reinstalled in their original location, however, they were placed into a more prominent and visible position within the gallery, and given new labelling – adapted from the *Maqdala 1868* display texts – which explicitly references their Maqdala provenance and the ongoing restitution debate.

Turner has explored how the 'legacies of colonialism' are manifest in institutional knowledge through museum documentation and digitization.[53] Before my departure from the V&A to begin my doctoral research, I ensured that all labels from the display, including those written by the focus group, were recorded in the museum's internal collections database and made available online, on the website's Explore the Collections pages.[54] Thoroughly and accurately recording and communicating the efforts of temporary projects is essential to longer-term progress,[55] and by recording these labels in the museum's databases I was able to ensure that they became part of the institutional record. The Director's blog post about the display also remains accessible on the museum's website,[56] and the display has been referenced in statements regarding the V&A's efforts to 'decolonize' its collections: in June 2020, as museums across the UK were pressured to release statements about their responses to the Black Lives Matter protests, *Maqdala 1868* was mentioned in a V&A blog post as one example of the museum's efforts to '[focus] on the history and legacy of its colonial past'.[57]

Conclusion

This chapter has demonstrated the inherently colonialist framework within which contemporary museum practice operates, an area which has been studied in far greater detail in volumes such as Claire Wintle's *Colonial Collecting and Display*.[58] It has also shown how museum personnel – across many different departments – play an active role as mediators of the archive, operating as part of 'complex networks of agency', as explored comprehensively in works such as the 2011 edited volume *Unpacking the Collections*.[59] The public response to *Maqdala 1868*, and the significant media attention it attracted, indicate that there is a strong demand for museums to publicly acknowledge these aspects of their histories, and temporary displays can be a powerful tool through which to do so. However, open and honest reflection on such efforts is vital, and it is essential to acknowledge the difficulty and even, at times, futility of attempting to address the 'legacies of colonialism' from within an inherently imperialist institution. It is my hope that the reflections on *Maqdala 1868* in this chapter will play a small role in allowing future curators to build upon this work and to begin to effect truly meaningful and long-lasting change.

Notes

1. Ann Laura Stoler, *Along the Archival Grain: Epistemic Anxieties and Colonial Common Sense* (Princeton: Princeton University Press, 2008), pp. 33–4.
2. Hannah Turner, *Cataloguing Culture: Legacies of Colonialism in Museum Documentation* (Vancouver: UBC Press, 2020).
3. Sarah Longair, 'The "Colonial Moment" in the Lives of Objects from the Swahili Coast', in Prita S. Meier and Allyson Purpura (eds), *Worlds on the Horizon: Swahili Arts across the Indian Ocean* (Champaign: Krannert Art Museum and Kinkead Pavilion, 2018), p. 132.
4. Nicholas Thomas, *Entangled Objects: Exchange, Material Culture and Colonialism in the Pacific* (Cambridge, MA: Harvard University Press, 1991), p. 4.
5. Thomas Osborne, 'The Ordinariness of the Archive', *History of the Human Sciences* 12. 2 (1999): 51–64.
6. Helen Mears and Wayne Modest, 'Museums, African Collections and Social Justice', in Richard Sandell and Eithne Nightingale (eds), *Museums, Equality and Social Justice* (London: Routledge, 2012), p. 295. Mears led the V&A's African Diaspora Research Project from 2005 to 2009.
7. For an overview of Britain's military involvement with Ethiopia, see Richard Pankhurst, *The Ethiopians: A History* (Oxford: Blackwell, 2001); and Bahru Zewde, *A History of Modern Ethiopia 1855–1991* (Oxford: James Currey Ltd, 2001).
8. Longair, 'Colonial Moment', p. 132.
9. Pankhurst, 'The Ethiopians', p. 154.
10. Quoted in David Appleyard and Richard Pankhurst, 'The Last Two Letters of Emperor Tewodros II of Ethiopia (April 11 and 12 1868)', *Journal of the Royal Asiatic Society of Great Britain and Ireland* 1 (1987), p. 38.
11. House of Commons Hansard Archive, 'Motion for an Address, 30 June 1871', 208 (1871): 939–40.

12   Henry Morton Stanley, *Coomassie and Magdala: The Story of Two British Campaigns in Africa* (London: Sampson Low, Marston, Low, & Searle, 1874), p. 470.
13   Jacques Mercier, 'The Gold Crown of Magdala', *Apollo Magazine*, December 2006, p. 52.
14   For a more thorough history of the V&A's Ethiopian collections, see Alexandra Jones, 'Ethiopian Objects at the Victoria and Albert Museum', *African Research and Documentation* 135 (2019): 8–24.
15   Tim Barringer, 'The South Kensington Museum and the Colonial Project', in Tim Barringer and Tom Flynn (eds), *Colonialism and the Object: Empire, Material Culture and the Museum* (London: Routledge, 1998), p. 21.
16   'Theodore the King', *The Gentleman's Magazine*, August 1868, p. 381. 'Mr Holmes' refers to Richard Rivington Holmes, an archaeologist and British Museum curator who accompanied the expedition and purchased material from Maqdala for the Museum's collection.
17   Annie E. Coombes, *Reinventing Africa: Museums, Material Culture and Popular Imagination in Late Victorian and Edwardian England* (New Haven: Yale University Press, 1994), p. 3.
18   Constance Classen and David Howes, 'The Museum as Sensecape: Western Sensibilities and Indigenous Artifacts', in Elizabeth Edwards, Chris Gosden and Ruth B. Phillips (eds), *Sensible Objects: Colonialism, Museums and Material Culture* (Oxford: Berg, 2006), p. 209.
19   Antoinette Burton, 'Introduction: Archive Fever, Archive Stories', in Antoinette Burton (ed.), *Archive Stories: Fact, Fictions, and the Writing of History* (Durham: Duke University Press, 2005), p. 7.
20   Mears and Modest, 'Museums, African Collections and Social Justice', p. 301.
21   Victoria and Albert Museum, *Exploring Hidden Histories* (display labels), 2012.
22   Sarah Longair and John McAleer (eds), *Curating Empire: Museums and the British Imperial Experience* (Manchester: Manchester University Press, 2012), p. 226.
23   For a more detailed account of the V&A's changing displays of Ethiopian material culture over the course of 150 years, see Jones, 'Ethiopian Objects', 8–24.
24   Longair, 'Colonial Moment', p. 138.
25   Tristram Hunt, 'Maqdala 1868', 4 April 2018. https://www.vam.ac.uk/blog/museum-life/maqdala-1868, accessed 28 March 2021.
26   Eithne Nightingale and Chandan Mahal, 'The Heart of the Matter: Integrating Equality and Diversity into the Policy and Practice of Museums and Galleries', in Richard Sandell and Eithne Nightingale (eds), *Museums, Equality and Social Justice* (London: Routledge, 2012), pp. 23–4.
27   Cf. Chapter 2: the role of community consultation at the Oriental Museum, Durham.
28   Nicola Stylianou, 'The Empress's Old Clothes: Biographies of African Dress at the Victoria and Albert Museum', in C. Nicklas and A. Pollen (eds), *Dress History: New Directions in Theory and Practice* (London: Bloomsbury Academic, 2015), p. 93.
29   Ibid., p. 93.
30   William Simpson, *Diary of a Journey to Abyssinia* (1868; Hollywood: Tsehai, 2002), p. 116.
31   James R. Ryan, *Picturing Empire: Photography and the Visualization of the British Empire* (London: Reaktion Books, 1997), p. 74.
32   House of Commons Hansard Archive, 'Motion for an Address', 948–51.

33 Victoria and Albert Museum, 'Writing Gallery Text at the V&A: A Ten Point Guide', 2018, https://www.vam.ac.uk/blog/wp-content/uploads/VA_Gallery-Text-Writing-Guidelines_online_Web.pdf.
34 Karen Exell, 'Community Consultation and the Redevelopment of Manchester Museum's Ancient Egypt Galleries', in V. Golding and W. Modest (eds), *Museums and Communities: Curators, Collections and Collaboration* (London: Bloomsbury Academic, 2013), p. 140.
35 Samuel Berhanu, label for gold chalice (V&A object M.26-2005), 2018.
36 For more on these displays, see Angus Patterson, 'Asante Goldweights: A New Display Highlighting Contested Heritage in Museums', https://www.vam.ac.uk/blog/design-and-society/asante-goldweights-a-new-display-highlighting-contested-heritage-in-museums, accessed 18 October 2019; and Jacques Schuhmacher, 'Concealed Histories: Uncovering the Story of Nazi Looting', https://www.vam.ac.uk/blog/museum-life/concealed-histories-uncovering-the-story-of-nazi-looting, accessed 15 November 2019.
37 Exell, 'Community Consultation', p. 139.
38 Anita Singh, 'For the V&A's Latest Show … Shamelessly Looted Treasure', *Daily Telegraph*, 15 February 2018, p. 3.
39 Charlie Kimber, 'Why Celebrate Britain's Murderous Past in Africa?', *Socialist Worker*, 22 March 2018, https://socialistworker.co.uk/art/46323/Why+celebrate+Britains++murderous+past+in+Africa, accessed 28 March 2021.
40 For example, Robert Dex, 'Ethiopian Treasures Brought to UK by British Army Could Be Lent Back after V&A Show', *Evening Standard*, 15 February 2018, https://www.standard.co.uk/culture/ethiopian-treasures-brought-to-uk-by-british-army-could-be-lent-back-after-v-a-show-a3766201.html, accessed 28 March 2021.
41 Ethiopian Embassy UK (@EthioEmbassyUK), Twitter (with video recording of His Excellency's speech), 6 April 2018, https://twitter.com/EthioEmbassyUK/status/982207211882479617, accessed 28 March 2021.
42 Ethiopian Embassy UK (@EthioEmbassyUK), Twitter (with video recording of Sissay's speech), 6 April 2018, https://twitter.com/EthioEmbassyUK/status/982225934047563776, accessed 28 March 2021.
43 Kerian Magloire, 'Reimagining Maqdala 1868', *Shades of Noir*, 17 May 2018, https://shadesofnoir.org.uk/reimagining-maqdala-1868, accessed 28 March 2021.
44 Ibid.
45 Anna Tulliach, 'Maqdala 1868', *Journal of Curatorial Studies* 8, no. 1 (2019): p. 105.
46 Charlotte Joy, *Heritage Justice* (Cambridge: Cambridge University Press, 2020), p. 42.
47 Rachel Morris (@MoMarcoPolo), Twitter, 29 July 2018, https://twitter.com/MoMarcoPolo/status/1023513402076004352, accessed 28 March 2021.
48 Tulliach, 'Maqdala 1868', p. 105.
49 Chris Hayes, 'What Should Be Done with Stolen Artworks?', *Dazed*, 8 May 2018, https://www.dazeddigital.com/art-photography/article/39974/1/what-should-be-done-with-stolen-artworks-ethiopia-nigeria-v-and-a-museum-debate, accessed 28 March 2021.
50 Tulliach, 'Maqdala 1868', p. 105.
51 Shaheen Kasmani (@SKbydesign), Twitter, 5 April 2018, https://twitter.com/SKbydesign/status/982004097887997952, accessed 28 March 2021.
52 Mears and Modest, 'Museums, African Collections and Social Justice', pp. 304–5.
53 Turner, 'Cataloguing Culture', p. 4.
54 https://www.vam.ac.uk/collections, accessed 28 March 2021.

55 Kimberley F. Keith, 'Moving beyond the Mainstream: Insight into the Relationship between Community-Based Heritage Organizations and the Museum', in Richard Sandell and Eithne Nightingale (eds), *Museums, Equality and Social Justice* (London: Routledge, 2012), pp. 45–58.
56 Hunt, 'Maqdala 1868'.
57 Tristram Hunt, 'Black Lives Matter: Race and Equality at the V&A', 4 June 2020, https://www.vam.ac.uk/blog/news/black-lives-matter-race-and-equality-at-the-va, accessed 28 March 2021.
58 Claire Wintle, *Colonial Collecting and Display: Encounters with Material Culture from the Andaman and Nicobar Islands* (New York: Berghahn Books, 2013).
59 Sarah Byrne, Anne Clarke, Rodney Harrison, and Robin Torrence (eds), *Unpacking the Collections: Networks of Material and Social Agency in the Museum* (New York and London: Springer, 2011).

Bibliography

Appleyard, David, and Richard Pankhurst. 'The Last Two Letters of Emperor Tewodros II of Ethiopia (April 11 and 12 1868)'. *Journal of the Royal Asiatic Society of Great Britain and Ireland* 1 (1987): 23–42.

Barringer, Tim. 'The South Kensington Museum and the Colonial Project'. In *Colonialism and the Object: Empire, Material Culture and the Museum*, edited by Tim Barringer and Tom Flynn, 11–27. London: Routledge, 1998.

Burton, Antoinette. 'Introduction: Archive Fever, Archive Stories'. In *Archive Stories: Fact, Fictions, and the Writing of History*, edited by Antoinette Burton, 1–24. Durham: Duke University Press, 2005.

Byrne, Sarah, Anne Clarke, Rodney Harrison, and Robin Torrence (eds). *Unpacking the Collections: Networks of Material and Social Agency in the Museum*. New York and London: Springer, 2011.

Classen, Constance, and David Howes. 'The Museum as Sensecape: Western Sensibilities and Indigenous Artifacts'. In *Sensible Objects: Colonialism, Museums and Material Culture*, edited by Elizabeth Edwards, Chris Gosden and Ruth B. Phillips, 199–200. Oxford: Berg, 2006.

Coombes, Annie E. *Reinventing Africa: Museums, Material Culture and Popular Imagination in Late Victorian and Edwardian England*. New Haven: Yale University Press, 1994.

Derillo, Eyob. 'Exhibiting the Maqdala Manuscripts: African Scribes: Manuscript Culture of Ethiopia'. *African Research and Documentation* 135 (2019): 102–16.

Dex, Robert. 'Ethiopian Treasures Brought to UK by British Army Could Be Lent Back after V&A Show'. *Evening Standard*. https://www.standard.co.uk/culture/ethiopian-treasures-brought-to-uk-by-british-army-could-be-lent-back-after-v-a-show-a3766201.html. Accessed 15 February 2018.

Exell, Karen. 'Community Consultation and the Redevelopment of Manchester Museum's Ancient Egypt Galleries'. In *Museums and Communities: Curators, Collections and Collaboration*, edited by V. Golding and W. Modest, 130–42. London: Bloomsbury Academic, 2013.

The Gentleman's Magazine. 'Theodore the King'. (August 1868): 377–86.

Hayes, Chris. 'What Should Be Done with Stolen Artworks?'. *Dazed*. https://www.dazeddigital.com/art-photography/article/39974/1/what-should-be-done-with-stolen-artworks-ethiopia-nigeria-v-and-a-museum-debate. Accessed 8 May 2018.

House of Commons Hansard Archive. 'Motion for an Address, 30 June 1871'. 208 (1871): 939–52.

Hunt, Tristram. 'Black Lives Matter: Race and Equality at the V&A'. https://www.vam.ac.uk/blog/news/black-lives-matter-race-and-equality-at-the-va. Accessed 4 June 2020.

Hunt, Tristram. 'Maqdala 1868'. https://www.vam.ac.uk/blog/museum-life/maqdala-1868. Accessed 4 April 2018.

Jones, Alexandra. 'Ethiopian Objects at the Victoria and Albert Museum'. *African Research and Documentation* 135 (2019): 8–24.

Joy, Charlotte. *Heritage Justice*. Cambridge: Cambridge University Press, 2020.

Keith, Kimberley F. 'Moving beyond the Mainstream: Insight into the Relationship Between Community-Based Heritage Organizations and the Museum'. In *Museums, Equality and Social Justice*, edited by Richard Sandell and Eithne Nightingale, 45–58. London: Routledge, 2012.

Kimber, Charlie. 'Why Celebrate Britain's Murderous Past in Africa?' *Socialist Worker*. https://socialistworker.co.uk/art/46323/Why+celebrate+Britains++murderous+past+in+Africa. Accessed 22 March 2018.

Longair, Sarah. 'The "Colonial Moment" in the Lives of Objects from the Swahili Coast'. In *Worlds on the Horizon: Swahili Arts across the Indian Ocean*, edited by Prita S. Meier and Allyson Purpura, 130–45. Champaign: Krannert Art Museum and Kinkead Pavilion, 2018.

Longair, Sarah, and John McAleer. *Curating Empire: Museums and the British Imperial Experience*. Manchester: Manchester University Press, 2012.

Magliore, Kerian. 'Reimagining Maqdala 1868'. *Shades of Noir*. https://shadesofnoir.org.uk/reimagining-maqdala-1868. Accessed 17 May 2018.

Mears, Helen, and Wayne Modest. 'Museums, African Collections and Social Justice'. In *Museums, Equality and Social Justice*, edited by Richard Sandell and Eithne Nightingale, 294–309. London: Routledge, 2012.

Mercier, Jacques. 'The Gold Crown of Magdala'. *Apollo Magazine* 164 (2006): 46–53.

Nightingale, Eithne, and Chandan Mahal. 'The Heart of the Matter: Integrating Equality and Diversity into the Policy and Practice of Museums and Galleries'. In *Museums, Equality and Social Justice*, edited by Richard Sandell and Eithne Nightingale, 13–37. London: Routledge, 2012.

Osborne, Thomas. 'The Ordinariness of the Archive'. *History of the Human Sciences* 12, no. 2 (1999): 51–64.

Pankhurst, Richard. *The Ethiopians: A History*. Oxford: Blackwell, 2001.

Patterson, Angus. 'Asante Goldweights: A New Display Highlighting Contested Heritage in Museums'. https://www.vam.ac.uk/blog/design-and-society/asante-goldweights-a-new-display-highlighting-contested-heritage-in-museums. Accessed 18 October 2019.

Ryan, James R. *Picturing Empire: Photography and the Visualization of the British Empire*. London: Reaktion Books, 1997.

Schuhmacher, Jacques. 'Concealed Histories: Uncovering the Story of Nazi Looting'. https://www.vam.ac.uk/blog/museum-life/concealed-histories-uncovering-the-story-of-nazi-looting. Accessed 15 November 2019.

Simpson, William. *Diary of a Journey to Abyssinia*, 1868. Reprint by Richard Pankhurst. Hollywood: Tsehai, 2002.

Singh, Anita. 'For the V&A's Latest Show ... Shamelessly Looted Treasure'. *Daily Telegraph* (15 February 2018): 3.

Stanley, Henry M. *Coomassie and Magdala: The Story of Two British Campaigns in Africa*. London: Sampson Low, Marston, Low, & Searle, 1874.

Stoler, Ann Laura. *Along the Archival Grain: Epistemic Anxieties and Colonial Common Sense*. Princeton: Princeton University Press, 2009.

Stylianou, Nicola. 'The Empress's Old Clothes: Biographies of African Dress at the Victoria and Albert Museum'. In *Dress History: New Directions in Theory and Practice*, edited by C. Nicklas and A. Pollen, 81–96. London: Bloomsbury Academic, 2015.

Thomas, Nicholas. *Entangled Objects: Exchange, Material Culture and Colonialism in the Pacific*. Cambridge, MA: Harvard University Press, 1991.

Tulliach, Anna. 'Maqdala 1868'. *Journal of Curatorial Studies* 8, no. 1 (2019): 102–6.

Turner, Hannah. *Cataloguing Culture: Legacies of Colonialism in Museum Documentation*. Vancouver: UBC Press, 2020.

Wintle, Claire. *Colonial Collecting and Display: Encounters with Material Culture from the Andaman and Nicobar Islands*. New York: Berghahn Books, 2013.

Zewde, Bahru. *A History of Modern Ethiopia 1855–1991*. Oxford: James Currey Ltd, 2001.

Part Two

Colonial power

5

Encountering 'colonial science' in the visual archive

The natural history paintings of Raja Serfoji II of Tanjore (1777–1832)

David Lowther

Introduction

In 1798, Raja Serfoji II Bhonsie (1777–1832) ascended the throne of the Maratha principality of Tanjore, in southern India. Although Serfoji lacked real power, having ceded the administration of his kingdom to the British East India Company, Tanjore enjoyed a remarkable cultural and intellectual 'golden age' during his reign. Educated by Danish and German missionaries, Serfoji was an active participant in colonial scientific networks, establishing Tanjore as a centre of natural history research, founded on an assemblage of South Asian and European practices of knowledge creation, in which visual culture played a prominent role.

This chapter focuses on a small visual archive, consisting of 117 paintings commissioned by Serfoji from court artists in the early 1800s, which depict zoological subjects. Dispatched by Serfoji in instalments between 1803 and 1807, and addressed to the former British Resident in Tanjore, Benjamin Torin (1768–1839), the paintings lay for many years in the Library and Museum of the East India Company (London), and were later donated to the British Library.[1] They have long been categorized as part of the wider genre of 'Company Art', a term which encompasses paintings commissioned by European officials from predominantly South Asian artists, and including topographical, ethnographic, architectural and natural history subjects.[2]

Serfoji's surviving archive, small though it is and as this chapter explores, can tell us much about archival practice during the nineteenth century, and the 'violence' wrought on material amassed in European colonial archives.[3] In Gayatri Spivak's persuasive formulation, the archive of European colonialism in South Asia from the mid-eighteenth century onwards must be seen as the result of the particular interests of the East India Company, which from 1757 to 1858 was the dominant territorial and political power on the subcontinent. Accordingly, and influenced too by postcolonial readings of colonial South Asian histories, subsequent interpretations of the Company's archives have challenged the notion that these archives can give a 'total' or 'objective' picture of the realities of Company rule.[4] Indeed, the archive itself has become a site where the practices of colonialism, including the diminution or the erasure of the Indigenous voice, were enacted, developed and perpetuated through the widespread omission (deliberate or otherwise) of sources accredited to non-Europeans.[5] Where collections created by South Asians were added to the Company's archive, they were, as in the case of Serfoji's collection, reordered according to contemporary European archival practice, relocated within wider collections reflecting the Company's largely mercantile interest in South Asian natural history, and largely forgotten.

I argue here that whilst Serfoji's collection shares visual similarities with other, comparable collections of natural history paintings commissioned from Indigenous artists by European figures in late-eighteenth and early-nineteenth century India, its holdings are also quite different. Executed in a synthetic style which drew both on European scientific conventions and the complex traditions of South Indian art, the paintings and the notes attached to them vividly record Serfoji's study of living nature, drawing upon but fundamentally distinct from contemporary colonial methods and preoccupations. Removed from their original context, Serfoji's paintings were thus transformed from artefacts of a sophisticated and distinctive syncretic intellectual outlook into mere curios displayed in a colonial archive. Inspired by research conducted and published by Savithri Preetha Nair and Indira Peterson, and drawing upon recent studies of Anglo-Indian artistic and scientific encounters and the radical transformation of South Asian historiography, it is demonstrated here how the reconsideration of Serfoji's collection, and others like it, can transform both our understanding of complex Indian responses to European science and the role of visual culture in the colonial encounter.[6]

The rulers of Tanjore and the East India Company, 1776–98

The East India Company established a British Residency in Tanjore in 1776 and, as both Moideen and Ramanujam have argued, waged a sustained financial campaign against the state that saw successive rulers become ever more deeply ensnared in debt to the Company.[7] Even before the state's annexation in 1799, Tanjore had effectively come under the rule of the Madras Presidency. In 1787 its ruler, Amar Singh, committed to pay the Company annual subsidies of 400,000 rupees in return for the Company's support against yet another rival claimant to the throne, partly for the maintenance of their troops, whilst also agreeing to loans extended by the Danish government.[8] Singh agreed that, should he default on any of his monthly payments, the Company also had the right 'to enter upon any of the districts of Tanjore' that appeared 'necessary to discharge the amount of the sum in arrears'.[9] The Company also took over the direct administration of Singh's annual tribute to the neighbouring Nawab of Arcot, which not only served to further enrich the Company's treasury but also neatly deprived the Nawab of any possible claim in Tanjore's affairs.

Tanjore's annexation to the Madras Presidency was, perhaps, a foregone conclusion given its indebtedness to the Company, but the process was further hastened by the Company's investigations into allegations of the Raja's mistreatment of his rival claimant to the throne. The latter, Serfoji, had been denied the throne in 1787 on the grounds of illegitimacy, within the terms of the same treaty by which the Company formalized its role as Tanjore's principal creditor. In a startling volte-face, the Company's growing disillusionment with Amar Singh prompted the Governor-General to order the re-investigation of Serfoji's legitimacy, a protracted process that called upon the legal expertise of *pandits* in Benares and Calcutta, and of Sir William Jones, the orientalist scholar and a judge of Calcutta's Supreme Court.[10] In 1795, Serfoji was proclaimed the rightful heir to the Tanjore throne, and in 1798, at the behest of the new Governor-General, Richard Wellesley, 2nd Earl of Mornington (1760–1842; he was soon to receive a step up in the Irish peerage as the Marquess Wellesley), Amar Singh was deposed and replaced by his adoptive nephew. A year later, on 25 October 1799, Tanjore's territories were wholly placed under the control of the Company, and Serfoji was reduced, in practice, from monarch to a vassal of the Governor of Madras.[11]

Raja Serfoji II: Contested perceptions

The new Raja, who reigned as Serfoji II, had spent most of his youth in Madras, safely out of Singh's reach and in the middle of a circle of European (predominantly German) intellectuals and Protestant missionaries. In her study of Serfoji's reign, and its impact on the arts and sciences in Tanjore, Savithri Preetha Nair highlights the importance of this network in shaping the young man's ideas and attitudes, not the least of which was his devotion to cultivating 'useful knowledge', both as a private passion and as a policy of state.[12] Whilst much attention has been devoted to the role of Charles Friedrich Schwartz (1726–98), a Prussian Lutheran missionary who acted as Serfoji's 'protector-regent and raja-guru', Serfoji also came under the influence of key Company officials during his time in Madras, including Lord Hobart, the Governor of Madras (1794–98), and successive Company surgeons.[13] Schwartz also played a formative role in introducing Serfoji to European naturalists. These included Patrick Russell (1727–1805), the East India Company's resident botanist and naturalist in Madras and later the author of pioneering works in Indian zoology; and William Roxburgh (1751–1815), a surgeon-naturalist who succeeded Russell as the Company's botanist in Madras and who in 1793 moved to Calcutta to take up post as Superintendent of the Sibpur Botanic Gardens.[14]

Whilst a holistic survey of Serfoji's educational reforms, his artistic and cultural patronage, and range of scientific interests is beyond the scope of this paper, Serfoji was renowned during his own lifetime as the model of an 'enlightened' ruler who engaged with the latest in European scholarship and ideas.[15] Peterson locates Serfoji's activities firmly within the context of eighteenth-century Enlightenment rationalism, pointing to the eclecticism of his collections as a South Indian facsimile of the *Kunstkammer*, or cabinet of curiosities, with which Schwartz would have been extremely familiar.

By 1798, the year of Schwartz's death and Serfoji's accession to the Tanjore throne, *Kunstkammern* were already becoming obsolete across Europe, superseded by the more specialized collections that developed alongside an increasing process of specialization that saw the division of natural history, and natural philosophy, into distinct scientific disciplines.[16] Peterson argues that Serfoji's continued adherence to the *Kunstkammer*, and the encyclopaedic survey of the universe that it represented, may be partially explained by a degree of overlap with Indigenous cosmologies. By contrast, Nair contends that Serfoji was a 'native counterpart' of Sir Joseph Banks (1743–1820), who was largely constructed as the archetypal European, 'enlightened' man of science. In direct contrast to Peterson, Nair states explicitly that Serfoji 'never attempted to create a cabinet of curiosities', instead adhering to 'an intuitive and sympathetic understanding of living nature … which blurred the boundaries between the object and observer', a rejection of the worldview which underpinned the ideals of the *Kunstkammer*.[17]

Natural history in India *c.* 1800

Against these contrasting interpretations of both Serfoji's intellectual originality and his collecting practices may be set an analysis of one facet of his interests – that relating to nature and natural history.[18] Serfoji's botanical practice was conventionally mercantilist. In line with his broader determination to promote 'useful knowledge', Nair notes that Serfoji quickly developed a 'medicinal garden' a decision which would have met with Banks's approbation.[19] As Adrian Thomas has described, by 1798 botanic gardens were a familiar feature across India, thanks in part to the success of the Calcutta Botanic Garden, established by William Kyd in 1786 with Banks's vigorous support. Banks exerted a powerful influence over the East India Company's directors; otherwise lukewarm in their support of any work that did not have a clear mercantile focus, they were persuaded of the garden's potential as a space to cultivate commercially 'useful' plants, as well as helping to uphold the Company's (otherwise tenuous) reputation as an 'enlightened' ruler.[20] Like many of his princely contemporaries, Serfoji maintained a number of court artists, and he directed them to make studies of the plants cultivated in his gardens, a practice which Banks and other contemporary botanists, such as William Roxburgh and Francis Buchanan (-Hamilton) (1762–1829) would also have recognized. The famous British traveller George Annesley, Lord Valentia (1770–1844) also visited Tanjore in 1804 and left a vivid account of some of these paintings as displayed in Serfoji's palace, alongside herbarium specimens and drawing materials.[21]

The roots and the extent of Serfoji's zoological interests are more difficult to trace. In European metropolitan scientific circles, zoology remained at a nascent stage of its development as a distinct discipline. In Britain, the Linnean Society of London, established in 1788 as Europe's first institution dedicated to natural history, resisted the calls of more zoologically minded fellows to set up a zoological research strand until 1822.[22] A further four years would elapse before the Zoological Society of London would be founded as the logical development of this earlier group.[23] In colonial scientific circles, progress in zoological research lagged far behind botany for want of official support and funding, and the lack of any central archive or repository which could act as a centre of knowledge formation and codification. For the most part, until well into the nineteenth century, zoological work was carried out in India as an adjunct to botanical work and, where not part of a survey, was the preserve of amateurs.

Although prepared to fund botanical research in the form of gardens and extensive surveys, the East India Company was far less inclined to support zoological studies due to their less obvious commercial application.[24] A rare exception was the Company's undertaking to cover the costs of the colour plates in Patrick Russell's pioneering account of Indian herpetology (the scientific study of reptiles and amphibians), published in two volumes between 1796 and 1810.[25] The first sustained attempt to encourage the study of zoology in India was the Barrackpore Menagerie, conceived by Wellesley in 1804 as the 'Institution for Promoting the Natural History of India', and located in the grounds of the Governor-General's palatial summer residence to the north of Calcutta. Although Wellesley, during his tenure as Governor-General, appears to have directly commissioned at least two volumes of bird paintings for his own collections, his motives in establishing the menagerie, soon viewed as an annex to the College he founded at Fort William for the training of newly arrived Company administrators, were primarily reputational.[26] Under Wellesley, vividly characterized by William Dalrymple in his recent history as 'the Empire-building cuckoo in the Company's corporate nest', Company troops waged an aggressive expansionist campaign across the sub-Continent, including the costly and controversial annexation of Mysore in 1799 and the capture of Delhi, the Mughal capital, in 1803.[27] Far from welcoming these conquests, which very nearly bankrupted the Company, the Court of Directors in London repeatedly confronted Wellesley and expressed dissatisfaction with his policies to the Board of Control (the government department responsible for Indian affairs and predecessor to the India Office).[28] Against this background, in a Minute written and despatched to the Company's directors in 1804, Wellesley loftily proclaimed that '[t]o facilitate and promote all enquiries to enlarge the boundaries of general science is a duty imposed on the British Government in India by its present exalted situation'.[29]

An indication of the relative backwardness of zoology is that Francis Buchanan-Hamilton, far better known for his botanical research and Wellesley's personal surgeon, was appointed the first superintendent of the new Barrackpore menagerie. The combination of Wellesley's support and Buchanan-Hamilton's drive and scientific reputation led to early success; Archer notes that 'specimens arrived from all over India' and a considerable amount of original research was carried out by Buchanan, William Fleming and Buchanan's successor William Gibbons. A fundamental aspect of Buchanan's research programme was to record specimens in both textual descriptions and in paintings, for which purpose he employed a number of Indigenous artists, including the highly accomplished Bengali artist Haludar, who also produced duplicate drawings for Wellesley's private collection.

Although draconian restrictions were set by the Company on Serfoji's freedom to travel – he would not visit Calcutta until the 1820s – it is highly likely that he would have been aware of Wellesley's venture through his official contacts with the Company's Resident in Tanjore, Benjamin Torin, who reported directly to the Governor-General, and may have sent specimens or drawings to Barrackpore. As discussed below, there are certainly intriguing similarities between some of the zoological images produced at Barrackpore and those commissioned by Serfoji, which were painted between c. 1802 and 1807. Serfoji also established his own menagerie, the *Vettai Mahal*, in the grounds of the *Saraswathi Mahal*, and, in common with Buchanan's practice at Barrackpore, commissioned his court artists to make detailed studies of the menagerie's residents.

The archive – Serfoji II as patron of art and science

The results of Serfoji's patronage, whilst more modest in number than those produced by the Barrackpore artists for Wellesley and Buchanan, are nevertheless highly significant. Although the exact number of the botanical and zoological paintings commissioned by Serfoji remains uncertain, records of those that are held in private and public collections in Tanjore and London indicate a sustained interest from 1798 to at least the 1820s. James White records ninety-one botanical paintings, royal folio size, that remain in the Saraswati Mahal Library in Tanjore. Divided unequally between three separate folios, they are described in the Library's archive as 'Botanical Pictures Painted by Serfogi's Artists' that 'include each species', with names provided in English, Tamil and Latin.[30] Highlighting the often contradictory, or at least shifting, archival practices relating to collections of visual materials, White notes that the ninety-one drawings he was able to identify in his own research fell 'far short of the 300 paintings reported' by the authors of a 1965 catalogue of Indian Botany.[31]

A similar slippage is seen in the various archival descriptions of the zoological drawings commissioned by Serfoji that are now held by the British Library. The collection itself has a fascinating history, and one that is still shrouded in some mystery. In common with his botanical paintings, Serfoji commissioned the zoological images directly from his artists. The majority of the sheets, again painted on royal folio size paper, are undated, although several individual paintings bear a 1796 watermark; it is not clear whether this indicates the date the paintings were created or, more likely, the year in which the paper itself was produced. As they are currently constituted in the British Library's Asian and African Studies Collections, the 117 images are bound together in a single volume entitled 'Mysore Drawings'. Archer, on whose 1962 description the British Library's note is directly based, noted that this inscription, added to the drawings c. 1879, is incorrect. The drawings contained in this single volume are, in fact, two volumes of zoological drawings commissioned and overseen by Serfoji entitled 'The Natural Products of Hindostan painted under the Direction of the Rajah of Tanjore and Presented to the Court by Mr Benjamin Torin' in 1807.

The title of this original binding is misleading, for the images do not represent the results of a sustained programme of research in the same way as, for example, a published illustrated scientific folio of the era. Instead, Serfoji presented and dispatched the paintings at intervals to Benjamin Torin, a Company official stationed in Madras during Serfoji's youth and the Company's Resident in Tanjore between 1798 and 1801. Following his retirement in 1801, Torin returned to London and, as Nair notes, thereafter acted as Serfoji's 'commercial agent' and 'the most important node in Serfoji's network'. Besides sending Serfoji invaluable treatises on medicine,

Torin also dispatched the most recent European works on natural history to Tanjore, engaging in a practice of reciprocal gift-giving that was already officially frowned upon by the Company as harking back dangerously to the worst excesses of the 'Nabobs' in the 1760s and 1770s. Torin himself wasted relatively little time in presenting them to the Company's Museum, though he was careful to couch his letter to Serfoji explaining this in the most appreciative of terms:

> I have not mentioned to your Excellency the several Pictures which you have had the goodness to send me from time to time presenting the various fish, Birds, Plants, Buildings etc. of Hindustan – Your Moochy [artist] has been so careful and correct in his representations that I thought these paintings deserving Public notice and as the Company are curious in their collection of all oriental objects, I thought the opportunity of presenting these paintings to them in your Ex[cellency]'s name too good to be overlooked and having them very handsomely formed into 2 books or two Large Portfolios I have sent them with the enclosed letter to the Court of Directors, who have been pleased to express their thanks and to give them a place in their Library.[32]

Of the 117 individual sheets, 30 are depictions of birds and predominantly of falcons and hawks – hunting birds. Further emphasizing the Raja's interests, several additional sheets depict falconer's paraphernalia, such as a falcon hood and bird traps. In addition, the collection includes thirteen depictions of mammals, of which the majority are again species used in hunting, including tigers – 'royal tigers' (Figure 5.1) –

Figure 5.1 NHD7/1035 Tiger. Watercolour on paper, *c.* 1802. Artist unknown, in 'Tanjore Style'. Raja Serfogee of Tanjore Collection, NHD7/1001–1116. Courtesy of the British Library: Visual Arts.

and caracals.[33] Of the remaining images, thirty-eight depict species of fish; twelve molluscs; nine reptiles; seven arthropods, mainly arachnids; frogs and toads, and a solitary marine invertebrate. Although each image is delineated and hand-coloured with a consistent attention to detail, it is noteworthy that only a minority bear any inscriptions (all in Serfoji's hand), and detailed inscriptions are reserved for those species of which Serfoji had detailed first-hand knowledge of their behaviour. These were animals that were used in hunts, or exotics, that resided in the *Vettai Mahal*.

A particularly fine example (Figure 5.2) is a painting of a caracal, or *syagosh*, a medium-sized cat then commonly used in India to hunt small mammals and birds. The cat is represented in this painting together with the trappings of captivity, a finely-worked red leather hood, used to keep the animal docile when not actively hunting, and a chain connected to a shackle around its leg. There are striking similarities here with paintings of the same species in the Wellesley/Buchanan-Hamilton collections, also held by the British Library and which are almost exactly contemporaneous. There are also similarities in the detailed descriptions of the caracal, which both emphasize its prowess as a hunter and – sometimes graphically – the 'correct' method of caring for it. For example, Serfoji notes:

Figure 5.2 NHD7/1034 Caracal. Watercolour on paper, *c.* 1802. Artist unknown, in 'Tanjore Style'. Raja Serfogee of Tanjore Collection, NHD7/1001–1116. Courtesy of the British Library: Visual Arts.

The great kings or Bautches, Nabaubs or Princes are fond to rear this, tho it was young or old to Chace upon the hare, rabbits and kites, but as for his fierceness, he will lay hold the Sheep but could not be able to tear it to pieces. This Animal will chace in these three Cool months, Viz December, January and Feb as for the other nine months the eyes of this Animal being covered with a leather socket and kept in in the Chain in a dark place upon a Cot, had this animal was tame and not well chaced, take a raw nut and grind it well and make a large pill keep it within the flesh and feed it, then a vomit and purge will take place by which it will be very diligent for hunting … The people who exercise this animal in regard to keep it under their possession instills four or five drops of urine of the man into his mouth, he becomes very soon in the possession of the man.[34]

We can compare this to the inscription on a similar painting of the caracal (Figure 5.3) in the Wellesley Collections:

From life, in possession of Marquis Wellesley – The animal is exactly double the size of this drawing. This animal was given to me by Rajah Mitter Jeet Singh a Zimindar of Bahar. – It is useful in hunting, principally the Hares – I have also seen it used at Lucknow by the Nawaub Vizier in hunting Deer; it springs with great velocity and strength, and also runs with astonishing fleetness for a short distance – if it misses its prey in the first spring it relinquishes the chase. – It is called Siah Goshe – [signed] W. 1802.[35]

Figure 5.3 NHD32/7 Caracal. Watercolour on paper, *c.* 1798–1805. Artist unknown, in 'Bengal Style'. Wellesley Collection, NHD26–31. Courtesy of the British Library: Visual Arts.

A keen hunter in both his native Ireland and during his tenure as Governor-General, Wellesley, like Serfoji, reserved his personal commentary on the paintings in his collection to those species that were particularly exotic or unusual, particularly if they were drawn from live specimens in the menagerie or Wellesley's personal possession. An intriguing example is an image of an Indian rhinoceros calf, the caption to which states: 'From the life, about 9 months old – in the possession of the Earl of Mornington'.[36] This dates the painting to between 1799 and 1801, when Wellesley was elevated to his marquessate, and which predates the establishment of a menagerie at Barrackpore by several years. Wellesley also had a clear interest in hunting animals. These are commonly depicted with chains, hoods and other restraints, such as an almost Stubbsian depiction of a cheetah depicted against an idealized, pastoral landscape. Curiously, the substantial number of paintings depicting birds of prey, including goshawks, peregrine falcons and besras (a hawk in the same genus as the more familiar sparrowhawk), all depicted somewhat formulaically in profile view chained to a padded perch, are not accorded the same attention.

Compositional similarities can also be seen between the depiction of a Malayan Giant Squirrel in Serfoji's album (Figure 5.4) and that of the Indian Giant Squirrel in the Wellesley Collection (Figure 5.5). Both images show the animals in full, left to right

Figure 5.4 NHD7/1040 Malayan Giant Squirrel/Black Giant Squirrel. Watercolour on Paper, *c.* 1802. Artist unknown, in 'Tanjore Style'. Raja Serfogee of Tanjore Collection, NHD7/1001–1116. Courtesy of the British Library: Visual Arts.

Figure 5.5 NHD33/19 Indian Giant Squirrel. Watercolour on Paper, c. 1798–1805. Artist unknown, in 'Bengal Style'. Wellesley Collection, NHD26–31. Courtesy of the British Library: Visual Arts.

profile view, set against a blank background. Whereas the composition of the Wellesley image is more sophisticated, showing the squirrel's tail curved elegantly across the animal's rear legs, both images privilege the overall form of the animal and exhibit a minute attention to detail. This can be seen to particular effect in the treatment of the squirrels' whiskers, body fur and long tails, in which the artists have taken great care to delineate each strand using the finest of single-hair brushes.

There were scientific reasons for this acute, objective focus on detail. In the late-eighteenth and early nineteenth centuries, the extent of European knowledge of natural history expanded exponentially, a process driven by colonial expansion and the subsequent flow of information, in the form of written descriptions, images and physical botanical and zoological specimens (alive and dead) into private and public museum collections. As well as having a profound effect on how European naturalists viewed and understood nature, resulting in a proliferation of competing taxonomic systems developed from Linnaean classification, this flow of information placed a greater emphasis on 'accurate' and 'objective' depictions of plants and animals. At a time when methods of preservation of physical specimens, particularly zoological specimens, were rudimentary, illustrations captured the physical characteristics of species necessary for classification in a form that was far less susceptible to the depredations of pests and the effects of climate.[37]

The increasing importance accorded to imagery in the classificatory process had an attendant consequence on the appearance of images used for these purposes. Where possible, subjects were depicted as near to life-size as possible, often in full-profile view, and against a blank or near-featureless background, focusing the attention of the viewer on those salient anatomical characteristics that were used to compare against other, known species in order to aid the process of classification. This stripping away of extraneous features, as Lorraine Daston and Peter Galison have demonstrated, is inherently and aggressively selective, and was intended to look beyond the individual variations visible in populations of the same species in order to get to the underlying form, or 'type'.[38] As Daston and Galison note, the type was viewed as closer to the real natural form of the species, unaffected by environmental factors, and therefore more 'real' than any individual specimen.[39]

Where the artists who painted these images did not themselves possess detailed knowledge of current European scientific practices, they worked under the close supervision of naturalists who directed their efforts. Daston and Galison term this process 'four-eyed sight', which aptly captures the constant back and forth between artist and naturalist as the latter sought to ensure that his scientific vision was accurately transferred to paper.[40] This process could lead to considerable tensions, artistic and inter-personal, between artist and naturalists, and was further complicated where European naturalists working in colonized territories commissioned artists from entirely different cultural backgrounds, and whose own artistic training was based on long-established aesthetic systems that were often impenetrable to European understanding.

Such conflicts are often only fleetingly alluded to in surviving documentation. For example, in the British Library's Wellesley Collections are two watercolours of the 'gyal' (gayal, a variety of large domestic cattle common across India), executed in very different styles. The first depicts the animal with considerable skill and accuracy, shaded to demonstrate the gayal's bulk. The second, a beautiful and stylized image against a pastoral background that is highly reminiscent of a Mughal miniature, bears the laconic inscription 'a bad figure of a Gyal'.[41] Brian Houghton Hodgson (1800–94), an East India Company diplomat and prolific amateur naturalist stationed in Nepal between 1820 and 1845, partially circumnavigated some of these difficulties in his relations with the Nepalese *chitrakars* who worked for him by introducing the use of a *camera lucida*. This allowed the artist to project an image of a specimen, or extant drawing, onto a sheet of paper and draw and colour over the image.[42] This eliminated, in theory at least, any vagaries of the artist's pencil or imagination.

A possible demonstration of this attempt to get to the underlying form can be seen in Serfoji's zoological albums in the formulaic depictions of hunting birds, and in particular the paintings of the Northern Goshawk and the Peregrine. Listed consecutively in the British Library's catalogue, the two depictions of the Goshawk, a female bird, differ substantively from one another only in the shape of the perches on which the bird sits. The depictions of the birds themselves, from the angle of the head down to the placement of wing feathers and the characteristic barred pattern across the birds' breasts and underparts, are depicted almost identically. Although neither picture is signed, the striking similarity in composition as well as colouring strongly suggests that both were the work of a single artist. The same artist is also likely to have executed the three images of the peregrines, which are again extremely similar in composition though evidently, on the basis of their different plumage colouring, depict three different birds.[43]

Where duplicate, or markedly similar, images exist within the same collections, there may be a number of divergent explanations. Brian Houghton Hodgson's extensive collection of zoological images, amassed over the course of at least twenty years, is now divided between the Zoological Society of London and Natural History Museum, with the latter holding more highly finished duplicates of the 'working drawings', many liberally covered in notes, in the ZSL collections. These later duplicates were the final pattern images intended for Hodgson's uncompleted 'Zoology of Nipal', which he projected as a multi-volume, illustrated zoological folio in the same manner as John Gould's highly successful folios published from the 1830s onwards.

As Mildred Archer noted sixty years ago, one of the most fascinating aspects of Serfoji's collection of zoological images is their status as 'Company Art' commissioned 'not by a Company servant' but by the head of an Indian princely house.[44] Serfoji was far from unusual amongst his contemporaries in maintaining a number of artists in his court; however, he was almost unique in directing them to depict natural history subjects in a broadly European, 'Company' style.

The treatment of animals as subjects of scientific interest, rather than for their religious symbolism or decorative possibilities, was uncommon in 'Indian Art' more broadly, and rarer still in South Indian, Tamil traditions. The most famous examples contrary to this trend date from the Mughal imperial painting tradition during the reign of Shah Jahangir (reigned 1605-27). Entranced by the naturalism of northern European Renaissance prints presented to him as gifts by Jesuit missionaries and European diplomats, Jahangir directed the artists in his *ateliers* to faithfully copy these images and incorporate European naturalistic devices into their own work. Combined with Jahangir's interest in the natural world, an interest he shared with his predecessors Babur (reigned 1526-30) and, to a lesser extent, Akbar (reigned 1556-1605), this exchange resulted in some extraordinarily beautiful zoological images, which adopted European perspective and naturalism whilst retaining the Mughal miniature tradition's meticulous detail and the use of traditional painting materials.[45]

Of the artists Serfoji employed to create his natural history images, we know relatively little. The British Library paintings are unsigned, in common with the majority of comparable images commissioned by European patrons and naturalists in the same period. Some indication of the artists' background can be drawn from Torin's use of the term 'moochie'. In his extensive study of the Cleghorn Collection of botanical paintings, amassed by the Scottish botanist Hugh Cleghorn (1820-95) in South India during the 1840s and 1850s, Henry Noltie notes that 'moochies' were frequently employed as artists by British patrons in Madras from the late eighteenth century onwards. Many 'moochies' appear to have been leather-workers and had originally moved southwards from Andhra to Madras and its surrounding areas, including Tanjore, following the dissolution of the Vijayanagar empire, which formerly extended across the whole of southern India, in the sixteenth century.[46] A further indication of the 'moochies' background comes from a portrait now in the British Museum's collections, and which originated in the collections of the Rev. Robert Liddell (1808-88). Dating from *c.* 1830 and executed by an anonymous Tanjore artist, this shows 'A Moochy or Painter' and a female figure, possibly his wife. Significantly the painter holds over his arm a leather saddle, symbolic of his status.[47] Others may have been textile painters or sandalwood carvers.[48]

Although there is similarly little evidence relating to the training of these artists to paint in a broadly European style, it is highly likely that they became acquainted with the conventions of European scientific illustration through making copies of European prints and published works of natural history, working under the supervision of a trained naturalist. This was a common practice favoured by European naturalists, such as Brian Houghton Hodgson (1800–94), a Company administrator and diplomat who amassed a large collection of zoological drawings whilst stationed in Kathmandu, Nepal, between 1820 and 1845.

As a zoological collector, Serfoji's practice can be compared with that of a near-contemporary, Rajendra Mullick (1819–87). The adopted son of a wealthy Calcutta merchant, Mullick is now most famous for his philanthropic activities in Calcutta and for the design and construction of the Marble Palace, a lavish private residence in the north-eastern quarter of the city which also functioned as an exhibition space for Mullick's collections of European art. The palace also included a menagerie in its grounds, in which Mullick maintained a sizeable collection of exotic animals.

Mullick's passion for natural history was sustained by his correspondence with European scientific figures. One of the most influential, thanks to his position in London's metropolitan circles and his own, was Edward Stanley, the thirteenth Earl of Derby (1775–1851), who from 1828 to 1833 was President of the Linnean Society of London, and from 1833 to his death was President of the Zoological Society of London. Founded as both a forum for 'serious' zoological research and as a public menagerie, under Derby's stewardship the Zoological Society further developed a global network of corresponding collectors and researchers, by whose services a constant stream of live acquisitions, as well as prepared specimens, arrived at the Regent's Park menagerie.[49] Derby facilitated this process by also maintaining his own private menagerie on his estate at Knowsley, on the outskirts of Liverpool, keeping up a regular exchange of animals between Knowsley and London. This habit was the cause of some resentment amongst the more politically radical of the Zoological Society's membership, who viewed this trade as exploiting the Society's resources.[50]

From Knowsley, Derby kept up a constant correspondence with the Society's officers and with a network of European naturalists working across South Asia, including Nathaniel Wallich (1786–1854), superintendent of the Sibpur Botanic Garden from 1817 to his retirement in 1846; Dr John McClelland (1805–83), of the Bengal Medical Service and superintendent of the Barrackpore Menagerie; and Edward Blyth (1810–73), a pioneering zoologist and the frequently irascible curator of the Asiatic Society of Bengal's museum in Calcutta.[51] Rajendra Mullick also corresponded regularly with Derby on zoological matters towards the end of the earl's life, predominantly regarding the exchange of animals between their two private zoos, with Blyth often acting as an intermediary in these transactions.

Whilst these letters demonstrate the nature of Mullick's zoological interests, which appear to have been focused exclusively on collecting 'exotic' species such as macaws and curassows rather than for any specialist research, they also cast light on how Mullick's collecting efforts were regarded by his influential European contemporaries. Although Mullick was to be made a Fellow of the Zoological Society in 1859, his relations with Blyth appear to have been strained, and Blyth's references to 'the Baboo' in his letters to Derby strongly suggest that the British naturalist did not take his Bengali contemporary seriously. Mullick's Hindu faith, apparent lack of knowledge of animal husbandry, partiality to aristocratic figures and lack of knowledge of contemporary taxonomy all, at various points, came in for Blyth's sub-acid commentary. On 22 January 1850, in a long letter to Derby, Blyth noted:

> There seems to have been some misapprehension about the procural of the Yak, and from one of yr lordship's letters I learn that the Baboo had promised to obtain a bull for you. Now to me he always politely enough but positively refused to have ought to do with sending away a Bovine animal, until very recently (since I last wrote yr lordship), when he suffered me to persuade him, though still with the understanding that they should be procured and kept here in my name! I was accordingly surprised at his having made such a promise to your lordship and he now tells me he did so in my name. The fact is, I believe, that he originally ordered Yaks for himself but has since allowed himself to be persuaded to spare some for your lordship. As an orthodox Hindoo he is obliged to keep up appearances among his countrymen, & bow to prejudices of creed that to us appear ridiculous in the extreme, not so, however, to a Hindoo. But now that he has undertaken to send some Yaks, they will cost yr lordship nothing beyond the freight.[52]

This passage highlights the often-grudging attitude to Indian intellectuals that gained further ground after the dissolution of the Company in 1858 and the assumption of all executive control over its former territories by the British Crown. Although prominent figures such as Sir Sayyid Ahmad Khan (1817–98) would be active in setting up new scientific societies in the 1860s, David Arnold notes that the British authorities ensured that these did not intrude on the growing monopoly of Europeans in scientific research in India.[53] By the 1890s, despite the Asiatic Society of Bengal including 112 Indian members, including the geologist and industrialist Pramatha Nath Bose (1855–1934), racist assumptions about Indians' perceived physical and intellectual inferiority were commonplace amongst British scientists, as reflected in the marked disparities in their pay, position and opportunities for promotion.[54]

By comparison, Serfoji's activities appear to have met with the near-universal approbation of both his countrymen and his European and Company correspondents. This disparity in attitudes may be attributed to several factors, not the least of which was Serfoji's princely status and the Company's recognition that, even when stripped of all but the most ceremonial of powers, he played a prominent role in Tanjore's internal affairs. Serfoji's activities also occurred before the Anglicist-Orientalist debates of the 1830s, which did much to discourage scholarly cross-cultural co-operation in favour of the gradual imposition of British cultural, educational and judicial practices.

Serfoji's practice differed with Mullick's in one further key respect. Although an avid collector of European art, and counting at least one of Reynolds' portraits amongst his private collection, Mullick does not appear to have been an active patron of Indian artists, and still less interested in commissioning natural history images. Again, external factors and shifting scientific methodologies likely played a role here. Although the European market for lavishly illustrated botanical and zoological works remained buoyant until well into the 1860s, the increasing specialization of both disciplines, as well as the ruinous costs involved in the publication of large-scale illustrated works, placed a greater emphasis on scientific journals and textual descriptions as the preferred forum for new discoveries and descriptions.

Conclusion

Unlike the comparable collections amassed by Wellesley and Buchanan-Hamilton, which can be framed within the wider context of an imperial project of cataloguing and categorization, Serfoji's paintings were not the product of a systematic survey. Gifted in tranches over the space of several years to a valued friend and associate, they subsequently had imposed upon them a system of archival and scientific classification that lent them a form and meaning quite different to Serfoji's original intention. However, and fortunately for modern scholars, Serfoji's 'voice' remains in the occasional, detailed notation inscribed on some of the images, which reveal a little of both the man and the ways in which he incorporated European scientific methodologies into South Indian traditions of seeing and understanding the natural world.

As an archive, and on an initial reading, Serfoji's paintings are an important record of living animals, and the ways in which they were valued as expressions of Court power. As we have seen, certain species exerted a perennial fascination for both Indian princes and the British state; images of big cats and birds of prey, hooded and chained, were visual metaphors both of the dominion of 'man' over the natural world and, from at least the middle of the eighteenth century, of Europe's ascendancy in South Asia. However, Serfoji's interests clearly ranged more widely to the less obviously charismatic, to snakes, frogs and spiders, animals that rarely, or if ever, featured in the tropes of South Indian art, or the schools of northern and central India. Here we can more clearly see the influence of Serfoji's European education, at a time of burgeoning and expanding interest in zoology.

Viewed within the broader archival holdings in which they are currently located, the paintings also offer scholars a valuable window into shifting archival practices and the potential pitfalls inherent in taking an archival record at face value. Without taking into account the context in which they were originally created and their subsequent shaping into reassuringly recognizable folios, Serfoji's archive of zoological paintings could quite easily be understood simply as another 'Company Art' collection, albeit an idiosyncratic one. Serfoji certainly drew upon the practices and techniques of European naturalists. As a patron, for example, he exercised a close supervision over the work of his 'moochies', that process of 'four-eyed sight' and intervention by which artists constructed a 'typical' zoological image. However, these images were not put to the same purposes as others commissioned by European naturalists, whether to serve as proxies for physical zoological specimens or as the basis for printed scientific works, as their current archival composition and close resemblance to comparable European collections might suggest. Nor were they intended to. As we have seen, successive generations of British archivists, beginning with Torin himself, brought the individual paintings together into albums, then into folios and christened them with one title and then another, resulting finally in a small collection which fits uncomfortably within the India Office records and archives. Their archival beginnings as the manifestation of a very personal interest in the natural world, and rich intellectual context, are lost.

Much work remains to be done in the area of Anglo-Indian visual culture, particularly relating to the role of Anglo-Indian images in contemporary classifications of the natural world, and their status as expressions of a highly complex and ongoing aesthetic and epistemological exchange, and many thousands of comparable paintings and drawings lie undisturbed in archives worldwide.[55] This chapter has sought to demonstrate that the analysis of image archives from this period not only sheds light onto the impact of shifting archival practices on our understanding of such collections, but has also the potential to transform our understanding of the ways in which scientific knowledge was mediated and communicated across cultural boundaries.

Notes

1   The East India Company established Residencies throughout the Indian subcontinent, stationing officials in major and regional centres to act as representatives of the Governor-General. Although nominally performing a similar function to ambassadors to local courts, in practice Residents had a far more active role and in some instances wielded considerable political power.

2   The literature into 'Company Art', and the developing debates on the term itself, is an expanding field amongst European and South Asian scholars. The first sustained research into collections of paintings and drawings commissioned by European patrons in South Asia, and the categorization 'Company Art', was initiated by Mildred and William Archer in the 1940s and 1950s, and their work remains foundational for modern scholars. The list below is by no means exhaustive, but represents a good starting point. Mildred Archer, *Natural History Drawings in the India Office Library* (London: HMSO, 1962); and, *Indian Popular Painting in the India Office Library* (London: HMSO, 1977); William Dalrymple and Yuthika Sharma (eds), *Princes and Painters in Mughal Delhi, 1707–1857* (New York: Asia Society Museum, 2010); William Dalrymple (ed.), *Forgotten Masters: Indian Painting for the East India Company* (London: Philip Williams Publishing, 2020); B. N. Goswamy, *The Spirit of Indian Painting: Close Encounters with 101 Great Works 1100–1900* (London: Thames & Hudson, 2016); Jeremiah P. Losty, *Sita Ram's Painted Views of India: Lord Hastings' Journey from Calcutta to the Punjab, 1814–15* (London: Thames & Hudson, 2015); John McAleer, *Picturing India: People, Places and the World of the East India Company* (London: The British Library, 2017); Henry J. Noltie, *Indian Botanical Drawings 1793–1868, From the Royal Botanic Garden Edinburgh* (Edinburgh: Royal Botanic Garden Edinburgh, 1999); Pratapaditya Pal, and Vidya Dehejia, *From Merchants to Emperors: British Artists and India 1757–1858* (Ithaca: Cornell University Press, 1986); Alison Smith and Derek Brown (eds), *Artist and Empire: Facing Britain's Imperial Past* (London: Tate Publishing, 2015).

3   See, for example, Gayatri Chakravorty Spivak, 'Can the Subaltern Speak?' in Cary Nelson and Lawrence Grossberg (eds), *Marxism and the Interpretation of Culture*

(Urbana: University of Illinois Press, 1988), pp. 271–313; and 'The Rani of Sirmur: An Essay in Reading the Archives', *History and Theory* 24 (1985): 247–72.

4   For example, see Tony Ballantyne's important chapter 'Rereading the Archive and Opening up the Nation-State: Colonial Knowledge in South Asia (and Beyond)', in Antoinette Burton (ed.), *After the Imperial Turn: Thinking With and Through the Nation* (Durham, NC: Duke University Press, 2003), pp. 102–24. Ballantyne rejects the centre-periphery model of colonial knowledge networks, advocating instead for a complex web of interconnecting and reciprocal flows of information between colonies and colonizer.

5   Thomas Richards, *The Imperial Archive: Knowledge and the Fantasy of Empire* (London: Verso, 1993); and Eugene F. Irschick, *Dialogue and History: Constructing South India, 1795–1895* (Berkeley: University of California Press, 1994). There is a developing literature on the roles played by South Asian intermediaries in European knowledge networks in South Asia. Christopher Bayly, *Empire and Information: Intelligence Gathering and Social Communication in India, 1780–1870* (Cambridge: Cambridge University Press, 1996), which emphasized the active role played by a wide range of South Asian intermediaries, from *pandits* to runners, remains the standard work. See also Alena Alamgir, '"The Learned Brahmen, Who Assists Me": Changing Colonial Relationships in 18th and 19th Century India', *Journal of Historical Sociology* 19. 4 (2006): 419–46; Brian Hatcher, 'What's Become of the Pandit? Rethinking the History of Sanskrit Scholars in Colonial Bengal', *Modern Asian Studies* 39. 3 (2005): 683–723; Thomas Trautmann, 'Dr Johnson and the Pandits: Imagining the Perfect Dictionary in Colonial Madras', *The Indian Economic and Social History Review* 38. 4 (2001): 375–97; and Philip Wagoner, 'Precolonial Intellectuals and the Production of Colonial Knowledge', *Comparative Studies in Society and History* 45. 4 (2003): 783–814.

6   Savithri Preetha Nair, 'Native Collecting and Natural Knowledge (1798–1832): Raja Serfoji II of Tanjore as a "Centre of Calculation"', *Journal of the Royal Asiatic Society* Third Series 15. 3 (2005): 279–302; '"… Of Real Use to the People": The Tanjore Printing Press and the Spread of Useful Knowledge', *The Indian Economic and Social History Review* 48. 3 (2011): 497–529; Indira Viswanathan Peterson, 'The Cabinet of King Serfoji II of Tanjore', *Journal of the History of Collections* 11. 1 (1999): 71–93.

7   The English East India Company was founded as a joint-stock trading company in 1600, under a Royal Charter granted by Elizabeth I. By the late eighteenth century, it had transformed into a vast mercantile corporation with quasi-governmental powers over swathes of South East Asia. In the aftermath of the Indian Rebellion in 1857, and following successive financial scandals, the British government 'nationalized' the Company and took over the direct governance of the Company's territories, marking the beginning of the British Raj. For an introduction and overview of the history of the East India Company, see John Keay, *The Honourable Company: A History of the East India Company* (London: HarperCollins, 1993); S. Khaja K. Moideen, 'Inherited Debts: Raja Amarasimha of Tanjore, Private Creditors and East India Company', *Proceedings of the Indian History Congress* 69 (2008): 592–602; and C. S. Ramanujam, 'British Relations with Tanjore (1848–1799)' (PhD, University of London, School of Oriental and African Studies, 1968).

8   IOR/H/57, BL. Papers concerning the Danes (1737–1816). 7, pp. 95–104.
9   Home Misc. Series, Vol. 634, pp. 103–6.
10 IOR/Z/E/4/37/B337, BL. India Office Records and Private Papers. Also IOR/H/571, Papers on Kurnool, Coorg and Tanjore (1784–95), pp. 183–213, which outlines the negotiations and proceedings in which Charles Schwarz acted as an interpreter.

11 IOR/H/635, BL. 13, pp. 203–16. Wellesley has been surprisingly poorly-served by biographers. The standard work remains Iris Butler, *The Eldest Brother: The Marquess Wellesley* (London: Hodder and Stoughton, 1973).
12 Nair, 'Native Collecting and Natural Knowledge', pp. 279–302.
13 Ibid., pp. 283–4; and Robert Eric Frykenberg, 'The Legacy of Christian Friedrich Schwartz', *International Bulletin of Missionary Research* 23. 3 (1999): 130–5.
14 Adrian P. Thomas, 'The Establishment of Calcutta Botanic Garden: Plant Transfer, Science and the East India Company, 1786–1806', *Journal of the Royal Asiatic Society* 16. 2 (2006): 165–77.
15 On Serfoji's scholarship, see for example Mss Eur C887, BL, India Office Records. A letter in which Serfoji requests of his correspondent (identity now unknown) the final volume of Robert Orme, *A History of the Military Transactions of the British Nation in Indostan from 1745* (Madras: Pharoah, 1861–2).
16 For a detailed analysis, see Scott Atran, *Cognitive Foundations of Natural History: Towards an Anthropology of Science* (Cambridge: Cambridge University Press, 1990).
17 Nair, 'Native Collecting and Natural Knowledge', p. 294.
18 The available literature on the study and development of natural history in South Asia, both in the pre-colonial and colonial periods, has increased hugely in the past two decades in both quantity and sophistication. Of Indian rulers, the Mughal emperor Jahangir is a primary focus for historians due to the resources he devoted to the study of nature and his engagement with European methods; see Ebba Koch, 'Jahangir as Francis Bacon's Ideal of the King as an Observer and Investigator of Nature', *Journal of the Royal Asiatic Society* 19. 3 (2009): 293–338. George Basalla, 'The Spread of Western Science', *Science* 156. 3775 (1967): 611–22, remains a seminal if contested interpretation of the centre-periphery model of the spread of 'western' scientific method and theory to the colonial peripheries. This model was developed and critiqued by Deepak Kumar, 'Patterns of Colonial Science in India', *Indian Journal of the History of Science* 15. 1 (1980): 105–13, and D. Raina, 'From West to Non-West?: Basalla's Three-Stage Model Revisited', *Science as Culture* 8. 4 (1999): 497–516. These and other studies have provided the basis for much subsequent work which assesses the dissemination of European scientific culture across the subcontinent. The works identified here are far from an exhaustive list but are identified as excellent starting points and studies in themselves: Kapil Raj, *Relocating Modern Science: Circulation and the Construction of Knowledge in South Asia and Europe, 1650–1900* (Basingstoke: Palgrave Macmillan, 2007); and 'Colonial Encounters and the Forging of New Knowledge and National Identities: Great Britain and India, 1760–1850', *Osiris* 15 (2000): 119–34; Jessica Ratcliff, 'The East India Company, the Company's Museum, and the Political Economy of Natural History in the Early Nineteenth Century', *Isis* 107, no. 3 (2016): 495–517; Satpal Sangwan, 'Reordering the Earth: The Emergence of Geology as a Scientific Discipline in Colonial India', *The Indian Economic and Social History Review* 31. 3 (1994): 291–310; Phillip Wagoner, 'Pre-colonial Intellectuals'; David Arnold, *Science, Technology and Medicine in Colonial India* (Cambridge: Cambridge University Press); Pratik Chakraborty, *Western Science in Modern India: Metropolitan Methods, Colonial Practices* (Delhi: Permanent Black, 2004); and David Cohn, *Colonialism and Its Forms of Knowledge* (Princeton, NJ: Princeton University Press, 1996).
19 Savithri Preethan Nair, 'Illustrating Plants at the Tanjore Court', *Marg: A Magazine of the Arts* (1 December 2018): https://marg-art.org/.
20 Thomas, 'Calcutta Botanic Garden', pp. 165–77.

21 G. Annesley, *Voyages & Travels to India, Ceylon, the Red Sea, Abyssinia and Egypt in the Years 1802, 1803, 1804, 1805, and 1806*, Vol. 1 (London: [no publisher], 1809), pp. 358-63.
22 Adrian Desmond, 'The Making of Institutional Zoology in London, 1822–1836', *History of Science* 23 (1985): 153-85.
23 Takashi Ito, *London Zoo and the Victorians, 1828–1859* (Woodbridge: The Boydell Press, 2014), pp. 21-6.
24 See John Matthew, 'To Fashion a Fauna for British India' (PhD, Harvard University, 2011).
25 Rajesh Kochhar, 'Natural History in India during the 18th and 19th Centuries', *Journal of Biosciences* 38. 2 (2013): 204.
26 See NHD26-27, 'Hindoostan Birds', British Library. These two volumes bear the inscription 'Originally prepared by Order of Marquis Wellesley when Governor-General of India', and comprise some seventy separate images of Indian birds.
27 William Dalrymple, *The Anarchy: The Relentless Rise of the East India Company* (London: Bloomsbury, 2019), p. 389.
28 Ibid.
29 Cited in *The Asiatic Annual Register for the Year 1807: Or, A View of the History of Hindustan, and the Politics, Commerce, and Literature of Asia, Vol. IX, for the Year 1807* (London: Cadell and W. Davies, 1809), p. 110.
30 J. J. White, 'Three Botanical Albums in the Thanjavur Maharaja Serfoji's Saraswati Mahal Library in India', *Huntia: A Journal of Botanical History* 9. 2 (1996): 161-3.
31 Ibid., p. 161.
32 TDR Vol. No. 3492. Benjamin Torin to Serfoji II of Tanjore, 15 September 1807.
33 A fine, profile view annotated as depicting a 'Royal Tiger' highlights the symbolism latent in the presence of these animals in princely menageries. BL, NHD 7/1035.
34 NHD7/1034 Caracal. BL Raja Serfojee of Tanjore Collection.
35 NHD32/7 Caracal. BL Wellesley Collections.
36 NHD32/46 Indian rhinoceros. BL Wellesley Collections.
37 See Peter Lawrence Farber, 'The Development of Taxidermy and the History of Ornithology', *Isis* 68. 4 (1977): 550-66, for a detailed discussion of methods of taxidermy and the impact on improvements in the late eighteenth and early nineteenth centuries on the progress of zoological classification.
38 Lorraine Daston and Peter Galison, *Objectivity* (New York: Zone Books, 2010).
39 Ibid., p. 60.
40 Ibid., pp. 84-98.
41 NHD 33/27-28, Gyal. Wellesley Collections, Quadrupeds of India.
42 David Lowther, 'The Art of Classification: Brian Houghton Hodgson and the "Zoology of Nipal"', *Archives of Natural History* 46. 1 (2019): 6-7.
43 NHD7/1010-1012, Peregrine Falcons. BL Raja Serfojee of Tanjore Collection NHD7/1001-1116.
44 Archer, *Natural History Drawings*, p. 13.
45 The historiography on the development of Mughal art in Jahangir's reign is extensive. For reference to his overlapping interest in European art and natural history, see Milo Cleveland Beach, 'The Mughal Painter Abu'l Hasan and Some English Sources for His Style', *The Journal of the Walters Art Gallery* 38 (1980): 6-33; and Milo Cleveland Beach, *Mughal and Rajput Painting* (Cambridge: Cambridge University Press, 1992); Ebba Koch, 'Jahangir', pp. 293-338.

46 Henry J. Noltie, *The Cleghorn Collection: South Indian Botanical Drawings 1845 to 1860* (Edinburgh: Royal Botanic Garden Edinburgh, 2016), pp. 6–9.
47 British Museum, Asia Collections, 1884, 0913, 0.37.
48 Dalrymple, *Forgotten Masters*, pp. 12–13.
49 See Ito, *London Zoo and the Victorians*.
50 See Desmond, 'Making of Institutional Zoology', pp. 153–85.
51 Ref. to correspondence in NML.
52 Edward Blyth to Lord Derby, 22 January 1850. 25/4. 'Tin Trunk' correspondence, NML.
53 Arnold, *Science, Technology and Medicine in Colonial India*, pp. 157–8.
54 Ibid., pp. 138–41. See also Deepak Kumar, 'Racial Discrimination & Science in Nineteenth-Century India', *The Indian Economic & Social History Review* 19. 1 (1982): 67–70.
55 For work on the intersections between colonialism, empire, science and art, or combinations therein, see: Hermoine de Almeida and George Gilpin, *Indian Renaissance: British Romantic Art and the Prospect of India* (London: Routledge, 2016); John Guy, *The Art of India: 1550–1900* (London: V&A Publications, 2004); McAleer, *Picturing India*; Partha Mitter, *Much Maligned Monsters: A History of European Reactions to Indian Art* (Oxford: Clarendon Press, 1977); Beth Tobin, 'Imperial Designs: Botanical Illustration and the British Botanic Empire', *Studies in Eighteenth-Century Culture* 25 (1996): 265–92; Sujit Sivasundaram, 'Trading Knowledge: The East India Company's Elephants in India and Britain', *The Historical Journal* 48. 1 (2005): 27–63; and Anne Secord, 'Botany on a Plate: Pleasure and the Power of Pictures in Promoting Early Nineteenth-Century Scientific Knowledge', *Isis* 93. 1 (2002): 28–57.

Bibliography

Alamgir, Alena. '"The Learned Brahmen, Who Assists Me": Changing Colonial Relationships in 18th and 19th Century India'. *Journal of Historical Sociology* 19, no. 4 (2006): 419–46.
de Almeida, Hermoine, and George Gilpin. *Indian Renaissance: British Romantic Art and the Prospect of India*. London: Routledge, 2016.
Annesley, G. *Voyages & Travels to India, Ceylon, the Red Sea, Abyssinia and Egypt in the Years 1802, 1803, 1804, 1805, and 1806*. Vol. 1. London: [no publisher], 1809.
Archer, Mildred. *Natural History Drawings in the India Office Library*. London: HMSO, 1962.
Archer, Mildred. *Indian Popular Painting in the India Office Library*. London: HMSO, 1977.
Arnold, David. *Science, Technology and Medicine in Colonial India*. Cambridge: Cambridge University Press, 2000.
The Asiatic Annual Register for the Year 1807: Or, a View of the History of Hindustan, and the Politics, Commerce, and Literature of Asia, Vol. IX, for the Year 1807. London: Cadell and W. Davies, 1809.
Atran, Scott. *Cognitive Foundations of Natural History: Towards an Anthropology of Science*. Cambridge: Cambridge University Press, 1990.

Ballantyne, Tony. 'Rereading the Archive and Opening up the Nation-State: Colonial Knowledge in South Asia (and Beyond)'. In *After the Imperial Turn: Thinking With and Through the Nation*, edited by Antoinette Burton, 102–24. Durham, NC: Duke University Press, 2003.

Basalla, George. 'The Spread of Western Science'. *Science* 156, no. 3775 (1967): 611–22.

Bayly, Christopher. *Empire and Information: Intelligence Gathering and Social Communication in India, 1780–1870*. Cambridge: Cambridge University Press, 1996.

Beach, Milo Cleveland. 'The Mughal Painter Abu'l Hasan and Some English Sources for His Style'. *The Journal of the Walters Art Gallery* 38 (1980): 6–33.

Beach, Milo Cleveland. *Mughal and Rajput Painting*. Cambridge: Cambridge University Press, 1992.

Butler, Iris. *The Eldest Brother: The Marquess Wellesley*. London: Hodder and Stoughton, 1973.

Chakraborty, Pratik. *Western Science in Modern India: Metropolitan Methods, Colonial Practices*. Delhi: Permanent Black, 2004.

Cohn, David. *Colonialism and Its Forms of Knowledge*. Princeton, NJ: Princeton University Press, 1996.

Dalrymple, William. *The Anarchy: The Relentless Rise of the East India Company*. London: Bloomsbury, 2019.

Dalrymple, William (ed.). *Forgotten Masters: Indian Painting for the East India Company*. London: Philip Williams Publishing, 2020.

Dalrymple, William, and Yuthika Sharma (eds). *Princes and Painters in Mughal Delhi, 1707–1857*. New York: Asia Society Museum, 2010.

Daston, Lorraine, and Peter Galison. *Objectivity*. New York: Zone Books, 2010.

Desmond, Adrian. 'The Making of Institutional Zoology in London, 1822–1836'. *History of Science* 23 (1985): 153–85.

Farber, Peter Lawrence. 'The Development of Taxidermy and the History of Ornithology'. *Isis* 68, no. 4 (1977): 550–66.

Frykenberg, Robert Eric. 'The Legacy of Christian Friedrich Schwartz'. *International Bulletin of Missionary Research* 23, no. 3 (1999): 130–5.

Goswamy, B. N. *The Spirit of Indian Painting: Close Encounters with 101 Great Works 1100–1900*. London: Thames & Hudson, 2016.

Guy, John. *The Art of India: 1550–1900*. London: V&A Publications, 2004.

Hatcher, Brian. 'What's Become of the Pandit? Rethinking the History of Sanskrit Scholars in Colonial Bengal'. *Modern Asian Studies* 39, no. 3 (2005): 683–723.

Irschick, Eugene F. *Dialogue and History: Constructing South India, 1795–1895*. Berkeley: University of California Press, 1994.

Ito, Takashi. *London Zoo and the Victorians, 1828–1859*. Woodbridge: The Boydell Press, 2014.

Keay, John. *The Honourable Company: A History of the East India Company*. London: HarperCollins, 1993.

Koch, Ebba. 'Jahangir as Francis Bacon's Ideal of the King as an Observer and Investigator of Nature'. *Journal of the Royal Asiatic Society* 19, no. 3 (2009): 293–338.

Kochhar, Rajesh. 'Natural History in India during the 18th and 19th Centuries'. *Journal of Biosciences* 38, no. 2 (2013): 201–24.

Kumar, Deepak. 'Patterns of Colonial Science in India'. *Indian Journal of the History of Science* 15, no. 1 (1980): 105–13.

Kumar, Deepak. 'Racial Discrimination & Science in Nineteenth-Century India'. *The Indian Economic & Social History Review* 19, no. 1 (1982): 67–70.

Losty, Jeremiah P. *Sita Ram's Painted Views of India: Lord Hastings' Journey from Calcutta to the Punjab, 1814-15*. London: Thames & Hudson, 2015.

Lowther, David. 'The Art of Classification: Brian Houghton Hodgson and the "Zoology of Nipal"'. *Archives of Natural History* 46, no. 1 (2019): 1-23.

Mathew, J. 'To Fashion a Fauna for British India'. PhD, Harvard University, 2011.

McAleer, John. *Picturing India: People, Places and the World of the East India Company*. London: The British Library, 2017.

Mitter, Partha. *Much Maligned Monsters: A History of European Reactions to Indian Art*. Oxford: Clarendon Press, 1977.

Moideen, S. Khaja. 'Inherited Debts: Raja Amarasimha of Tanjore, Private Creditors and East India Company'. *Proceedings of the Indian History Congress* 69 (2008): 592-602.

Nair, Savithri Preetha. 'Native Collecting and Natural Knowledge (1798-1832): Raja Serfoji II of Tanjore as a "Centre of Calculation"'. *Journal of the Royal Asiatic Society* Third Series 15, no. 3 (2005): 279-302.

Nair, Savithri Preetha. '"… Of Real Use to the People": The Tanjore Printing Press and the Spread of Useful Knowledge'. *The Indian Economic and Social History Review* 48, no. 3 (2011): 497-529.

Nair, Savithri Preetha. 'Illustrating Plants at the Tanjore Court'. *Marg: A Magazine of the Arts* (1 December 2018): https://marg-art.org/.

Noltie, Henry J. *Indian Botanical Drawings 1793-1868, From the Royal Botanic Garden Edinburgh*. Edinburgh: Royal Botanic Garden Edinburgh, 1999.

Orme, Robert. *A History of the Military Transactions of the British Nation in Indostan from 1745*. Madras: Pharoah, 1861-2.

Pal, Pratapaditya, and Vidya Dehejia. *From Merchants to Emperors: British Artists and India 1757-1858*. Ithaca: Cornell University Press, 1986.

Peterson, Indira Viswanathan. 'The Cabinet of King Serfoji II of Tanjore'. *Journal of the History of Collections* 11, no. 1 (1999): 71-93.

Raina, D. 'From West to Non-West?: Basalla's Three-Stage Model Revisited'. *Science as Culture* 8, no. 4 (1999): 497-516.

Raj, Kapil. 'Colonial Encounters and the Forging of New Knowledge and National Identities: Great Britain and India, 1760-1850'. *Osiris* 15 (2000): 119-34.

Raj, Kapil. *Relocating Modern Science: Circulation and the Construction of Knowledge in South Asia and Europe, 1650-1900*. Basingstoke: Palgrave Macmillan, 2007.

Ramanujam, C. S. 'British Relations with Tanjore (1848-1799)'. PhD, University of London, School of Oriental and African Studies, 1968.

Ratcliff, Jessica. 'The East India Company, the Company's Museum, and the Political Economy of Natural History in the Early Nineteenth Century'. *Isis* 107, no. 3 (2016): 495-517.

Richards, Thomas. *The Imperial Archive: Knowledge and the Fantasy of Empire*. London: Verso, 1993.

Sangwan, Satpal. 'Reordering the Earth: The Emergence of Geology as a Scientific Discipline in Colonial India'. *The Indian Economic and Social History Review* 31, no. 3 (1994): 291-310.

Secord, Anne. 'Botany on a Plate: Pleasure and the Power of Pictures in Promoting Early Nineteenth-Century Scientific Knowledge'. *Isis* 93, no. 1 (2002): 28-57.

Sivasundaram, Sujit. 'Trading Knowledge: The East India Company's Elephants in India and Britain'. *The Historical Journal* 48, no. 1 (2005): 27-63.

Smith, Alison, and Derek Brown (eds). *Artist and Empire: Facing Britain's Imperial Past*. London: Tate Publishing, 2015.

Spivak, Gayatri Chakravorty. 'The Rani of Sirmur: An Essay in Reading the Archives'. *History and Theory* 24 (1985): 247–72.

Spivak, Gayatri Chakravorty. 'Can the Subaltern Speak?'. In *Marxism and the Interpretation of Culture*, edited by Cary Nelson and Lawrence Grossberg, 271–313. Urbana: University of Illinois Press, 1988.

Thomas, Adrian P. 'The Establishment of Calcutta Botanic Garden: Plant Transfer, Science and the East India Company, 1786–1806'. *Journal of the Royal Asiatic Society* 16, no. 2 (2006): 165–77.

Tobin, Beth. 'Imperial Designs: Botanical Illustration and the British Botanic Empire'. *Studies in Eighteenth-Century Culture* 25 (1996): 265–92.

Trautmann, Thomas. 'Dr Johnson and the Pandits: Imagining the Perfect Dictionary in Colonial Madras'. *The Indian Economic and Social History Review* 38, no. 4 (2001): 375–97.

Wagoner, Philip. 'Precolonial Intellectuals and the Production of Colonial Knowledge'. *Comparative Studies in Society and History* 45, no. 4 (2003): 783–814.

White, J. J. 'Three Botanical Albums in the Thanjavur Maharaja Serfoji's Saraswati Mahal Library in India'. *Huntia: A Journal of Botanical History* 9, no. 2 (1996): 161–3.

6

Enclosing archival sound: Colonial singing as discipline and resistance

Erin Johnson-Williams

Conversations about decolonization have created a lot of noise recently. As a historian of sound, it often strikes me that such dialogues also create a significant opportunity to think critically about the colonial legacies of *silence* – and the power of the archive to silence or (re)sound forms of colonial experience.[1] Indeed, there has been a growing tendency to interrogate the power imbalances latent in western institutional structures – from the #MeToo movement, to the rise of Black Lives Matter protests and threats of fake news, to critiques of the ways in which the pressures of digital surveillance and capitalist globalization increasingly shape modern life. Alongside this questioning of and resistance to hierarchical structures, there is an emergent commitment to attend to voices previously silenced through the processes of archival curation, and to narratives (and forms of expression) that have traditionally been omitted from canonical discourses. Likewise, new academic readings of the imperial archive are under pressure to 'give voice to' those who have been systemically silenced by structural power imbalances.[2] Yet conversations about 're-sounding' the past necessarily start with a critical interrogation of who has the institutional *ability* to archive colonial sound. From the perspectives of sound studies and, more specifically, musicology, how can colonial archives both 'sound' and 'give voice to' histories of violence and resistance, particularly when the colonial archive is arguably a 'silencing' structure by its very nature?

Focusing on the idea of the nineteenth-century archive as both a space and an archive of carceral 'enclosure',[3] this chapter examines how music – particularly in the form of settler colonial hymn-singing – functioned to both 'sound' and 'silence' the ambiguities of the colonial archive within spaces of disciplinary enclosure. In much existing musicological scholarship, the role of singing within institutions of settler colonial biopolitical containment – such as Indigenous residential schools, concentration camps and prisons – has largely been archived as a strategic tool for religious conversion and/or social control.[4] By the same token, there has been a relatively long-standing association in historical musicology of the genre of the hymn with congregational (and stylistic) conformity, resulting in the devaluing of the hymn's potential as a form of both personal self-expression and potentially violent coercion.[5]

By providing a case for a 're-archiving' of nineteenth-century technologies of sonic incarceration, I suggest that the flexibility and accessibility of the nineteenth-century hymn – a genre that 'sounded' simple, beautiful and even child-like to Victorian ears[6] – reinforced yet challenged the atrocities of settler colonialism. Effectively, acts of silencing, sounding and archiving thus go hand in hand: the use of English-language hymns as a form of discipline in colonial residential schools and prisons created sonic spaces for conformity while actively silencing Indigenous singing traditions. Therefore, the archiving of the hymn as a tool of imperial 'enclosure' in colonial institutions was part of a larger movement to 'silence' colonized voices, often (in the context of religious mission) through the 'sounding' of English-language hymns. To erase the colonial hymn from histories of the past would be to lose the opportunity to find moments within these histories where colonial subjects were able to sound – and, effectively, re-archive – their own experiences of oppression or resistance.[7]

Drawing on material relating to acts of colonial 'disciplining' in late nineteenth-century Canada and twentieth-century South Africa, I challenge Foucauldian analyses of institutional power by exploring how the biopolitics of hymn singing in spaces of colonial enclosure both reinforced and resisted the silence of the imperial archive, and, later, through Truth and Reconciliation initiatives, how new 'soundings' were made possible through the processes of decolonial re-archiving.[8] Hymn-singing in environments such as colonial residential schools and prisons simultaneously evaded – and yet also nuanced – a top-down 'sounding' of the archival silences that were brought about by western carceral institutions. I propose that while the violence of the colonial hymn may have been largely silenced by the archive of empire, its enduring traces bear witness to the power of singing as a form of liberation, and ultimately, a sonic 're-archiving' of imperial discipline.

Sound as enclosure/archive as silence

In the summer of 2021, a series of unmarked graves were uncovered in Canada. Holding the bones of hundreds of Indigenous children, this discovery generated heated discussions about the long-silenced history of Canada's Indigenous Residential Schools (1883–1996), which have recently culminated in the Canadian government pledging $31.5 billion to repair the system that supported these atrocities and to compensate the families of those affected.[9] These schools had previously been declared a site of 'cultural genocide' by the Canadian Truth and Reconciliation Commission (TRC),[10] but the sudden visibility of the graves also sparked a call within the UK to acknowledge the responsibility of the British Empire for the existence of these disciplinary spaces. On 2 July 2021, for example, an article entitled 'The Toxic Legacy of the British Empire in Canada's Residential Schools' appeared in the *Guardian*, claiming that '[t]he destruction of Indigenous lifeways was necessary for the British corporations whose interest in timber and other natural resources drove many of the actions of crown officials in that era', and that:

> it was British money that funded much of the early missionary work that eventually became the religious institutions that would go on to bury children in unmarked graves. Maybe a little more reckoning with the UK's own past is in order.[11]

This link between racial capitalism and empire sets the scene for how missionary imperialism provided a humanitarian and moral justification for institutional racism, whether the institutions were justified as pedagogical, carceral or commercial.[12] Within the Canadian residential schools, hundreds of children died due to unsanitary conditions and physical and sexual abuse. Those who attempted to speak or sing in their Indigenous language were severely punished.[13] Indigenous Canadians have long mourned the horrific conditions at these 'compulsory' residential schools, where children were forcibly separated from their families by governmental authorities, yet the discovery of the mass graves has sparked new attention from the press internationally, and the resulting conversations have joined a broader dialogue about decolonization, and how the atrocities of imperialism have been archived and made available (or not) for the public.[14]

The singing of English-language hymns was used within these spaces of colonial incarceration as a mandatory form of religious and pedagogical discipline. And yet archives relating to music within Canadian residential schools are almost non-existent, except to indicate that mandatory English-language hymn singing occurred at regular intervals throughout the day.[15] Similar archival gaps – perhaps because of an implicit ambiguity of hymn singing as an effective tool for coercion and conversion, despite the (silenced) risk that communities might use singing as a means of reformist solidarity[16] – occur when examining the broader presence of music in other spaces of colonial incarceration, such as prisons, military camps and concentration camps.[17] At the same time, more recent Truth and Reconciliation initiatives, particularly in the contexts of Canada and South Africa that I examine here, have placed Indigenous-language singing as crucial to processing transgenerational trauma.[18] Taking western imperial structures of institutional 'enclosure' as a starting point, I propose that a re-consideration of how sound operated as a form of 'disciplinary enclosure' in settler colonial contexts might provide a way to start to fill the gaps left by archival silences.[19]

A topical, performative 're-sounding' of hymn singing within Canadian residential schools appeared in 2019 in the popular Canadian Broadcasting Corporation (CBC) drama (now on Netflix) *Anne With an E*: a striking re-imagining of the beloved Edwardian novel *Anne of Green Gables*, where the themes of mental health, trauma, sexual consent, race, gender and empire are all foregrounded. The content of much of the third season, in a notable departure from the novels by L. M. Montgomery, is about power, race and consent. In episode 4 of Season 3 (aired 13 October 2019), the character of Anne's Indigenous Canadian friend Ka'kwet is forcibly removed from Avonlea to a residential school, and a powerful central scene shows the Indigenous children (who are literally locked into the school as prisoners) being forced to sing the

Victorian hymn 'Praise him! Praise him, Jesus, our Blessed Redeemer'. Anne, oblivious to the coercion in the school, unsuccessfully attempts to pay a visit to Ka'kwet. As she approaches the schoolhouse, the doleful sound of children reluctantly singing the hymn resonates in the background. The nun who greets Anne at the door refuses to let her in because 'the children are in choir practice'. When Ka'kwet tries to break out of the hymn singing session by protesting in her own language, she is physically assaulted by the nun, who slaps her across the face, saying: 'speak English: your heathen tongue is forbidden. Now, sing to the Lord'.[20] When Ka'kwet refuses to sing a second time, the nun brings in a male priest, Father Beck, who gives her the belt because she was 'behaving like a stupid Indian'.[21]

Notably, the other children stop singing the hymn when the physical abuse begins. This is a telling dramatic moment in the television script because the sonic archive that it (re)creates is effectively a record of how Indigenous voices were silenced, and how the students themselves 'silenced' the English hymn by tentatively showing a mute solidarity for Ka'kwet. Because it is challenging to theorize the 'silencing' properties of the colonial musical archive, there has been relatively little space, musicologically, to explore what role music and sound played in the lives of the Indigenous school children, and it has taken a CBC/Netflix production to dramatize what a hymn-as-violent-coercion might actually have sounded like. Indeed, if hymns have been traditionally dismissed from being a 'serious' genre of musicological study *because* they still retain Victorian associations of simplicity and benevolence, then such aesthetic sidelining has also reinforced how hymns can be used as a form of (and a cover for) institutional abuse.[22] It is also notable that the producers of *Anne With an E* chose to have the mandatory 'choir practice' in full swing at the moment when Anne arrives. In Anne's white, Protestant experience, hymn singing is a 'noble', holy and thus an entirely acceptable (and ostensibly compassionate) pursuit; an apparently innocent reason for why Ka'Kwet could not be allowed visitors. Because of the veneer of hymn singing as benevolent, therefore, the sound of the hymn, at least to Anne's ears, effectively covers up the abuse happening behind locked doors. Even though Anne, in this dramatization, is a character who is extraordinarily perceptive about structures of abuse across virtually all of the other storylines, as a white settler she is effectively deaf to the silencing properties of the Protestant hymn in the context of residential schools. The presence of hymn singing in this upsetting scene, therefore, both reveals and conceals the abusive structures of Indigenous incarceration: a hymn as melodically and harmonically innocuous (to Anne's ears, at least) as 'Praise him! Praise him, Jesus, our Blessed Redeemer!' can for Ka'kwet imply a context of torture and coercion, even though to Anne, that the children are in 'choir practice' at all is 'marvellous', as 'singing is a great fortifier for the spirit'.[23]

One of the reasons why the residential school scene in *Anne With an E* is so powerful, and has generated discussion on the internet,[24] is the rarity of portrayals of how hymn singing functioned as both a tool of humanitarian benevolence as well as disciplinary violence within spaces of colonial incarceration. Anne's obliviousness to the various overlapping levels of coercion going on at the school is a jarring metaphor for the colonial archive's silencing potential, for up to this point in the drama the viewer has been primed to believe that Anne would be able to see through violent, hierarchical structures. The idea of hymn singing as wholly benevolent is therefore indelibly linked to Anne's white racial frame.

Returning, then, to the place of Canadian residential schools within recent conversations about decolonization, perhaps the 'sounding' of an archive of enclosure is a powerful way to see the archive as a disciplinary space that *must* engage with sound because silence is at the heart of how many colonial archival spaces were created. Historians of music, however, have often struggled with how to 'sound' historical discourses about biopolitical enclosure, when music is so often virtually absent from the archives of such disciplinary spaces. How, then, can a history of incarcerated colonial music-making be 'enclosed' in the nineteenth-century archive, and ultimately 'disclosed' through a decolonial hearing of archival gaps? Indeed, institutional spaces of empire, whether they be camps, prisons or cultural institutions, all to varying degrees *enclose*, frame and control their holdings. By implication, such institutions also have an extraordinary power to silence. Music – through its flexible parameters to both sound *and* silence an environment – is a potentially useful, if at times elusive, way to bring the material archives of nineteenth-century imperialism into dialogue with the reparative potential of decolonization. Musical sound, at least in a nineteenth-century western construction, allegedly constituted an inherently subjective artform, but at the same time music-in-practice has been a profoundly disciplining force throughout the history of the British Empire. In this way, the lived experience of colonial singing was in one sense at odds with the textual, recorded histories of nineteenth-century art music, while also being the unheard soundtrack to the daily lives of the peoples represented in institutional holdings.[25]

Such tensions have been described by Beverley Diamond as the 'doubleness of sound' in Canadian residential schools.[26] Diamond claims that the presence of hymn singing in the schools 'functioned as a mechanism of assimilation and control, but also as a form of student resistance and resilience'.[27] As students might refuse to sing, or use the genre of the hymn for their own subjective expression, music is therefore an ambiguous, although potentially very revealing, way to enter the nineteenth-century colonial archive. Diamond makes the case that the existing archives of Canadian residential schools provide a very limited understanding of the range of traumas that were possible with hymn singing, noting that '[m]ost information available about music in the schools was written for school newsletters, often by students under the close supervision of teachers and administrators. These articles presented the schools in a positive light, as if they were the equivalent of other schools across the country'.[28] While the transient nature of music may seem, on the surface, to be at odds with an institutional archive's claims to permanence, the tensions of absence and presence that pervade utopian discourses about nineteenth-century western music as a civilizing force and those that uphold archival spaces of institutional enclosure stem from remarkably parallel impulses.[29] The same might be said of the kinds of disciplining discourses that were applied to music, sound and archival curation in colonial contexts.[30] Thus, the nineteenth-century archiving of empire was fundamentally in tension with Eurocentric understandings of the place of music in the world, leaving acts of colonial musical archiving to be at once implicit attempts of hierarchical control, as well as opportunities for sonic ambivalence.

Constructions of the archive as a form of silencing, as explored across the essays in this volume, are far from new. What I am interested in here is what the inverse of archival silencing would sound like – and whether the heroic assumptions about 're-sounding' lost voices that many scholars adopt can in fact reinforce neo-imperial, salvationist assumptions.[31] An implication across a lot of recent literature on decolonization is that the inverse of archival silencing is to create space for sound(ing)s to happen.[32] The next step, I suggest, is to consider critically what form(s) this might take: to state the obvious, whenever sound occurs, it has the effect of silencing what was there before, even if what was already there was actually silence (or even silent protest), which is then filled by the (sometimes non-consensual) regulation of organized sound, a technique widely used as a torture device in Guantanamo Bay.[33] Music, therefore, can be both a form of historical erasure and its own kind of 'disciplinary enclosure', as well as a vehicle of potential emancipation. Furthermore, the colonial hymn still offered the possibility of asserting and expressing group identity for its singers, creating musical spaces that are therefore difficult to 'archive' as strictly oppressive or liberative.

In academic discourses the idea of the archive as a disciplinary, silencing space has been explored from a variety of perspectives, although there is room for links between silence, sound and music to be forged *beyond* Foucauldian discourses of institutional archives as forms of top-down hierarchical dominance.[34] In approaching the idea of the 'enclosed' subject, Chris Waller argues that Victorian singing goes hand in hand with the tensions between control and resistance within many nineteenth-century carceral institutions.[35] As Waller reminds us, Henry Mayhew was famously moved by hearing hymns sung at London's Pentonville prison, although, even there, the 'singing of hymns and psalms wasn't always as earnest, with some prisoners taking the rare opportunity of physical proximity to their fellow inmates to communicate', using the 'raucous noise of the hymns' to act as a cover for subversive speech.[36] Other prisoners would likewise 'implant their own words over those of the hymns to subvert the acoustical authority of the service'.[37] As a result, hymn singing in Pentonville prison was sometimes banned.[38] Mayhew's account is a powerful indication of the potential of the hymn to both demonstrate and resist conformity in contexts of imprisonment. By extension, in colonial contexts Kofi Agawu has shown that hymns in postcolonial practice are constantly reappropriated, and thus they are prone to be in tension with the colonizer.[39]

What could be helpful here would be to extend the idea of the panoptical powers of (archival) enclosure to ways of understanding the function of music in colonial institutions in light of what la paperson has termed 'technologies of indigenous erasure'.[40] While la paperson does not write about music, imagining the hymn as a 'technology' of Indigenous erasure fits well within a paradigm of settler colonial institutions that define themselves through performative projects of 'cultural assimilation' that reflect 'desires for a colonizer's future and, paradoxically, desires for Indigenous futures'.[41] Enforced hymn singing within spaces of colonial incarceration can thus be constructed as a kind of performative aspiration towards Indigenous 'erasure', although – and this is where music creates a particularly reflexive archive – I would argue that through colonial hymnic reappropriation, space may be created for resistance.[42] Taking on Michel-Rolph Trouillot's idea in *Silencing the Past* of how history is a form of storytelling that reflects the hierarchies of the past while replicating and reinforcing new power structures,[43] I suggest that the hymn within spaces of colonial biopolitical enclosure can operate within what Daniel Nemser has described as a form of relational infrastructure, where '[w]hat appears as infrastructure – what *dis*appears from view – necessarily does so in relation to specific subject positions or practices'.[44] In Nemser's formulation, such racial infrastructures are learned, and 'the habitual practices that congeal around them are themselves constructive of collective norms. If familiarity can generate a shared sense of belonging to a community of users, engaging with unfamiliar infrastructures can yield the unsettling sense of being out of place'.[45] Applying this framework to musical practice, the underlying unfamiliarity of English-language hymn singing within spaces of colonial incarceration had the potential to yield an unsettling sense of being 'out of place', while at the same time requiring conformity and offering the possibilities of collective belonging.

Enclosing and disclosing the hymn

Effectively, the imposition of hymn singing within spaces of colonial incarceration had a double effect of presence and absence, belonging and unbelonging: what we might call a 'sounding into disappearance' of Indigenous agency.[46] The presence of imposed music (here, hymns) as a way to obstruct the possibility of resistance is all the more troubled in settler colonial records because historians are so often looking *to* the institutional archive to fill a sonic void. As Bryanne Young evocatively describes of her experience in conducting archival research on the Canadian residential schools, 'I continue to find more resonant significance in the effect of those documents blurring together than I do in the records themselves. Walking out of The Archives at the end of that day, into the clamor of the capital city at rush hour, I realized how deeply I had been aching for *sound*'.[47] Similarly, in *The Silence of the Archive*, David Thomas, Simon Fowler and Valerie Johnson claim that archival silences can also be starting points: 'certain voids in archives may also function as positive or humanly necessary spaces – tacit agreements and ellipses designed to leave unsaid or let slip away things that may be too painful, too problematic, too love-laden or too explicit to capture'.[48]

Archival silences, too, are reminders that institutional collections are constructed and curated by people with their own agendas and fallibilities. As Thomas et al. continue, '[s]ources and archives are neither neutral nor natural. They are created. It is this that is the reason for so many silences. Archival creation is, of course, a human process'.[49] Such tensions can also lead to what Simon Fowler has referred to as a history of 'enforced silences',[50] where associations between utopia and institutional incarceration run deep.[51] It is no coincidence that in nineteenth-century British colonial prisons, concentration camps and residential schools, hymn singing at chapel services was mandatory (a practice in line with Victorian schools, that still continues, somewhat controversially, in many British schools today),[52] and framed as a wholly moral pursuit.[53]

Becca Whitla's concept of 'hymnic coloniality'[54] is a useful way to navigate the kinds of sonic gaps that are left in a Foucauldian discourse of carceral biopolitical power, particularly within post/colonial contexts.⁵⁵ Moreover, it is worth remembering that many of the early biopolitical initiatives of 'concentration' were originally framed as so-called protective measures: as Laleh Khalili notes, concentration camps, first used by the Spanish, British and US militaries in Cuba, South Africa and the Philippines, were 'originally conceived as mechanisms for removing the civilians from a battlefield, the entirety of the countryside, thus allowing maximum firepower to the conquering European armies'.⁵⁶ With regard to the Canadian context, Jennifer Graber argues that the incarceration of Indigenous subjects was framed within a series of theological justifications, and that imprisonment was thought of as a compassionate, reformative activity, where Indigenous American inmates singing hymns was offered up as an example of benevolent incarceration.⁵⁷

The colonial hymn thus functioned in these carceral contexts as an ostensibly 'protective' framing device: it silenced Indigeneity under the guise of humanitarian benevolence. Music as a means of initiating mandatory colonial 'congregation' in this way also reinforces Nemser's claim that concentration operates as 'the enabling ground for racialization'.⁵⁸ As Nemser elaborates, 'concentration literally emerges through the construction of a colonial "peace"'.⁵⁹ In this formulation, spaces of colonial enclosure, even those resulting in genocide, were framed under an imperial veneer of 'peace'. If Victorian hymn singing represented conformity and social harmony, then it was an ideal way to 'silence' Indigeneity within carceral spaces: its fragmented existence in colonial archives in the form of hymn books and mandatory singing timetables therefore implies a benign and co-operative soundscape that enclosed, and curated, an ideological edifice of administrative innocence. Rather than covering up the coercive use of the hymn, then, the settler colonial archive implies a righteous belief that silencing Indigenous languages through singing English-language hymns was right, and even necessary, for the success of empire. If the archive of colonial hymnody shielded and protected carceral institutions from being culpable of musical coercion, then by extension sonic 'disclosures' need to come to terms with their archival omissions. A significant obstacle here is that of language: while a lot of hymns were translated into Indigenous languages by nineteenth-century British missionaries, the hymn in the context of residential schools was sung in English, necessarily reflecting what Whitla has described as an '(English) coloniality – the all-encompassing residual web of colonizing processes, tendencies, and practices',⁶⁰ a phenomenon she refers to as 'musicoloniality'.⁶¹

Canadian residential schools therefore created a context where Christian rituals, presented as being fulfilling and redemptive, were detrimental to the Indigenous students' understanding of their own languages and musical cultures. As Johnson notes, rituals of hymn singing in Canadian residential schools 'embodied disciplines that functioned as technologies of power, self, and community'.⁶² Whitla, moreover, characterizes hymn singing in the residential schools as an example of 'a cultural-genocidal project of "taking the Indian out of the child"'.⁶³ Searching for agency within this history is complex. As Diamond recounts, in examining the 'historical record' for the 'multiple functions – oppressive, assimilative, or resistant – that music served within the schools', she found that '[a]gency is prominent ... but includes the agency of several different players: the Canadian government, church authorities, teachers and IRS [Indian Residential Schools] administrators, and the children themselves'.[64]

I argue that hymn singing is a potentially flexible enough genre to create a way to explore multiple forms of resistance to colonial carceral institutions. While the teachers and administrators would have brought their own associations of 'hymnic coloniality' to the residential schools, students may have engaged with Christian hymnody to varying degrees later in life, or not at all. More complex are historical moments where a hymn text or tune was composed within a context of limited agency. As Volume 1 of the 2015 Canadian TRC report noted with regard to the residential schools, '[i]n the classroom, Aboriginal children were given a constant drilling in English, and spent much of their time memorizing and reciting religious texts and hymns'.[65] The same TRC report also describes an Indigenous student, renamed Henry Budd (first taken into the residential school system in the 1820s), who wrote the text of a hymn 'with a verse that reflected both his new language proficiency and the new attitude he had been encouraged to develop towards his own native culture':

> Oh let a vain and thoughtless race,
> Thy pardning [sic.] mercy prove;
> Begin betimes to seek thy face
> And thy commandments love.[66]

Effectively, the TRC report created a new, postcolonial archive in which materials such as hymns are given space and recontextualization. The supervised inscription in Budd's text of directing one's own 'vain and thoughtless race' towards the 'pardning [sic.] mercy' of a benevolent Christian God is in line with the silencing structures of the settler colonial archive. The TRC report also revealed the ubiquity of hymn singing as a structural device within a carceral environment, providing the following description of how time was ordered and punctuated by hymn-singing on a daily basis. Quoting from a Methodist report given about the school at Mount Elgin in 1914:

> The bell rings at 5 a.m. when the children rise, wash, dress and are made ready for breakfast. At 5:30 they breakfast; after which they all assemble in the last schoolroom and unite in reading the Scriptures, singing and prayer. From 6–9 a.m. the boys are employed and taught to work on the farm, and the girls in the house. At 9, they enter their schools. At 12 they dine and spend the remaining time till one in recreation. At one they enter school, where they are taught till 3:30, after which they resume their manual employment till six. At six, they sup and again unite in reading the Scriptures, singing and prayer. In the winter season, the boys are engaged in the Evening school and girls are taught needle-work until 9, when all retire to rest. They are never left alone, but are constantly under the eye of some of those engaged in this arduous work.[67]

In this timetable, communal Scripture reading, singing and prayer punctuate the school day. Taking the TRC's report as an archive of how sound was manipulated to be a disciplinary tool, hymn singing plays the role of a structural device of sounding *and* silencing that is both benevolent and corrective.

Listening, liberating and re-archiving

Looking forward to how the legacies of nineteenth-century sonic archives have impacted more recent calls for decolonization in the twentieth and twenty-first centuries, it is worth noting that the Canadian TRC report is relatively unique for the depth of its historical remit. In the twentieth century perhaps the most famous Truth and Reconciliation Commission was initiated in South Africa in 1995. While the South African TRC focused primarily on the twentieth-century events of Apartheid, the legacies of nineteenth-century colonial atrocities were left relatively untouched. As Dirkie Smit and Elna Mouton claim, therefore, the 'sufferings with which the Truth and Reconciliation Commission had to deal were, to a large extent, caused by the fact that the sufferings of the Anglo-Boer War had not been dealt with adequately'.[68] In other words, nineteenth-century archival silences are still shaping decolonial attempts to re-archive post/colonial trauma. Further, the structures of racialized carceral 'encampment' that were normalized in nineteenth-century South Africa naturally influenced the institutionalization of racial separatism that would pervade South Africa for much of the twentieth century.[69]

I have examined elsewhere how the tensions between Dutch and English-language hymn singing created spaces for theological and racial negotiation in the concentration camps of the South African War (1899–1902).[70] In these carceral spaces, where the British set up separate camps for white (then 'Boer'; now 'Afrikaner') and Black inmates, I hold that hymn singing was used as a way to establish colonial rivalry between the British and Afrikaner soldiers and civilians, and, as British missionaries were often more evangelical in spreading the genre of hymn singing to Black South Africans, the sonic vestiges of colonial concentration camp musicality largely equated Black hymn singing in South Africa with an allegiance to English, rather than Dutch, hymnic traditions.[71] The ways in which missionary hymns have been translated and reclaimed by Black South Africans during the Apartheid era have largely been framed as a positive narrative about Black musical agency within a context of postcolonial resistance.[72] Yet, drawing on Smit and Mouton's claim that the South African TRC did not reckon with (or, effectively, provide an 'archive of') the nineteenth-century legacies of trauma and suffering that had created such entrenched racial cultures of separation and incarceration in the first place, the fact that Nelson Mandela sang hymns in prison as a means of expressing personal faith and solidarity for Black resistance also speaks to a silenced history of sonic incarceration and colonial hymnic appropriation that predates the Apartheid era.[73]

Many of the existing records of South African concentration camps reveal, firstly, that hymn singing is primarily given archival space in relation to 'white' carceral subjects.[74] A lot of this is due to the fact that interest in the camps from within Britain was largely generated by concern over the considerable number of 'Boer' women and children who were starving in the camps, spawning wide press coverage about the unprecedented scale of white suffering – even if the 'Boers' were, like the Irish, generally regarded in Britain as a degenerate white race.[75] By contrast, very little coverage or military history at the time gave attention to the Black concentration camps.[76] In terms of available information on music in the camps, by extension, while there are numerous references to and descriptions of the prevalence (both positive and negative) of Dutch psalm and hymn-singing within the white camps, virtually no archive exists for Black hymn singing within colonial carceral spaces.[77] This is a striking archival silence, considering the prevalence of hymn singing on South African mission stations throughout the nineteenth century, and the rich traditions of Black South African sacred choralism that were already pervasive during the war.[78]

It is compelling to think about TRC reports worldwide as a powerful form of decolonial 're-archiving' of the systemic imbalances, exclusions and absences of the nineteenth-century archive.[79] Indeed, the growth of TRC movements since the late twentieth century provides a unique opportunity for a critical 'listening' to nineteenth-century archival silences as a way to generate new modes of hearing the past. In the South African TRC reports, for example, hymn singing in spaces of Apartheid imprisonment acts as a way of 'sounding' many of the same ambiguities of oppression and resistance that can be read into the accounts of Canadian residential schools, despite the differences in context. As Volume 3 of the South African TRC recounts, one of the witnesses who had been imprisoned, a Mr Mopeloa, told the Commission that while he was being tortured:

> They said I should sing and I was singing a song 'God we praise you', and they put a hose-pipe in my mouth, they said 'You are singing nonsense, why don't you sing the Mandela song, we want to listen to that' ... I said to them, 'I do not have an idea of what you are talking about, I can't even sing those songs'. They forced me to sing and I kept on singing the hymns.[80]

In this account Mr Mopeloa's torturers, who try to coerce him into performing 'Mandela' freedom songs, attempt to rob him of any musical agency. Instead, he resists, by continuing to sing the hymns that he wants to sing, although he has already been accused of 'singing nonsense'. What is notable here is that the Victorian imperial construction of hymns as a 'benevolent' form of discipline has been effectively 're-archived' and 're-sounded' as Black resistance *to* carceral space: an imperial musical structure once justified as a 'compassionate' way to silence Indigenous musical traditions is now reframed through the TRC archives as the very solace that helps prisoners endure their incarceration. As one TRC testimonial described the conditions on Death Row at Pretoria Maximum Security Prison, those sentenced to death were sent to the 'Pot', where 'the traditional silence of Death Row was broken – with singing day and night. Singing mostly of traditional and religious hymns but sometimes of freedom songs'.[81] Further examples abound of protesters being shot and killed while singing hymns and protest songs.[82]

In the re-archiving of these accounts, I suggest that the postcolonial hymn *can* be become newly reconfigured as musical resistance once it has exited the nineteenth-century carceral framework. The fact that the 'Black' hymn, by the late twentieth century, was such a powerful tool for protest that it no longer 'belonged' to white structures of disciplinary enclosure is perhaps one explanation for why written accounts of Black hymn singing in the concentration camps of the South African War are so rare, compared to the re-archiving of the hymn as a form of Black expressive agency during and since the anti-Apartheid movement. In Canada, too, singing has been at the forefront of recent attempts at reconciliation and reparation for victims of the residential schools.[83] Such powerful attempts at filling archival voids with songs not only reveal the limitations of the colonial archives that have silenced or downplayed the role of singing for processing trauma, but they also speak to a powerful reframing of the Victorian hymn as a revitalizing decolonial genre that, once sounded, will reshape the legacies of 'who' gets to speak (or sing) out against (and within) violent spaces.

The idea of the subaltern singing back against the empire is what Whitla calls the 'flipping' of hymns to take forms ranging from 'a subtle act of subversion or a direct act of defiance.'[84] What exact forms a decolonial archiving of musical sound will take in the future remains to be seen, for in one sense to archive (or, returning to the carceral metaphor, to 'enclose') sound is to colonize it. Conversely, to forget, or to erase, the silencing properties of the nineteenth-century archive from postcolonial musical experience is to obstruct the possibility of sonic liberation. To return once more to la paperson's concept of 'technologies of indigenous erasure,'[85] it is worth considering where a decolonial fracture in the musical archives of settler colonialism can most effectively happen. In the context of the Canadian residential schools, English-language hymn singing violently erased Indigenous identity; in the South African prisons, a reappropriated and arguably decolonial form of hymn singing challenged the white prison guard's unsuccessful attempts to frame 'Mandela's' songs as a mode of performative torture. Perhaps to liberate and decolonize the sound of colonial incarceration is, ultimately, to come to terms with how many of the silences of the nineteenth-century archive are, ultimately, the loudest moments of all.

Acknowledgements

Research for this chapter is a part of a larger project funded by a Leverhulme Early Career Fellowship grant. Special thanks must go to my co-editor Rachel Bryant Davies, for such thoughtful support as my ideas for this piece developed. Bennett Zon, Tim Barringer and Kamala Schelling also provided writing feedback on earlier drafts.

Notes

1   The impulse in musicology to focus on what has been *sounded* and *written about*, rather than what has been *silenced* and *not written about*, is of course understandable, but perhaps it goes part of the way to explaining why historical musicology (as opposed to ethnomusicology) has been relatively slow to engage with decolonial conversations. Coming to terms with what has been silenced also directly challenges the all-too-often-nostalgic 'sounding' of much-loved musical repertoires, creating what William Fourie

has referred to as a 'cultural amnesia' in Britain and in British musicology about the existence of the empire. See William Fourie, 'Musicology and Decolonial Analysis in the Age of Brexit', *Twentieth-Century Music* 17. 2 (2020): 197–211. Relatedly, on the institutional barriers to decolonization in musicological institutions in North America, see Tamara Levitz, 'The Musicological Elite', *Current Musicology* 102 (2018): 9–80.

2   The growing academic literature that addresses the systemic effects of 'archival silencing' includes, but is not limited to: Saidiya Hartman, 'Venus in Two Acts', *Small Axe* 26 (2008): 1–14; and *Scenes of Subjection: Terror, Slavery, and Self-Making in Nineteenth-Century America* (New York and Oxford: Oxford University Press, 1997); Christina Sharpe, *In the Wake: On Blackness and Being* (Durham: Duke University Press, 2016); David Thomas, Simon Fowler, and Valerie Johnson (eds), *The Silence of the Archive* (Chicago: Neal-Schuman, 2017); Evelyn Araluen Corr, 'Silence and Resistance: Aboriginal Women Working Within and Against the Archive', *Journal of Media & Cultural Studies* 32. 4 (2018): 487–502; Carolyn Steedman, *Dust: The Archive and Cultural History* (New Brunswick: Rutgers University Press, 2002); and 'After the Archive', *Comparative Critical Studies* 8. 2–3 (2011): 321–40; and Ann Laura Stoler, *Along the Archival Grain: Epistemic Anxieties and Colonial Common Sense* (Princeton and Oxford: Princeton University Press, 2009).

3   I understand the concept of 'enclosure' to refer to both incarceration and salvationist, paternalistic discourses of imperialism that saw the carceral institution as not just disciplinary but 'humanitarian' and 'benevolent' as well. Aidan Forth has compellingly drawn parallels between the so-called 'humanitarian' justifications for the concentration camps that the British set up during the South African War and broader rationalizations for carceral enclosure as part of an ethical, liberal humanitarianism. See Aidan Forth, *Barbed-Wire Imperialism: Britain's Empire of Camps, 1876–1903* (Oakland: University of California Press, 2017).

4   On the British colonial hymn as a tool for conversion and control, see Charles McGuire, 'Christianity, Civilization and Music: Nineteenth-Century British Missionaries and the Control of Malagasy Hymnology', in Martin Clarke (ed.), *Music and Theology in Nineteenth-Century Britain* (Burlington: Ashgate, 2012), pp. 79–96; Grant Olwage, 'Scriptions of the Choral: The Historiography of Black South African Choralism', *SAMUS: South African Journal of Musicology* 22. 1 (2002): 29–45; and 'Discipline and Choralism: The Birth of Musical Colonialism', in Annie J. Randall (ed.), *Music, Power, and Politics* (London: Routledge, 2004), pp. 25–46.

5   Musicology is increasingly making room for empire and postcolonialism: see, for example, Jeffrey Richards, *Imperialism and Music: Britain, 1876–1953* (Manchester: Manchester University Press, 2017); and Ronald Radano and Tejumola Olaniyan (eds), *Audible Empire: Music, Global Politics, Critique* (Durham: Duke University Press, 2016). Studies of the hymn as a signifier of cultural and stylistic ideology are very recent but are gradually gaining traction; see, for example, Kofi Agawu, 'Tonality as a Colonizing Force in Africa', in Ronald Radano and Tejumola Olaniyan (eds), *Audible Empire: Music, Global Politics, Critique* (Durham: Duke University Press, 2016), pp. 334–55; *Representing African Music: Postcolonial Notes, Queries, Positions* (New York and London: Routledge, 2003); Becca Whitla, *Liberation, (De)Coloniality, and Liturgical Practices: Flipping the Song Bird* (Basingstoke: Palgrave Macmillan, 2020); and Laura Rademaker, *Found in Translation: Many Meanings on a North Australian Mission* (Honolulu: University of Hawai'i Press, 2018).

6   On the strong associations in nineteenth-century Britain between hymns and children (and by extension, the children of empire), see Alisa Clapp-Itnyre, *British Hymn Books for Children, 1800–1900: Re-Tuning the History of Childhood* (Farnham: Ashgate, 2016).

7   The potential for hymn singing to express and enact postcolonial liberation has recently been explored by Whitla, *Liberation, (De)Coloniality*.
8   Michel Foucault most famously discussed the concept of biopower, or the 'administration of life', in *The History of Sexuality: An Introduction, Vol. 1*, translated by R. Hurley (New York: Random House: 1978). In bringing Foucault's Eurocentric discussions of biopolitical enclosure into dialogue with post/colonial contexts, where I expand the notion of 'the human' to one that was heavily racialized in nineteenth-century carceral spaces, I have drawn heavily upon Alison Howell and Melanie Richter-Montpetit, 'Racism in Foucauldian Security Studies: Biopolitics, Liberal War, and the Whitewashing of Colonial and Racial Violence', *International Political Sociology* 13 (2019): 2–19.
9   Amber Bracken, 'Canada Pledges $31.5 Billion to Settle Fight over Indigenous Child Welfare System', *The New York Times* (5 January 2022), https://www.nytimes.com/2022/01/04/world/canada/canada-indigenous-children-settlement.html, accessed 13 January 2022.
10 See Sarah Kathleen Johnson, 'On Our Knees: Christian Ritual in Residential Schools and the Truth and Reconciliation Commission of Canada', *Studies in Religion* 47. 1 (2019), p. 5.
11 David Stirrup and James Mackey, 'The Toxic Legacy of the British Empire in Canada's Residential Schools', https://www.theguardian.com/world/2021/jul/02/the-toxic-legacy-of-the-british-empire-in-canadas-residential-schools, accessed 17 August 2021. See also BBC News, 'Canada: 751 Unmarked Graves Found at Residential School', https://www.bbc.co.uk/news/world-us-canada-57592243, accessed 5 August 2021; The Economist, 'What Happened at Residential Schools for Indigenous Children in North America?', https://www.economist.com/the-economist-explains/2021/07/26/what-happened-at-residential-schools-for-indigenous-children-in-north-america, accessed 5 August 2021; Paula Newton, 'More Unmarked Graves Discovered in British Columbia', https://edition.cnn.com/2021/07/13/americas/canada-unmarked-indigenous-graves/index.html, accessed 5 August 2021; and Ian Austen, 'How Thousands of Indigenous Children Vanished in Canada', https://www.nytimes.com/2021/06/07/world/canada/mass-graves-residential-schools.html, accessed 5 August 2021. References to spaces of colonial incarceration are also made in the chapters by Roisín Laing and Jemima Short in this volume.
12 See Andrew Porter, '"Cultural Imperialism" and Protestant Missionary Enterprise, 1780–1914', *The Journal of Imperial and Commonwealth History* 25. 3 (1997): 367–91.
13 BBC News, 'Canada: 751 Unmarked Graves'.
14 See Eric Hanson, Daniel P. Games, and Alexa Manuel, 'The Residential School System', *Indigenous Foundations*, https://indigenousfoundations.arts.ubc.ca/residential-school-system-2020/, accessed 17 August 2021.
15 As quoted in Truth and Reconciliation Commission, *Canada's Residential Schools: The History, Part 1: Origins to 1939, Volume 1* (Montreal, Kingston, London and Chicago: Published for the Truth and Reconciliation Commission by McGill-Queen's University Press, 2015), p. 79.
16 For example, singing as a form of communal solidarity has been well-documented with regard to Victorian mass choral movements: see Charles McGuire, *Music and Victorian Philanthropy: The Tonic Sol-fa Movement* (Cambridge: Cambridge University Press, 2009). On the communal protest singing of the anti-Apartheid movement, see Omoyato Jolaosho, 'Singing Politics: Freedom Songs and Collective Protest in Post-Apartheid South Africa', *African Studies Review* 62. 2 (2019): 6–29.

See also Mark Malisa and Nandipha Malange, 'Songs for Freedom: Music and the Struggle against Apartheid', in Jonathan C. Friedman (ed.), *The Routledge History of Social Protest in Popular Music* (New York: Routledge, 2013), pp. 304–18.

17 See Erin Johnson-Williams, 'Singing, Suffering and Liberation in the Concentration Camps of the South African War', in Esther Morgan-Ellis and Kay Norton (eds), *The Oxford Handbook of Community Singing* (forthcoming, Oxford University Press, 2023).

18 For example, singing has been a fundamental tool for trauma recovery in initiatives to help former students of the Canadian residential schools process their experiences. In a poignant 2015 BBC video on the Canadian victims, a former student ended his interview by singing a First Nations song in his Indigenous language, as a symbol of moving forward. See Micah Luxen, 'Survivors of Canada's "Cultural Genocide" Still Healing', https://www.bbc.co.uk/news/magazine-33001425, accessed 17 August 2021. On the South African context, see Omotayo Jolaosho, 'Political Aesthetics and Embodiment: Sung Protest in Post-Apartheid South Africa', *Journal of Material Culture* 20. 4 (2015): 443–58.

19 On the tensions between music, race and archival silences, see Janet Topp Fargion, 'African Music in the World and Traditional Music Section at the British Library Sound Archive', *History in Africa* 31 (2004): 447–54; and Alessandra Raengo and Lauren McLeod Cramer, 'The Unruly Archives of Black Music Videos', *Journal of Cinema and Media Studies* 59. 2 (2020): 138–44. See also Thomas et al., *Silence of the Archive*, pp. 5–6.

20 'A Hope of Meeting You in Another World', *Anne With an E*, Season 3, Episode 4, CBC Television, 13 October 2019. *Netflix*, https://www.netflix.com/search?q=anne%20with%20an%20e&jbv=80136311, accessed 18 August 2021.

21 Ibid.

22 It is worth noting that while hymns have received substantial coverage in scholarship on theology and congregational worship music, including topics of de/colonization, there has yet to be a sustained incorporation of colonial hymns in the discipline of 'historical musicology', where they could be studied alongside genres such as symphonies, string quartets and operas; there is also room for the congregational studies scholarship to engage more specifically with historical legacies of contemporary traditions. For example, hymnody as a practice is virtually absent (as is empire and colonialism) from the landmark 'music history' textbooks such as Richard Taruskin, *The Oxford History of Western Music*, 5 vols. (Oxford: Oxford University Press, 2005); and J. Peter Burkholder, Donald J. Grout and Claude V. Palisca, *A History of Western Music* (New York: W. W. Norton, 2010). For key concepts in hymnody and congregational music studies, see the essays in Monique M. Ingalls, Carolyn Landau and Tom Wagner (eds), *Christian Congregational Music: Performance, Identity and Experience* (London: Routledge, 2013); and Andrew Mall, Jeffers Engelhardt and Monique M. Ingalls (eds), *Studying Congregational Music: Key Issues, Methods, and Theoretical Perspectives* (London: Routledge, 2021).

23 'A Hope of Meeting You in Another World'.

24 See, for example, Tara Grier, '"Anne With an E" Acknowledges Indigenous Residential Schools in New Episodes', *The Whit Online*, https://thewhitonline.com/2019/10/arts-entertainment/anne-with-an-e-acknowledges-indigenous-residential-schools-in-new-episodes/, accessed 18 August 2019; and Amala Reddie, 'Anne With An E: A Reflection on Representation', https://cambridgeeditors.wordpress.com/2020/09/04/anne-with-an-e-a-reflection-on-representation/, accessed 18 August 2021.

25 As the famous twentieth-century musicologist Carl Dahlhaus noted, a 'neglect of the text' was at the cornerstone of western Romantic musical aesthetics during the nineteenth century, which had devastating consequences for the historiography of vocal traditions, because the assumption was that 'great' music was without text. As a consequence, historical musicology is still catching up in terms of writing a history of nineteenth-century sung traditions. Carl Dahlhaus, *Nineteenth-Century Music*, translated by J. Bradford Robinson (Berkeley: University of California Press, 1989), p. 5. By implication, this 'neglect of text' also led to an internalized assumption that the 'greatness' of western art music could not really be archived (despite the rise in the nineteenth century of a fetishization of the printed score).

26 Beverley Diamond, 'The Doubleness of Sound in Canada's Indian Residential Schools', in Victoria Lindsay Levine and Philip V. Bohlman (eds), *This Thing Called Music: Essays in Honor of Bruno Nettl* (Lanham: Rowman & Littlefield, 2015), pp. 267–79.

27 Ibid., p. 267.

28 Ibid., p. 272.

29 For further reading, particularly on the idea of music as a form of civilization in colonial contexts, see Veit Erlmann, '"Africa Civilised, Africa Uncivilised": Local Culture, World System and South African Music', *Journal of Southern African Studies* 20. 2 (1994): 165–79.

30 See Philip Burnett, Erin Johnson-Williams, and Yvonne Liao, 'Music, Empire, Colonialism: Sounding the Archives: Introduction', *Postcolonial Studies* (forthcoming, 2022).

31 I am referring here to what Saidiya Hartman has called the 'romance' of trying to construct resurrected narratives of resistance from marginalized voices: Hartman, 'Venus in Two Acts', p. 9.

32 This trend has arguably taken off more in ethnomusicology than in historical musicology, and the integration of conversations about decolonization between these two subdisciplines is certainly a pressing issue. For calls towards decolonial 'soundings' in ethnomusicology, see Elizabeth Mackinlay, 'Decolonization and Applied Ethnomusicology: "Story-ing" the Personal-Political-Possible in Our Work', in Svanibor Pettan and Jeff Todd Titon (eds), the *Oxford Handbook of Applied Ethnomusicology* (Oxford: Oxford University Press, 2015). https://doi.org/10.1093/oxfordhb/9780199351701.013.14.

33 See Suzanne G. Cusick, '"You Are in a Place That Is Out of the World … "': Music in the Detention Camps of the 'Global War on Terror', *Journal of the Society for American Music* 2. 1 (2008): 1–26.

34 For further reading see Britta Lange, 'Archival Silences as Historical Silences', *SoundEffects* 7. 3 (2017): 47–60.

35 Chris Waller, '"Darker Than the Dungeon": Music, Ambivalence, and the Carceral Subject', *International Journal of the Semiotics of Law* 31 (2018): 275–99.

36 Ibid., p. 281.

37 Ibid.

38 Ibid.

39 Agawu, 'Tonality as a Colonizing Force', pp. 334–55.

40 la paperson, *A Third University Is Possible* (Minneapolis: University of Minnesota Press, 2017), p. 11.

41 Ibid., pp. 11, xiii.

42 See Grant Olwage, 'John Knox Bokwe, Colonial Composer: Tales about Race and Music', *Journal of the Royal Musical Association* 131 (2006): 1–37.
43 Michel-Rolph Trouillot, *Silencing the Past: Power and the Production of History* (Boston: Beacon, 1995).
44 Daniel Nemser, *Infrastructures of Race: Concentration and Biopolitics in Colonial Mexico* (University of Texas Press, 2017), p. 17. Emphasis original.
45 Ibid.
46 I have used 'sounding into disappearance' here in relation to the phrase 'writing into disappearance', which has been used by Bryanne Young, 'Killing the Indian in the Child: Materialities of Death and Political Formations of Life in the Canadian Indian Residential School System', (PhD: University of North Carolina at Chapel Hill, 2017), p. iv. Another scholar who uses the phrase 'writing into disappearance' is William Viney, 'T. S. Eliot and the Textualities of the Discarded', *Textual Practice* 28. 6 (2014), p. 1071.
47 Young, 'Killing the Indian', p. 32. Emphasis original.
48 Thomas et al., *Silence of the Archive*, p. xvi.
49 Ibid., pp. 1–2.
50 Ibid.
51 See Andrew Scull (ed.), *The Asylum as Utopia: W. A. F. Browne and the Mid-Nineteenth Century Consolidation of Psychiatry* (London: Routledge, 1991).
52 The singing of hymns in Church of England schools in Britain today has received criticism and backlash, reflecting controversies over religious traditionalism versus secularism. See, for example, Nicola Woolcock and Kaya Burgess, 'Don't Sing Hymns That Are Too Preachy, Church of England Schools Told', https://www.thetimes.co.uk/article/dont-sing-hymns-that-are-too-preachy-church-of-england-schools-told-h6b6f69b3, accessed 18 August 2021.
53 Relatedly, see Rosemary Golding, '"Appeasing the Unstrung Mental Faculties": Listening to Music in Nineteenth-Century Lunatic Asylums', *Nineteenth-Century Music Review* 17. 3 (2020): 403–25. See also Alan Maddox, 'On the Machinery of Moral Improvement: Music and Prison Reform in the Penal Colony on Norfolk Island', *Musicology Australia* 34. 2 (2012): 185–205; Helen Rogers, 'Singing at Yarmouth Gaol: Christian Instruction and Inmate Culture in the Nineteenth Century', *Prison Service Journal* 199 (2011): 35–43; and Janice Schroeder, 'Inside Voice: Talk, Silence, and Resistance in the Victorian Prison', *Victorian Review* 46. 1 (2020): 9–13.
54 On 'hymnic Coloniality', see Whitla, *Liberation, (De)Coloniality*, pp. 94–110.
55 A useful example here, although it does not focus on music, is Teresa Dirsuweit, 'Carceral Spaces in South Africa: A Case Study of Institutional Power, Sexuality and Transgression in a Women's Prison', *Geoforum* 30. 1 (1999): 71–83.
56 Laleh Khalili, *Time in Shadows: Confinement in Counterinsurgencies* (Stanford: Stanford University Press), p. 174. See also Klaus Mühlhahn, 'The Concentration Camp in Global Historical Perspective', *History Compass* 8. 6 (2010): 543–61.
57 Jennifer Graber, 'Natives Need Prison: The Sanctification of Racialized Incarceration', *Religions* 10 (2019), p. 3.
58 Nemser, *Infrastructures of Race*, p. 168.
59 Ibid.
60 Whitla, *Liberation, (De)Coloniality*, p. 79.
61 Ibid., p. 80.
62 Johnson, 'On Our Knees', p. 3.

63   Whitla, *Liberation, (De)Coloniality*, p. 118.
64   Diamond, 'Doubleness of Sound', p. 270.
65   Truth and Reconciliation Commission, *Canada's Residential Schools*, p. 86.
66   A hymn text written by an Indigenous student in a Canadian Residential School. As quoted in Truth and Reconciliation Commission, *Canada's Residential Schools*, p. 86.
67   Ibid., p. 79.
68   Dirkie Smit and Elna Mouton, 'Shared Stories for the Future? Theological Reflections on Truth and Reconciliation in South Africa', *Journal of Reformed Theology* 2 (2008), p. 41.
69   Ibid.
70   Johnson-Williams, 'Singing, Suffering and Liberation'.
71   Ibid.
72   See Omoyato. 'Singing Politics', pp. 6–29.
73   Smit and Mouton, 'Shared Stories', 41. See also Johann S. Buis, 'Music and Dance Make Me Feel Alive: From Mandela's Prison Songs and Dances to Public Policy', *Torture* 23. 2 (2013): 55–67.
74   For example, see the focus on white subjects in Anne-Marie Gray, 'Vocal Music of the Anglo-Boer War (1899–1902): Insights into Processes of Affect and Meaning in Music' (PhD: University of Pretoria, 2004).
75   See Van Wyk Smith, 'The Boers and the Anglo-Boer War (1899–1902) in the Twentieth-Century Moral Imaginary', *Victorian Literature and Culture* 31. 2 (2003): 429–46.
76   See, for example, the lack of archiving of Black experience in histories compiled at the time, such as Richard Danes, *Cassell's History of the Boer War, 1899–1902* (London: Cassell, 1902).
77   Even in the subsequent rise of scholarship on Black experience and the war, music is notably absent: see, for example, Peter Warwick, *Black People and the South African War, 1899–1902* (Cambridge: Cambridge University Press, 1983); and Bill Nasson, *Abraham Esau's War: A Black South African War in the Cape, 1899–1902* (Cambridge: Cambridge University Press, 1991).
78   On Black chroralism in South Africa, see Olwage, 'Scriptions of the Choral', pp. 29–45. On hymns and South African mission stations see Philip Burnett, 'Music and Mission: A Case Study of the Anglican-Xhosa Missions of the Eastern Cape, 1854–1880' (PhD: University of Bristol, 2020).
79   For further reading, see Antjie Krog and Nosisi Mpolweni, 'Archived Voices: Refiguring Three Women's Testimonies Delivered to the South African Truth and Reconciliation Commission', *Tulsa Studies in Women's Literature* 28. 2 (2009): 357–74.
80   Truth and Reconciliation Commission of South Africa, *Truth and Reconciliation Commission of South Africa Report* Volume 3 (1998), https://www.justice.gov.za/trc/report/finalreport/Volume%203.pdf, p. 619.
81   Truth and Reconciliation Commission of South Africa, *Truth and Reconciliation Commission of South Africa Report* Volume 4 (1998), https://www.justice.gov.za/trc/report/finalreport/Volume%204.pdf, p. 214.
82   See Truth and Reconciliation Commission of South Africa, *Truth and Reconciliation Commission of South Africa Report* Volume 7 (1998), https://www.justice.gov.za/trc/report/finalreport/victims_10to300_vol7.pdf.
83   Luxen, 'Survivors of Canada's "Cultural Genocide"'.
84   Whitla, *Liberation, (De)Coloniality*, p. 126.
85   la paperson, *A Third University*, p. 11.

Bibliography

Agawu, Kofi. *Representing African Music: Postcolonial Notes, Queries, Positions*. New York and London: Routledge, 2003.

Agawu, Kofi. 'Tonality as a Colonizing Force in Africa'. In *Audible Empire: Music, Global Politics, Critique*, edited by Ronald Radano and Tejumola Olaniyan, 334–55. Durham: Duke University Press, 2016.

Austen, Ian. 'How Thousands of Indigenous Children Vanished in Canada'. https://www.nytimes.com/2021/06/07/world/canada/mass-graves-residential-schools.html. Accessed 5 August 2021.

BBC News. 'Canada: 751 Unmarked Graves Found at Residential School'. https://www.bbc.co.uk/news/world-us-canada-57592243. Accessed 5 August 2021.

Bracken, Amber. 'Canada Pledges $31.5 Billion to Settle Fight over Indigenous Child Welfare System'. *The New York Times* (5 January 2022). https://www.nytimes.com/2022/01/04/world/canada/canada-indigenous-children-settlement.html. Accessed 13 January 2022.

Buis, Johann S. 'Music and Dance Make Me Feel Alive: From Mandela's Prison Songs and Dances to Public Policy'. *Torture* 23, no. 2 (2013): 55–67.

Burkholder, J. Peter, Donald J. Grout and Claude V. Palisca. *A History of Western Music*. New York: W. W. Norton, 2010.

Burnett, Philip. 'Music and Mission: A Case Study of the Anglican-Xhosa Missions of the Eastern Cape, 1854–1880'. PhD: University of Bristol, 2020.

Burnett, Philip, Erin Johnson-Williams, and Yvonne Liao. 'Music, Empire, Colonialism: Sounding the Archives: Introduction'. *Postcolonial Studies* (forthcoming, 2022).

Clapp-Itnyre, Alisa. *British Hymn Books for Children, 1800–1900: Re-Tuning the History of Childhood*. Farnham: Ashgate, 2016.

Corr, Evelyn Araluen. 'Silence and Resistance: Aboriginal Women Working within and Against the Archive'. *Journal of Media & Cultural Studies* 32, no. 4 (2018): 487–502.

Cusick, Suzanne G. '"You Are in a Place That is Out of the World ... ": Music in the Detention Camps of the "Global War on Terror"'. *Journal of the Society for American Music* 2, no. 1 (2008): 1–26.

Dahlhaus, Carl. *Nineteenth-Century Music*, translated by J. Bradford Robinson. Berkeley: University of California Press, 1989.

Danes, Richard. *Cassell's History of the Boer War, 1899–1902*. London: Cassell, 1902.

Dirsuweit, Teresa. 'Carceral Spaces in South Africa: A Case Study of Institutional Power, Sexuality and Transgression in a Women's Prison'. *Geoforum* 30, no. 1 (1999): 71–83.

The Economist. 'What Happened at Residential Schools for Indigenous Children in North America?'. https://www.economist.com/the-economist-explains/2021/07/26/what-happened-at-residential-schools-for-indigenous-children-in-north-america. Accessed 5 August 2021.

Erlmann, Veit. '"Africa Civilised, Africa Uncivilised": Local Culture, World System and South African Music'. *Journal of Southern African Studies* 20, no. 2 (1994): 165–79.

Fargion, Janet Topp. 'African Music in the World and Traditional Music Section at the British Library Sound Archive'. *History in Africa* 31 (2004): 447–54.

Forth, Aidan. *Barbed-Wire Imperialism: Britain's Empire of Camps, 1876–1903*. Oakland: University of California Press, 2017.

Foucault, Michel. *The History of Sexuality: An Introduction, Vol. 1*, translated by R. Hurley. New York: Random House: 1978.

Fourie, William. 'Musicology and Decolonial Analysis in the Age of Brexit'. *Twentieth-Century Music* 17, no. 2 (2020): 197–211.

Graber, Jennifer. 'Natives Need Prison: The Sanctification of Racialized Incarceration'. *Religions* 10 (2019): 1–12.

Gray, Anne-Marie. 'Vocal Music of the Anglo-Boer War (1899–1902): Insights into Processes of Affect and Meaning in Music'. PhD: University of Pretoria, 2004.

Grier, Tara, '"Anne With an E" Acknowledges Indigenous Residential Schools in New Episodes'. *The Whit Online*. https://thewhitonline.com/2019/10/arts-entertainment/anne-with-an-e-acknowledges-indigenous-residential-schools-in-new-episodes/. Accessed 18 August 2019.

Golding, Rosemary. '"Appeasing the Unstrung Mental Faculties": Listening to Music in Nineteenth-Century Lunatic Asylums'. *Nineteenth-Century Music Review* 17, no. 3 (2020): 403–25.

Hanson, Eric, Daniel P. Games, and Alexa Manuel. 'The Residential School System'. *Indigenous Foundations*. https://indigenousfoundations.arts.ubc.ca/residential-school-system-2020/. Accessed 17 August 2021.

Hartman, Saidiya. *Scenes of Subjection: Terror, Slavery, and Self-Making in Nineteenth-Century America*. New York and Oxford: Oxford University Press, 1997.

Hartman, Saidiya. 'Venus in Two Acts'. *Small Axe* 26 (2008): 1–14.

'A Hope of Meeting You in Another World'. *Anne With an E*, Season 3, Episode 4, CBC Television, 13 October 2019. *Netflix*. https://www.netflix.com/search?q=anne%20with%20an%20e&jbv=80136311. Accessed 18 August 2021.

Howell Alison and Melanie Richter-Montpetit. 'Racism in Foucauldian Security Studies: Biopolitics, Liberal War, and the Whitewashing of Colonial and Racial Violence'. *International Political Sociology* 13 (2019): 2–19.

Ingalls, Monique M., Carolyn Landau, and Tom Wagner (eds). *Christian Congregational Music: Performance, Identity and Experience*. London: Routledge, 2013.

Johnson, Sarah Kathleen. 'On Our Knees: Christian Ritual in Residential Schools and the Truth and Reconciliation Commission of Canada'. *Studies in Religion* 47. 1 (2019): 3–24.

Johnson-Williams, Erin. 'Singing, Suffering and Liberation in the Concentration Camps of the South African War'. In *The Oxford Handbook of Community Singing*, edited by Esther Morgan-Ellis and Kay Norton. Forthcoming, Oxford University Press, 2023.

Jolaosho, Omoyato. 'Singing Politics: Freedom Songs and Collective Protest in Post-Apartheid South Africa'. *African Studies Review* 62, no. 2 (2019): 6–29.

Khalili, Laleh. *Time in Shadows: Confinement in Counterinsurgencies*. Stanford: Stanford University Press.

Krog, Antjie, and Nosisi Mpolweni. 'Archived Voices: Refiguring Three Women's Testimonies Delivered to the South African Truth and Reconciliation Commission'. *Tulsa Studies in Women's Literature* 28, no. 2 (2009): 357–74.

Lange, Britta. 'Archival Silences as Historical Silences'. *SoundEffects* 7, no. 3 (2017): 47–60.

Levitz, Tamara. 'The Musicological Elite'. *Current Musicology* 102 (2018): 9–80.

Luxen, Micah. 'Survivors of Canada's "Cultural Genocide" Still Healing'. https://www.bbc.co.uk/news/magazine-33001425. Accessed 17 August 2021.

Mackinlay, Elizabeth. 'Decolonization and Applied Ethnomusicology: "Story-ing" the Personal-Political-Possible in Our Work'. In *The Oxford Handbook of Applied Ethnomusicology*, edited by Svanibor Pettan and Jeff Todd Titon. https://doi.org/10.1093/oxfordhb/9780199351701.013.14. Oxford: Oxford University Press, 2015.

Maddox, Alan. 'On the Machinery of Moral Improvement: Music and Prison Reform in the Penal Colony on Norfolk Island'. *Musicology Australia* 34, no. 2 (2012): 185–205.

Malisa, Mark, and Nandipha Malange. 'Songs for Freedom: Music and the Struggle Against Apartheid'. In *The Routledge History of Social Protest in Popular Music*, edited by Jonathan C. Friedman, 304–18. New York: Routledge, 2013.

Mall, Andrew, Jeffers Engelhardt and Monique M. Ingalls (eds). *Studying Congregational Music: Key Issues, Methods, and Theoretical Perspectives*. London: Routledge, 2021.

McGuire, Charles. *Music and Victorian Philanthropy: The Tonic Sol-fa Movement*. Cambridge: Cambridge University Press, 2009.

McGuire, Charles. 'Christianity, Civilization and Music: Nineteenth-Century British Missionaries and the Control of Malagasy Hymnology'. In *Music and Theology in Nineteenth-Century Britain*, edited by Martin Clarke, 79–96. Burlington: Ashgate, 2012.

Mouton, Elna, and Dirkie Smit. 'Shared Stories for the Future? Theological Reflections on Truth and Reconciliation in South Africa'. *Journal of Reformed Theology* 2 (2008): 40–62.

Mühlhahn, Klaus. 'The Concentration Camp in Global Historical Perspective'. *History Compass* 8, no. 6 (2010): 543–61.

Nasson, Bill. *Abraham Esau's War: A Black South African War in the Cape, 1899–1902*. Cambridge: Cambridge University Press, 1991.

Nemser, Daniel. *Infrastructures of Race: Concentration and Biopolitics in Colonial Mexico*. University of Texas Press, 2017.

Newton, Paula. 'More Unmarked Graves Discovered in British Columbia'. https://edition.cnn.com/2021/07/13/americas/canada-unmarked-indigenous-graves/index.html. Accessed 5 August 2021.

Olwage, Grant. 'Scriptions of the Choral: The Historiography of Black South African Choralism'. *SAMUS: South African Journal of Musicology* 22, no. 1 (2002): 29–45.

Olwage, Grant. 'Discipline and Choralism: The Birth of Musical Colonialism'. In *Music, Power, and Politics*, edited by Annie J. Randall, 24–46. London: Routledge, 2004.

Olwage, Grant. 'John Knox Bokwe, Colonial Composer: Tales about Race and Music'. *Journal of the Royal Musical Association* 131 (2006): 1–37.

la paperson. *A Third University Is Possible*. Minneapolis: University of Minnesota Press, 2017.

Porter, Andrew. '"Cultural Imperialism" and Protestant Missionary Enterprise, 1780–1914'. *The Journal of Imperial and Commonwealth History* 25, no. 3 (1997): 367–91.

Radano, Ronald, and Tejumola Olaniyan (eds). *Audible Empire: Music, Global Politics, Critique*. Durham: Duke University Press, 2016.

Rademaker, Laura. *Found in Translation: Many Meanings on a North Australian Mission*. Honolulu: University of Hawai'i Press, 2018.

Raengo, Alessandra, and Lauren McLeod Cramer. 'The Unruly Archives of Black Music Videos'. *Journal of Cinema and Media Studies* 59, no. 2 (2020): 138–44.

Reddie, Amala. 'Anne with An E: A Reflection on Representation'. https://cambridgeeditors.wordpress.com/2020/09/04/anne-with-an-e-a-reflection-on-representation/. Accessed 18 August 2021.

Richards, Jeffrey. *Imperialism and Music: Britain, 1876–1953*. Manchester: Manchester University Press, 2017.

Rogers, Helen. 'Singing at Yarmouth Gaol: Christian Instruction and Inmate Culture in the Nineteenth Century'. *Prison Service Journal* 199 (2011): 35–43.

Schroeder, Janice. 'Inside Voice: Talk, Silence, and Resistance in the Victorian Prison'. *Victorian Review* 46, no. 1 (2020): 9–13.

Scull, Andrew (ed.). *The Asylum as Utopia: W. A. F. Browne and the Mid-Nineteenth Century Consolidation of Psychiatry*. London: Routledge, 1991.

Sharpe, Christina. *In the Wake: On Blackness and Being*. Durham: Duke University Press, 2016.

Smith, Van Wyk. 'The Boers and the Anglo-Boer War (1899–1902) in the Twentieth-Century Moral Imaginary'. *Victorian Literature and Culture* 31, no. 2 (2003): 429–46.

Steedman, Carolyn. *Dust: The Archive and Cultural History*. New Brunswick: Rutgers University Press, 2002.

Steedman, Carolyn. 'After the Archive'. *Comparative Critical Studies* 8, no. 2–3 (2011): 321–40.

Stirrup, David, and James Mackey. 'The Toxic Legacy of the British Empire in Canada's Residential Schools'. https://www.theguardian.com/world/2021/jul/02/the-toxic-legacy-of-the-british-empire-in-canadas-residential-schools. Accessed 17 August 2021.

Stoler, Ann Laura. *Along the Archival Grain: Epistemic Anxieties and Colonial Common Sense*. Princeton and Oxford: Princeton University Press, 2009.

Taruskin, Richard. *The Oxford History of Western Music*, 5 vols. Oxford: Oxford University Press, 2005.

Thomas, David, Simon Fowler and Valerie Johnson (eds). *The Silence of the Archive*. Chicago: Neal-Schuman, 2017.

Truth and Reconciliation Commission. *Canada's Residential Schools: The History, Part 1: Origins to 1939, Volume 1*. Montreal, Kingston, London and Chicago: Published for the Truth and Reconciliation Commission by McGill-Queen's University Press, 2015.

Truth and Reconciliation Commission of South Africa. *Truth and Reconciliation Commission of South Africa Report* Volumes 1–7 (1998). https://www.justice.gov.za/trc/report/.

Viney, William. 'T. S. Eliot and the Textualities of the Discarded'. *Textual Practice* 28, no. 6 (2014): 1057–75.

Waller, Chris. '"Darker Than the Dungeon": Music, Ambivalence, and the Carceral Subject'. *International Journal of the Semiotics of Law* 31 (2018): 275–99.

Warwick, Peter. *Black People and the South African War, 1899–1902*. Cambridge: Cambridge University Press, 1983.

Whitla, Becca. *Liberation, (De)Coloniality, and Liturgical Practices: Flipping the Song Bird*. Basingstoke: Palgrave Macmillan, 2020.

Woolcock, Nicola, and Kaya Burgess. 'Don't Sing Hymns That Are Too Preachy, Church of England Schools Told'. https://www.thetimes.co.uk/article/dont-sing-hymns-that-are-too-preachy-church-of-england-schools-told-h6b6f69b3. Accessed 18 August 2021.

Young, Bryanne. 'Killing the Indian in the Child: Materialities of Death and Political Formations of Life in the Canadian Indian Residential School System'. PhD: University of North Carolina at Chapel Hill, 2017.

7

The infantilization of Indigeneity in colonial Australia

Roisín Laing

This chapter quotes from nineteenth-century texts which use offensive and derogatory language. It also contains reference to Indigenous Australian people who have died. I use the terms 'Indigenous Australians'/'Indigenous Australian peoples' to refer collectively to the diverse societies and peoples living on mainland Australia and Tasmania prior to British invasion. I intend this terminology respectfully. However, I recognise that it is not universally accepted; as I hope the conclusion to this chapter suggests, I also recognise some of the reasons why this is the case.

Introduction

Jeannie Gunn's *The Little Black Princess* (1905) has been described by its publishers as an 'Australian classic', 'beloved' by 'generations of Australians'. This might come as a surprise to the many Australians who have never heard of it. *The Little Black Princess* is currently in print only in the same volume as Gunn's considerably more famous work, *We of the Never-Never* (1908). The two works were first published separately, then reissued, combined and abridged, in 1982. The 1905 edition of *The Little Black Princess* was made available online in 2016. This partial availability reflects how dubious its canonical status is. As John Guillory argues, canonicity is a judgement made by an imaginary 'group of readers, defined by a common social identity and common values'.[1] Its publishers imply that *The Little Black Princess* has a place in the Australian literary canon by, first, imagining a group of readers united by their supposed Australianness, and then, circularly, suggesting that this 'Australian' classic is the very text in which these imaginary Australians can find their common – national – identity epitomized.

Recognized, accessible and beloved: a nation's literary canon is (at least ostensibly) all that its archives, conventionally conceived, are not. As Achille Mbembe suggests, the archive – defined both as a building and as the documents it houses – grants 'privileged status' to its own documents.[2] Through this status, archived documents are imbued with the power to define, in Ann Laura Stoler's words, 'what knowledge should be valued and what their readers should know'.[3] By thus categorizing other knowledge as 'disqualified', archives erase 'the facts of subjugation' in colonial contexts.[4] According to this model, canonical literature is the beloved expression of an uncomplicated national identity, and is (or should be) read by all Australians; archived documents, by contrast, are 'rhetorical sleights-of-hand', and require a reader capable of reading 'against their grain'.[5]

Of course, literary fiction is essentially an extended exercise in rhetorical sleights of hand. *The Little Black Princess* is its author's account of her relationship with the eponymous child, Bett-Bett. As such, it individuates a specific and ubiquitous model of the relationship between settler and Indigenous Australian in nineteenth-century Australia: that of parent and child.[6] In this chapter, I will apply what Aleida Assmann has called 'the strategy of the archive' to the literary text, placing it 'back in its historical context … side by side with other texts of the epoch' to analyse the rhetorical devices through which *The Little Black Princess* idealizes that model.[7]

Following Stoler's suggestion, furthermore, that when reading archives 'we explore the grain with care and read along it first', I suggest that many archived texts – those which are kept behind physical or, increasingly, digital, walls – articulate quite explicitly both the ideology underlying the parent-child model of settler-Indigenous relations, and its colonial functions.[8] This reading of archived texts demonstrates that infantilization is a common trope in late nineteenth-century settler depictions of, and interactions with, Indigenous Australians, and that it presents Indigeneity as a transient state, so that its counterpart, paternalism, complements colonial efforts to eradicate Indigenous peoples.

Assmann differentiates the canon – 'the actively circulated memory that keeps the past present' – from the archive – 'the passively stored memory that preserves the past past'.[9] To elevate *The Little Black Princess* to the status of a literary classic is to naturalize, in the present day, the prevailing, infantilizing mode of depicting Indigenous Australians evident in the archives of the colonial era. When this text is eulogized as an Australian classic, Australian national identity is re-constituted for today's readers, as it was constituted in the colonial period, as white.

Archived documents by settlers thus articulate the ideology underpinning the literary canon. Archived Indigenous writing complicates the hegemony of settler Australia itself. As Evelyn Araluen Corr has argued, for many Indigenous peoples, '"the archive" is a material and symbolic space of imperial violence'.[10] Produced under colonial, coercive conditions, articles written by Indigenous Australians for the *Flinders Island Chronicle* (1836–7) deny their authors 'the right to experience and articulate their contemporary and ancestral heterogeneities without resistance'.[11] Notwithstanding the coercive 'resistance' to Indigenous articulation evident throughout them, however, I suggest that these articles represent a (partial, fragmentary) challenge to the white Australia constructed by the settler infantilization of Indigeneity.

Several scholars have demonstrated the systematic neglect of Indigenous sources from the historiography of colonialism.[12] This situation is both reflected and compounded by the relative availability of canonical literature, archives of settler writing and archives of Indigenous writing. Canonical literature is, almost by definition, easily accessed. The limited accessibility of physical archives, meanwhile, has been overcome by the digitization of much archival material by settlers in colonial Australia (and elsewhere). However, this digital – and thus relatively accessible – nineteenth-century imperial archive is, as Adeline Koh suggests, 'largely *white*'.[13]

This hierarchy of availability has two major effects. First, it substantiates and perpetuates Leonie Stevens's claim that Indigenous voices are also at the bottom of a hierarchy of credibility.[14] Second, it dictates an analytical framework within which scholars simply cannot 'adequately represent or interrogate the important historical interconnections of nineteenth-century colonialism and the existence of people of colour'.[15] In an effort to represent more fully the fact of Indigenous presence in a colonial discourse predicated on the 'disappearance' or 'extinction' of the first owners of Australian lands,[16] I evaluate the dialogue between canonical literature, archived writing by settlers, and archived writing by Indigenous Australians. I read (purportedly) canonical literature in search of what is hidden under its rhetoric. With Stoler, I then read archived writing by settlers along its grain: not for its omissions of Indigenous experience, but as a partial record of how Indigenous peoples and settlers were imagined in the colonial period. A comparative analysis of these readings demonstrates that one ubiquitous trope in settler depictions of Indigeneity – infantilization – is consonant with the ideological construction of a white Australia, and therefore with historical acts of genocide associated with this ideology. I then turn to writings by Indigenous Australians. Keeping the violence which frames the production of Indigenous writing in nineteenth-century Australia in view, I argue that the fragments of Indigenous voices we can access through their archived writing imbue the trope of infantilization with an ambivalent significance. These fragments complicate, though they never quite contradict, the white Australia implied by infantilization in white literary canons and archives.

Infantilization in the literary classic

The Little Black Princess has been classified in academic discourse as 'children's literature'.[17] Children's literature is typically defined as literature *for* children. However, as Jacqueline Rose has famously argued, 'the question of what we mean by that "for"' – the question 'of what the adult desires ... in the very act of construing the child as the object of its speech' – is of vital significance.[18] This chapter will not attempt to debate whether *The Little Black Princess* actually *is* for children. Rather, it will analyse the significance of 'the phantom child – implied, addressed, represented, assumed ... lurking' behind the *idea* that it is.[19]

Many analyses of children's literature since Rose argue that these texts speak both to an implied child reader, and – over that child's head – to an implied adult reader.[20] As Marah Gubar has outlined, 'the power imbalance' inherent to the 'adult author-child reader relationship' and exacerbated by this double address has led to a school of thought in which children's literature is actually seen as a form of colonialism.[21]

Notwithstanding this theoretical analogy between children's literature and colonialism, and a wealth of research into explicitly or implicitly colonial themes in children's literature, little has been written on the *literal* colonial significance of the act of writing for children. Thus, although Clare Bradford, for example, explicitly categorizes *The Little Black Princess* as a work for children, and outlines several ways in which the text is imbued with more than merely 'superficial features of racism', she only briefly notes, in the final sentence of her discussion of the text, that its 'positioning of white children as amused and superior observers' is perhaps its most powerfully racist feature.[22]

In other words, Bradford identifies but does not fully evaluate the interaction between genre and ideology in *The Little Black Princess*. What does it mean, not just for our understanding of a particular text but also for our understanding of colonialism, to describe that text as *for* children? Or, to modify Rose's question, what is the colonial significance of construing 'the child' as the object of a particular text's speech? Elsewhere, Bradford has demonstrated that *The Little Black Princess* depicts two (racialized) communities: an Indigenous community, 'them', raced, as the book's title suggests, 'black', and the settler community, 'us', implicitly raced 'white'.[23] I suggest that the features which mark *The Little Black Princess* as *for* children facilitate an emphatically colonial depiction of the relationship between these imagined communities. Through what I will demonstrate is a racialized representation of relative age, *The Little Black Princess* not only depicts and justifies a paternalistic interaction between settler and Indigenous people in Australia, but actually contributes to a genocidal project of colonization. The metaphorical colonization which many critics claim is enacted by children's literature in general becomes literal in the white adult's address to the child in *The Little Black Princess*.

Since children's literature is notable for the dual or at least ambivalent age of its implied audience, Gunn's implied readers might be *either* – or both – child and/or adult. This uncertainty about the age of the implied reader, combined with the certainty about her race which Bradford identifies, together epitomize the literally colonizing significance of *The Little Black Princess*. It is not the racially defined groups 'us' and 'them' alone but the relative age of these imagined groups which marks Gunn's depiction of the colonial encounter as consonant with the genocidal ideology underpinning that encounter in the nineteenth century.

The following passage illustrates Gunn's depiction of age as a function of race. Gunn has made Bett-Bett a red dress:

> But oh dear, the fuss she made … In funny pidgin English, and with much waving of her arms, she said that, if you had on a red dress when there was a thunderstorm, the debbil-debbil who made the thunder would 'come on' and kill you 'deadfellow'. When I heard this, of course I made a pink dress, as I didn't want the Thunder-Debbil-debbil to run off with her.[24]

Neither Gunn nor the *adult* readers partially addressed in this passage believe in Bett-Bett's devil. In this respect – insofar as she addresses an adult reader – Gunn uses a child's voice to provoke adult laughter at children, in keeping with the charge laid at children's authors in general by Rose and others.

However, white children would neither share the specifically Indigenous fear experienced here by Bett-Bett, nor use the 'funny pidgin English' in which that fear is articulated. This means that the passage is equally accessible, on the same level, to a white *child* as to a white adult reader: white children replicate the position white adult readers assume in relation to Bett-Bett in this passage. Gunn does not adopt Bett-Bett's point of view to provoke adult laughter at children's fears. She ventriloquizes the Indigenous child to provoke white laughter at 'black' fears, and she does so by narrating Indigenous beliefs in the voice of a child, and positioning white readers of any age as the (indulgent, amused) adult listener.

Bradford claims that an earlier work of Australian children's literature, Charlotte Barton's *A Mother's Offering to her Children* (1841), is 'unambiguously a children's book', in part because 'the children outside the book can align themselves with the children within, who listen to stories told by the authoritative, knowledgeable female narrator'.[25] In the case of *The Little Black Princess*, the children 'outside the book' are invited to align themselves not with the child within, but with the authoritative, knowledgeable, adult narrator, and this alignment is predicated on the racial profile, not the age, of Gunn's implied child readers. The readers of *The Little Black Princess* are addressed as adults, because they are white, and are aligned against the child within, because she is not.

In keeping with a long tradition in children's literature criticism, Bradford points to the way this strategy 'flatters' the text's white child readers.[26] As in her claim that *A Mother's Offering* 'seeks to colonise the nineteenth-century child readers of the book into viewing themselves as engaged, along with their parents, in the imperial enterprise', Bradford focuses exclusively on how children's literature 'colonizes' the white child reader.[27] Of course, colonial writing for children also speaks to the colonization of Indigenous peoples, though in a different – and less metaphorical – way.

This is most apparent when Gunn turns from Bett-Bett to other, older Indigenous people. As the use of the definite article in the title – The *Little Black Princess* – suggests, Bett-Bett stands in for Indigenous Australian peoples as a whole, who are thus collectively infantilized. There is, therefore, no change in tone when Gunn changes subject from Bett-Bett to her (adult) uncle:

> The white people had nicknamed him 'Goggle-eye'; and he was very proud of his 'whitefellow name', as he called it. You see, he didn't know what it meant … The first time I met Google Eye, he was weeding my garden, and I didn't know he was king … It takes a good deal of practice, to tell a king at a glance – when he's naked and pulling up weeds.
>
> (pp. 12–13)

Once again, Gunn depicts the Indigenous character as childish, and implies a community of readers united by their amusement at this childishness and, thus, by their relative maturity. The actual age of any character or reader is less important than the metaphorical age they acquire by virtue of their race.

The Little Black Princess thereby constructs two mutually reinforcing equivalences: between Indigeneity and childhood, and concomitantly between whiteness and adulthood. Claudia Castañeda suggests that the idea of 'the child' as 'an adult in the making' is 'so apparently self-evident that it seems almost impossible to imagine an alternative'.[28] A cursory glance at nineteenth-century literature and history complicates this, since both are populated with dead children. The child is 'a potentiality rather than an actuality', as Castañeda argues, but that potentiality has one, and only one, alternative: death.[29] The child is defined, above all, not by its potentiality (the adult), but by its provisionality: whether in adulthood or in death, childhood by definition comes to an end.

Through infantilization, then, Indigeneity is likewise defined as a provisional, transient state. Concomitantly, as well as validating settler authority over Indigenous peoples, the analogy between whiteness and adulthood asserts that to be an adult is to be white. In short, if children either grow up or die, Indigenous people either grow *white* or die. This is the central underlying message which *The Little Black Princess* communicates, and it does so through the interaction of its genre and its ideology, by positioning itself as *for* children, and depicting age as a function of race rather than chronology. This message is made visible by reading canonical fiction against its grain, by reading it as another archived document, which gives privileged status to certain, colonial ways of thinking.

Infantilization in the settler archive

The status of *The Little Black Princess* as canonical literature invites the study of its literary qualities: its fictionality, its position in literary history, its genre. This is the 'timeless framework' described by Assmann, and it obscures both the text's value as a (fictionalized) record of actual historical events, and its continuity with colonial Australian history.[30] I will now situate *The Little Black Princess* in dialogue with more literally archived, more explicitly historical records of the infantilizing practices implemented during Australia's colonial period. Through this, I will argue that *The Little Black Princess* can be understood not only as a romanticized depiction of paternalism, but as a participant in the genocidal violence of Australia's colonial era.

The Aborigines Protection Society (APS) was formed in 1836. Its journal, *The Aborigines' Friend, or Colonial Intelligencer*, ran from 1847 to 1909. The connection between the infantilization of Indigenous Australians and their attempted annihilation is exemplified in the establishment of so-called Training Schools – institutions for 'The Religious Instruction and Moral Training of Aboriginal Natives' – which the Archdeacon of Adelaide, Mathew Hale, advocates for in a contribution to the *Aborigines' Friend*:

> Our natives ... will be ... removed from the influence which the elders of their own tribes at present influence over them ... We shall give to the married couples their own hut, their own plot of ground, their regular, though light and easy, daily employment ... And above all, we shall strive to make them feel the value of a settled mode of life, as affording them the means of religious instruction, and of enabling them to attend to those things which concern their everlasting welfare.[31]

Both Hale's objective – to impose a 'settled' (that is, settler) mode of life – and his paternalistic tone signpost his motivating idea: British civilization is the cultural adulthood towards which Indigenous peoples ought to be enabled to grow.[32]

Training Schools were presented as a moral imperative because they were seen as the best way to slow, halt or reverse the rapid decline in Indigenous populations across Australia, in accounts which ignore the exact coincidence of this decline with the period of colonialism. Training Schools do not only constitute protective, moral action in the settler imagination. They also present such action as necessitated not by colonialism but by Indigeneity.

Of course, the effect of Hale's infantilization is not merely to justify cultural imperialism or whitewash settler culpability for the decline in Indigenous populations across Australia. Because it equates whiteness with adulthood, and designates Indigeneity as a transient state which will end either in this adult-whiteness or in death, infantilization simultaneously obscures and celebrates an emphatically racial form of ethnic cleansing. The endeavour to 'civilize' Indigenous Australians is an effort to cultivate white Australians, in intent as well as in effect.[33]

An analysis of the scientific theory propounded by one of the APS's staunchest supporters demonstrates this. James Cowles Prichard was a passionate opponent of slavery, and a beacon, even today, of all that was at least well-intentioned about British colonial practices.[34] His principle scientific work, *Researches into the Natural History of Mankind* (1813), is a sustained defence of monogenism, predicated on the theory that culture produces race. This theory is clear in Prichard's analysis of the supposed differences between slaves and domestic servants with African heritage in the United States:

> The field slaves live on the plantations, and retain pretty nearly the rude manners of their African progenitors. The third generation in consequence preserve much of their original structure, though their features are not so strongly marked as those of imported slaves. But the domestic servants of the same race are treated with lenity, and their condition is little different from the lower class of white people. The effect is that in the third generation they have the nose raised, the mouth and lips of moderate size, the eyes lively and sparkling, and often the whole composition of features extremely agreeable.
>
> (p. 227)

It is clear which 'manners' Prichard sees as more civilized, and which physical 'structure' he sees as superior. Furthermore, the perceived correlation between cultural practices and racial characteristics is described as causation: 'the *effect*' of the difference in culture between 'African progenitors' and 'domestic servants' is a difference in their 'composition of features', which remain 'original' or become 'agreeable', respectively.[35]

Prichard's clear preference for the physical characteristics of those who have been in servitude rather than in slavery casts a less flattering light on his opposition to slavery than many critics suggest. He may have opposed slavery because he recognized the humanity of the enslaved people, but he argues against it on the grounds that its abolition will eradicate the racial features which characterize them and their 'savage' counterparts.[36] In his work, if not actually in his thought, Prichard does not take issue with slavery itself, but rather with slavery as one manifestation of that absence of civilization which keeps certain groups of the human race in a 'primitive state': in the racial condition he calls 'Negro' (p. 233).

This means that the introduction of British culture complements the annihilation of Indigenous Australians as a racial group, despite the APS's purported objective of preventing this.[37] When Prichard, Hale and others advocate for the (enforced) introduction of British civilization as the way to ensure the survival of Indigenous Australian peoples, they are covertly advocating for the development of Indigenous peoples into white Australians. Hale is not particularly covert about this. His article on Training Schools includes an almost Edenic depiction of an Australia purged of its Indigenous peoples. He claims that 'The Anglo-Saxon race are deriving countless wealth from the sunny hills and dales of South Australia: we have acquired here a noble country, destined, perhaps, to sustain its millions of population in prosperity and power'.[38] The paternalistic ideology underpinning Training Schools expunges the genocidal means through which this white Australia was to be achieved, by implying that Australia's Indigenous populations were not annihilated by its settlers; they were 'trained' to grow up into settlers themselves.

According to the representational strategy of infantilization, white Australia is the natural consequence of Indigenous racial and cultural inferiority, not because Indigenous Australians have been exterminated by settlers, but because they have either died, as was their inevitable fate anyway, or been enabled, by settler benevolence, to grow from 'black' to 'white'. This idea is theorized at the start of the nineteenth century in scientific work like Prichard's, advocated for throughout the century by philanthropists through the APS, and, finally, romanticized in canonical literature like *The Little Black Princess*.

Infantilization in the Indigenous archive

One of the most infamous 'Training Schools' was the settlement on Flinders Island, an island off the coast of Van Diemen's Land. This settlement, known as Wybalenna, was devised in 1834 as a sanctuary, and/or prison, for those Indigenous peoples who had eluded systematic massacre on Van Diemen's Land in the preceding decades.[39] The goal of Wybalenna was to civilize Indigenous peoples, by replacing their culture with nineteenth-century British peasant culture including, most importantly for its commandant George Robinson, Christianity.[40]

Intermittently between September 1836 and December 1837, two Indigenous teenagers, Thomas Brune and Walter George Arthur, wrote and edited a newspaper at Wybalenna, the *Flinders Island Chronicle*. Given the conditions of its production, the *Chronicle* requires what Benjamin Miller describes as a 'two-part reading strategy'.[41] First, 'to avoid overwriting colonial violence, [it] needs to be carefully contextualised'.[42] Much of this context is visible within the *Chronicle* itself. Indeed, as Stevens argues, 'there is little doubt' that its prospectus was 'dictated to Brune by the Commandant'.[43] This prospectus, and some of the earlier issues of the *Chronicle*, consequently both exude and extol the infantilization and paternalism implicit in this dynamic. The claim that 'The object of this journal is to promote christianity civilisation and Learning among the Aboriginal Inhabitants at Flinders Island ... which it is hoped may induce Emmulation in writing excite a desire for useful knowledge and promote Learning generally' [sic], for example, is written in Brune's hand, but more plausibly represents Robinson's voice.[44] As such, it is an unusually clear statement of 'the incomplete nature of a supposedly complete record'; 'the archive' of the *Flinders Island Chronicle* is a very limited repository of Indigenous knowledges and histories.[45]

However, the second part in the reading strategy Miller proposes 'to avoid obliterating Aboriginal presence', is that 'the potential effort of Aboriginal authors might be imagined even as that effort is consumed by the archive'.[46] Subsequent issues of the *Chronicle* suggest that Robinson became either more permissive or less diligent in his censorship, and these issues facilitate this second, more imaginative interpretative work. This is, crucially, not an attempt to 'provide a (fictionalised) account of [Brune's] motives and intentions from this fragment – to pretend to know [Brune] based on limited information'.[47] It is, rather, an interpretation of an archival fragment, into which Indigenous resistance might be imagined in part through the 'violence of [its] partial archival representation'.[48] I read this 'Indigenous archive' not as an articulation of Brune's or Arthur's views – much less of 'Indigenous' views – but as a trace of Indigenous presence within, and reduced to, two spaces of coercion, incarceration and colonial violence: Flinders Island, and the colonial archive.

On 17 November 1837, Brune appears to praise Robinson, claiming that he is 'so kind to you he gives you everything that you want … he brought you out of the bush because … he knowed the white men was shooting you and now he has brought you to Flinders Island where you get everything and when you are ill tell the Doctor immediately and you get relief' [sic].[49] This passage is as much about the brutality of white men in general as it is a testimony to the safety of Flinders Island and the protection offered by Robinson. It obliquely points out that Flinders Island represents less a safe haven than a last resort.

Brune's tone becomes more ambivalent, even ominous, in following paragraphs:

… Yes my friends you should thank the Commandant yes you should thank the Commandant. There is many of us dying my friends we must all die and we ought to pray to God before we get to heaven yes my friends if we dont we must have eternal punishment … Let us hope … that something may be done for us poor people they are dying away the Bible says some of all shall be saved but I am much afraid none of us will be live by and by as then as nothing but sickness among us. Why don't the black fellows pray to the king to get us away from this place.[50]

This passage invites us to imagine Brune's despair and anger at the hypocrisy of the ideology behind Wybalenna in two ways. First, it once again gives us a description of the colonial context and some of its devastating effects: sickness and death. Such passages justify Robert Hughes's claim that Wybalenna foreshadowed the concentration camps which the British would systematize during the South African War (also known as the Second Boer War) at the end of the century.[51]

Second, the passage is a clear instance of what Amanda Nettlebeck calls 'Indigenous participation in "protection talk"'.[52] I have demonstrated that the paternalistic idea of protection contributed to the ideological and practical subjection of Indigenous Australians, since it was predicated on Indigeneity as a transient state which would end either in death or in maturation into whiteness. As Nettlebeck argues, however, the participation of Indigenous people themselves in such discourse reflects 'some of the more nuanced positions that Indigenous groups took up inside settler colonial states, and across changing political climates, than can be encapsulated by the familiar binary of colonial race relations defined by either resistance or accommodation'.[53]

When he appeals to his readers to 'pray to the king', Brune invokes protection as both 'a moral imperative' dictated by Christianity and 'a legal imperative' dictated by 'the Crown itself'.[54] On one level, then, Brune invokes the infantilization-paternalism dynamic to claim the Indigenous rights and settler responsibilities it implies, and in doing so he acts, as Penny van Toorn has argued, as a 'mediator of the coloniser's doctrine'.[55] However, in telling his readers to pray to the king, Brune depicts God and the king as two (inseparable) manifestations of the same thing: namely, paternalism.

Of course, paternalism already had a physical, embodied presence at Wybalenna, in its Commandant; as Van Toorn has argued, Robinson had already discursively placed himself 'into the same position as God' in early editions of the *Chronicle*.[56] This, combined with the slippage from Brune's instruction that his readers 'thank the Commandant' to an injunction that we 'pray to God', and with the subsequent elision of God and the king, all operate to align Robinson with the king, and both with God. Since Robinson's power to protect the Indigenous peoples at Wybalenna had, by this stage of the project, already been revealed as dubious, to align him with God and the king casts doubt on the power of these other iterations of paternalistic power.

Furthermore, Christianity was only selectively adopted by some Indigenous people at Wybalenna, and not adopted at all by others. It is therefore doubtful that many of Brune's readers would have simply accepted the idea that prayer or, by extension, God, had any power to protect them. Brune's suggestion that 'the black fellows pray to the king' conflates the protection afforded by the Crown with that afforded by a God who has limited, if any, power for his Indigenous audience. Thus, on one level Brune can be seen to capitalize on the fact that their infantilization affords certain rights to the Indigenous peoples at Wybalenna. On another level, however, his writing points to the ideological continuity between Robinson, the King and God. The *Chronicle* thereby corroborates a colonial idea of infantilized Indigeneity, even as it also depicts paternalism as ineffectual; whether in the embodied form of Robinson or in the sublime form of God, it has failed to protect the Indigenous people at Wybalenna from sickness and death. Concomitantly, since paternalism might equally be manifested in Robinson, or the King, or God, it becomes, in Brune's writing, a repository for any individuals and any ends.

Ultimately, this suggests that this protean, empty father figure can be a repository for Indigeneity too. By appropriating the imaginative and linguistic strategies used to represent Indigeneity as a transient phase on the route to whiteness, Brune asserts his rights as a child and Robinson's failures as a father. In short, Brune depicts himself as a 'black-child' in order to chastise his 'white-father', and he does so through the very language, medium and representational strategies which epitomize the father's authority. Brune thereby becomes not (or not only) 'a willing accomplice' to Robinson, as Stevens suggests, but instead (or also) his double.[57] Brune's writing contributes to the construction of the imaginary racial binary of (white) settler-father and Indigenous-child. However, both by the very act of writing, and in what he writes, Brune becomes a father figure too. His writing thereby also invokes the possibility that the racial profile of each figure in that binary might easily be reversed. Paradoxically, the very act of participating in his own infantilization constitutes, at the same time, an act of resistance to it.

Conclusion

Edward Said argues that, after the period of 'primary resistance' to colonialism – the effort to retain or recover 'geographical territory' – comes a period of 'secondary, that is ideological resistance', the effort to 'reconstitute' the community after colonialism.[58] The 'partial tragedy of this resistance' is 'that it must to a certain degree work to recover forms already established or at least influenced or infiltrated by the culture of empire'.[59] For Said, 'To achieve recognition is to rechart and then occupy the place in imperial cultural forms reserved for subordination'.[60] Brune's writing does just this; by occupying a recharted form of the infantilized Indigenous figure, Brune invites his readers both to equate and to reimagine infantilization and Indigeneity. Following Miller's suggestion that we approach such archival fragments as an 'opportunity to fill silence with the potential of a reimagined life while acknowledging the damage of colonial ideologies that frame' it, I have argued that the archive of Indigenous writing represented by *The Flinders Island Chronicle* both mediates, and invites its reader to imagine resistance to, colonial ideology.[61]

As outlined in the introduction to this chapter, however, the *Flinders Island Chronicle* is considerably more difficult to access than Gunn's dubious 'classic', or settler representations of Indigeneity like Hale's in the *Aborigines' Friend*, neither of which holds prime position in the hierarchy of availability in Australian literary culture either. That position is reserved for established literary classics, of which Ethel Turner's *Seven Little Australians* (1894) is among the most loved.[62] 'In Australia', Turner begins, 'the land and the people are young-hearted together, and the children's spirits are not crushed and saddened by the shadow of long years' sorrowful history. There is a lurking sparkle of joyousness and rebellion and mischief in nature here, and therefore in children'.[63] In Turner's work, Indigenous Australians are expunged from Australian history, and this obscures Britain's genocidal efforts to remove them from Australia itself.

As Assmann has argued, 'The canon stands for the active working memory of a society that defines and supports the cultural identity of a group': a nation's identity is imaginatively constructed, in part, through its literary classics.[64] *Seven Little Australians* might be a regrettable component of Australian national identity, but it is not clear that it is aberrant. Successive Australian governments throughout the twentieth century upheld a policy, now notorious as the Stolen Generations, whereby Indigenous Australian children were forcibly removed from their families and communities and placed with white families. The Stolen Generations epitomizes the catastrophic consequences of infantilization for Indigenous Australian peoples.[65] This practice is consonant with the pernicious ideas that Indigeneity itself is the cause of any difficulties faced by Indigenous Australians, that they must be protected by white Australians, and ultimately that they must grow up, into white Australians themselves.

This chapter has discussed texts published from 1813 to 1905. It has suggested that infantilization endured as a representational strategy throughout the nineteenth century. The lasting popularity of *Seven Little Australians* and the attempted canonization of *The Little Black Princess* suggest that the infantilization of Indigenous Australians and their cultures endures to an extent in Australia today; these novels are the canonical surface of the archive of infantilized Indigeneity from which Australia itself emerges. *Seven Little Australians* depicts the racist fantasy underneath the Stolen Generations and the imaginary scene in which *The Little Black Princess* is canonically 'Australian': the fantasy that Australia is white, or at least will be when it grows up.

By reading literary texts as archives of the enduring trope of infantilization, we can see that 'sparkle of joyousness' in Turner's Australia for what it is: not the absence of 'long years' sorrowful history', but the erasure of genocide. An analysis of literary classics in dialogue with settler and Indigenous archives decodes the discursive practices through which paternalistic representational strategies like Gunn's or Hale's complement colonial efforts to eradicate not just Indigenous Australian cultures, but Indigenous Australian peoples. It also reveals Indigenous peoples' appropriation of the same representational strategies in their efforts to respond to, and resist, the existential threat represented by colonialism.

As Aileen Moreton-Robinson has argued, 'Resistance by the oppressed is the influence they have on their relationship with the oppressors'; within the literary archive examined here, Indigeneity exists only through Brune, who himself exists only in relation – opposition or submission – to colonial power.[66] Brune's knowledge and experience – beyond the possibility of his opposition to colonial incarceration – are uncertain, but as Miller has suggested, 'Careful close readings of the frames that influence subaltern records can produce silence through failed representation'.[67] Silence and failure, in other words, are 'valuable outcomes' of research like this, since they acknowledge Indigenous presence and subjectivity prior to and outside colonial knowledge systems.[68]

The Australian Institute of Aboriginal and Torres Strait Islander Studies is developing an archive of intangible Indigenous heritage, but as Tran Tran and Clare Barcham argue this must be 'embedded in the practice of a lived culture'.[69] This 'living archive' makes impossible what Thomas Richards calls 'the basic animating project of the imperial archive, namely, the organization of all knowledges into a coherent imperial whole'.[70] The infantilization of Indigeneity in colonial Australia is a failed representation of Indigeneity, but as such points to the partiality of the conventional colonial archive, and its public-facing counterpart, the literary canon. The fragmentary nature of the 'Indigenous archive' examined in this chapter bears witness to the violence underpinning colonial ways of knowing, and to the partial and limited knowledge of Indigenous peoples and histories produced through the tangible, the textual, the literary archive. It also leaves a gaping, visible space: the failures of what Richards calls the imperial archive, or, rather, the knowledges, histories and cultures of the living Indigenous archive which persist outside the frame.

Acknowledgements

I am grateful to Matthew Sussman and the Interdisciplinary Nineteenth-Century Studies Group at the University of Sydney for their comments on an earlier draft of this research, and particularly to Benjamin Miller for his insights into the use of archival material by Indigenous Australians.

Notes

1. John Guillory, *Cultural Capital: The Problem of Literary Canon Formation* (Chicago: University of Chicago Press, 1993), p. 28.
2. Achille Mbembe, 'The Power of the Archive and its Limits', in Carolyn Hamilton, Verne Harris, Jane Taylor, Michele Pickover, Graeme Reid, and Razia Saleh (eds), *Refiguring the Archive* (Dordrecht: Springer Science+Business Media, 2002), pp. 19–26, at p. 19.
3. Ann Laura Stoler, *Along the Archival Grain: Epistemic Anxieties and Colonial Common Sense* (Princeton: Princeton University Press, 2009), p. 44, referring to Ranajit Guha, *Dominance without Hegemony: History and Power in Colonial India* (Cambridge: Harvard University Press, 1997).
4. Ibid., p. 47.
5. Ibid., pp. 20, 47. See also Sas Mays, 'Introduction', in Sas Mays (ed.), *Libraries, Literatures, and Archives* (New York: Routledge, 2014), pp. 1–19 on the difference between archives and libraries: namely, the 'collection of imaginative literary texts' which characterizes the latter (Mays, p. 3).
6. See Margaret D. Jacobs, *White Mother to a Dark Race: Settler Colonialism, Maternalism, and the Removal of Indigenous Children in the American West and Australia, 1880–1940* (Lincoln: University of Nebraska Press, 2009), for a detailed account of the paternalistic settler practice of forced child removal in Australia and America.
7. Aleida Assmann, 'Canon and Archive', in Astrid Erll, Ansgar Nünning, and Sara Young (eds), *A Companion to Cultural Memory Studies* (Berlin and New York: de Gruyter, 2008), pp. 97–107, at p. 102.
8. Stoler, *Archival Grain*, p. 46.
9. Assmann, 'Canon and Archive', p. 98.
10. Evelyn Araluen Corr, 'Silence and Resistance: Aboriginal Women Working within and Against the Archive', *Continuum: Journal of Media and Cultural Studies* 32. 4 (2018): 487–502, at p. 487.
11. Ibid., p. 487.
12. See Leonie Stevens, '*Me Write Myself*': *The Free Aboriginal Inhabitants of Van Diemen's Land at Wybalenna, 1832–47* (Melbourne: Monash University Press, 2017), esp. pp. xxiv–xlii. This neglect encompasses written sources, of course, but also extends to the wealth of non-textual sources of Indigenous history.
13. Adeline Koh, 'Inspecting the Nineteenth-Century Literary Digital Archive: Omissions of Empire', *Journal of Victorian Culture* 19. 3 (2014): 385–95, at p. 394, emphasis in original. See also Rachel Bryant Davies's observations in this volume on the illusory 'wholeness' of digital archives.
14. Stevens, '*Me Write Myself*, p. xxvi.

15 Koh, 'Digital Archive', p. 394.
16 See Russell McGregor, *Imagined Destinies: Aboriginal Australians and the Doomed Race Theory, 1880–1939* (Carlton South: Melbourne University Press, 1997).
17 *The Little Black Princess* features in Clare Bradford's *Reading Race: Aboriginality in Australian Children's Literature* (Melbourne: Melbourne University Press, 2001), pp. 88–91, and 'Australian Children's Literature', in Peter Pierce (ed.), *The Cambridge History of Australian Children's Literature* (Cambridge: Cambridge University Press, 2009), pp. 282–302.
18 Jacqueline Rose, *The Case of Peter Pan, or; The Impossibility of Children's Literature* (Philadelphia: University of Pennsylvania Press, 1984), p. 2.
19 Julia Mickenberg and Lynne Vallone, 'Introduction', in Julia Mickenberg and Lynne Vallone (eds), *The Oxford Handbook of Children's Literature* (Oxford: Oxford University Press, 2011), pp. 4–23, at p. 5.
20 See, for example, Barbara Wall, *The Narrator's Voice: The Dilemma of Children's Fiction* (New York: Palgrave Macmillan, 1991).
21 Marah Gubar, *Artful Dodgers: Reconstructing the Golden Age of Children's Literature* (Baltimore: Johns Hopkins University Press, 2007), p. 71. Rose's is the seminal analysis of children's literature as a form of colonialism (Rose, *The Case of Peter Pan*, esp. pp. 42–65). Gubar offers a persuasive counterargument.
22 Bradford, *Reading Race*, pp. 89, 91. See also, for example, Don Randall, *Kipling's Imperial Boy: Adolescence and Cultural Hybridity* (Basingstoke: Palgrave, 2000).
23 Bradford, 'Australian Children's Literature', in Peter Pierce (ed.), *The Cambridge History of Australian Children's Literature* (Cambridge: Cambridge University Press, 2009), p. 297. Of course, this dialectic entirely erases the many peoples in turn of the century Australia who were racialized neither as 'white' nor as 'black'. I use the term 'black' in inverted commas, rather than the capitalized 'Black' used elsewhere in this collection, because I am describing the nineteenth-century racialization of Indigenous Australians as 'black', not describing or identifying Indigenous Australians as Black.
24 Jeannie Gunn, *The Little Black Princess* (London: De la More Press, 1905), p. 6.
25 Bradford, 'Australian Children's Literature', p. 282.
26 Bradford, *Reading Race*, p. 91.
27 Clare Bradford, 'The Wise Colonial Child: Imperial Discourse in *A Mother's Offering to Her Children*', *New Literatures Review* 33 (1997): 39–50, at p. 33.
28 Claudia Castañeda, *Figurations: Child, Bodies, Worlds* (Durham and London: Duke University Press, 2002), p. 1.
29 Ibid.
30 Assmann, 'Canon and Archive', p. 101.
31 Mathew Hale, 'Prospectus of an Institution About to be Formed at Port Lincoln for the Religious Instruction and Moral Training of Aboriginal Natives', in *The Colonial Intelligencer or Aboriginal's Friend* 3 (1850–1): 214–17, at pp. 213; 216.
32 Hale here repeats an idea, which persists today, that Indigenous Australians were not already 'settled' prior to colonialism. See Bruce Pascoe, *Dark Emu: Aboriginal Australia and the Birth of Agriculture* (Broome: Magabala Books, 2014), on the evidence for pre-colonial Indigenous Australian agriculture.
33 See Jacobs, *White Mother to a Dark Race*, pp. 63–73. See also Warwick Anderson, *The Cultivation of Whiteness: Science, Health, and Racial Destiny in Australia* (Durham: Duke University Press, 2006).

34 See, for example, H. F. Augstein, *James Cowles Prichard's Anthropology: Remaking the Science of Man in Early Nineteenth-Century Britain* (Amsterdam: Rodopi, 1999). See also Efram Sera Shriar, *The Making of British Anthropology, 1813-1871* (Pittsburgh: University of Pittsburgh Press, 2016), esp. p. 52 on empire and ethnography.
35 See Lara Atkin, 'Review: The Architects of the Study of Man', *Journal of Victorian Culture*, 19. 1 (2014): 123-6, on the symbiotic relationship between the missionary and the ethnographer, which are seamlessly amalgamated in Prichard himself. See Colin Kidd, *The Forging of Races; Race and Scripture in the Protestant Atlantic World, 1600-2000* (Cambridge: Cambridge University Press, 2006), esp. pp. 121-67, on race and religion in the nineteenth century. Stephen Jay Gould, *The Mismeasure of Man* (New York: Norton, 1981) is the essential work on what is now called 'scientific racism', a genre to which Prichard was an early, if unwitting, contributor.
36 This casts doubt on Kidd's claim that the 'mainstream version of race science in the British world during the first half of the nineteenth century' – in which Prichard was pre-eminent – 'was anti-racist in its motivations' (Kidd, *Forging of Races*, p. 135).
37 See Patrick Wolfe, *Settler Colonialism and the Transformation of Anthropology: The Politics and Poetics of an Ethnographic Event* (London: Cassell, 1999) on the 'logic that was common to the ostensibly separate projects of ethnography and ethnocide' in the context the emergence of the assimilation policy in late nineteenth-century Australia (Wolfe, *Settler Colonialism*, p. 11).
38 Hale, 'Prospectus', p. 216.
39 See N. J. B. Plomley, *Weep in Silence: A History of the Flinders Island Aboriginal Settlement, with the Flinders Island Journal of George Augustus Robinson, 1835-1839* (Hobart: Blubber Head Press, 1987), p. 4.
40 See 'Robinson, George Augustus (1791-1866)', *Australian Dictionary of Biography* (Canberra: Australian National University Press, 1967), http://adb.anu.edu.au, accessed 11 December 2020; and Patrick Brantlinger, *Taming Cannibals: Race and the Victorians* (Ithaca: Cornell University Press, 2011), p. 52. See also Erin Johnson-Williams in this collection on the interaction of Christianity and incarceration in colonial contexts.
41 Benjamin Miller, 'Fragments of the Archive: The Subaltern Protests of Charles Never', *Journal of Australian Studies* 47. 4 (2021): 491-506, at p. 500.
42 Ibid. David Lowther similarly demonstrates the value of meticulous contextualization when researching colonial archives in his contribution to this collection.
43 Stevens, '*Me Write Myself*', p. 64.
44 Thomas Brune and Walter Juba Martin, 'The Aboriginal or Flinders Island Chronicle Under Sanction of the Commandant', in Michael Rose (ed.), *For the Record: 160 Years of Aboriginal Print Journalism* (St. Leonards: Allen and Unwin, 1996), pp. 3-19, at p. 3.
45 Miller, 'Fragments of the Archive', p. 493. Tran Tran and Clare Barcham, '(Re)defining Indigenous Intangible Cultural Heritage', *AIATSIS Research Discussion Paper 37* (2018), examine the forms and complexities of Indigenous knowledges, revealing just how inadequate a conventional archive – a collection of documents in a building – is for developing, preserving and providing access to Indigenous heritages. See also Philip Burnett's discussion in this volume of Christian Cole's 'scattered and invisible' archival presence.
46 Miller, 'Fragments of the Archive', p. 500.
47 Ibid. Judith Phillips's contribution to this collection asks whether it is *permissible* to expose private lives to public gaze; Miller asks whether it is *possible* to 'expose'

an Indigenous person's motives or intentions from the traces that remain in the archive, without obfuscating and thus repeating the violence of these archival representations.

48 Miller, 'Fragments of the Archive', p. 493.
49 Brune, *'Flinders Island Chronicle'*, p. 17.
50 Ibid. See Stevens, *'Me Write Myself'*, pp. 134–5, on this passage.
51 Robert Hughes, *The Fatal Shore: A History of the Transportation of Convicts to Australia, 1787–1868* (London: Pan Books, 1987), p. 423. See pp. 414–24 for an overview of the context in which Wybalenna, the 'benign concentration camp', was created.
52 Amanda Nettelbeck, '"We Are Sure of Your Sympathy": Indigenous Uses of the Politics of Protection in Nineteenth-Century Australia and Canada', *Journal of Colonialism and Colonial History* 17. 1, (2016), n.p. https://doi.org/10.1353/cch.2016.0009.
53 Ibid.
54 Ibid.
55 Stevens, *'Me Write Myself'*, p. xxxvii.
56 Penny Van Toorn, *Writing Never Arrives Naked: Early Aboriginal Cultures of Writing in Australia* (Canberra: Aboriginal Studies Press, 2006), p. 107.
57 Stevens, *'Me Write Myself'*, p. 66.
58 Edward Said, *Culture and Imperialism* (New York: Knopf, 1993), p. 134.
59 Ibid., p. 135, quoted in Corr, 'Silence and Resistance', p. 493.
60 Ibid.
61 Miller, 'Fragments of the Archive', p. 494.
62 Bradford notes that *Seven Little Australians* is 'the only nineteenth-century text still read by children' in Australia. Bradford, 'Australian Children's Literature', p. 287.
63 Ethel Turner, *Seven Little Australians* (London: Penguin, 2010), pp. 1–2.
64 Assmann, 'Canon and Archive', p. 106.
65 See 'The Stolen Generation', *Australians Together*, https://australianstogether.org.au/discover/australian-history/stolen-generations, accessed 17 November 2020; 'The Stolen Generations', *AIATSIS*, https://aiatsis.gov.au/stolen-generations, accessed 19 November 2020; 'Who Are the Stolen Generations?', *The Healing Foundation*, https://healingfoundation.org.au/resources/who-are-the-stolen-generations, accessed 19 November 2020; and 'The Stolen Generations', *Common Ground*, https://commonground.org.au/learn/the-stolen-generations, accessed 19 November 2020, for overviews and accounts of the Stolen Generations and its devastating effects.
66 Aileen Moreton-Robinson, 'Introduction: Resistance, Recovery and Revitilization', in Michèle Grossmann (ed.), *Blacklines: Contemporary Critical Writing by Indigenous Australians* (Carlton: Melbourne University Press, 2003), pp. 127–31, at pp. 128–9, quoted in Corr, 'Silence and Resistance', p. 439.
67 Miller, 'Fragments of the Archive', p. 506.
68 Ibid. See Stevens, *'Me Write Myself'*, p. 90, on silences and absences in the archived school reports from Flinders Island.
69 Tran and Barcham, '(Re)defining Indigenous Intangible Cultural Heritage', p. 19. See Jemima Short in this volume, however, on the challenges and ethical issues of researching communal histories as an 'outsider'.
70 Ibid., pp. 18–20; and Thomas Richards, *The Imperial Archive: Knowledge and the Fantasy of Empire* (London: Verso, 1993), p. 7.

Bibliography

AIATSIS. 'The Stolen Generations'. *AIATSIS*. https://aiatsis.gov.au/stolen-generations. Accessed 19 November 2020.

Anderson, Warwick. *The Cultivation of Whiteness: Science, Health, and Racial Destiny in Australia*. Durham: Duke University Press, 2006.

Assmann, Aleida. 'Canon and Archive'. In *A Companion to Cultural Memory Studies*, edited by Astrid Erll, Ansgar Nünning, and Sara Young, 97–107. Berlin and New York: de Gruyter, 2008.

Atkin, Lara. 'Review: The Architects of the Study of Man'. *Journal of Victorian Culture*, 19, no. 1 (2014): 123–6.

Augstein, H. F. *James Cowles Prichard's Anthropology: Remaking the Science of Man in Early Nineteenth-Century Britain*. Amsterdam: Rodopi, 1999.

Australian Dictionary of National Biography. 'Robinson, George Augustus (1791–1866)'. In *Australian Dictionary of Biography*. Canberra: Australian National University Press, 1967. http://adb.anu.edu.au. Accessed 11 December 2020.

Australians Together. 'The Stolen Generation'. *Australians Together*. https://australianstogether.org.au/discover/australian-history/stolen-generations. Accessed 17 November 2020.

Bradford, Clare. 'The Wise Colonial Child: Imperial Discourse in *A Mother's Offering to Her Children*'. *New Literatures Review* 33 (1997): 39–50.

Bradford, Clare. *Reading Race: Aboriginality in Australian Children's Literature*. Melbourne: Melbourne University Press, 2001.

Bradford, Clare. 'Australian Children's Literature'. In *The Cambridge History of Australian Children's Literature*, edited by Peter Pierce, 282–302. Cambridge: Cambridge University Press, 2009.

Brantlinger, Patrick. *Taming Cannibals: Race and the Victorians*. Ithaca: Cornell University Press, 2011.

Brune, Thomas, and Walter Juba Martin. '*The Aborginal or Flinders Island Chronicle* under Sanction of the Commandant'. In *For the Record: 160 Years of Aboriginal Print Journalism*, edited by Michael Rose, 3–19. St. Leonards: Allen and Unwin, 1996.

Castañeda, Claudia. *Figurations: Child, Bodies, Worlds*. Durham and London: Duke University Press, 2002.

Common Ground. 'The Stolen Generations'. *Common Ground*. https://commonground.org.au/learn/the-stolen-generations. Accessed 19 November 2020.

Corr, Evelyn Araluen. 'Silence and Resistance: Aboriginal Women Working within and Against the Archive'. *Continuum: Journal of Media and Cultural Studies* 32, no. 4 (2018): 487–502.

Gould, Stephen Jay. *The Mismeasure of Man*. New York: Norton, 1981.

Gubar, Marah. *Artful Dodgers: Reconstructing the Golden Age of Children's Literature*. Baltimore: Johns Hopkins University Press, 2007.

Guillory, John. *Cultural Capital: The Problem of Literary Canon Formation*. Chicago: University of Chicago Press, 1993.

Gunn, Jeannie. *The Little Black Princess: A True Tale of Life in the Never-Never Land*. London: De la More Press, 1905.

Hale, Mathew. 'Prospectus of an Institution about to Be Formed at Port Lincoln for the Religious Instruction and Moral Training of Aboriginal Natives'. *The Colonial Intelligencer or Aboriginal's Friend* 3 (1850–1851): 214–17.

Healing Foundation. 'Who Are the Stolen Generations?'. *The Healing Foundation.* https://healingfoundation.org.au/resources/who-are-the-stolen-generations. Accessed 19 November 2020.

Hughes, Robert. *The Fatal Shore: A History of the Transportation of Convicts to Australia, 1787–1868.* London: Pan Books, 1987.

Jacobs, Margaret D. *White Mother to a Dark Race: Settler Colonialism, Maternalism, and the Removal of Indigenous Children in the American West and Australia, 1880–1940.* Lincoln: University of Nebraska Press, 2009.

Kidd, Colin. *The Forging of Races; Race and Scripture in the Protestant Atlantic World, 1600–2000.* Cambridge: Cambridge University Press, 2006.

Koh, Adeline. 'Inspecting the Nineteenth-Century Literary Digital Archive: Omissions of Empire'. *Journal of Victorian Culture* 19, no. 3 (2014): 385–95.

Mays, Sas. 'Introduction'. In *Libraries, Literatures, and Archives*, edited by Sas Mays, 1–19. New York: Routledge, 2014.

Mbembe, Achille. 'The Power of the Archive and Its Limits'. In *Refiguring the Archive*, edited by Carolyn Hamilton, Verne Harris, Jane Taylor, Michele Pickover, Graeme Reid, and Razia Saleh, 19–26. Dordrecht: Springer Science+Business Media, 2002.

McGregor, Russell. *Imagined Destinies: Aboriginal Australians and the Doomed Race Theory, 1880–1939.* Carlton South: Melbourne University Press, 1997.

Mickenberg Julia, and Lynne Vallone. 'Introduction'. In *The Oxford Handbook of Children's Literature*, edited by Julia Mickenberg and Lynne Vallone, 4–23. Oxford: Oxford University Press, 2011.

Miller, Benjamin. 'Fragments of the Archive: The Subaltern Protests of Charles Never'. *Journal of Australian Studies* 45, no. 4 (2021): 491–506.

Moreton-Robinson, Aileen. 'Introduction: Resistance, Recovery and Revitilization'. In *Blacklines: Contemporary Critical Writing by Indigenous Australians*, edited by Michèle Grossmann, 127–31. Carlton: Melbourne University Press, 2003.

Nettelbeck, Amanda. '"We Are Sure of Your Sympathy": Indigenous Uses of the Politics of Protection in Nineteenth-Century Australia and Canada'. *Journal of Colonialism and Colonial History* 17, no. 1 (2016): n.p. https://doi.org/10.1353/cch.2016.0009.

Pascoe, Bruce. *Dark Emu: Aboriginal Australia and the Birth of Agriculture.* Broome: Magabala Books, 2014.

Plomley, N. J. B. *Weep in Silence: A History of the Flinders Island Aboriginal Settlement, with the Flinders Island Journal of George Augustus Robinson, 1835–1839.* Hobart: Blubber Head Press, 1987.

Randall, Don. *Kipling's Imperial Boy: Adolescence and Cultural Hybridity.* Basingstoke: Palgrave, 2000.

Richards, Thomas. *The Imperial Archive: Knowledge and the Fantasy of Empire.* London: Verso, 1993.

Rose, Jacqueline. *The Case of Peter Pan, or; The Impossibility of Children's Literature.* Philadelphia: University of Pennsylvania Press, 1984.

Sera Shriar, Efram. *The Making of British Anthropology, 1813–1871.* Pittsburgh: University of Pittsburgh Press, 2016.

Stevens, Leonie. *'Me Write Myself': The Free Aboriginal Inhabitants of Van Diemen's Land at Wybalenna, 1832–47.* Melbourne: Monash University Press, 2017.

Stoler, Ann Laura. *Along the Archival Grain: Epistemic Anxieties and Colonial Common Sense.* Princeton: Princeton University Press, 2009.

Toorn, Penny Van. *Writing Never Arrives Naked: Early Aboriginal Cultures of Writing in Australia.* Canberra: Aboriginal Studies Press, 2006.

Tran, Tran, and Clare Barcham. '(Re)defining Indigenous Intangible Cultural Heritage'. *AIATSIS Research Discussion Paper* 37 (2018): 1–24.
Turner, Ethel. *Seven Little Australians*. London: Penguin, 2010.
Van Toorn, Penny. *Writing Never Arrives Naked: Early Aboriginal Cultures of Writing in Australia*. Canberra: Aboriginal Studies Press, 2006.
Wall, Barbara. *The Narrator's Voice: The Dilemma of Children's Fiction*. New York: Palgrave Macmillan, 1991.
Wolfe, Patrick. *Settler Colonialism and the Transformation of Anthropology: The Politics and Poetics of an Ethnographic Event*. London: Cassell, 1999.

8

'Some nameless, dreadful wrong'

Reading the silencing of police rape in the Indian colonial archive

Deana Heath

In February 1921, Medai Tamboli of Madhpuri, in the Raebareli district of the United Provinces, went to Gaura Bazar with two and a half rupees to buy a bullock. Not finding one that he liked, he was returning home when he realized that he had left his money on the parapet of a well at which he had stopped to wash; on returning to collect it, however, he found it gone.[1] Assuming that two children who had been nearby – an eleven-year-old boy, Raghbir, and his older sister, Sukhdeia – had taken the money, Tamboli went to their mother, a poor agricultural labourer named Mussamat Itwaria, to demand it back. In the face of her denial at having committed the theft, Tamboli turned to the police for help. But with the money still not forthcoming, the local *chaukidars* (village police), along with two police constables and a local *zamindar* (landlord) determined, in the words of Sessions Judge E. M. Nanavutty, in his judgement on the trial of six police officers and *chaukidars* under section 330 of the Indian Penal Code for causing hurt to extort a confession, to 'disgrace Mussamat Itwaria'.[2] They did so by throwing her on the ground, removing her lower garment and then holding apart her legs, while one of the *chaukidars*, in Nanvutty's words, 'sprinkled powdered chillies with his hand on her private parts'.[3] The *chaukidars* and one of the constables, according to Nanavutty, then 'took the girl Sukhdeia to a ruined house close by and "maltreated" her'.[4] In describing the treatment to which Mussamat Itwaria and her daughter had been subject by the Indian police, acting in concert with a local elite, simply as a form of 'disgrace' or 'mistreatment', Nanavutty's language thus served to erase the sexual violence to which both had been subject – not only from his judgement, but from the Indian colonial archive.

It did so despite the fact that the ordeal of Mussamat Itwaria and her presumably adolescent daughter did not end there (although Sukhdeia is referred to in the judgement as both a 'woman' and a 'child', and once as 'Mussamat Sukhdeia', and hence as a married woman, since the judgement contains no reference to a husband, she was probably a young adolescent and was either widowed or unmarried). Later that night they were taken to a pond, stripped and made to stand naked in cold water, 'up to their breasts', for an hour.⁵ Nanvutty's judgement remains silent as to what happened to Mussamat Itwaria and her daughter that night – possibly because the chief witness, Raghbir, was unaware as to what may have transpired – but according to Raghbir's testimony, the next morning the hair of Mussamat Itwaria and her daughter 'was tied together and they were made to stand ... on a *chabutra* [a raised platform] and ... to pull in different directions'.⁶ Nanavutty's judgement refers to this as 'a form of torture' that lasted until midday, at which point constable Mahngu Ram and police sub-inspector Jai Dayal, who had taken charge of the proceedings, promised to release mother and daughter upon the payment of five rupees.⁷ Mussamat Itwaria then went to her employer, Darshan Brahman, and begged him for five rupees to give to her tormentors to protect her from further oppression, as well as for some food to eat, since neither she nor her children had been fed during their ordeal. Brahman gave her some unhusked rice, which she presumably cooked and fed to her children before throwing her son into a well and then, as the judge put it, 'mother and daughter, locked into one another's embrace, jumped into the well to find in a watery grave that peace and rest which they had been denied on earth' – a joint suicide that, as we shall see, was to play an important role in bringing this case to trial.⁸ While both Itwaria and her daughter died, Raghbir managed to survive by clinging to a brick on the inside of the well.

Mussamat Itwaria was both low-caste (she was from the predominantly agricultural *Lodh* community) and, presumably, a widow, since no husband is mentioned in the documents relating to the trial of her tormentors. Both her caste status and her lack of a male protector would have made her particularly vulnerable to men who were in a position to abuse their authority, such as village officials, the police and local *zamindars* – not least since the *Lodhs*, or *Lodhis*, who had been organizing for recognition of higher caste status since the late nineteenth century, had claimed the higher-caste name *Lodhi-Rajput* at the All-India *Lodhi* conference in Fategarh the same year as the terrible ordeal suffered by Mussamat Itwaria and her family (a claim that, in threatening the primacy of the upper castes, doubtless fuelled caste tensions at the village level and added to the vulnerability of *Lodh* women).⁹ Since judge Nanavutty had, however, clearly internalized the conviction that members of marginal groups, particularly women, had 'a "habitual disregard for the truth"' (a conviction that, while intrinsic to the colonial judicial system, also built on dominant perceptions of the lower castes and *Dalits*, particularly of lower-caste or *Dalit* women, held by upper-caste Hindu men), the fact that most of the witnesses to the ordeal of Mussamat Itwaria and her daughter were almost all *Lodhs* automatically rendered them unreliable.¹⁰ Although Nanavutty admitted that 'On *a priori* grounds one may reasonably suspect that violence and beating ... must have been used ... in order to make the women ... confess their guilt and give up or restore the money of Medai Tamboli', he regarded the incidents that the witnesses had described as being simply too improbable in light of the circumstances (namely that they took place in broad daylight, in front of witnesses, and that, since Mussamat Itwaria clearly did not have Tamboli's money, the purported violence inflicted upon her would have been purely gratuitous).¹¹ For the judge, therefore, there was no evidence regarding what he referred to as 'the *simple hurt*' (emphasis added) inflicted upon mother and daughter.¹² What prevented Nanavutty from throwing the case out, however, was the evidence of the one Brahman witness in the trial, Darshan Brahman, whose high caste status clearly gave him credibility. It was, in particular, Brahman's account of what Mussamat Itwaria had said to him when she begged for his help – namely '*kise karm ke no rahe*' (sic.; lit., 'we are left good for nothing') – that Nanavutty found particularly compelling, since he maintained that, when uttered by an Indian woman in this context, it could only mean: 'our chastity has been violated'.[13] But rather than giving a name to such a violation – namely that mother and daughter had been raped – for Nanavutty there were 'strong reasons for suspecting that some *nameless*, dreadful wrong' (emphasis added) had been committed on Musamat Itwaria and her daughter.[14] Moreover, instead of convicting their oppressors for rape or torture, or any other forms of hurt to extort a confession, he convicted them, instead, for wrongful confinement.[15] In essentially admitting that Mussamat Itwaria and her daughter had been raped, albeit refusing to explicitly name such violation or to punish it, Nanavutty thus undermined British colonial perceptions of the falsity of the truth claims of Indian rape victims, particularly those who were lower-caste – although he nonetheless followed the common colonial precedent of coding rape as a different type of crime.

My aim in this chapter is to understand how acts of rape committed by what I have elsewhere referred to as the *violence workers* of the British colonial state – in this case, by members of the Indian police – have been coded in the colonial archive. While the term 'colonial archive' is undoubtedly fraught (not least because of differing conceptions of 'the archive' and 'archives' among humanities and archival studies scholars), in using it I am not positing an essentialist notion of how such an archive is constituted; rather, I agree with Charu Gupta's contention that '[t]he archive is anything of which a set of questions is asked and the nature of the archive is largely, but not entirely, defined by the nature of questions asked of it'.[16] In conjunction with the chapters by Erin Johnson-William and Roisín Laing, in this volume, I wish to interrogate, furthermore, how acts of violence, omission and silencing in the colonial archive can or should be interpreted, and what they reveal about the nature of colonialism. For when it came to the rape of Indian women by the police, Nanavutty's stance, namely refusing to name and thus prosecute rape, and to categorize it as another form of crime, was the norm (although as I have demonstrated elsewhere, this was also largely the case in regard to the rape of men).[17] In both the Indian press and the official sphere in colonial India, rape was generally referred to in euphemistic terms – in the case of police rape, generally through euphemisms such as 'the vilest ill-treatment' or 'torture … of the worst kind' – although since rape had to be named in order to be prosecuted it was deemed acceptable to refer explicitly to it in legal documents and literature such as judgements or medical jurisprudence texts.[18]

But since rape trials in India, as Pratiksha Baxi argues, serve not to bring justice for rape victims but to reinforce 'deeply entrenched phallocentric notions of "justice"', Nanavutty's verdict should, perhaps, be unsurprising, particularly considering the low conviction rates for rape trials in India in the colonial era.[19] Yet Nanavutty issued his judgement during a period in which the British colonial government in India was being subject to considerable pressure regarding the prevalence of police brutality, not least about the employment of sexual violence by the police as an investigatory tactic – both, as in Mussamat Itwaria's case, to secure confessions from them, as well as to obtain confessions from men anxious to protect their womenfolk and, with it, what they regarded as *their* honour (which according to one critic was a method 'as ingenious as it was atrocious').[20] That he chose to refuse to name, let alone punish, the rape of Mussamat Itwaria and her daughter is, therefore, significant. If, as Michel Foucault argues, the archive is 'the law of what can be said', I thus seek to understand the 'law' of what could be said about police rape in the Indian colonial archive.[21] Such an endeavour necessitates mining the silences within the colonial archive to theorize what Stephanie Smallwood terms the 'counterfact', namely the 'fact the archive is seeking to ignore, marginalize and disavow', while acknowledging – since colonial archives are inherently gendered – that the process of making sexual violence visible in the colonial archive also reveals the limits of such visibility.[22] As Ann Laura Stoler has urged, it necessitates reading, furthermore, *along* rather than *against* the archival grain, not only because without a clear-cut understanding of what is signified by the 'grain' the idea of reading *against* it 'becomes nothing more than a prescriptive call to treat the documentary fragment as though it stands apart from and outside, rather than structurally embedded within, the politics of knowledge production', but because reading along the grain makes it possible to reveal not only the power dynamics behind the production of the archive, and the particular institutions that it served, but the threat the archive posed to the very state that it helped to construct.[23]

To understand how police rape was coded in the Indian colonial archive we need to begin, then, by looking both at colonial attitudes towards rape and how rape was treated in Indian courts. As scholars have demonstrated, colonial officials regarded violence against Indian women not only as part of the private sphere, and therefore not subject to criminal jurisdiction, but as 'a social problem that should be handled by Indians themselves ... not by the colonial state'.[24] Those forms of gendered violence that did attract the attention of British liberal reformers, like *sati* (widow immolation) – which, in contrast to rape, drew attention because they were sensational and thus confirmed British perceptions of Indian difference – were therefore framed in cultural and religious terms, not that of criminal justice.[25] But the need to entrench a moral framework within the colonial Indian judicial system 'also meant that the realm of sexual-social regulation could not', for the British, be 'entirely ... abandoned to [Indian] society'.[26] The development of colonial legal institutions in India from the late eighteenth century onwards thus drew the British into policing crimes against women, but in ways that reinforced both their own political authority and that of Indian patriarchy – albeit one shorn of what the British regarded as its more excessive features by its embedment within the colonial rule of law.[27] The Indian penal code, for example, made rape subject to wide magisterial discretion, since it carried a punishment of between two to ten years (on the grounds that the sentence for the rapist of a high-caste woman by a low-caste man, for example, should be high in comparison to that of a low-caste woman, who was presumed to be 'without character'; the injury of rape was therefore presumed to be 'infinitely less' against low-caste victims like Mussamat Itwaria).[28] As I have already noted, conviction rates were, moreover, low, and continued to decline from the late nineteenth century onwards; rape was, in fact, less likely to be prosecuted than any other embodied crime.[29] In addition to treating the claims of female Indian rape victims with scepticism – and even to declaring such charges as false and charging victims with adultery – British judges also regarded rape as a violation of male codes of honour, which led them to treat acts of violence committed by Indian men in response to the sexual disgrace of a wife or other female relative with considerable leniency (which served to highlight, in addition, their perception of Indian women as the property of their husbands, rather than as individuals capable of experiencing pain and suffering).[30]

Scholars such as Elizabeth Kolsky, Radhika Singha and Ishita Pande have offered a range of compelling reasons why the British were reluctant to intervene in cases of sexual violence against women in India, ranging from their uncertainty and fear about interfering in Indian culture to their desire 'to conserve police and judicial agencies for [their] own priorities of rule', not to mention anxieties about being able to control their low-paid, poorly educated police.[31] But the scholarship on rape in colonial India focuses primarily upon the law and its implementation – in other words, on the rare rape cases that were actually prosecuted in colonial India (and that, moreover, were heard on appeal in the higher courts), rather than those that were not. The colonial state also appears in such accounts to be, at the very least, prejudiced and callous when it came to the violation of Indian women, and at worst as using rape as a trope of difference to justify and sustain its rule.[32] Such an approach underestimates, however, the role of rape as a technology of colonial rule, particularly when perpetrated by the colonial regime's violence workers, as well as the ways in which the archive served to reinforce this.

To understand the centrality of rape to the maintenance of British rule in India we need to begin, however, not with rape but with torture. As I have argued elsewhere, police torture had become systematized as a tactic of colonial governance in India by the late nineteenth century because it benefitted the British; not only did it serve to terrorize, and thus quell, the Indian population, but also to justify the civilizing rhetoric of colonialism through displacing blame for such acts of violence onto so-called 'depraved' and 'barbaric' Indian men.[33] Since sexual violence is (and has historically been) 'used by authoritarian regimes to discourage dissent and to demonstrate power', rape thus became a key component of such a process, namely a means through which the Indian police could torture suspects and their families through humiliating, degrading and intimidating them.[34] As Marnia Lazreg argues in the case of the torture of Front de libération nationale (FLN) suspects by French security forces during the Algerian War of Independence (1954–62), when it came to the torture of women, 'torture seldom took place without rape'.[35] Yet although rape as an aspect of torture was facilitated in Algeria by the legal vacuum surrounding the implementation of France's 'antisubversive' doctrine, for the French authorities, not to mention the French media, rape was not regarded as an aspect of torture, since it could not be justified as part of France's purportedly legitimate 'counter-revolutionary war' against Algerians.[36]

In colonial India, as in colonial Algeria, it was both the prevalence of rape as a torture tactic by the state's violence workers and the legal vacuum surrounding torture that made it possible for acts of rape committed by police officials to be coded as either 'unnameable' in the colonial archive or simply as other forms of violence, since although torture was illegal it was accommodated in the colonial criminal justice system as an extra-legal 'custom of the law'.[37] That the British were aware, from at least the early nineteenth century, of the sexually predatory nature of their police forces in India is clear in enactments such as Regulation 7 of 1811: according to this, a complaint regarding rape and other sexual offences had to be lodged with a magistrate, at whose discretion it was to be investigated, rather than with the police.[38] While such a measure was ostensibly designed, on the one hand, to prevent such complaints from being simply dismissed, and on the other to impede the police from submitting victims of sexual violence to further violation, there was never any real attempt to put a stop to such predation. When not reconceptualized, for example, as a seemingly more benign offence, such as 'seduction', rape accusations against police officers were largely dismissed as being 'false', or as incapable of being substantiated for lack of evidence.[39] This was particularly the case in regard to women who were lower caste or otherwise marginal, on the grounds that 'an "attempt to outrage modesty" could not be perpetrated on a woman who had none'.[40] Moreover, by the 1920s, the time that Mussammat Itwaria and her daughter suffered their horrific ordeal, the requirement that rape cases be corroborated – that is, that a woman's testimony alone was not sufficient to secure a conviction – had become a 'general rule' in the high courts.[41] In refusing to acknowledge and name acts of rape committed by the state's violence workers, the judicial system in colonial India thus not only made women more vulnerable to being raped, but made rape central to what Walter Benjamin has termed the 'law-preserving violence' of colonial rule.[42]

Numerous scholars have demonstrated the falsity of the purported mission of British colonialism in India, as Gayatri Spivak has memorably phrased it, of 'saving brown women from brown men'.[43] The intersections between torture and rape thus further underline the impossibility of such a mission in light of the fact that, as Lazreg has highlighted for Algeria, 'rape was an essential part of state terror'.[44] In the case of Mussamat Itwaria and her daughter, that they were tortured by the police essentially rendered their rape invisible. That their torturers were, however, prosecuted – a relatively rare occurrence in colonial India – was not just because the victims died (which elevated torture, very problematically for the British, into scandal) but, I would argue, because they committed suicide. While colonial officials were generally dismissive of India's high female suicide rate, arguing that Indian women simply had a propensity to commit suicide for 'trivial domestic reasons' (although they did find the number of mothers who jumped into wells with their children in their arms 'astounding'), they were forced to pay it some regard when it came to rape, since a woman's willingness to commit the ultimate act of embodied violence *against herself* offered the ultimate proof that she had, indeed, been raped.[45] It was the suicide of Mussamat Itwaria and her daughter, in short, that led to the prosecution of a police sub-inspector, two constables, and three *chaukidars* for 'voluntarily causing hurt to extort confession' – not, for reasons I have already noted, for rape.[46] But although Nanvutty gave such officers what were, in colonial India, fairly harsh sentences (although for wrongful confinement, not torture) these were reduced on appeal. Sub-Inspector Jai Dayal's three-year sentence of rigorous imprisonment was reduced to nine months and the two constables' two-year sentences of rigorous imprisonment to six months, while the *chaukidars* were sentenced merely to three months' simple imprisonment and a fine of 100 rupees (although one received a mere one-day sentence).[47]

I would like to conclude by considering a question posed by Rajeswari Sunder Rajan in response to Spivak's seminal article 'Can the Subaltern Speak?' that highlights how the process of making sexual violence visible in the colonial archive also demonstrates the constraints of such visibility, namely: what does it mean that the subaltern, in this case, died, and that she did so through committing suicide?[48] Representing such a death, as Rajan notes, requires certain affective and ethical responses in light of the fact that it was the deaths of Musammat Itwaria and her daughter that make it possible for them to emerge into historical discourse. The difficulty that a subaltern suicide poses, for historians, is that while suicide is, on the one hand, an act of free will, it also serves to foreclose meaning, particularly for women; in the case of Musammat Itwaria, her suicide was interpreted by colonial officials as a sign that she was innocent of the charges made against her, and it was her self-proclaimed embodied innocence, I would suggest, that led her torturer-rapists to be prosecuted.[49] The problem is not, then, that the subaltern cannot speak – remember Musammat Itwaria's '*kise karm ke no rahe*' – but that we fail to hear her. We fail to hear her because the subaltern can speak but has been silenced by western history. Like the archive of slavery, the colonial archive, as Spivak argues, 'rests upon a founding violence', one which determines what can be said about colonialism in addition to creating 'subjects and objects of power'.[50] It is for this reason, as Tiziana Morosetti demonstrates in her chapter in this volume, that attempts to recover the lived experiences of colonized women from the colonial archive can serve as acts of ventriloquism that mask the absence of their voices from such an archive. But it is also a result of such power dynamics that the historicity of subaltern women, to borrow from Marissa Fuentes, is 'mutilated', since they largely enter the colonial archive as objects to whom violence has been done.[51] We thus fail to hear the subaltern woman even as she speaks through her body in the only way open to her in the face of a socio-cultural system in which gendered violence is enshrined through the demands placed on female chastity, namely to take her own life.[52]

It is not only, however, the way in which the sexed subject is constituted in such a system that ensures that, while 'the singularity of [her] death demands from us an effort of understanding and [a] gesture of mourning ... the gendered subaltern will resist such recuperation'.[53] An additional reason is the power dynamics inherent in the colonial archive. This is because, for the British colonial state, Mussamat Itwaria could only enter the archive as a victim of her own act of self-destruction, not of rape, as a result of the threat the archive poses to the state that constructs it – since, as Achille Mbembe puts it, 'the power of the state rests on its ability to consume time, that is, to abolish the archive and anaesthetise the past'.[54] In other words, it was vital for the British to keep the truth that its violence workers were routinely raping Indian women from entering the Indian colonial archive, since this would undermine a key justification for colonial rule. But to borrow from Saidiya Hartman, who contends that it is the state of emergency to which Black bodies continue to be subject that makes the study of historic acts of violence against Black women so pressing, what makes the need to resist such anesthetization of the past imperative is the ongoing 'zones of emergency' inscribed onto the bodies of subaltern women, and the brutal sexual violence to which they continue to be subject not just in India, but globally.[55]

Notes

1. Home, Police, B, February 39, 1921, National Archives of India (NAI).
2. Ibid.
3. Ibid.
4. Ibid.
5. Ibid.
6. Ibid.
7. Ibid.
8. Ibid.
9. See Brij Raj Chauhan, *Extending the Frontiers of Sociological Learning* (Meerut: Meerut University, Institute of Advanced Studies, 1980).
10. Cited in Douglas Peers, 'Torture, the Police, and the Colonial State in the Madras Presidency, 1816-55', *Criminal Justice History: An International Annual* 12 (1991): 33. See also Charu Gupta, 'Writing Sex and Sexuality: Archives of Colonial North India', *Journal of Women's History* 23. 4 (2011): 25-6.
11. Home, Police, B, February 39, 1921, NAI.
12. Ibid.
13. Ibid.
14. Ibid.
15. Ibid. See Elizabeth Kolsky, 'The Rule of Colonial Indifference: Rape on Trial in Early Colonial India, 1805-57', *The Journal of Asian Studies* 69. 4 (2010): 1101-14; Elizabeth Kolsky, '"The Body Evidencing the Crime": Rape on Trial in Colonial India, 1860-1947', *Gender & History* 22. 1 (2010): 115-18; and Jonathan Saha, 'The Male State: Colonialism, Corruption and Rape Investigations in the Irrawaddy Delta c. 1900', *The Indian Economic and Social History Review* 47. 3 (2010): pp. 343-376.
16. Gupta, 'Writing Sex and Sexuality', p. 15. See also Michelle Caswell, '"The Archive" Is Not an Archives: Acknowledging the Intellectual Contributions of Archival Studies', *Reconstruction* 16. 1 (2016): *UCLA*. https://escholarship.org/uc/item/7bn4v1fk, accessed 18 January 2021.
17. Deana Heath, 'Torture, the State and Sexual Violence against Men in Colonial India', *Radical History Review*, 126 (2016): 122-33.
18. See Ameer Ali, Enclosure No. 3, p. 7, IOR/L/PJ/6/1368, file 1823, 1914, British Library (BL); '"Police Torture"', *The Times of India*, 19 April 1889; and Bhupendranath Basu, Legislative Council Debates, 28 February 1912, p. 265. See also Kolsky, '"The Body Evidencing the Crime"', p. 124; and Ishita Pande, 'Phulmoni's Body: The Autopsy, The Inquest and the Humanitarian Narrative on Child Rape in India', *South Asian History and Culture* 4. 1 (2013): 9-30.
19. Pratiksha Baxi, *Public Secrets of Law: Rape Trials in India* (Delhi: Oxford University Press, 2014), p. xlvi. See also Kolsky, 'The Rule of Colonial Indifference', p. 1095; and Saha, 'The Male State', p. 367. Baxi is referring, here, to post-colonial India, but

her observations apply equally well to the colonial era. Although the case that I am analysing here was not prosecuted as a rape case, in effectively erasing the rape of Mussamat Itwaria and her daughter it essentially enforced the phallocentric notions of justice that Baxi describes.

20 Heath, *Colonial Terror*, Ch. 3 and Conclusion; Ameer Ali, Enclosure No. 3, 7, IOR/L/PJ/6/1368, file 1823, 1914, BL; 'Editorial', *The Times of India*, 12 October 1880; and Radhika Singha, 'Making the Domestic More Domestic: Criminal Law and the "Head of the Household"', 1772-1843', *The Indian Economic and Social History Review* 33. 3 (1996): 314.

21 Michel Foucault, *The Archaeology of Knowledge and the Discourse on Language*, translated by A. M. Sheridan Smith (New York: Pantheon Books, 1972), p. 129.

22 Stephanie E. Smallwood, 'The Politics of Accountability and History's Accountability to the Enslaved', *History of the Present: A Journal of Critical History* 6. 2 (2016): p. 125; Marisa J. Fuentes, *Dispossessed Lives: Enslaved Women, Violence and the Archive* (Philadelphia: University of Pennsylvania Press, 2016), p. 10; Saha, 'The Male State', p. 345; and Anjali Arondekar, *For the Record: On Sexuality and the Colonial Archive in India* (Durham and London: Duke University Press, 2009), p. 3.

23 Anne Laura Stoler, 'Colonial Archives and the Arts of Governance', *Archival Science* 2 (2002): 101, 107; and Smallwood, 'The Politics of Accountability'. See also Achille Mbembe, 'The Power of the Archive and Its Limits', in Carolyn Hamilton, Verne Harris, Jane Taylor, Michele Pickover, Graeme Reid, and Razia Saleh (eds), *Refiguring the Archive* (Dordrecht: Kluwer Academic Publishers, 2002), p. 23.

24 Kolsky, 'The Rule of Colonial Indifference', p. 1099.

25 Ibid., p. 1096; and Lata Mani, 'Contentious Traditions: The Debate on Sati in Colonial India', *Cultural Critique* 7 (1987): 119-56.

26 Radkhia Singha, *A Despotism of Law: Crime and Justice in Early Colonial India* (New Delhi: Oxford University Press, 1998), p. 141.

27 Kolsky, 'The Rule of Colonial Indifference', p. 1094; Singha, *A Despotism of Law*, p. 136; and Singha, 'Making the Domestic More Domestic', p. 310.

28 Kolsky, 'The Rule of Colonial Indifference', p. 1099.

29 Ibid., p. 1095.

30 Singha, *A Despotism of Law*, pp. 143-4; and Kolsky, 'The Rule of Colonial Indifference', pp. 106, 1112. See also Daniel Grey, 'Importing Gendered Legal Reasoning from England: Wife Murders in Early Colonial India, 1805-1857', *Cultural and Social History* 14. 4 (2017): 483-98.

31 Singha, *A Despotism of Law*, p. 123; and Heath, *Colonial Terror*, pp. 122-6, 148-58, 166.

32 The rape of child-wives, in particular, was used to justify colonialism as humanitarian intervention while also, as Isihita Pande argues, 'brush[ing] over the horror or the violence of rape as such'. Pande, 'Phulmoni's Body', p. 25.

33 Heath, *Colonial Terror*; and Deana Heath, 'Bureaucracy, Power and Violence in Colonial India: The Role of Indian Subalterns', in Peter Crooks and Timothy Parsons (eds), *Empires & Bureaucracy in European History: From Late Antiquity to the Modern World* (Cambridge University Press, 2016), pp. 515-56.

34 Michael Peel, 'Introduction', in Michael Peel (ed.), *Rape as a Method of Torture* (Manchester: Medical Foundation for the Care of Victims of Torture, 2004), p. 11. As Peel argues, when rape 'is carried out in an organized manner [this] aggravates the humiliating and degrading treatment such that it can be considered torture'. Ibid., p. 12.

35 Marnia Lazreg, *Torture and the Twighlight of Empire: From Algiers to Baghdad* (Princeton and Oxford: Princeton University Press, 2008), p. 160.
36 Ibid., pp. 165–6.
37 Heath, 'Torture, the State and Sexual Violence against Men'; Heath, *Colonial Terror*, pp. 106–39; and Iltudus Prichard, *The Chronicles of Budgepore; or, Sketches of Life in Upper India* (first published in 1870, London: Richard Edward King Limited 1893), p. 167.
38 Singha, *A Despotism of Law*, p. 141.
39 Saha, 'The Male State', pp. 363–5. Jonathan Saha has detailed a horrific case in colonial Burma (then governed as part of British colonial India), for example, almost a century after the passage of Regulation 7, in which a woman who went to her village headman to report being raped was then raped two more times, first by a police sergeant and then the headman. Saha, 'The Male State', p. 365.
40 Kolsky, 'The Body Evidencing the Crime', p. 118.
41 Ibid., p. 116.
42 Ibid., p. 123; and Walter Benjamin, 'Critique of Violence', in *Reflections: Essays, Aphorisms, Autobiographical Writings*, translated by Edmund Jephcott (New York: Shocken, 1978), p. 284.
43 Gayatri Chakravorty Spivak, 'Can the Subaltern Speak?', in Patrick Williams and Laura Chrisman (eds), *Colonial Discourse and Post-Colonial Theory: A Reader* (Hertfordshire: Harvester Wheatsheaf, 1994), p. 93.
44 Ibid., p. 167.
45 Cited in Singha, *A Despotism of Law*, p. 137; *Administration Report of the Madras Police for the Year 1868* (Madras: The Scottish Press, 1869), p. 10; and Kolsky, 'The Body Evidencing the Crime', p. 117.
46 Home, Police, B, February, 39, 1921, NAI; The Indian Penal Code, Act no. 45 of 1860.
47 Ibid.
48 Rajeswari Sunder Rajan, 'Death and the Subaltern', in Rosalind Morris (ed.), *Can the Subaltern Speak? Reflections on the History of an Idea* (Columbia: Columbia University Press, 2010), p. 119. On the significance of the suicide of the subaltern woman see also Spivak, 'Can the Subaltern Speak?', revised edn, pp. 21–78.
49 Ibid., p. 125.
50 Saidiya Hartman, 'Venus in Two Acts', *Small Axe* 26 (2008): 10.
51 Fuentes, *Dispossessed Lives*, p. 7. See also Smallwood, 'The Politics of Accountability', p. 124. Cf. Chapter 3, which discusses how/if it is possible to display objects associated with slavery, without perpetuating narratives.
52 See Donna Landry and Gerald MacLean, 'Reading Spivak', in Donna Landry and Gerald Maclean (eds), *The Spivak Reader* (New York: Routledge, 1996), pp. 1–14; and Concetta Principe, 'Spivak's Fantasy of Silence: A Secular Look at Suicide', *Journal for Cultural Research* 17. 3 (2013): 234–54.
53 Rajan, 'Death and the Subaltern', p. 127. See also Gayatri Chakravorty Spivak, 'The Rani of Sirmur: An Essay in Reading the Archives', *History and Theory* 24. 3 (1985): 247–72.
54 Mbembe, 'The Power of the Archive', p. 23.
55 Saidiya Hartman, 'The Dead Book Revisited', *History of the Present: A Journal of Critical History* 6. 2 (2016): 210–11; see also Hartman, 'Venus in Two Acts', and Baxi, *Public Secrets of Law*, p. xlvii.

Bibliography

Arondekar, Anjali. *For the Record: On Sexuality and the Colonial Archive in India*. Durham and London: Duke University Press, 2009.

Baxi, Pratiksha. *Public Secrets of Law: Rape Trials in India*. Delhi: Oxford University Press, 2014.

Benjamin, Walter. 'Critique of Violence'. In *Reflections: Essays, Aphorisms, Autobiographical Writings*, translated by Edmund Jephcott, 277–300. New York: Shocken, 1978.

Caswell, Michelle. '"The Archive" Is Not an Archives: Acknowledging the Intellectual Contributions of Archival Studies'. *Reconstruction* 16, no. 1 (2016): https://escholarship.org/uc/item/7bn4v1fk.

Chauhan, Brij Raj. *Extending the Frontiers of Sociological Learning*. Meerut: Meerut University, Institute of Advanced Studies, 1980.

Foucault, Michel. *The Archaeology of Knowledge and the Discourse on Language*, translated by A. M. Sheridan Smith. New York: Pantheon Books, 1972.

Fuentes, Marisa J. *Dispossessed Lives: Enslaved Women, Violence and the Archive*. Philadelphia: University of Pennsylvania Press, 2016.

Grey, Daniel. 'Importing Gendered Legal Reasoning from England: Wife Murders in Early Colonial India, 1805–1857'. *Cultural and Social History* 14, no. 4 (2017): 483–98.

Gupta, Charu. 'Writing Sex and Sexuality: Archives of Colonial North India'. *Journal of Women's History* 23, no. 4 (2011): 12–35.

Hartman, Saidiya. 'Venus in Two Acts'. *Small Axe* 26 (2008): 1–14.

Heath, Deana. 'Bureaucracy, Power and Violence in Colonial India: The Role of Indian Subalterns'. In *Empires & Bureaucracy in European History: From Late Antiquity to the Modern World*, edited by Peter Crooks and Timothy Parsons, 515–56. Cambridge University Press, 2016.

Heath, Deana. 'Torture, the State and Sexual Violence against Men in Colonial India'. *Radical History Review* 126 (2016): 122–33.

Heath, Deana. *Colonial Terror: Torture and State Violence in Colonial India*. New York: Oxford University Press, 2021.

Huggins, Martha, Mika Haritos-Fatouros, and Philip G. Zimbardo (eds). *Violence Workers: Police Torturers and Murderers Reconstruct Brazilian Atrocities*. Berkeley: University of California Press, 2002.

Kolsky, Elizabeth. '"The Body Evidencing the Crime": Rape on Trial in Colonial India, 1860–1947'. *Gender & History* 22, no. 1 (2010): 109–30.

Kolsky, Elizabeth. 'The Rule of Colonial Indifference: Rape on Trial in Early Colonial India, 1805–57'. *The Journal of Asian Studies* 69, no. 4 (2010): 1218–46.

Landry, Donna, and Gerald MacLean. 'Reading Spivak'. In *The Spivak Reader*, edited by Donna Landry and Gerald Maclean, 1–14. New York: Routledge, 1996.

Lazreg, Marnia. *Torture and the Twilight of Empire: From Algiers to Baghdad*. Princeton and Oxford: Princeton University Press, 2008.

Madras (Presidency), Police Department. *Administration Report of the Madras Police for the Year 1868*. Madras: The Scottish Press, 1869.

Mani, Lata. 'Contentious Traditions: The Debate on Sati in Colonial India'. *Cultural Critique* 7 (1987): 119–56.

Mbembe, Achille. 'The Power of the Archive and Its Limits'. In *Refiguring the Archive*, edited by Carolyn Hamilton, Verne Harris, Jane Taylor, Michele Pickover, Graeme Reid, and Razia Saleh, 19–26. Dordrecht: Kluwer Academic Publishers, 2002.

Pande, Ishita. 'Phulmoni's Body: The Autopsy, The Inquest and the Humanitarian Narrative on Child Rape in India'. *South Asian History and Culture* 4, no. 1 (2013): 9–30.

Peel, Michael. 'Introduction'. In *Rape as a Method of Torture*, edited by Michael Peel, 3–13. Manchester: Medical Foundation for the Care of Victims of Torture, 2004.

Peers, Douglas. 'Torture, the Police, and the Colonial state in the Madras Presidency, 1816–55'. *Criminal Justice History: An International Annual* 12 (1991): 29–56.

Prichard, Iltudus. *The Chronicles of Budgepore; or, Sketches of Life in Upper India*. London: Richard Edward King Limited: [1870] 1893.

Principe, Concetta. 'Spivak's Fantasy of Silence: A Secular Look at Suicide'. *Journal for Cultural Research* 17, no. 3 (2013): 234–54.

Rajan, Rajeswari Sunder. 'Death and the Subaltern'. In *Can the Subaltern Speak? Reflections on the History of an Idea*, edited by Rosalind Morris, 117–38. Columbia: Columbia University Press, 2010.

Saha, Jonathan. 'The Male State: Colonialism, Corruption and Rape Investigations in the Irrawaddy Delta c. 1900'. *The Indian Economic and Social History Review* 47, no. 3 (2010): 343–76.

Singha, Radhika. 'Making the Domestic More Domestic: Criminal Law and the "Head of the Household", 1772–1843'. *The Indian Economic and Social History Review* 33, no. 3 (1996): 309–43.

Singha, Radhika. *A Despotism of Law: Crime and Justice in Early Colonial India*. New Delhi: Oxford University Press, 1998.

Smallwood, Stephanie E. 'The Politics of Accountability and History's Accountability to the Enslaved'. *History of the Present: A Journal of Critical History* 6, no. 2 (2016): 117–32.

Spivak, Gayatri Chakravorty. 'The Rani of Sirmur: An Essay in Reading the Archives'. *History and Theory* 24, no. 3 (1985): 247–72.

Spivak, Gayatri Chakravorty. 'Can the Subaltern Speak?'. In *Colonial Discourse and Post-Colonial Theory: A Reader*, edited by Patrick Williams and Laura Chrisman, 66–111. Hertfordshire: Harvester Wheatsheaf, 1994.

Stoler, Anne Laura. 'Colonial Archives and the Arts of Governance'. *Archival Science* 2 (2002): 87–109.

Part Three

Biographical silences

9

Completing the mosaic: Sara Baartman and the archive

Tiziana Morosetti

Introduction

In an essay for the edited collection *The Postcolonial Enlightenment*, Daniel Carey has argued that Saidian contrapuntal readings of *Robinson Crusoe* – the superimposition of the historical and fictional narratives (as critics have looked for what the novel does *not* tell us) – have ultimately generated a trend to re-inscribe into the text what the text does not say. The problem for Carey does not lie with the practice of contrapuntal reading *per se*, but rather with its implications:

> The justification for such a scheme derives from an imperative to redress historical injustices ... Yet it runs the risk of appropriating literature as a mere allegory of history while assigning to criticism the task of determining the ways in which such texts represent historical truths outside themselves .... [A] temptation accompanies this critical approach, in which it is not enough to describe what the text excludes; rather, a tendency exists to write what is excluded back into the text itself. At this stage, counterpoint gives way to palimpsest.[1]

Carey refers here to the issue of slavery, as '[f]or critics it is not enough to demonstrate the text's ample engagement with colonialism and slavery ...; the relationship between Crusoe and Friday must also be implicated and specifically defined as that of master and slave'[2] – which, however, is not the case in the novel, unless the term 'slavery' acquires loose and generic meaning.

In this chapter, I apply Carey's approach to readings of Sara Baartman that, preoccupied with a contemporary political agenda,[3] reinscribe into the 'text' of her life 'historical truths outside' itself, or rather, as I will discuss, our own perceptions of her historical context, as well as of what *we* imagine must have been her acts, thoughts or even feelings. It is unsurprising that Baartman, a South African (Khoekhoe) woman infamously exhibited as the 'Hottentot Venus' in London in 1810, should have become an allegory of exploitation, racism and constructions of cultural and bodily 'difference' both in imperial Britain and in France, where she died in 1815. Baartman had 'the dubious honour of being an original, having served, in turn, as an object of entertainment, an object of media attention, a "sexualized" object, a monstrous object, and a scientific object'.[4] Her display won publicity when Zachary Macaulay of the African Institution accused her exhibitors in London, Alexander Dunlop and Hendrick Caesars, of having taken Baartman to Britain against her will, despite the 1807 Act for the Abolition of the Slave Trade. The later involvement of Georges Cuvier, who examined and dissected her body – the remains of which were displayed at the Musée de l'Homme in Paris and only repatriated to South Africa in 2002 – was another key factor in the sustained interest for Baartman, whose alleged 'apron' (*hypertrophied nymphae*) and steatopygia (enlargement of the buttocks) were presented as typical traits of the females of her 'race'.

Nor is it surprising that, in retracing the steps of Baartman, scholarship should have been driven by 'an imperative to redress historical injustices', to use Carey's words, while advancing the understanding of the display of human beings in nineteenth-century Europe, where sister forms of entertainment such as the freak show and the ethnological exhibition were central tools in articulating ideas of Otherness, hierarchy and power. Scholarly journeys into these subjects, from Robert Bogdan's seminal *Freak Shows* (1988) to Sadiah Qureshi's *Peoples on Parade* (2011), share necessary caution and a concern that their studies may represent 'an opportunity for modern voyeurism'.[5] Approaches to the colonial archive are of paramount importance: how do we interrogate the primary sources so that no new insult is added to the injury of the past? How do we share sources with other scholars without inviting voyeurism? How does the location, collection and retrieval of these sources, which often sit in imperial institutions, inform the direction of our investigation? And, last but not least, what could the implications of the investigation of the past be for our present time?

As a white scholar from the North writing at a moment of heightened debate about racism, I find these questions particularly pressing. My chapter, however, suggests that a way to prevent mis-appropriations of the past is in fact by prioritizing, in our enquiries, archival evidence over political agendas, approaching primary sources in a way that does not de-contextualize them or align them to *expectations* of what they should be telling us.

This point itself is not new; in an illuminating article, Zine Magubane has discussed what she terms the 'fetishization'[6] of Baartman by scholarship that 'saw [in her] not only racial and sexual alterity but also a personification of current debates about the right to liberty versus the right to property'.[7] More recently, Kellen Hoxworth has pointed to how Baartman's 'Blackness' has been reinterpreted in contemporary debates: 'many different racial groups claim Baartman as a symbol of their traumatic pasts …. She is variably reanimated as Coloured, "Hottentot," Khoekhoe, Khoisan, African, brown, and black'.[8] Echoing Magubane's concerns, Hoxworth observes how if

> Gilman's essay [1985] and its broad circulation generate an indexical Sara Baartman, which functions as the effigy of black female subjection … in [Hershini Bhana] Young's *Haunting Capital* [2006] this indexical Sara Baartman reappears … as the ghostly link between transatlantic scenes of subjection, the common tissue connecting African diasporas and transnational blacknesses.[9]

Yet, 'it is crucial to remember that the colonialist term "Hottentot" has long functioned as a derogatory signifier for *nonblack* indigenous peoples, especially the Khoekhoe, whose "yellow" or "brown" skin positioned them in shifting relations with blackness and whiteness'.[10]

Building on these preliminary observations by Magubane and Hoxworth, I will expand on two areas in which I find scholarship actively re-inscribes contemporary understandings into the archival 'text' of Baartman. The first is scholarship's uses of de-contextualized notions of 'whiteness' or 'Europeanness' – what I call a 'European exotic' – to further support narratives of Baartman's 'Blackness' and highlight her symbolism in current debates. These notions, as I illustrate in the first section, emerge especially in relation to Cuvier and to Baartman's sexual alterity, and reveal a fragmentary approach to the archive that conflates the early nineteenth century and the Victorian age.

The second point concerns scholarship's attempts to ventriloquize for Baartman. While this trend emerges from the dissatisfaction with a fundamental injustice – the stark absence of Baartman's own voice from the archive – I suggest it runs into the contradiction of reiterating the power structures that are being critiqued. The silencing of Baartman starts in fact in the archive itself, and this section will point to the several actors involved in this process: Baartman's interviewers in the examination conducted during the trial; the African Institution, in the charges brought forward against her exhibitors; and Anne Mathews in her recollection of her husband's encounter with Baartman. I posit that contemporary scholars, in positioning their own work as an opportunity for Baartman's voice to be finally 'heard', therefore also deny the dignified, *active* silences she opposed during the questionings she faced in her lifetime.

In my conclusions, I will briefly illustrate contrasting approaches to the archive by focusing on the research of Crais and Scully, which integrates the western archives with those in South Africa, and some recent work by Gordon-Chipembere in particular, which instead dismisses the 'charismatic nature' of the archive as 'useless and superfluous'.[11] I ultimately argue that a non-judgemental reappraisal of the archive in its entirety and *within* its context is a vital move towards restoring a more balanced consideration of Baartman, and that key to this is an acceptance of both her silences and those of the archive itself.

Baartman's context: The creation of a 'European exotic'

Jean Young and Natasha Gordon-Chipembere have pointed to the 'commodification' of Baartman on the part of the creative writing that has emerged around her story, especially Suzan-Lori Parks's *Venus* (1996), in which Baartman's relation with Cuvier is constructed as erotic: he 'plays out a "love" scenario on a giant, vertical white satin bed amid his own spasms of uncontrollable lust'.[12] Diana Ferrus's poem, 'I've Come to Take You Home' (1998), similarly presents '[t]he medical gaze … as penetrative – masculinised and sexualised'.[13] The depiction of Cuvier as predatory and sexually motivated, a form of ventriloquism in its own right, is an example of the tendency to reinscribe into Baartman's 'text' mis/understandings of the nineteenth century that reflect contemporary constructions of race, gender and sexuality. Gordon-Chipembere, while criticizing Parks for depicting Baartman as complicit in her romantic relation to Cuvier, expresses no doubt that the latter's observations in the autopsy should 'contain their own porno-erotic perspective'.[14] Rachel Holmes's study similarly describes Cuvier as someone who

> 'coaxed Saartje with chivalry ... [He] made little jokes which made her laugh in spite of herself. All of this disarming behaviour concealed Cuvier's true intentions. ... [H]e conceived a passion for Saartje that would not be satisfied until he possessed her completely. ... Through this most famous Venus the scientist enacted his rage against all women'.[15]

Robin Mitchell further reaffirms the notion that Cuvier's interest for Baartman 'went beyond his scientific authority'.[16] This idea finds no evidence in the archive; Holmes's statements are even based, by her own admission, on Henri de Blainville's *Sur une femme de la race hottentote* (1816), which does not mention Cuvier at all.[17] On their part, Cuvier's *Extrait d'observation*, overlooked in the examples above, does not reveal erotic or romantic undertones, even in the only passage that describes Baartman alive[18] – unless, that is, we decide to read an autopsy's description of body parts as proof of such interest. The overall tone of Cuvier's report is undeniably triumphalist and betrays the self-assuredness of a powerful man in sharing with the scientific community findings that (despite tenuously evidenced) he presents as conclusive evidence of the much-talked 'apron'. That Cuvier's assertions on the 'anomalies' of Khoekhoe women would have been contradicted later in the century[19] does not detract from the opportunity – horrific as it was – that the chance of dissecting Baartman represented for him within his work at the Muséum d'Histoire Naturelle. While we cannot exclude that the man Cuvier formed an erotic interest in Baartman, the self-satisfaction of the scientist Cuvier is reasonably explained by professional ambition and evidenced by the primary sources. Far from wishing to defend Cuvier, my concern is that reducing his relation to Baartman to a vignette of white-on-Black sexual violence does in fact invite, rather than avoid, voyeuristic approaches (cf. Adiva Lawrence's and Deana Heath's chapters in this volume), thus trivializing the significance of Baartman's dissection within early nineteenth-century science. As Magubane has observed, Cuvier's stance would in this context 'be better understood if ... analyzed in relation to nineteenth-century European class dynamics, rather than simply concluding that his actions reflect the generalized psychological dispositions ... of European men'.[20]

Furthermore, discussions of Cuvier conflate early nineteenth-century attitudes to race with Victorian scientific racism. In Gilman's study (also in its 2002 expansion)[21] Cuvier's positions are discussed as representative of the whole century, while Fausto-Sterling suggests that "[b]y naming Baartman as a Bushwoman, Cuvier created her as the most primitive of all humans – a female exemplar of a degenerate, barely human race. Despite his lack of belief in evolution, he constructed her as the missing link between humans and apes".[22] McKittrick has further observed how 'in [Baartman's] life *and afterlife*, it has been biological determinism and scientific racism – evolutionary reports, missing-link tales ... – that have descriptively coded her'.[23] Not only does Cuvier's *Extrait d'observation* not mention the missing link (an expression first used by Charles Lyell only in 1851),[24] but even if for him Baartman 'was as close as possible to an ape',[25] describing this with the vocabulary of Victorian science again speaks to present-day debates on race alongside, arguably, contemporary understandings of nineteenth-century science.

Similar generalizations also inform discussions of the sexual alterity represented by Baartman as the 'Hottentot Venus'. Gould has argued that part of a reason for the titillation offered by Baartman's show, in which she wore a tight costume designed to suggest nakedness, should be found in the contrast with '[a]dvanced humans (read modern Europeans), [who] are refined, modest, and sexually restrained (not to mention hypocritical for advancing such a claim)'.[26] The point is reiterated by Abrahams's observation that 'in an age where a glimpse even of female ankles was regarded as indecent, the exhibition of Sarah Bartman's legs clearly set her apart from white females'.[27] These statements come in disregard of differences in class, background and nationality that informed constructions of whiteness in nineteenth-century Europe, and again reinscribe understandings of the Victorian age – or rather, renowned stereotypes of Victorian prudishness[28] – into the early-nineteenth-century context. In so doing, these scholars suggest straightforward juxtapositions that are, however, complicated both by the 'transitional and contested position'[29] of Baartman's display – as it sat, long before the established business of Victorian 'human zoos', between freak show and ethnological exhibition – and by notions of individual and racial ab/normalcy conveyed by the posters of Baartman's show.[30]

Furthermore, if Baartman's attire was in clear contrast with Georgian fashion, as suggested also by Anne Mathews's *Memoirs of Charles Mathews, Comedian* (1839), a closer look at what this fashion entailed provides room for alternative readings of Baartman's attire. Mathews opens her account of Baartman by saying that '[i]n those days, when *bustles* were *not*, she was a curiosity, for English ladies then wore no shape but what Nature gave …; and the Grecian drapery was simply thrown upon the natural form, without whalebone or buckram to distort or disguise it'.[31] The absence of bustles, however, does not imply that the bodies of 'English ladies' should be invisible beneath their garments. The pseudo-classical style in fashion between 1790 and 1810 was in fact, as pointed by A. D. Harvey, 'less constricting and shape-disguising than earlier styles', with plenty of flesh visible: '[t]he shoulders and arms were bared … The décolletage became low and wide, and the stays were sometimes arranged to thrust up the breasts'.[32] Importantly, the posterior of women was not supposed to disappear, but rather appear without artifice, as suggested by Mathews herself when she states that women at the show even poked Baartman to verify whether her posterior was '*nattral*'.[33] The *Memoirs* therefore suggest in hindsight (and probably building in part on the numerous caricatures that followed Baartman's show, as Mathews herself never attended it) that the interest of audiences should be in the alleged size of Baartman's rear, not in the unusual sight of a woman's posterior. As Harvey again notes, 'it is surely more than a coincidence that the 1800s, which were one of the periods when rumps were highly visible, at least in outline, also saw the establishment of flagellation as a major component of the commercial sex industry'.[34]

In superimposing contemporary understandings of Victorian culture on aspects of early nineteenth-century culture, scholars therefore again overlook Baartman's historical context, while partaking of a wider tendency to dismiss 'the Victorians' experience [the whole nineteenth century in fact] as less honest, less sophisticated, less self-cognisant than our own'.[35] In doing so, they betray an anxiety to draw a line between 'us' and 'them' that derives, as mentioned, from a wish to redress the injustices and the long-lasting legacy of nineteenth-century racialist and racist ideas. In the process, however, not only are important details diminished – the relevance of Baartman's posterior in both her iconography and the scientific discourses that ultimately led to her dissection is lost, for example, in Abrahams's focus on her legs. But, importantly, scholarship also inadvertently contributes to reiterating the vocabulary of human display, as using Baartman 'as a focal point for discussions of race and gender' risks, in Qureshi's words, 're-establishing her as a curiosity merely renamed as cultural icon.'[36]

The quest for the 'real' Sara: Ventriloquizing Baartman's voice

Abrahams's is also an example of work that explicitly wishes to engage with the person of Baartman, as she writes that 'while reams have been written about the various uses of Sara Bartman as a metaphor, a freak show, or a piece of evidence for scientific racist theories, little interest has been displayed in Sara Bartman the human being'.[37] Similarly, Gordon-Chipembere's edited collection on Baartman aims at establishing a close connection with the 'personhood' of 'Auntie Sarah',[38] while in her most recent publication on the subject Hershini Bhana Young strives to 'imagine Baartman's will'[39] in a 'political act that does not overlook [her will's] ultimate illegibility'.[40] While it is somewhat inevitable that an interest in the historical figure of Baartman should conflate with a quest for the 'real' Sara, ventriloquizing for Baartman has the problem, alongside perpetuating her silencing, of also silencing or de-contextualizing archival primary sources in the process.

An example can be found in discussions of the trial, the documents of which are central to our knowledge of Baartman's show as the 'Hottentot Venus' but also revealing of the silencing of Baartman's voice in the archive itself – as her testimony in this circumstance is, compared to others, not only indirect and incomplete but also tellingly short. In the deposition of Samuel Solly and John George Moojen – who represented Macaulay, Dunlop and Caesars, respectively, and who interviewed Baartman at her residence on 27 November 1810 – three hours of conversation in Dutch are summarized in English in a few hundred words. The document briefly describes Baartman's background, gives some sense of her routine in London, and outlines her exhibition as one for which 'she is to receive one half of the money'– while on Baartman's freedom to disengage from her exhibitors, had she so wanted, no 'satisfactory answer' can be obtained.[41] Some information provided by this document has been challenged,[42] and the agreement that Baartman is said to have produced during this interview is, furthermore, only dated 29 October 1810, which has prompted scholars to wonder whether Baartman may have been issued with a more favourable agreement in light of the forthcoming trial. The contents of the agreement are not in any case disclosed, and Baartman, who is said to be unable to read and write, reportedly 'understands very little' of it. Even as it does not provide conclusive evidence of whether or not Baartman had willingly signed a contract, this source therefore offers enough ground for us to doubt her willing engagement; at the very least, it speaks to a subjugation and exploitation that the label of freedom, even if ascertained, would certainly not erase.

Yet, as for *Robinson Crusoe*, the issue of Baartman's slavery remains problematic; and if our interest today 'must partly lie in her relevance to discussions of slavery',[43] a dissatisfaction with the outcome of the trial – as the Court concluded she was *not* a slave – also arguably characterizes scholarship. Abrahams amongst others challenges the credibility of Baartman's interview on the ground that this was a situation in which 'the white man asked the questions and the brown woman answered'.[44] This being the case, '[Baartman] would have done her utmost to discover what her interlocutors wished to hear, which responses would get her into least trouble, and which might conceivably ameliorate her situation. She would have thought like that *because she spoke a slave language* shaped by a culture forced to develop under slavery'.[45] Thus, the evidence on Baartman's interview, however fragmentary or unreliable, is hushed to make place for the assumption that the language Baartman spoke, which stemmed from a context of slavery but was not incidentally her main language,[46] should have determined her individual thinking *as* that of a slave in those particular circumstances. Baartman's association with slavery – which holds political significance not least in South Africa[47] – is further reinforced by the speculation that '[h]ad she [Baartman] arrived in the 1780s, she might have met the likes of Olaudah Equiano and Sancho Ignatius, black people with … an understanding of slave cultures'.[48] Differences in class, gender, background and experience between Black individuals across decades are thus erased to appeal to common goals that speak to the present day rather than Baartman's time.

Hershini Bhana Young similarly shifts the focus away from archival evidence; because conditions of enforced labour would equal *de facto* slavery, she finds 'the question of whether Baartman had signed a contract of secondary importance'[49] and wonders 'what happens if we think of [Baartman] as performing not only while on display but also as she testifies in front of a group of men *who are determined to cast her in obvious ways*'.[50] The possibility advanced by Young is not only intriguing but has the merit, like Abrahams's work, of fully acknowledging Baartman's Khoekhoe status, as the colonial power relation replicated by the interview cannot be underestimated when approaching the documents of the trial. It is striking, however, that no such doubt applies to the affidavit of Zachary Macaulay, Thomas Gisborne Babbington and Peter Van Wageninge, who on the other hand contend Baartman was a slave, despite their testimony resulting from a similar interview.

In the affidavit, Baartman is described as sullen and sighing, looking visibly distressed 'during the time they [Macaulay et al.] were present';[51] a statement that has been widely read as indicative of her *general* state of mind, but may also, as convincingly advanced by Helen Davies, 'inadvertently reveal that she is behaving differently due to having an *especially* interrogative audience'.[52] Macaulay had in fact visited the show twice, remaining more than an hour in the room; and because Caesars failed to produce, on Macaulay's first visit, the required permission by Lord Caledon to bring Baartman to Europe, an interview was arranged that saw her questioned by white men in the manner of the later interview with Solly and Moojen. Furthermore, Baartman's voice is notably and regrettably absent also in the affidavit, ventriloquized by someone whose antislavery positions may indeed 'have predisposed [them] to see the relationship [between Baartman and her exhibitors] as one of slavery'.[53] The interest of the African Institution, which offered to 'bear all expenses of restoring [Baartman] to her Country and friends',[54] must also be read in the context of its general purpose, which was 'to introduce the blessings of civilized society among a people sunk in ignorance and barbarism'.[55]

In short, the men that interviewed Baartman on this occasion may well have been as 'determined to cast her in obvious ways' as Solly and Moojen. It is furthermore worth remembering that it was Baartman's legal status that interested Macaulay, not her individual circumstances, so that 'when Lord Ellenborough invited the possibility of a second prosecution on these grounds [public decency], it was never taken up by the defenders of Saartjie Baartman'.[56] The show thus went on to the provinces before Baartman ended up in Paris, where she died.

I should like to stress that I do not doubt the contents of the affidavit, as primary sources are overall consistent in pointing to Baartman's distress and exploitation; rather, my concern is with certain sources being taken at face value over others. This is also, importantly, the case with the already mentioned *Memoirs of Charles Mathews, Comedian*, which, because it offers detailed insights into the show (such as that Baartman could be touched by the audience without an extra fee),[57] has been regularly quoted from Richard Altick's *The Shows of London* (1978) onwards. But that the nature of this source – a four-volume recollection of Charles Mathew's life published by his widow some thirty years after Baartman's show – should have gone unquestioned by scholarship is all the more surprising, as it provides one of the boldest attempts to ventriloquize Baartman: by putatively quoting her own voice.

The description of Charles Mathews's and John Philip Kemble's encounter with the 'Hottentot Venus' in the *Memoirs* is in fact arguably more about Kemble than Baartman herself. From the description of his theatrical entrance to the close-up on the tragedian's face ('he gazed at the woman, with his under-lip dropped for a minute. His beautiful countenance then underwent a sudden change, and at length softened almost into tears of compassion. "Poor, *poor* creature!"').[58] Kemble is depicted in very emotional tones. His countenance is contrasted with that of the working classes, 'our own barbarians', as well as that of Baartman, whose 'sullen and occasionally ferocious expression' with the common public changed 'the moment she looked in Mr Kemble's face, [as] her own became placid and mild'.[59] It is a gendered and politicized gaze that is described in this symbolic tableau, which also importantly illustrates the hierarchies of theatre: the white man's 'fine face', that of the most famous tragedian of the time, bestows some grace upon the sullen features of the 'Hottentot' woman, engaged in a freak show – while Mathews, the renowned comedian, stands aside, silent between the two.

Such is the delight of Baartman to see Kemble that 'patting her hands together, and holding them up in evident admiration, uttered the unintelligible words "Oh, ma Babba! Oh, ma Babba!" gazing at the face of the tragedian with unequivocal delight'.[60] Is this Baartman's delight or Charles Mathews's, or could this be what his wife – herself an actress – presumes must have been anyone's reaction, let alone that of a 'Hottentot', to the interest of a stage celebrity such as Kemble? And what language would indeed Baartman speak that is 'unintelligible' but perfectly apt for transcription, so that the word 'babba' is even understood by Kemble to mean *'papa'*?[61] In short, I would argue this source reflects far more Anne Mathews's own interpretation, as someone familiar with the stage who, as mentioned, did not herself attend the show, than Charles Mathews's recollection of that particular encounter (which, incidentally, is absent from biographies of Kemble).

This, again, is not to suggest that the misery of Baartman's show must not have been as described. Indeed, if one lines up the bare events as they are outlined, it is a bleak picture that emerges: Baartman is harassed by her audience; Kemble addresses Baartman and then 'minutely question[s] the man [Caesars?] about the state of mind, disposition, comfort &c. of the Hottentot';[62] Kemble then turns to Charles Mathews and starts talking to him; Baartman addresses Kemble. This is a woman that – taken aback, or scared perhaps, by yet another intervention of a white man whom in all likeliness she did not know but who seemed very interested in knowing about *her* – may have simply tried to engage in a conversation otherwise going on over her head. These two different interpretations (a Baartman that is impressed by Kemble, and one that merely tries to affirm her agency; to which, following Young's suggestion above, we may even add that of a *performing* Baartman) co-exist in this source, and we can only suspect which is the nearest to reality.

Conclusions

So far my chapter, in considering scholarship from a variety of backgrounds, from anthropology to history to literary studies, has examined approaches to the archive that consider primary sources located in Britain and France. I should now like to briefly consider the work of Crais and Scully (2008), which, while attracting mixed criticism, has represented a turning point in scholarship on Baartman, in that their extensive research in South Africa – Cape Town, especially – has effectively integrated the western sources. This has resulted in reassessing the study of Baartman in three main directions.

The first concerns Baartman's time in South Africa, which comes out in fuller picture – her date of birth, assumed to be around 1789, being retroceded to the 1770s to account for her pregnancy in 1796. Secondly, the representation of Baartman as a passive subject is challenged on the ground of the aquatints produced for Baartman's show, for two of which Bartmann was recognized as the publisher: itself a rarity in the history of human displays, and one that leaves some room for Baartman's agency, because '[i]f [she] was the publisher of the prints, she had legal title to the proceeds derived from their sale'.[63] Furthermore, Baartman herself may have contributed to the costume shown in the aquatints; this is a mixture of imagined and real elements from Gonaqua culture, which, however, was not known to Dunlop and Caesars: the latter 'never ventured outside Cape Town. Nor could the men easily consult descriptions of Gonaqua. [Caesars] could not read'.[64] Thirdly, Caesars, who the 'London public perceived ... as a white Boer, a Dutch settler',[65] is suggested to be a free Black, enlisted as such in the Cape 1807 census, as well as in the tax rolls.[66] While this may not mean

Caesars was indeed Black,[67] the possibility substantially complicates readings of Baartman's experiences in London, as also does her contradictory lifestyle, including the presence of the two Black boys that Solly and Moojen affirm attended to her.[68]

These findings may not radically alter how we feel regarding Baartman's show, as they do not prove she was free nor that she profited from her show (Crais and Scully themselves doubt that Baartman ever received any of the due royalties from the aquatints). But Baartman's legal position in the matter cannot altogether be dismissed, and Caesars's potential ethnicity certainly casts a different light even on Macaulay's demand that he produce the necessary documents.[69] However, because these findings still rely 'solely on the authority of the colonial records',[70] they are rejected by scholars like Gordon-Chipembere, who, in her review of Crais and Scully's book and *Sara Baartman and the Hottentot Venus: A Ghost Story and a Biography* (2008), challenges the agency attributed to Baartman in relation to the aquatints once again on the ground of Baartman's supposed thoughts: 'Why Sara would contribute to the reductive, racist caricatures of herself ... is never problematized'.[71] This is an interesting question that reveals, however, the assumption that Baartman should have had notions of racism in the terms we do today, and ultimately re-establishes the narrative of Baartman as entirely passive.

Gordon-Chipembere's work, like that of Hershini Bhana Young and Siphiwe Gloria Ndlovu, who contributed to her 2011 edited collection on Baartman, is representative of recent work that overall contests the use of the colonial archive *as such*; as Gordon-Chipembere affirms, 'testimonies in Europe [but, arguably, South Africa too] ... are through the voices/written words of [Baartman's] European translators and owners. They remain questionable in regard to agenda and intent. I am not willing to surrender my knowledge of Sarah Baartman to these texts'.[72] To be clear, the point raised is essential, and speaks to power dynamics that it is paramount to interrogate when it comes to the colonial archive (see the contributions in part 2 of this volume); but if on the one hand Gordon-Chipembere's edited collection raises more questions than it answers (does 'wrong' intent, for instance, necessarily lead to inaccuracy?), on the other it also ends up relying on the archives it purports to reject: which ultimately, I would argue, demonstrates in many ways the *inescapability* of the archive itself.

For example, the goal of not using 'racist and sexist caricatures of Sarah from old aquatints and British and French newspapers',[73] as expressed in Gordon-Chipembere's 'Introduction', is contradicted by the individual contribution of Siphiwe Gloria Ndlovu, as she relies on but these very visual materials when affirming that '[w]hen I first saw Saartje Baartman – naked, looking directly at me – I saw a woman full of grace. *It was only when I started reading the text beneath the image* that I realized the picture pointed to a body in pain, a body ashamed, and a body violated'.[74] The quotation highlights a dual interpretation of Baartman's iconography that is indeed poignant: if we separate the image from the accompanying text we may indeed have different interpretations. But what are the principles that guide the assessment of what is reliable and what is not between text and image?

Ndlovu also goes on by acknowledging that Crais and Scully in particular

> make a worthy effort of retrieving Sara Baartman ... However, this Sara Baartman seems to be shaped by the archive, and by extension (Euro) history. I strongly suspect that before there was ... a woman with a past, that is, a woman who had lived

through events that shaped her life, some of which were written down and entered in the archive, but most of which simply happened and in time were forgotten.[75]

The point again rightly questions the limits of historical investigation, above all in regard to a distinction between the person and the *persona* of Baartman; but where is the connection 'by extension' between the archive and Euro history? And how can we then measure the significance of the silences, 'the kind of testimony that doesn't make it onto the reports',[76] to say it with Edward Said, if we refuse to engage in the first instance with that which *did* make it?

As I hope to have illustrated, *because* Baartman is a 'cypher of minimal presence'[77] in what is a reluctant archive, the testimonies of those that met her, however questionable, and the scattered evidence of her life between South Africa and Europe must remain an essential guide for us to acknowledge her story and assess its significance. Attempting to integrate this archive *on her behalf* is an operation which at once risks overshadowing the specificity of that particular page of history, while diminishing the complex dynamics of contemporary racism to read them through an icon whose own story can never fully explain them. To use Said's words again, rather than 'condemning or ignoring [the primary sources'] participation in what was an *unquestioned* reality in their societies',[78] a fruitful way to address and challenge the colonial archive would be, as Crais and Scully's work demonstrates, to extend one's engagement with *all* available sources – the further investigation of which is due also, and not least, to explore the history of the other 'Hottentot Venuses' that have so far remained in the shade.[79]

Acknowledgements

I should like to thank my husband and our daughter for their patience while I was working on this chapter, as the topic of Sara Baartman has absorbed me for quite some time. Some early research leading to this chapter has received funding from the People Programme (Marie Curie Actions) of the European Union's Seventh Framework Programme (FP7/2007–2013) under REA grant agreement no. 299000.

Notes

1 Daniel Carey, 'Reading Contrapuntally: *Robinson Crusoe*, Slavery, and Postcolonial Theory', in D. Carey and L. Festa (eds), *The Postcolonial Enlightenment: Eighteenth-Century Colonialism and Postcolonial Theory* (Oxford: Oxford University Press, 2008), pp. 105–36; pp. 109–11.
2 Ibid., p. 129.
3 I use 'contemporary' to refer to late twentieth-century and present-day debates and scholarship.
4 Gilles Boëtsch and Pascal Blanchard, 'The Hottentot Venus: Birth of a "Freak"', in P. Blanchard, N. Bancel, G. Boëtsch, E. Deroo, S. Lemaire and C. Forsdick (eds), *Human Zoos: Science and Spectacle in the Age of Colonial Empires* (Liverpool: Liverpool University Press, 2008), pp. 62–72, p. 62.

5. Sadiah Qureshi, *Peoples on Parade: Exhibitions, Empire, and Anthropology in Nineteenth-Century Britain* (Chicago and London: The University of Chicago Press, 2011), p. 10.
6. Zine Magubane, 'Which Bodies Matter? Feminism, Poststructuralism, Race, and the Curious Theoretical Odyssey of the "Hottentot Venus"', *Gender and Society* 15. 6 (2001): 816–34, p. 821.
7. Ibid., p. 827.
8. Kellen Hoxworth, 'The Many Racial Effiges of Sara Baartman', *Theatre Survey* 58. 3 (2017): 275–99, p. 276.
9. Ibid., p. 278.
10. Ibid., p. 279. My emphasis.
11. Natasha Gordon-Chipembere, *Representation and Black Womanhood: The Legacy of Sarah Baartman* (New York: Palgrave Macmillan, 2011), pp. 25–6.
12. Jean Young, 'The Re-objectification and Re-commodification of Saartjie Baartman in Suzan Lori Parks's *Venus*', *African American Review* 31 (1997): 699–708, p. 703.
13. Helen Davies, *Victorian Freakery: The Cultural Afterlife of the Victorian Freak Show* (Basingstoke: Palgrave, 2015), p. 24.
14. Natasha Gordon-Chipembere, '"Even with the Best Intentions": The Misreading of Sarah Baartman's Life by African American Writers', *Agenda: Empowering Women for Gender Equity*, 68 (2006): 54–62, p. 59.
15. Rachel Holmes, *The Hottentot Venus: The Life and Death of Saartje Baartman: Born 1789–Buried 2002* (London: Bloomsbury, 2008), pp. 149–50.
16. Robin Mitchell, *Vénus Noire: Black Women and Colonial Fantasies in Nineteenth-Century France* (Athens, GA: University of Georgia Press, 2020), p. 40.
17. Here the third person refers to de Blainville himself: 'M. de Blainville … la tourmentait davantage pour prendre les matériaux de sa description; au point que, quoique amant beaucoup l'argent, elle a refusé celui qu'il lui offrait, dans le but de la rendre plus docile' (Henri De Blainville, 'Sur une femme de la race hottentote', *Bulletin des sciences par la Société philomathique de Paris* (1816): 183–90, p. 189).
18. Georges, baron Cuvier, 'Extrait d'observations faites sur le Cadavre d'une femme connue a Paris et a Londres sous le nom de Venus Hottentotte', in G. Cuvier, *Discours, Révolutions du Globe, Étude sur l'ibis, et Mémoire sur la Vénus Hottentote* (Paris: Passard, 1864 [1817]), pp. 211–22, p. 214.
19. Von Luschka found in 1870 that in the case of Afandi, a 'bushwoman' said to have toured Germany in 1866, 'the anomalies seen in several parts of the skeleton of the Hottentot Venus were not observed' (Hubert von Luschka, A. Koch, E. Gortz, 'Anatomical Examination of a Bushwoman', *Anthropological Review* 8. 28 (1870): 89–91, 89.
20. Magubane, 'Which Bodies Matter?', p. 820.
21. Sander Gilman, 'Black Bodies, White Bodies: Toward an Iconography of Female Sexuality in Late Nineteenth-Century Art, Medicine, and Literature', in H. L. Gates Jr. (ed.), *Race, Writing, and Difference* (Chicago: University of Chicago Press, 1985), pp. 204–42, p. 235.
22. Anne Fausto-Sterling, 'Gender, Race, and Nation: The Comparative Anatomy of "Hottentot" Women in Europe, 1815–1817', in J. Terry and J. Urla (eds), *Deviant Bodies* (Bloomington: Indiana University Press, 1995), pp. 19–48, p. 36.
23. Katherine McKittrick, 'Science Quarrels Sculpture: The Politics of Reading Sarah Baartman', *Mosaic: An Interdisciplinary Critical Journal* 43. 2 (2010): 113–30, p. 114. My emphasis.
24. See also Magubane, 'Which Bodies Matter?', p. 821.

25 Sadiah Qureshi, 'Displaying Sara Baartman, the '"Hottentot Venus"', *History of Science* 42. 2 (2004): 233–57, p. 243.
26 Stephen Jay Gould, *The Flamingo's Smile: Reflections in Natural History* (New York-London: Norton & Company, 1985), p. 301.
27 Yvette Abrahams, 'Images of Sarah Bartman: Sexuality, Race, and Gender in Early-Nineteenth-Century Britain', in R. Roach Pierson and N. Chadhuri (eds), *Nation, Empire, Colony: Historicizing Gender and Race* (Bloomington: Indiana University Press, 1998), pp. 220–36, p. 226.
28 The notion that glimpses of the ankles were deemed indecent is suggested for instance in Captain Marryat's *Diary in America* (1839), which describes Americans (not Europeans) as so prudish that in the United States even piano legs were clothed to preserve the decency of the young girls. Warm thanks to Luke Seaber for pointing me to Marryat's work.
29 Z. S. Strother, 'Display of the Body Hottentot', in B. Lindfors (ed.), *Africans on Stage* (Bloomington: University of Indiana Press, 1999), pp. 1–61, p. 25.
30 While the three-quarter portrait of one poster (based on an aquatint by Frederick Christian) builds on the freak show tradition, informing 'prospective viewers ... of what they will actually see' (Strother, 'Display of the Body Hottentot', p. 27), in the second, which depicts Baartman in profile, 'the Hottentot's skin is darkened and her figure highly sexed' (ibid., 28).
31 Mrs Charles Mathews, *Memoirs of Charles Mathews, Comedian* (London: Richard Bentley, 1839), Vol. 4, p. 136. Emphasis original.
32 A. D. Harvey, *Sex in Georgian England: Attitudes and Prejudices from the 1720s to the 1820s* (New York: St. Martin's Press, 1994), p. 33.
33 Mathews, *Memoirs of Charles Mathews*, p. 137.
34 Harvey, *Sex in Georgian England*, p. 35.
35 Mathew Sweet, *Inventing the Victorians* (London: Faber, 2001), p. xv.
36 Qureshi, 'Displaying Sara Baartman', p. 251.
37 Yvette Abrahams, 'Disempowered to Consent: Sara Bartman and Khoisan Slavery in the Nineteenth-Century Cape Colony and Britain', *South African Historical Journal* 3–4 (1996): 89–114, p. 93.
38 Natasha Gordon-Chipembere, *Representation and Black Womanhood: The Legacy of Sarah Baartman* (New York: Palgrave Macmillan, 2011), p. 1, p. 10.
39 Hershini Bhana Young, *Illegible Will: Coercive Spectacles of Labor in South Africa and the Diaspora* (Durham, NC: Duke University Press, 2017), p. 66.
40 Ibid., p. 70.
41 Court Records regarding the Hottentot Venus, 21–28 November 1810, The National Archives (TNA): Public Record Office (PRO), King's Bench (KB) 1/36/4.
42 Baartman is reported to be twenty-two in the interview, not in her thirties as Crais and Scully's research suggests.
43 Qureshi, *Peoples on Parade*, p. 171.
44 Abrahams, 'Disempowered to Consent', p. 104.
45 Ibid., p. 109. My emphasis.
46 The slave language in question, Dutch, was spoken by Baartman because '[t]hey [the Baartmans] had to speak it to the settlers now owning the land and forcing them to work it as herders and domestic servants'. See Clifton Crais and Pamela Scully, 'Race and Erasure: Sara Baartman and Hendrik Caesars in Cape Town and London', *Journal of British Studies* 47. 2 (2008): 301–23, p. 307.

47 On Baartman's funeral (9 August 2002), Thabo Mbeki referred to hers as 'a story of our reduction to the status of objects that could be owned, used and disposed of by others'. http://www.dirco.gov.za/docs/speeches/2002/mbek0809.htm, accessed 20 February 2021.
48 Abrahams, 'Disempowered to Consent', p. 104.
49 Ibid., p. 30.
50 Ibid., p. 50. My emphasis.
51 Court Records … King's Bench (KB) 1/36/4.
52 Davies, *Victorian Freakery*, p. 31. My emphases.
53 Qureshi, *Peoples on Parade*, p. 147.
54 Court Records … King's Bench (KB) 1/36/4.
55 Whyte, *Zachary Macaulay 1768-1838: The Steadfast Scot in the British Anti-Slavery Movement* (Liverpool: Liverpool University Press, 2017), p. 107. Whyte adds that 'there was a suggestion that [Baartman] might be willing to attend Bible training before her return [to Africa] and act as a missionary agent on her return'. Ibid., p. 113.
56 Whyte, *Zachary Macaulay*, p. 113.
57 Mathews, *Memoirs of Charles Mathews*, pp. 137-9. Crais and Scully instead suggest a fee was asked.
58 Ibid., p. 137.
59 Ibid., p. 138.
60 Ibid.
61 Baartman's exhibitor instead assures Kemble she means 'you are a very fine man'. Ibid.
62 Ibid., pp. 137-8.
63 Crais and Scully, 'Race and Erasure', p. 318.
64 Ibid., p. 312.
65 Ibid.
66 See also Holmes, *The Hottentot Venus*, p. 29.
67 'Well into the nineteenth century, a classificatory system according to skin color did not operate explicitly as a marker of status'. Ibid., p. 310.
68 See ibid., p. 316.
69 Holmes claims that 'Macaulay knew that Caesars was of mixed ethnicity, as … in a letter to the *Examiner* … he compared Caesars with Shakespeare's Caliban. Desparing that the formerly oppressed might become a future oppressor, Macaulay attacked Caesars's greed: "… what, alas! will not avarice do? It is that "stamps the monster on the man", and leads him "to play such fantastic tricks as make the angels weep"'. Holmes, *The Hottentot Venus*, p. 88. The reference to Caliban is, however, inaccurate; the passage quoted by Macaulay is from *Measure for Measure* (II.2).
70 Natasha Gordon-Chipembere, 'Clifton Crais and Pamela Scully. 2009. Sara Baartman and the Hottentot Venus: A Ghost Story and Biography. Princeton: Princeton University Press', *Scrutiny2* 14. 2 (2009): 87-9, p. 87.
71 Ibid., p. 88.
72 Gordon-Chipembere, *Representation and Black Womanhood*, p. 4.
73 Ibid., p. 5.
74 Siphiwe Gloria Ndlovu, 'Body of Evidence: Saartje Baartman and the Archive', in N. Gordon-Chipembere (ed.), *Representation and Black Womanhood: The Legacy of Sarah Baartman* (New York: Palgrave Macmillan, 2011), pp. 17-30, pp. 17-18. My emphasis.
75 Ibid., p. 19.
76 Edward Said, *Culture and Imperialism* (London: Vintage Books, 2004 [1994]), p. 81.
77 Qureshi, 'Displaying Sara Baartman', p. 249.

78 Said, *Culture and Imperialism*, p. xv. My emphasis.
79 These include Tono Maria, a Brazilian woman exhibited in London in the 1820s as the 'Venus of South America'; a 'Hottentot Venus' that Gilman suggests was displayed at a ball for the Duchess of Berry in 1829; and Afandi, a South African woman who toured Germany in the 1860s (see note 19).

Bibliography

Primary Sources

De Blainville, Henri. 'Sur une femme de la race hottentote'. *Bulletin des sciences par la Société philomathique de Paris* (1816): 183–90.
Court Records regarding the Hottentot Venus, 21–28 November 1810, The National Archives (TNA): Public Record Office (PRO), King's Bench (KB) 1/36/4.
Cuvier, Georges. 'Extrait d'observations faites sur le cadavre d'une femme connue a Paris et a Londres sous le nom de Venus Hottentotte'. In *Discours, Révolutions du Globe, Étude sur l'ibis, et Mémoire sur la Vénus Hottentote*, in Georges Cuvier (Paris: Passard, 1864 [1817]), pp. 211–22.
Von Luschka, Hubert, A. Koch, and E. Gortz. 'Anatomical Examination of a Bushwoman'. *Anthropological Review* 8, no. 28 (1870): 89–91.
Mathews, Mrs Charles. *Memoirs of Charles Mathews, Comedian, Vol. 4*. London: Richard Bentley, 1839.
The Morning Post (29 October 1810), p. 3.

Secondary Literature

Abrahams, Yvette. 'Disempowered to Consent: Sara Bartman and Khoisan Slavery in the Nineteenth-Century Cape Colony and Britain'. *South African Historical Journal* 3–4 (1996): 89–114.
Abrahams, Yvette. 'Images of Sarah Bartman: Sexuality, Race, and Gender in Early-Nineteenth-Century Britain'. In *Nation, Empire, Colony: Historicizing Gender and Race*, edited by R. Roach Pierson and N. Chadhuri, 220–36. Bloomington: Indiana University Press, 1998.
Boëtsch, Gilles, and Pascal Blanchard. 'The Hottentot Venus: Birth of a "Freak"'. In *Human Zoos: Science and Spectacle in the Age of Colonial Empires*, edited by P. Blanchard, N. Bancel, G. Boëtsch, E. Deroo, S. Lemaire and C. Forsdick, 62–72. Liverpool: Liverpool University Press, 2008.
Carey, Daniel. 'Reading Contrapuntally: *Robinson Crusoe*, Slavery, and Postcolonial Theory'. In *The Postcolonial Enlightenment: Eighteenth-Century Colonialism and Postcolonial Theory*, edited by D. Carey and L. Festa, 105–36. Oxford: Oxford University Press, 2008.
Crais, Clifton, and Pamela Scully. 'Race and Erasure: Sara Baartman and Hendrik Caesars in Cape Town and London'. *Journal of British Studies* 47, no. 2 (2008): 301–23.
Davies, Helen. *Victorian Freakery: The Cultural Afterlife of the Victorian Freak Show*. Basingstoke: Palgrave, 2015.
Fausto-Sterling, Anne. 'Gender, Race, and Nation: The Comparative Anatomy of "Hottentot" Women in Europe, 1815–1817'. In *Deviant Bodies*, edited by J. Terry and J. Urla, 19–48. Bloomington: Indiana University Press, 1995.

Gilman, Sander. 'Black Bodies, White Bodies: Toward an Iconography of Female Sexuality in Late Nineteenth-Century Art, Medicine, and Literature'. In *Race, Writing, and Difference*, edited by H. L. Gates Jr., 204–42. Chicago: University of Chicago Press, 1985.

Gordon-Chipembere, Natasha. '"Even with the Best Intentions": The Misreading of Sarah Baartman's Life by African American Writers'. *Agenda: Empowering Women for Gender Equity* 68 (2006): 54–62.

Gordon-Chipembere, Natasha. 'Clifton Crais and Pamela Scully. 2009. Sara Baartman and the Hottentot Venus: A Ghost Story and Biography. Princeton: Princeton University Press', *Scrutiny2* 14, no. 2 (2009): 87–9.

Gordon-Chipembere, Natasha. *Representation and Black Womanhood: The Legacy of Sarah Baartman*. New York: Palgrave Macmillan, 2011.

Gould, Stephen Jay. *The Flamingo's Smile: Reflections in Natural History*. New York and London: Norton & Company, 1985.

Harvey, A. D. *Sex in Georgian England: Attitudes and Prejudices from the 1720s to the 1820s*. New York: St. Martin's Press, 1994.

Holmes, Rachel. *The Hottentot Venus: The Life and Death of Saartje Baartman: Born 1789-Buried 2002*. London: Bloomsbury, 2008.

Hoxworth, Kellen. 'The Many Racial Effigies of Sara Baartman'. *Theatre Survey* 58, no. 3 (2017): 275–99.

Magubane, Zine. 'Which Bodies Matter? Feminism, Poststructuralism, Race, and the Curious Theoretical Odyssey of the "Hottentot Venus"'. *Gender and Society* 15, no. 6 (2001): 816–34.

Mitchell, Robin. *Vénus Noire: Black Women and Colonial Fantasies in Nineteenth-Century France* (Athens, GA: University of Georgia Press, 2020).

McKittrick, Katherine. 'Science Quarrels Sculpture: The Politics of Reading Sarah Baartman'. *Mosaic: An Interdisciplinary Critical Journal* 43, no. 2 (2010): 113–30.

Ndlovu, Siphiwe Gloria. 'Body of Evidence: Saartje Baartman and the Archive'. In *Representation and Black Womanhood: The Legacy of Sarah Baartman*, edited by N. Gordon-Chipembere, 17–30. New York: Palgrave Macmillan, 2011.

Qureshi, Sadiah. 'Displaying Sara Baartman, the "Hottentot Venus"'. *History of Science* 42, no. 2 (2004): 233–57.

Qureshi, Sadiah. *Peoples on Parade: Exhibitions, Empire, and Anthropology in Nineteenth-Century Britain*. Chicago and London: The University of Chicago Press, 2011.

Said, Edward. *Culture and Imperialism*. London: Vintage Books, 2004 [1994].

Strother, Z. S. 'Display of the Body Hottentot'. In *Africans on Stage*, edited by B. Lindfors, 1–61. Bloomington: University of Indiana Press, 1999.

Sweet, Mathew. *Inventing the Victorians*. London: Faber, 2001.

Whyte, Iain. *Zachary Macaulay 1768-1838: The Steadfast Scot in the British Anti-Slavery Movement*. Liverpool: Liverpool University Press, 2017.

Young, Jean. 'The Re-objectification and Re-commodification of Saartjie Baartman in Suzan Lori Parks's *Venus*'. *African American Review* 31 (1997): 699–708.

Young, Hershini Bhana. '"Rude" Performances: Theorizing Agency'. In *Representation and Black Womanhood: The Legacy of Sarah Baartman*, edited by N. Gordon-Chipembere, 47–63. New York: Palgrave Macmillan, 2011.

Young, Hershini Bhana. *Illegible Will: Coercive Spectacles of Labor in South Africa and the Diaspora*. Durham, NC: Duke University Press, 2017.

10

Mercury, sulphur baths and fine art

Censorship and the sexual health of John and Joséphine Bowes, founders of The Bowes Museum

Judith Phillips

The Bowes Museum at Barnard Castle, County Durham opened to the public in 1892, nearly ten years after the death of John Bowes and nearly twenty years after the death of his wife Joséphine.[1] At its inception in the 1860s, this privately financed, publicly accessible museum presented a radical approach, for which John gave Joséphine the full credit: 'It must be remembered that thanks only are due to my late Wife, as the idea, & project of the Museum, & Park originated entirely with her'.[2] Museums were usually found in large cities, managed by the state, educational institutions or local societies, or were still personal collections of individuals or families, often with restricted public access.[3]

This essay explores a very personal aspect of this nineteenth-century couple – their sexual health – which lies in the shadows, self-censored by John Bowes, rarely mentioned outright and only within the very limited and specific archive of the Boweses' private papers held in The Bowes Museum. The Boweses' childlessness, probably due to the infertility of one or both as a side effect of a sexually transmitted infection, is potentially a significant factor in the creation of the museum.

John and Joséphine Bowes were marginalized during their lives by illegitimacy and social class perceptions, and their narrative has in some instances been censored through selective dissemination and interpretation of the archives. While the previous essay explored the absence of a person's voice from the archive and subsequent essays explore other marginalizations in the archival discourse, here I consider archival information and its interpretation by biographers and museum curators in the light of (un)conscious censorship by the archive creator and its potential implications for the museum today.

A trope in modern discussions on collecting and museum creation as a legacy project is the founder(s)' childlessness, seeing the collection and/or museum as a replacement or surrogate child.[4] It is simplistic to suggest that childlessness in itself was the reason for the Boweses' collecting and museum creation but, given that it has been postulated as a possible catalyst for creating the museum, it is pertinent to look at potentially significant factors for their childlessness. John Bowes (1811–85) and his wife Joséphine (1825–74) are conspicuously missing from (or only slightly mentioned in) the collection/museum creation historiography, largely due to missing or previously unavailable archives, unlike well-documented and researched collectors. The surviving Boweses' archival material gives little information on the emotional and intellectual motivations behind the practicalities; the lack of surviving letters from Joséphine to dealers and to John himself creates a significant lacuna in the archive which has affected modern judgements about their activities, abilities and motivations.

The Boweses were actively collecting art by the early 1860s, when Joséphine was in her late thirties with a history of poor health; at the same time they were acquiring land in Barnard Castle, for the proposed museum for the collection.[5] The reality of childlessness changed John and Joséphine's lives. If John predeceased Joséphine, his English estates would revert to the Earls of Strathmore and the Bowes-Lyon family; in 1767 John Lyon, ninth Earl of Strathmore, married Mary Eleanor Bowes, a wealthy heiress, and took the additional surname Bowes, as stipulated by her father's will.[6] Joséphine would have no claim on these estates, although their French properties could be bequeathed to her. Building the museum on the outskirts of Barnard Castle, and the subsequent growth and curation of a display of objects, would provide Joséphine with a substantial and public-spirited task for her widowhood, replete with 'social capital', with living accommodation included.[7] An article in *The Builder* magazine in 1871 described the proposed building as 'Mrs Bowes' Mansion and Galleries' and outlined a suite for Joséphine within the building.[8]

Charles Hardy (1897–1989), author of the first substantial study of the museum's history, displays a reticence towards discussing intimate sexual matters, and the Friends of The Bowes Museum, who arranged the original publication of Hardy's book in 1970 and its reprint in 1989, may have had similar concerns. A continuous film in the museum giving visitors background information about the museum and its founders implies childlessness as a motive but does not speculate further. It was only in 2010 that the connection between a sexually transmitted infection, infertility and the museum's creation was made explicit by Caroline Chapman, who used archival medical evidence for John's condition.[9] This book was 'also' supported by the Board of Trustees who had succeeded Durham County Council as responsible for the museum, and it is interesting to speculate on the change in attitude that allowed such openness, reflecting societal changes in the intervening forty years. In the 2017 exhibition *Joséphine Bowes: Woman of Fashion and Influence*, John's sexual activity was openly discussed and explicitly linked to infertility and childlessness within the museum narrative for the first time. As individuals and as a couple, the Boweses are not unique collectors/museum creators. Consideration of this aspect of their lives and the effect it might have had on their decision-making and legacy illuminates them within the wider picture of nineteenth-century society, collecting and museum creation.[10]

Recent critical scholarly research and writings have raised fundamental questions about the reliability of the nineteenth-century archive, largely in terms of conscious and unconscious bias and censorship in creation, appraisal, disposal, retention and the random survival of original material and its subsequent re-use for wide-ranging research purposes.[11] Ann Laura Stoler considers how narrative inconsistencies should be read, particularly balancing official accounts with contradictory personal archives, highlighting selectivity bias in the archive creators as well as researchers. She asks, 'how deeply [historical] renderings went along – or bristled against – their grain'.[12] Carolyn Steedman similarly warns that archives are 'made from selected and consciously chosen documentation from the past and also the mad fragments that no one intended to preserve'.[13] The power imperatives behind the growth and institutionalization of archive creation in the nineteenth century have influenced the survival of original material. These often reflected contemporary attitudes at the various stages in the life-cycle of the archive despite the growing intellectualization and systematization of archival processes, and the development of archivists' professionalism in the twentieth century and beyond.[14] An archive was created to serve practical needs, subsequently often modified to serve managers, archivists, researchers and others.

Contemporary researchers have used nineteenth-century archives for new purposes, investigating and recovering 'hidden stories', such as Hallie Rubenhold's study of the women killed by Jack the Ripper.[15] These perspectives illuminate aspects of history and groups previously obscured, ignored, misunderstood or deliberately removed from the historical record. They include the physically, mentally and financially disadvantaged (usually subjugated within institutions and/or recorded through interaction with the legal and government systems), ethnic minorities (often the ruled class in the colonial empires of the nineteenth century), the working-classes (usually seen only through observation by and interaction with other classes) and women (legally subservient to fathers, husbands or other male relatives for much of the nineteenth century).[16] Attitudes, conscious and unconscious, of the 'powerful' affected descriptions of 'others' in the archives, in what was recorded, how people and actions were described and in documented decisions.

Research is framed by and within the significant limitations of the surviving archival material. The Bowes Museum archives reflect all these considerations and limitations. It is unclear when the documents held in The Bowes Museum were acquired; arrangements for the records are not mentioned in John's correspondence, the Trustees' minutes or the Curators' correspondence.[17] The Trustees acquired hundreds of letters sent by John, though without any identifiable transaction record: 'Your Curator has spent many hours in arranging some 3,000 letters of John Bowes, to his agent and solicitors. These letters were added about 1919'.[18] Several letters sent before the introduction of envelopes and stamps are incomplete, with the final sheet (or part-sheet) removed, possibly to sell for postmark information and/or John's franking signature.[19] Other letters sent to John by friends, family and servants, together with estate records and personal records relating to activities in England, form part of the Strathmore Estate archive held in the Durham County Record Office and at Glamis Castle, sometimes overlapping with records at the museum.[20] Between 1956 and 2000, when the museum was administered by Durham County Council, some records were transferred from the museum to the nascent county archive service.[21]

'As historians of women frequently find, there are very few documents that have been kept relating to Joséphine Bowes'.[22] This statement is only true in the sense of immediately personal records; there are no extant diaries for either John or Joséphine. Only one letter from Joséphine to John (and none from him to her) survives, although John's letter diaries indicate that they wrote constantly to each other when they were apart; and only a hundred or so letters – a relatively small number – addressed to

Joséphine by friends and servants are preserved, mainly dating to her prolonged absence in England between 1869 and 1871.[23] John wrote letters constantly, maintaining contact with his friends, land agents and solicitors.[24] He also kept bills and receipts of expenditure for his French households for over three decades.[25]

A substantial historiography exists of nineteenth-century European collectors, such as Richard Wallace (1818–90), Lady Charlotte Schreiber (1812–95) and the Duc d'Aumale (1822–97), with many publications focussing on the contents of collections, history of their acquisition and later display or dispersal and the narrative history of the collector's life.[26] The Boweses collected through dealers, agents, visits to exhibitions, factories, auction previews, commissioning work and patronizing new and established artists and craftspeople, although the boundary between collecting for domestic use and the museum project was porous and constantly shifting. From the 1860s the childless Boweses spent about 275,000 francs (nearly £1,000,000 at current value), buying around 15,000 objects for their proposed museum, as evidenced by the hundreds of bills and letters from dealers.[27]

John Bowes (1811–85)

John Bowes was the semi-legitimate son of the tenth Earl of Strathmore and Mary Milner, a local Teesdale estate servant; his parents married the day before his father's death in 1820. The inheritance was challenged and the title and Scottish estates were awarded to John's uncle; John inherited his father's English estates in Durham and Yorkshire.

In a letter series in 1833 to Mr Wheldon, his local solicitor, John referred to an 'unfortunate little disease' and 'that confounded disease of mine' which he had suffered for three or four years, that is, from about 1829 or 1830.[28] He probably contracted it as a student at Trinity College, Cambridge where he studied from 1829.[29] Little is known about John's student life but students at Cambridge consorting with prostitutes was described in the 1840s as 'natural, excusable and perhaps to most men necessary'.[30] John confessed in 1833 that he had been persuaded to consult 'Brodie', and Caroline Chapman has argued convincingly that this was Sir Benjamin Brodie (1783–1862), a specialist in diseases of the bones and joints.[31] Brodie described patients suffering a triad of purulent urethral discharge, purulent conjunctivitis and arthritis, particularly affecting the knees, ankles and feet, which he attributed to gonorrhoea.[32] John also mentions consulting a medical man called Vance, possibly George Vance, who has not yet been identified.[33] In later life, John complained of eye problems and suffered from mobility difficulties; both may be related to gonorrhoea but could be contingent on aging.[34]

John claimed that his condition was not infectious but he did not name it or identify it as a sexually transmitted infection; although the phrase 'not clap' appears in one of his letters, the page is partially torn off and it is not certain that the phrase refers to John.[35] Chapman argues that he was suffering a severe attack of gonorrhoea, rather than syphilis.[36] Gonorrhoea would have involved a painful and unpleasant discharge from the genital area, possibly with lesions, as well as a range of subsidiary irritating symptoms. In 1854, Dr Wilhelm Gollmann addressed gonorrhoea in his book *Homeopathic Guide to all Diseases of the Urinary and Sexual Organs* and noted that gonorrhoea was common in prostitutes in large cities. Gollmann recommended the following as cures: aconite to cure 'shooting pains with soreness and inflammation'; mercury 'for pain with purulent discharge'; *nux vomica* (strychnine) and sulphur 'when the symptoms are complicated with haemorrhoids and stricture of the rectum' and other remedies including silver nitrate, belladonna and phosphorus, most of which could be considered poisonous.[37] Sea-bathing was a recommended treatment, although it is likely this offered palliative relief rather than a cure; John mentions undertaking a course of sea-bathing in Bognor in 1833.[38]

John was also obliquely recommended to consult Professor Claude François Lallemand 'as there is no man in Europe equal to Monsieur Lallemand of Montpellier for disorders of the urethra.'[39] Lallemand (1790–1854) was noted for his work on urogenital pathology.[40] This recommendation came, probably via William Hutt, John's step-father and friend, from George and Charles Silvertop, members of a well-established Durham family with local Teesdale connections to the Witham family of Lartington; Monsignor Witham was John's life-long friend and served as one of the original museum Trustees.[41] This suggests John's condition was known outside his immediate family but kept within his social class.[42] John refers to the proposed treatment as 'their plan is most violent ... being the use of an injection of caustic soda strong enough to dislodge the devil himself', and later claims: 'I have given a trial to every sort of injection, bougies, caustic [soda ...] the confounded thing has fairly beat them all.'[43] In 1842 he was still complaining about his 'infernal complaint', and there is a hint that he was still having health issues in 1844: 'I have not much profited by my visit here [Richmond] in the way of health.'[44]

Despite his encounter with a sexually transmitted infection, John continued to be sexually active. In 1834, his butler wrote: 'I think there will be racers this year as the last but it is not firmly settled. Noe Lady was with Mr Bowes', implying an unusual absence.[45] In London and in Paris, John was a frequent visitor to theatres, and he maintained a French actress as his mistress – certainly between 1842 and 1846 and possibly as early as 1840.[46] John was not singular in having a mistress from the world of the theatre; actresses and dancers in London and Paris were regarded as little different from prostitutes and regularly exchanged sexual favours for money, gifts and protection from male patrons.[47]

Throughout the 1830s and particularly the 1840s John regularly visited Paris as well as maintaining a residence in London to enable him to engage in his parliamentary duties – serving as Member of Parliament for South Durham from 1832 to 1847 – and to indulge his interest in the theatrical world. In both cities he could have availed himself of services offered by brothels and prostitutes; a report in 1867 calculated that there was twice as much prostitution in London as in Paris although that might reflect the tighter control of Paris brothels under the Second Empire.[48] From 1847 John established himself in Paris, visiting England and his estates regularly. In Paris he invested heavily in the Théâtre des Variétés where Joséphine Coffin Chevallier acted under the stage name of Mademoiselle Delorme. Fourteen years John's junior, Joséphine soon became his mistress and then, in 1852, his wife.

Joséphine Bowes (1825–74)

Joséphine Coffin Chevallier was born in Paris, the daughter of a clock- or watchmaker and his wife, both migrants to the capital from their separate birthplaces. Almost nothing is known about her life until she appears in 1846 as a new actress on the Paris stage and in 1847 as occupying an apartment in the same building as John Bowes, not far from the Boulevard Montmartre in an area of Paris with a raffish reputation where theatres and other amusements abounded.[49] By spring 1847 Joséphine appears in John's letter diaries and on the payroll of the Théâtre des Variétés as an actress, perhaps as a favour to the owner. John set Joséphine up as his mistress in a 'cottage' in the country at Auteuil, then on the edge of the city, and a shared apartment at Cité d'Antin, very close to the theatre.[50]

French novels of the period show that many young women were expected to have a financial protector or patron, usually in return for sexual favours.[51] Working in the theatrical world in Paris, and in London, offered women limited security and independence although securing financial independence through shrewd dealing with a protector and/or social respectability through marriage was possible.[52] Emile Zola's novel *Nana* used the Théâtre de Variétés – once Joséphine's stage – as the backdrop to the story of an actress whose sexual identity is already compromised by an illegitimate child but who uses her main asset – her beauty – to acquire a wealthy protector. The identification of a leading theatrical performer with a life of combined sexual liberty (an unmarried mother having affairs with married men) and sexual dependence (married lovers supported her financially with gifts of money and estates) highlights contemporary attitudes to women from the *demi-monde*, a social entity more prominent and accepted in France than in England.[53]

Lives of fictional and real courtesans provide some possible parallels with Joséphine's life. The poor or working-class background and the theatrical theatre offer immediate connections but one must be wary of being dogmatic or stereotypical. Joséphine appeared regularly on stage in roles that could be construed as potentially immoral, reinforcing generic public perception of the actress as closely identified with the prostitute.[54] She performed the can-can and the *camargo*, dances considered outrageous and decadent; she appeared as a mistress and as a disreputable dancer; she impersonated Madame de Pompadour, one of the most iconic French royal mistresses; and she played roles, including her debut, that required cross-dressing in masculine clothes, providing an opportunity to show off an actress's legs (usually unseen under the fashionable long skirts).[55] Even her stage name, Mademoiselle Delorme, invited connection with Marion Delorme, a famous seventeenth-century courtesan and heroine of a play by Victor Hugo that debuted in Paris in 1831. After her marriage to John in 1852 moved her into a different social class, she never re-appeared on stage. If, as seems likely, Joséphine was part of the theatrical *demi-monde* before her liaison with John, she may have contracted a sexually transmitted infection then, or perhaps she was infected by John. Her health was a matter of concern throughout her relationship with John but it is unclear whether her health issues pre-dated their relationship, nor are the causes of her various health issues specified. John's letters to his friends and others frequently mention her health (usually hoping it will improve) but in unspecific terms.[56] This is a pattern also found in letters from friends to John and Joséphine from the 1850s through to Joséphine's death in 1874.[57]

A visit to Arran in Scotland in 1858 included sea-bathing for Joséphine.[58] As John was advised to take sea-baths in 1833 as part of his treatment for gonorrhoea, this may be an indication that sea-bathing was a medical treatment for Joséphine.[59] There are several references to her dislike – even fear – of the sea, and it is unlikely that she would have chosen sea-bathing as a form of relaxation.[60] More sea-bathing was planned during a stay at the Hotel Frascati in Le Havre in June 1861: 'I am anxious Mrs Bowes should get as much Sea-Bathing as possible, & there are great facilities for that, & the treatment of her case in the Establishment connected with this hotel'.[61] What was 'her case'? Around the same time John refers to it as 'a surgical case requiring a constant, & I am afraid long treatment', but no further information is given.[62]

Augustus Hare, a gossipy writer and a distant connection of the Bowes family, recorded a visit to the Boweses at Streatlam Castle in 1861.[63] Hare described Joséphine as follows: 'Madame appears, having painted the underlids of her eyes with belladonna'.[64] This was probably employed as a beauty treatment to enhance the appearance of the eyes as it enlarged the pupils and made eyes sparkle, but belladonna was also used as an anti-inflammatory and as a treatment for gonorrhoea.[65] More intriguingly he also recalled: 'she is then reclining in a bath of coal-black acid, which "refreshes her system", but leaves her finger-nails black'.[66] In 1865 John wrote to Mr Dent at Streatlam: 'I think Mrs Bowes may perhaps have to take sulphur Baths. The old Wash House had better be white washed, & cleaned as before'.[67] These comments probably indicate a Barèges bath, usually a solution of potassium sulphide but also diluted sulphuric acid. Laroze, a Parisian pharmacist who regularly supplied Joséphine with medicines, sent recipes for both types to a London pharmacist in 1862, presumably for Joséphine's use in England.[68] The bath treatment was frequently used to cure skin complaints which may be symptoms of a sexually transmitted infection.

An archival research path is offered by the retention of many bills from chemists and pharmacists in Paris and seaside towns such as Boulogne-sur-Mer, Calais and Le Havre where Joséphine spent long periods waiting for a calm Channel crossing.[69] Unfortunately, in the detailed bills, several items appear only as numbers that refer to the individual pharmacist's recipe book. The general tenor of the items in the bills suggests that Joséphine suffered from stomach ailments, rheumatic ailments, chest infections and skin irritation; all these could indicate the side effects of a sexually transmitted infection.[70] The marriage remained childless, and, as far as is known, Joséphine never became pregnant nor did John father any children.[71]

A legacy of childlessness?

A connection between collecting and health had been commonplace since at least 1847 when Balzac coined the term '*bricabracomanie*' in his novel *Cousin Pons* to refer to 'collectors who were considered mad because of their single-minded focus on accumulating'.[72] Art objects were no longer defined by aesthetics but by the social role of art 'denoting or conferring distinction and cachet upon its possessor'.[73] Sarah Kane's early article on Joséphine Bowes describes Joséphine's collecting habit in potentially pejorative terms, referring to 'a period of furious acquisition', 'a mere collector of bibelots', a 'chaotic and random accumulation of objects' and 'readiness to buy in bulk', implying lack of discrimination and a rather unhealthy attitude to acquisition.[74]

A contemporary visitor to the museum would be unaware of the personal issues around sexual health that affected the museum's founders unless they read the most recent guidebook.[75] Whether this reticence is because the topic is felt to be too personally intrusive, irrelevant to the objects in the collections or, more opaquely, unacceptably in bad taste is unclear, but the result is conscious or sub-conscious censorship. Visitors' sensibilities have already exerted some conscious censorship.[76] There are no warnings or censorship of paintings and objects in the museum collections showing fully (or partially) naked human bodies, usually female, and images of religious, mythological or historical violence, and historically public reaction against such images has been limited.[77] The possibility of the pendulum of 'taste and propriety' swinging in the opposite direction has to be taken into account, with a temptation to apply an equivalence of 'actress and prostitute' in Joséphine's case to titillate and catch the public's attention.

Barbara Caine usefully points out that biography has historically constructed narratives of lives in different ways in different eras, modelling lives by inclusions and omissions, with nineteenth-century writers stressing propriety and modern writers more concerned with the whole life, acknowledging failures and weaknesses.[78] Sexual orientation or proclivity, once ignored and/or censored, now regularly features in biographies. In the context of John and Joséphine Bowes, should the public narrative include the reality of their sexual lives and the potentially significant part that this may have played in the creation of the museum? Does omitting contested elements in their lives amount to censorship, Carlyle's 'mealy mouth' of English biography?[79] Is it permissible to throw light on the shadows surrounding the personal and sexual lives of deceased individuals and, using privately-created archives, expose private lives to public gaze? Does this enhance and increase the interpretation and understanding of their lives, motives, agency, collections and legacy? Now that the sexual health of John and Joséphine Bowes is a recognized element in the narrative of their lives, and therefore part of the museum narrative even if not obviously referenced within the museum's public spaces, there is perhaps a need to debate how the museum could strike a balance between prurient intrusion and nuanced explanation in bringing the topic into the public narrative of The Bowes Museum.

Acknowledgement

I would like to thank the Trustees, staff and volunteers at The Bowes Museum for their encouragement, help and support over the years.

Notes

1   For a general history of John and Joséphine Bowes and The Bowes Museum, see Charles E. Hardy, *John Bowes and The Bowes Museum* (Bishop Auckland: Friends of

The Bowes Museum, 1970, reissued 1989); and Caroline Chapman, *John & Joséphine: The Creation of The Bowes Museum* (Barnard Castle: The Bowes Museum, 2010).

2 Letter from John Bowes to Mr Dent, 5 October 1874 (JB/2/1/42/21).
3 Anne Higonnet, *A Museum of One's Own: Private Collecting, Public Gift* (Pittsburgh and New York: Periscope Publishing Ltd., 2009); Kate Hill, *Culture and Class in English Public Museums, 1850–1914* (Aldershot: Ashgate, 2005); Daniel J. Sherman, *Worthy Monuments: Art Museums and the Politics of Culture in Nineteenth-Century France* (Cambridge, MA and London: Harvard University Press, 1989).
4 E.g. Higonnet, *A Museum of One's Own*, pp. 125, 127. See also Judith Phillips, 'National Identity, Gender, Social Status and Cultural Aspirations in Mid-Nineteenth Century France and England: Joséphine Bowes (1825–1874), Collector and Museum Creator' (PhD diss., Teesside University, 2020), pp. 271–3.
5 E.g. Higonnet, *A Museum of One's Own*, pp. 125, 127. See also Phillips, 'National Identity', pp. 271–3.
6 The surname Lyon-Bowes was changed to Bowes-Lyon in the late-nineteenth century.
7 Jen Webb, Tony Schirato and Geoff Denaher, *Understanding Bourdieu* (London: SAGE, 2002), especially Chapter 2, 'Cultural Field and the Habitus', pp. 21–44.
8 'Mrs Bowes' Mansion and Galleries', *The Builder*, January 1871 (JB/6/3/7).
9 Chapman, *John & Joséphine*, pp. 19–20, 51.
10 E.g. Higonnet, *A Museum of One's Own* considers the Duc d'Aumale, Sir Richard Wallace and Isabella Stewart Gardner, among others.
11 E.g. Ann Laura Stoler, *Along the Archival Grain: Epistemic Anxieties and Colonial Common Sense* (Princeton, NJ and Oxford: Princeton University Press, 2009); and Carolyn Steedman, *Dust* (Manchester: Manchester University Press, 2001).
12 Stoler, *Along the Archival Grain*, p. 184.
13 Steedman, *Dust*, p. 68.
14 (Sir) Hilary Jenkinson, *A Manual of Archive Administration* (London: Lund, Humphries & Co., 1922) was reissued several times and provided the foundation on which others built and continue to build: for example, Michael Cook, *The Management of Information from Archives* (Aldershot: Gower, 1986; Abingdon: Routledge, Taylor & Francis Group, 2016); and Caroline Williams, *Managing Archives: Foundations, Principles and Practice* (Oxford: Chandos, 2006).
15 Hallie Rubenhold, *The Five: The Untold Lives of the Women Killed by Jack the Ripper* (London: Doubleday, 2019).
16 E.g., Simon Schama, *Citizens: A Chronicle of the French Revolution* (London: Penguin, 1989); Rozsika Parker and Griselda Pollock, *Old Mistresses: Women, Art and Ideology* (London: Routledge & Keegan Paul, 1989; London: I.B. Tauris, 2013); and Carolyn Steedman, *An Everyday Life of the English Working Class: Work, Self and Sociability in the Early Nineteenth Century* (Cambridge: Cambridge University Press, 2013).
17 John's correspondence with his land agent and others, 1860–85 (JB/2/1/29-51); Trustees' minute books, 1885–1956 (TBM/1/1/1/1-4); correspondence files of Owen Scott and Sidney Harrison, Curators 1884–1922, 1922–45 (TBM/7/1/1-2).
18 Curator's report to Trustees covering 1921–7, p. 12 (TBM/1/1/5/2).
19 John's letters, 1820s–1840 (JB/2/1/1–9 *passim*).
20 Strathmore Estate archive at Durham County Record Office (D/St: online catalogue at www.durham.recordoffice.org.uk); for Glamis Castle archives, see www.glamis_castle.co.uk/the-castle/archives. The Bowes Museum catalogues for museum objects, the reference library and the archives are available at https://www.thebowesmuseum.org.uk/Collection/Collections_Search.

21 Bowes Museum material deposited in Durham County Record Office in August 1961 (D/Bo/E 1-41: online catalogue at www.durham.recordoffice.org.uk).
22 Clarissa Campbell Orr, 'Introduction', in Clarissa Campbell Orr (ed.), *Women in the Victorian Art World* (Manchester and New York: Manchester University Press, 1995), p. 30, n. 54.
23 Joséphine's letter to John, September 1867 (JB/2/3/1); John's letter diaries, 1840–53 (D/St/C 1/16-32); letters from housekeepers, 1870–1 (JB/8/1/7/1–43); letters from friends, 1869–71 (JB/8/1/3/1-3; JB/8/1/11/1–7; JB/8/1/13/1-6; JB/8/1/20/1–33).
24 Letters mainly from John to his land agent and his solicitor, 1824–85 (JB/2/1/1–51); letters to John from friends etc., 1857–84 (JB/2/4–10; JB/9/3).
25 Household bills, 1855–85 (JB/3/3/1–33).
26 For example, Frank Herrmann, *The English as Collectors: A Documentary Source Book* (London: John Murray, 1999); Jacqueline Yallop, *Magpies, Squirrels & Thieves: How the Victorians Collected the World* (London: Atlantic Books, 2011); and Higonnet, *A Museum of One's Own*.
27 Dealers' bills and letters, 1861–73 (JB/3/3/JB/5/3–13). The current value has been calculated using www.measuringworth.com. For a detailed analysis of dealers' bills, see Phillips, 'National identity', Appendix 6.
28 John's letters to Mr Wheldon, June to November 1833 (JB/2/1/2/9–31 *passim*); John's letters to Mr Wheldon 22 July and 8 August 1833 (JB/2/1/2/9; JB/2/1/2/14). Chapman, *John & Joséphine*, p. 20 incorrectly calculates that John had suffered from the disease since the age of twenty-two or twenty-three.
29 *Cambridge University Calendar, 1829* (The Bowes Museum Library, 914.259/CAM); John appears as a Fellow Commoner in the Undergraduates section, p. 337.
30 Charles Astor Bristed, *Five Years in an English University* (1852), republished as *An American in Victorian Cambridge*, ed. Christopher Stray (Exeter: University of Exeter, 2008), pp. 303–4.
31 John's letters to Mr Wheldon, 25 July and 8 August 1833 (JB/2/1/2/12; JB/2/1/2/14); Chapman, *John & Joséphine*, pp. 19–20.
32 Sir Benjamin Collins Brodie (1783–1862), 'Heberden Historical Series', *Rheumatology* 42. 5 (2003), pp. 689–91. www.academic.oup.com/rheumatology/issue/42/5.
33 John's letters to Mr Wheldon, 25 July and 8 August 1833 (JB/2/1/2/12; JB/2/1/2/14).
34 For example, letters referring to eye problems 15 March 1862 and 29 February 1872 (JB/2/1/31/1; JB/2/1/40/36); letters referring to problems with leg and foot throughout 1875 (JB/2/1/43 *passim*).
35 John's letters to Mr Wheldon, 8 August and 5 November 1833 (JB/2/1/2/14; JB/2/1/2/31). 'Clap' was a well-known term for gonorrhoea.
36 Chapman, *John & Joséphine*, p. 19.
37 Dr Wilhelm Gollmann, *Homeopathic Guide to All Diseases of the Urinary and Sexual Organs*, translated by Charles J. Hempel (Philadelphia: Rademacher & Sheek, 1855), pp. 54–5, 66–7.
38 John's letters to Mr Wheldon, 1833 (JB/2/1/2 *passim*).
39 George Silvertop's letter to Mr Wheldon, 12 October 1833 was filed with William Hutt's letters (JB/9/3/1/5).
40 J. Poirier, 'Claude François Lallemand (1790–1854)', *Journal of Neurology*, 257 (2010), pp. 681–2.
41 Wills of Joséphine and John Bowes, 1871 and 1884 (TBM/2/1/1–2); Trustees Minute Book, 1886–1906 (TBM/1/1/1/1).

42 John never mentioned his 'disease' to his land agent, addressed as 'Dear Sir'; only to his solicitor, addressed as 'My Dear Sir', a more socially equal form of address. John's letters to his solicitors and land agents, 1830s–1880s (JB/2/1/1-51 *passim*).
43 John's letters to Mr Wheldon, 25 July and 8 August 1833 (JB/2/1/2/12; JB/2/1/2/14).
44 John's letter to Mr Wheldon, 19 May 1842 (JB/2/1/11/28); John's letter to Mr Dent, 27 August 1844 (JB/2/1/13/68).
45 Letter from Malcom [*sic*.] [no surname given] to Mr Dent, 8 July 1834 (JB/2/1/3/17).
46 John's letter diaries, 1840–1847 (DCRO, D/St/C 1/16/16-21).
47 Emile Zola, *Nana* (originally published 1880), translated by George Holden (London: Penguin 1972); Theodore Zeldin, *France 1848–1945: Ambition and Love* (Oxford: Oxford University Press, 1979), Chapter 13, 'Women', pp. 343–62; Tracy C. Davis, *Actresses as Working Women: Their Social Identity in Victorian Culture* (London: Routledge, 1991), especially Chapter 3, 'The Social Dynamic and "Respectability", Actresses and Prostitutes', pp. 78–86; F. W. J. Hemmings, *The Theatre Industry in Nineteenth-Century France* (Cambridge: Cambridge University Press, 1993), especially Chapter 13, 'The Difficult Life of the Actress', pp. 199–209.
48 Rupert Christiansen, *Tales of the New Babylon: Paris 1869–1875* (London: Sinclair-Stevenson, 1994), pp. 85–6.
49 Lindsay Macnaughton, 'Beyond the Bowes Museum: The Social and Material Worlds of Alphonsine Bowes de Saint-Amand', *19: Interdisciplinary Studies in the Long Nineteenth Century* 31 (2020): 19, cites two references to Mademoiselle Delorme relating to the Théâtre Français in Paris (*Le Mercure des théâtres*, 29 January and 24 December 1846, https://gallica.bnf.fr/ark:/12148/bpt6k5444161b/f4; and https://gallica.bnf.fr/ark:/12148/bpt6k54443507/f2.item); notices (congés) about leaving apartments in 8 rue Rougemont, 30 March 1850 (DCRO, D/St/C5/088/34-35), with thanks to Professor John Findlay for bringing these to my attention. John's letters are dated from 8 rue Rougemont 1847–1850 (JB/2/1/16-19 *passim*).
50 John's letter diary, 1847 (DCRO, D/St/C 1/16/21); theatre wages book, 1846–7 (JB/7/5/1).
51 Chapman, *John & Joséphine*, p. 38; bills from Monbro fils aîné including Auteuil and 7 Cité d'Antin, 1851–5 (JB/4/6/1, 5–6); John's letters addressed from 7 Cité d'Antin, 1850–5 (JB/2/1/19-24 *passim*).
52 Honoré de Balzac's series of novels about nineteenth-century Paris, *La Comédie humaine* [*The Human Comedy*] (Paris: 1829–50); Emile Zola's Rougon-Macquart sequence of novels covering the period of the Second Empire in Paris and southern provincial France (Paris: 1871–93).
53 For a general view, see Davis, *Actresses as Working Women*, pp. 78–86; Hemmings, *The Theatre Industry*, pp. 199–209; Kimberley White, *Female Singers on the French Stage, 1830–1848* (Cambridge: Cambridge University Press, 2019), Chapter 4 'La vie bourgeoise', pp. 88–112. For example, for Alice Ozy from the Théâtre des Variétés, see Virginia Rounding, *Grandes Horizontales: The Lives and Legends of Four Nineteenth-Century Courtesans* (London: Bloomsbury, 2003), pp. 112–13.
54 Zola's novel *Nana* was written in the 1870s but set in the late 1860s; see also n. 47, above. 'Demi-mondaine – Femme née dans un monde distingué sans en respecter les lois. Le succès d'une pièce de Dumas fils a créé le mot. – "On écrit en toutes lettres que vous régnez sur le demi-monde."' (Woman of the *demi-monde* – A woman who was born into a distinguished world but does not respect its laws. The success of a play by Dumas the younger created the word. – 'Everyone writes in all their letters

that you reign over the *demi-monde.*'): Lorédan Larchey, *Dictionnaire historique, étymologique et anecdotique de l'argot parisien: sixième édition des excentricités du langage, mise à la hauteur des révolutions du jour* [Paris, 1875] (The Bowes Museum Library, F.447/LA).

55 Can-can dancer in *La Mariée de Poissy* (The Married Woman of Poissy) (JB/7/12//1/10); dancer in *Le Mari d'une Camargo* (The Husband of a Camargo Dancer) (JB/7/12/1/11); mistress in *Les Métamorphoses de Jeanette* (The Transformation of Jeanette) (JB/7/12/1/8); Madame de Pompadour in *Pomponette et Pompadour* (Pomponette and Pompadour) (JB/7/12/1/12); cross-dressing in her debut performance in *Mademoiselle Grabutot* (JB/7/12/1/1), and *Le Chevalier de Pézenas* (The Lord of Pézenas) (JB/7/12/1/13).

56 John's letters, 1850s–1874 (JB/2/1/20–42 *passim*).

57 Letters to John, 1850s–1874 (JB/2/4–10 *passim*); letters to Joséphine, 1870–1871 (JB/8/1/1–23 *passim*).

58 John's letters to Mr Dent, 26 July and 9 August 1858 (JB/2/1/27/60; JB/2/1/27/63).

59 It might be significant that John's second wife also took a course of sea-bathing – see John's letters to Mr Holmes (successor to Mr Wheldon), 14 July and 16 September 1879 (JB/2/1/47/95; JB/2/1/47/98).

60 Letters to Joséphine from Comtesse Fabre de l'Aude, January to March 1870 (JB/8/1/11/1-5); letters to Joséphine from Ellen Piétri, undated [1870], 25 November 1870 (JB/8/1/20/4; JB/8/1/20/20).

61 John's letter to Mr Dent, 27 June 1861 (JB/2/1/30/54).

62 John's letter to Mr Dent, 11 June 1861 (JB/2/1/30/49).

63 Hare quoted in Hardy, *John Bowes*, pp. 136–7.

64 Hare quoted in Ibid., p. 137.

65 Gollmann, *Homoeopathic Guide*, p. 102.

66 Hare quoted in Hardy, *John Bowes*, p. 137.

67 John's letter to Mr Dent, 30 July 1865 (JB/2/1/34/22).

68 The recipe suggested dissolving 125 grammes of sulphur of potassium or 125 grammes of sulphuric acid in a bath of 300 litres. Letter from François Laroze to Savory & Moore, 18 August 1862 (JB/2/10/3/16).

69 For example, pharmacists' bills in annual bundles of household bills, 1849–74 (JB/3/3/1–22 *passim*).

70 I am grateful to John Elliott, retired chemist and volunteer at The Bowes Museum, for this opinion.

71 The film commentary about the museum and its founders in the museum hints at possible hopes of a pregnancy but gives no supporting reference.

72 Elizabeth Emery, *Photojournalism and the Origins of the French Writer House Museum 1881–1914* (Farnham: Ashgate, 2012), p. 108.

73 René G. Saisselin, *Bricabracomania: The Bourgeois and the Bibelot* (London: Thames and Hudson, 1985), p. xiv.

74 Sarah Kane, 'Turning Bibelots into Museum Pieces: Josephine Coffin-Chevallier and the creation of The Bowes Museum, Barnard Castle'. *Journal of Design History* 9. 1 (1996): pp. 6, 10.

75 'This [childlessness] was possibly the result of a venereal infection John had suffered before meeting Joséphine.' Andrew Burnet, *The Bowes Museum* (Peterborough: Jarrold Publishing, 2015), p. 12.

76 In 2011, public reaction to one phallic shoe in a Vivienne Westwood touring exhibition led to warning notices posted in the museum, and in 2018 pre-emptive

censorship warned visitors about graphic depictions of surgical operations in an exhibition. Exhibitions at The Bowes Museum: *Vivienne Westwood Shoes: A World Wide Exhibition* (2011), *Skin Deep* by Jonathan Yeo (2018).
77 Cf. Guerilla Girls' poster 'Do Women Have to Be Naked to Get into the Met. Museum?', 1989 (www.nga.gov/collection/art-object-page.139856.html).
78 Barbara Caine, *Biography and History* (Basingstoke: Palgrave Macmillan, 2010), esp. Section 2, 'A History of Biography', pp. 27–46. See also Steedman, *Dust*, pp. 149–50.
79 Thomas Carlyle, quoted in Caine, *Biography and History*, p. 33.

Bibliography

Primary Sources

Archives of The Bowes Museum in The Bowes Museum (TBM).
Bowes Museum material in Durham County Record Office (D/Bo).
Papers of John and Joséphine Bowes in The Bowes Museum (JB).
Strathmore Estate Archive in Durham County Record Office (D/St).

Secondary literature

Balzac, Honoré de. *La Comédie' humaine (The Human Comedy)*. Paris, 1829–50.
Bristed, Charles Astor. *Five Years in an English University*. 1852. Republished as *An American in Victorian Cambridge*, edited by Christopher Stray. Exeter: University of Exeter, 2008.
Burnet, Andrew. *The Bowes Museum*. Peterborough: Jarrold Publishing, 2015.
Caine, Barbara. *Biography and History*. Basingstoke: Palgrave Macmillan, 2010.
Cambridge University Calendar, 1829. [Cambridge]: 1829. The Bowes Museum Library, 914.259/CAM.
Chapman, Caroline. *John & Joséphine: The Creation of The Bowes Museum*. Barnard Castle: The Bowes Museum, 2010.
Christiansen, Rupert. *Tales of the New Babylon: Paris 1869–1875*. London: Sinclair-Stevenson, 1994.
Cook, Michael. *The Management of Information from Archives*. Aldershot: Gower, 1986; Abingdon: Routledge, Taylor & Francis Group, 2016.
Davis, Tracy C. *Actresses as Working Women: Their Social Identity in Victorian Culture*. London: Routledge, 1991.
Emery, Elizabeth. *Photojournalism and the Origins of the French Writer House Museum 1881–1914*. Farnham: Ashgate, 2012.
Gollmann, (Dr) Wilhelm. *Homeopathic Guide to all Diseases of the Urinary and Sexual Organs*, translated by Charles J. Hempel. Philadelphia: Rademacher & Sheek, 1855.
Guerilla Girls' Poster. 'Do Women Have to Be Naked to Get into the Met. Museum?', 1989. www.nga.gov/collection/art-object-page.139856.html.
Hardy, Charles E. *John Bowes and the Bowes Museum*. Bishop Auckland: Friends of The Bowes Museum, 1970, reissued 1989.
Heberden Historical Series. *Rheumatology* 42, no. 5 (2003). www.academic.oup.com/rheumatology/issue/42/5.

Hemmings, F. W. J. *The Theatre Industry in Nineteenth-Century France*. Cambridge: Cambridge University Press, 1993.

Herrmann, Frank. *The English as Collectors: A Documentary Source Book*. London: John Murray, 1999.

Higonnet, Anne. *A Museum of One's Own: Private Collecting, Public Gift*. Pittsburgh and New York: Periscope Publishing Ltd., 2009.

Hill, Kate. *Culture and Class in English Public Museums, 1850–1914*. Aldershot: Ashgate, 2005.

Jenkinson, (Sir) Hilary. *A Manual of Archive Administration*. London: Lund, Humphries & Co., 1922; 2nd edn. 1937, reissued 1965.

Kane, Sarah. 'Turning Bibelots into Museum Pieces: Josephine Coffin-Chevallier and the Creation of the Bowes Museum, Barnard Castle'. *Journal of Design History* 9, no. 1 (1996): 1–21.

Larchey, Lorédan. *Dictionnaire historique, étymologique et anecdotique de l'argot parisien: sixième édition des excentricités du langage, mise à la hauteur des révolutions du jour*. [Paris: 1875]. (The Bowes Museum Library, F.447/LA).

Macnaughton, Lindsay. 'Beyond the Bowes Museum: The Social and Material Worlds of Alphonsine Bowes de Saint-Amand'. *19: Interdisciplinary Studies in the Long Nineteenth Century* 31 (2020): https://doi.org/10.16995/ntn.3348.

Orr, Clarissa Campbell. 'Introduction'. In *Women in the Victorian Art World*, edited by C. C. Orr, 1–30. Manchester and New York: Manchester University Press, 1995.

Parker, Rozsika, and Griselda Pollock. *Old Mistresses: Women, Art and Ideology*. London: Routledge & Keegan Paul, 1989; London: I.B. Tauris, 2013.

Phillips, Judith. 'Nationality, Gender, Social Status and Cultural Aspirations in Mid-Nineteenth Century England and France: Joséphine Bowes (1825–1874), Collector and Museum Creator'. PhD dissertation, Teesside University, 2020.

Poirier, J. 'Claude François Lallemand (1790–1854)'. *Journal of Neurology* 257 (2010): 681–2.

Rounding, Virginia. *Grandes Horizontales: The Lives and Legends of Four Nineteenth-Century Courtesans*. London: Bloomsbury, 2003.

Rubenhold, Hallie. *The Five: The Untold Lives of the Women Killed by Jack the Ripper*. London: Doubleday, 2019.

Saisselin, René G. *Bricabracomania: The Bourgeois and the Bibelot*. London: Thames and Hudson, 1985.

Schama, Simon. *Citizens: A Chronicle of the French Revolution*. London: Penguin, 1989.

Sherman, Daniel J. *Worthy Monuments: Art Museums and the Politics of Culture in Nineteenth-Century France*. Cambridge, MA and London: Harvard University Press, 1989.

Steedman, Carolyn. *Dust*. Manchester: Manchester University Press, 2001.

Steedman, Carolyn. *An Everyday Life of the English Working Class: Work, Self and Sociability in the Early Nineteenth Century*. Cambridge: Cambridge University Press, 2013.

Stoler, Ann Laura. *Along the Archival Grain: Epistemic Anxieties and Colonial Common Sense*. Princeton and Oxford: Princeton University Press, 2009.

Webb, Jen, Tony Schirato, and Geoff Denaher. *Understanding Bourdieu*. London: SAGE, 2002.

White, Kimberley. *Female Singers on the French Stage, 1830–1848*. Cambridge: Cambridge University Press, 2019.

Williams, Caroline. *Managing Archives: Foundations, Principles and Practice*. Oxford: Chandos, 2006.
Yallop, Jacqueline. *Magpies, Squirrels & Thieves: How the Victorians Collected the World*. London: Atlantic Books, 2011.
Zola, Emile. *Rougon-Macquart Sequence of Novels*. Paris, 1871–93.
Zola, Emile. *Nana*. Paris, 1880. Translated by George Holden with an Introduction. London: Penguin, 1972.
Zeldin, Theodore. *France 1848–1945: Ambition and Love*. Oxford: Oxford University Press, 1979.

11

Empowering the invisible: The archival legacy of Christian Cole

Philip Burnett

It is hoped that sufficient matter can be collected, to publish for the information of the rising generation, the life of such a hard-working and industrious student.
'Death of Mr. Christian F. Cole', *The Sierra Leone Weekly News* (3 April 1886)

The limits of invisibility

In recent years, a great many books and articles have been written about the experiences that Black people of African descent had in Britain and the British Empire during the nineteenth century.[1] Both inside and outside the academy, and across a variety of disciplines and sub-disciplines, major reference works, institutions and curriculum developers have made concerted efforts to find and incorporate the stories of Black figures from the nineteenth century into the prevailing knowledge about the period. For example, when the *Dictionary of National Biography* was first published in 1885 it included virtually no accounts of Black lives, while its modern descendant, the *Oxford Dictionary of National Biography* has, by contrast, sought to address and expand its coverage to include figures of African heritage who have shaped British History.[2] From initiatives such as this one and many others like it there is no doubt that history and memory are all the richer and more inclusive. But such endeavours pose a significant methodological challenge, for almost all of the lives and experiences of Black people in the nineteenth century are written using small numbers of source material and archival records.[3]

Such is the case with Christian Frederick Cole, whose life provides a window into the experience of a Black African living in Britain during the nineteenth century. The extract at the beginning of this chapter is taken from an obituary for Cole, who was born in Sierra Leone in 1851–2 and died in Zanzibar in December 1885. In 1876 he became the first Black African to take the BA degree from the University of Oxford, and in 1883 he became a barrister, claiming that he was 'the first Negro who has ever pleaded at the bar of England'.[4] Despite the fame Cole achieved in his own time, constructing and piecing together a detailed account of his life is not easy: the 'sufficient matter' required to publish a full-length biography, as wished for in the opening quote above from the *Sierra Leone Weekly News*, does not exist.[5] In what follows I reflect on what might have been meant by 'sufficient matter'. The aim of this chapter, then, is less about examining what exceptionalized and distinguished Cole's life and his archival legacy over that of other Black individuals in nineteenth-century England. Rather, this chapter focuses more on the extent to which Cole's archival invisibility is emblematic of archival practice in the nineteenth century. In discussing what we can find about Cole in archives I consider how this matter is in/substantial, and how information about Cole's life might bring fresh insights and considerations into the argument that nineteenth-century archives sought to both control and curate knowledge in order to understand the vast amounts of information from 'new' parts of the world.[6]

Cole's scattered life

I first encountered Cole and began researching his life in 2016. While working in Oxford, I was handed a pamphlet entitled *Reflections on the Zulu War* (1879). I was told that the anonymous author was Cole, the first Black person to be awarded a degree from the University of Oxford. The pamphlet itself (see Figure 11.1), which circulated in London, Oxford and Sierra Leone, its topic, and the historical milieu in which it was written, quite simply incited curiosity and made me want to find out more. Finding out the story behind its author, the dedication it bore to W. E. Gladstone and the assemblage of quotations began a series of visits to archives following leads out of unanswered questions and missing pieces of information.

The other reason I found Cole compelling was the overlap with my own research interests. Many of the issues and topics had also come up in my research on missionary musicians on Anglican mission stations in nineteenth-century South Africa. An important strand of this research was understanding the reception of religious literacy which involved examining the contributions made by Black mission members to the composition of hymns.[7] Hymns and hymn writing, in particular the ways in which Indigenous converts responded to the repertoire formed an important part of this analysis.[8] Here, my source material was in the archive of the United Society for the Propagation of the Gospel, which in many respects is an incredibly rich historical resource, and reveals much evidence about the prominent role that Black mission members had in all aspects of mission music making, whether as teachers, performers or composers. The records, however, were largely written by missionaries of European descent, and there was very little available by way of first-hand accounts written by Black Christians.[9]

At first, there seemed to be the same problem with Cole, in that finding any information about him would be an impossible task. Part of the challenge with Cole is that his own words are largely absent from the archive. Apart from six pamphlets (see Table 11.1) and one letter, there is no other personal material.[10] Accounts of his life (or particular moments in it) are tied to other figures or institutions, notably the University of Oxford and the Inner Temple.[11] The six pamphlets, while a rich source for his politics and ideology, reveal little about his personal and day-to-day life. My

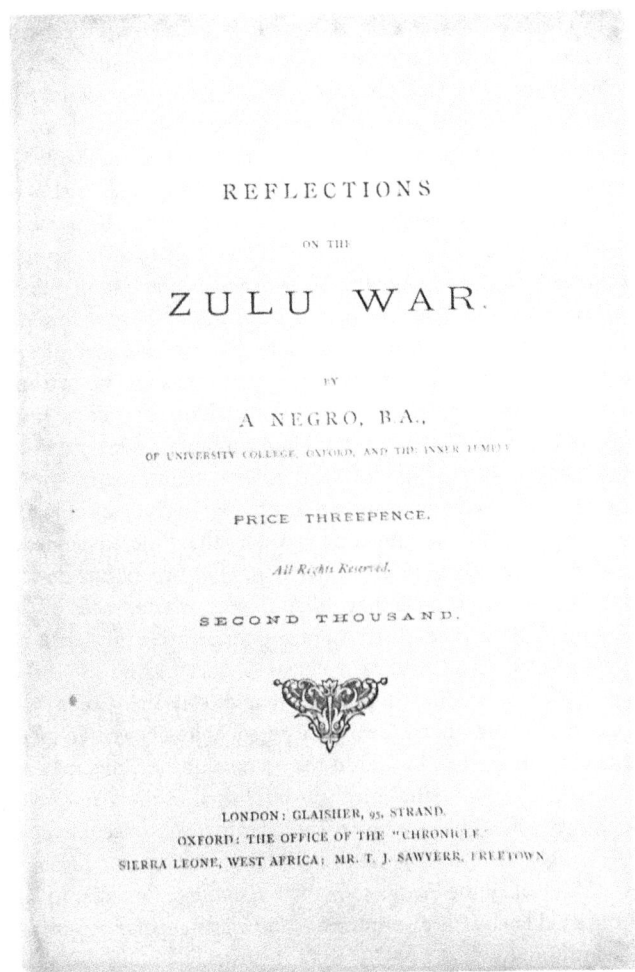

Figure 11.1 Title page of [Frederick Christian Cole], *Reflections on the Zulu War* (London: Glaisher; Oxford: The Office of the *Chronicle*; Sierra Leone: T. J. Sawyer, 1879). Courtesy of The Master and Fellows of University College Oxford.

aim became to find out who Cole knew, how he travelled and how he negotiated and understood his world. The main route into this world was through the partial glimpses of Cole through the recollections and chance remarks of people who knew or had encounters with him.

For instance, Nicholas, Cole's older brother, mentioned in his application for ordination in 1874 that Christian was 'keeping terms at Oxford, in the first principles of the Christian Faith.'[12] A few years earlier, G. A. Metzger, a trader in Freetown, made reference in his preface to Cole's pamphlet *Athletic Sports* that Cole had a 'Grecian mind'. This was a remark that not only characterized Cole's style of writing, which made heavy use of classical imagery and often referenced classical literature, but also pointed to Cole's own education at Fourah Bay College, Freetown, where the curriculum consisted almost entirely of the classics.[13] Throughout his time at Oxford, a period of roughly six years, Cole's presence was recorded in personal reminiscences and other miscellaneous types of documentation. For example, Thomas Wentworth Higginson (1846–1906) recorded in his journal that he had met Cole in Oxford in 1876.[14] Higginson did little more than note he had had 'some talk' with 'a conspicuous figure' and only referred to Cole by his nickname 'King Cole'. His name also appears in account books at University College, Oxford and in the University of Oxford Archives.[15] Charles Mallet's biography of Herbert Gladstone also mentioned Cole, as Gladstone had supported Cole and helped to fundraise money for him. Mallet made reference to a letter of gratitude from Cole, but no source was given for the original letter, and only to give an example of Gladstone's generosity and philanthropy.[16]

Cole is also represented in encounters with officialdom or specific institutions. At the end of his time in Oxford, the Oxford Union minute book noted that Cole had incurred a fine of £1 for placing a motion for debate but failing to turn up to defend it.[17] Another occasion when Cole found himself on the wrong side of officialdom was in 1883: several newspapers around England ran a story that Cole was sentenced to a fine of 40 shillings (approximately £140 in today's money) or twenty-one days.[18]

It is the world of nineteenth-century mission work where traces of Cole's life are most in evidence.[19] Cole was educated by missionaries in Sierra Leone and while at Oxford he became active in advocating overseas Anglican missions. Three sources of information produced by missionaries in Zanzibar shortly after Cole's death travelled a great distance to relay their news. Two were personal letters written by missionaries to Oxford contacts and are now found in the archive of the Universities' Mission to Central Africa (UMCA), while the third was published in the *Oxford Magazine*. All provide us with a snapshot of Cole's life in Zanzibar that is at once tantalizingly sparse but also richly insightful.[20] Cecil Pollard, a UMCA missionary educated at Oxford, tells us that Cole had taken the Pledge soon after arriving in Zanzibar in January 1885, that he had practised law while also tutoring, and was a regular congregant at Christ Church Cathedral (built by the UMCA) in Stonetown.[21] A multi-racial and religious congregation attended Cole's funeral, as well as notable figures in Zanzibar society. The two letters were buried in the UMCA archive and finding them was part luck, part hard work, sifting through vast quantities of letters and official papers. J. P. Farler, the archdeacon of Zanzibar, wrote in a letter to W. H. Penney, the secretary of the UMCA, that while in Zanzibar, Cole 'had done well and given no cause of offence'. Penney was at Oxford and like Cole was an unattached student, that is, a student not belonging to a specific Oxford college.[22] Percy Jones-Bateman, a missionary priest in Zanzibar, reported that Cole was teaching English, French and German classes, that he attended both the Swahili and English services, and was generally 'prospering', which Jones-Bateman explained to mean that Cole 'was winning the respect of many both Europeans & natives in his work'.[23]

There were other places where Cole left an imprint, even if it was transitory and not fully recorded in archival records. For instance, his career at the Oxford Union Society would have created an imprint on memories which were not often transferred into a documentary, textual form. Cole joined the Oxford Union on 19 February 1874.[24] The

Oxford Union, founded in 1823, was primarily a debating society and its membership was (then) made up of university students. Cole probably attended debates but it was only in 1878 and 1879 that he spoke in them, putting himself in a very public setting. It was also a place where Cole could present himself and his views, and where he would have been heard speaking. As Figure 11.2 shows, the speaker in a debate stood in front of a large group of people, usually members of the Union and fellow participants in the debate, while members of the public would watch from a gallery. The topics he spoke on (e.g. University discipline, capital punishment, the Press and Britain's foreign and imperial policy) suggest that Cole keenly followed current affairs both nationally and internationally.

Figure 11.2 The Oxford Union Society Debating Chamber in 1873. (The room depicted here is now the Union Library.) *The Graphic* (31 May 1873): 1. Photograph from author's collection.

The small amount of scattered material about Cole, when brought together, presents an image of him as highly educated, religious, ambitious and well-versed in the literature and culture of the British metropole. He lived in three different countries, and the traces he left behind in each, not to mention the archival testimonies of the experiences he had in them, provide glimpses into the complexities that characterized the life of this mobile, literate, religious and defiant man.

This image is confirmed in his pamphlets, in which he projected a strong sense of his own African identity and, because of his experience, expressed disdain towards the contradictions he saw in liberal British worldviews. This body of writing, although insubstantial, provided a significant amount of the 'sufficient matter' which helped to see the complexity of Cole's life. Mirrored in his own geographic experience is the breadth of the topics Cole considered and addressed. From the debates in which he took part or the topics on which he wrote, we are given insights into his views on topics ranging from cultural events and current affairs in Sierra Leone and the wider African

Table 11.1 Pamphlets authored by Christian Cole and their present locations (researched and prepared by Philip Burnett)

Location	Title	Publication details
School of Oriental and African Studies (SOAS) Library	What Do Men Say About Negroes? Being a Few Remarks on a Passage in 'Oxford Days: or, How Frank Ross Obtained his Degree'	London: Williams & Co. (1879)
School of Oriental and African Studies (SOAS) Library	The Athletic Sports at Falcon Bridge, Battery, Freetown, Sierra Leone, West Coast of Africa, on Friday 4 June 1869./ Graphically Sketched by Christian F. Cole	Freetown: J. Taylor (1870)
University of Birmingham, Special Collections	Education: A Lecture Delivered in Holy Trinity Church Schoolroom Kissey Road, Freetown, Sierra Leone	Manchester: John Heywood (1880)
University Library, Cambridge	Reflections on the Zulu War and the Future of Africa	London: Griffith & Farran (1883)
University College Library, Oxford	Reflections on the Zulu War. By a Negro, B.A., of University College, Oxford, and the Inner Temple (Second Thousand ed.)	London: Glaisher (1879)
Bodleian Library, Oxford	The Wall Case, Can Anything Good Come out of Sierra Leone? Being a Letter Addressed to Lord Derby ... on One or Two of the Burning West African Questions of the Hour	London: Griffith and Farran/Sierra Leone: T. J. Sawyerr (1883)
Yale University Library	Reflections on the Zulu War	London: Glaisher (1879)
	What Do Men Say About Negroes? Being a Few Remarks on a Passage in 'Oxford Days: or, How Frank Ross Obtained his Degree'	London: Williams & Co. (1879)
n/a	Colenso: A Threnody	Unknown

Source: The Author

continent, to racial attitudes in Victorian Britain, and verses which praised his role model, John Colenso, the dissident bishop of Natal.

The pamphlets provided Cole with a means to participate in the network of ideas that were emerging from the Pan-African movement during the second half of the nineteenth century.[25] He dedicated one of his pamphlets (*What Do Mean Say?*) to the statesman Edward Blyden (1832–1912), one of the key thinkers in the Pan-African movement, with whom there were several personal connections.[26] Blyden knew the Cole family in Sierra Leone, where he taught Cole's older brother, Nicholas, and Christian once signed in Blyden as his guest at the Oxford Union, where Cole was a member.[27] The quotations in Cole's pamphlets suggest he read works by Ruskin, Pater and Macaulay.[28] Despite his strong African identity, he was cosmopolitan and international in outlook, and his peers and acquaintances multi-racial, and it was out of this that he formed his social world. The spatial and conceptual geography of his life was inseparable from the British imperial world, which through its variety of technologies from print and the circulation of printed media, to shipping routes, let alone its cultural and religious footprints, formed and shaped the trajectory of Cole's life from Freetown, to Oxford, to Zanzibar.

Thus, Cole was a complex person in his day. The glimpses we see of his life, and the ambiguities of his self-image, and those of his supporters and peer groups, provide the thread that runs through the fragments of his documented narrative. He is at once present in the memorialization of his achievements in England, and yet in the archive he is absent. His existence there relies almost entirely on the words and descriptions of others. His story is an unusual and an important biography of a man who achieved prominence at a time when this was not the norm for some one of his race. In the 1870s, only one Black man before him (and in those days it could only have been a man) had been awarded a degree by the University of Oxford.[29] Yet Cole's exceptionalism, which he himself lauded, was predicated on a complex racial identity. He was, as he himself put it, 'the first Negro' to practise law in English courts, but he was not the first Black man: John Thorpe, a Sierra Leonean of 'Maroon' descent could also make this claim as he was called to the English bar in 1850.[30] Cole's life therefore also reveals the internal divisions and splintering of what might seem to be a coherent and monolithic racial identity.

What we can see

Cole's experiences, the ways in which he was (and is) seen, his reputational legacies and his archival invisibility can be explained by his short and mobile life, and these archival fragments offer a nuanced insight into much broader contexts than this chapter can address. His pamphlets, for instance, offer much to analyse for insights into the rise of Pan-Africanism and how this played out in a variety of settings. There are two distinct, yet interacting politics that emerge from this partial, invisible archive. The first is a politics of memory, where we see Cole through the eyes of those who knew him. While we don't know much about the day-to-day conversations he had with people, we do have his words and opinions which were read by his peers, and people who brought his pamphlets in Freetown, Oxford, London and wherever else they were distributed.[31]

People formed opinions of his actions and his words, and these can be found in newspapers, while his pamphlets, the most substantial body of Cole's own words, can be found in repositories around the world. The location of these sources in itself is an indication of the politics behind the creation (and curation) of memory.

Throughout his life, Cole found himself at the centre of various networks which generated and authored his archival legacy. Networks, generally, require participation, and they are where individuals can leave and create an imprint. Thus, in discovering more about Cole's networks, we are able to habilitate some of his own agency. The other point to note about networks is that, depending on their constitution, they offer support, and in Cole's case this is provided by those in his circle of missionary networks. His actions, personality and social status were observed and recorded, taking up space and inscribing him onto the historical record in what could be seen as at once both unexpected and obscure ways. Here through the perspectives of family members, teachers, friends, colleagues and anonymous clerks and bureaucrats we are given a glimpse of Cole's world, and his experience is given voice.

For example, one document in particular tells us a bit more about Cole's background and his time at Oxford. The document was a 'Statement' signed by Herbert Gladstone, George Bradley, the Master of University College, Oxford, and George Kitchin, the academic in charge of the Unattached Students.[32] All would have known Cole well as an undergraduate, and wrote the statement in 1877 asking for financial support on behalf of Cole. The statement noted Cole's 'praiseworthy steadiness and perseverance' during his studies, and is also the first known instance in print where Cole is referred to as 'the first negro graduate member of the University of Oxford', the way in which Cole styled himself when signing the pamphlets he authored in 1879 and 1883. In many ways, then, this document could almost be seen as evidence of the foundation of Cole's latter-day reputation, one predicated on race, and whose longevity has survived into the present.

A different, more insidious side of Cole's experience of being racially typecast can be seen in the reception of two of his pamphlets. *What Do Men Say* and *Reflections* were written during the second half of 1879, a year in which the Zulu War provided a topic for discussion not just in newspapers, but also at the Union. They articulate Cole's strong anti-racial and anti-imperial position. Both are short, taking up only twelve sides of paper, but are packed with quotations from well-known works of European literature and the Bible. *What Do Men Say* was written in the form of an essay as a response to racist stereotypes in a popular novel about Oxford life, while *Reflections* was in verse form, and launched an attack on British Imperial policy, specifically British foreign policy towards the Zulu.[33] Both pamphlets received uncomplimentary reviews in the student press which made racist and derogatory references to Cole.[34] In an issue of the *Oxford and Cambridge Undergraduates' Journal* two letters were published side by side, one from Cole and one from J. Renner Maxwell, a Sierra Leonean compatriot studying at Oxford.[35] Maxwell's letter denounced Cole's pamphlets on the grounds that because of them 'injustice will be done to a great many intelligent Africans in England at the present time, who are actuated by nobler motives'.[36]

The second politics that emerges is one of race and identity, both asserted, contested and debated by Cole on a personal and a social level. Cole's sense of his own identity is revealed in surprisingly complex terms given that there are only seven documents written in his words. From them emerges an image of Cole's sense of his place in the world(s) he inhabited. Although he had been educated at the 'Athens of West Africa' and presented with the culture and literature of the metropole, in England he suffered a battery of racial profiling and abuse. Documented in his own writings is a self-consciousness of his racial identity and his reactions to how he viewed himself as a citizen of Britain and its empire. If, as Achille Mbembe notes, the experience of Africans outside of Africa encountering Africans in Africa was characterized in part as one of encountering another's Other, then the archive becomes an important space in which Cole should be understood as an individual not only inhabiting one space, but many interlinking and seemingly disparate spaces, out of which arose a racial identity built on co-identification and solidarity through struggle.[37]

This politics of identity also emerges at moments when Cole represented himself as a devout Christian, and a supporter of mission work. In Oxford he was particularly active in promoting the cause of overseas mission work. As an undergraduate, Cole for a time represented the Unattached Students as their secretary on the committee for the Universities' Mission to Central Africa. Two newspaper reports from 1877 provide not only a glimpse of Cole's activities to help promote mission work but also show the reach of his newsworthiness, the interest being generated by his race. *Jackson's Oxford Journal*, a local newspaper, and *Riverine Grazier*, distributed in New South Wales, Australia, demonstrate that Cole's activities were known about further afield than Oxford. Both articles noted Cole's race, the *Riverine Grazier* noting that Cole was 'the first gentleman of color on whom the University of Oxford conferred a degree', while *Jackson's* more bluntly called its news piece 'A negro at the parish church'.[38] Both articles highlight Cole's own religious action as they report that Cole read the lessons at the Sunday services in St Mary Magdalene, Woodstock, and *Jackson's* added that Cole gave two talks on mission work in Sierra Leone to the Sunday School and at the Union Workhouse.

Cole's pamphlets also highlight the importance of Christianity for understanding his intellectual frameworks. Cole quoted directly from the Bible, but also drew on Biblical imagery for rhetorical effect. Christianity, it would seem, provided a framework by which Cole could articulate his understanding of the world, an understanding that was at times frustrated by the contradictions and disjunctions between a British Empire that was founded on Christian beliefs and practices, but that was at the same time oppressive and unequal. This is most evident in his poem, 'The Future of Africa', a thirty-six-line piece of verse published with the second edition of *Reflections on the Zulu War* (1883), which laments the treatment of Africa, and presents an optimistic vision for the continent's future. The influence of Christianity is seen in the imagery Cole uses in the poem. For instance, 'cease their weepings' (line 10), 'one trumpet-blast' (line 15) 'vanish like the early dew' (line 19) and 'oppression's yoke' (line 21) are allusions rich in Biblical association and meaning. There is another explicit, unexpected link to Africa through the poem's dedication to John Colenso, dissident bishop of Natal, and his family.[39] The poem is preceded by a biblical quotation: 'Let us hear the conclusion of the whole matter'.[40] This was the text which Colenso had used for the sermon he preached in Balliol College on 29 November 1874, when Cole was an undergraduate at Oxford. Whether Cole heard Colenso preach or not, this choice of epitaph, and the dedication to Colenso and his family, all of whom were vocal in their criticism of British military action in Zululand, suggest a politics in which race, religion and identity overlapped.

Christian Cole's family background had its origins in the West African slave trade, and the British-led establishment of colonies for freed slaves. The uprooting of his ancestors from their homelands meant that he was brought up in Sierra Leone, a culturally diverse Krio society which had heritage from West Africa, the Caribbean and Sierra Leone and developed through a complex interaction between these various cultures and western agents of change, namely missionaries, settlers and traders.[41] Through his missionary education he experienced the spread of British Christianity and its concomitant culture. On a personal level, Cole struggled with an addiction to alcohol and experienced financial troubles, through which he was helped by friends and acquaintances. He travelled great distances to receive education and to find work, during the course of which he was confronted with racial abuse, notably in Oxford and London. While the imperial world brought him closer to England, it also alienated him, and this is a theme that characterized his life.

Conclusion

The historian Olivette Otele has recently argued that in seeking to highlight 'Black presence', scholarship has tended to engage with exceptional individuals rather than collective experience.[42] Consequently, the achievements of Black individuals are seen as unique, which in turn continues to place Blackness in contrast to, rather than as a part of, European norms, whereas, certainly in the case of Britain there is a consistent Black presence in historical records.[43] It is tapping into these records and interpreting what is found that requires patience and skill. We might reflect on the ways in which archival silence, or absence, amplifies this tendency to exceptionalism, and how this is echoed in the portrayal and construction of individual lives such as Cole's.[44] Likewise, we are challenged to understand more about how the interpretations of what we find in archives have changed (or not) and to generate methods of sympathetically challenging and revisiting how historical figures could be re-imagined.[45]

What might the documentation of Cole tell us? Broadly speaking, the documents and records we have for Cole show how his life took some surprising turns that were indeed at times exceptional, at others spiritual, and at others quotidian, as he negotiated the imperial and colonial spaces he inhabited. He held steadfast to the culture of the Christian, 'English' upbringing and education he received in Sierra Leone, yet it was at Oxford, in many ways the heart of the educational and cultural world he inhabited, that he was made most aware of his outsider-ness and status as an 'Other'. As Kwezi Mkhize has shown, the colonial institutions that sustained Englishness and 'English' culture were often taken up with more enthusiasm in the colony than in the metropole because of the universal identity they offered to colonial subjects. Ultimately, this led to disillusionment as the myth of a universal imperial identity free of racial stratification unravelled.[46] Cole's embrace of the liberal values presented to him was loosened as he became aware of the contradictions that lay embedded in this supposedly open-to-all worldview.

If Cole's scattered and invisible presence in archival records is emblematic of his experience, we would do well to remember that, certainly during his time in Britain, he was moving against, rather than within, a society that was promising to move with him. The prevailing liberalism in Britain at the time had an idealized understanding of education and material progress, which, as it promised to be a liberating agent for Black colonial subjects, enabled new identities and politics to emerge. This was part of a larger shift too broad to summarize here, but understanding the causes behind these shifts and how they played out in individuals such as Cole are an antidote towards nuancing the experiences we find documented in the archives. Cole's own choice of words provides us with an interpretive starting point. In one of his pamphlets, quoting from the Bible, he made the appeal, 'Look not upon me because I am black'.[47] Perhaps this would appear how Cole wished for himself to be remembered.

Acknowledgements

This chapter is part of a much larger work in progress. I would like to thank the editors of this volume, Anne Winner for reading draft versions of the chapter, and also Pamela Roberts, Robin Darwall-Smith and Peter Gilliver for the conversations we had about Cole before I began writing this chapter. I am also grateful to the archivists who have helped me to track down material about Cole, and for those whose decision it was to preserve these precious records.

Notes

1. Some examples, amongst many, that deal exclusively or in part with the topic are Peter Fryer, *Staying Power: The History of Black People in Britain* (London: Pluto Press, 2010); David Killingray, 'Significant Black South Africans in Britain Before 1912: Pan-African Organisations and the Emergence of South Africa's First Black Lawyers', *South African Historical Journal* 64. 3 (2012): 393–417; Bongani Ngqulunqa, *The Man who Founded the ANC: A Biography of Pixley ka Isaka Seme* (Cape Town: Penguin, 2017); Brian Willan, *Sol Plaatje: A Life of Solomon Tshekisho Plaatje, 1876–1932* (Johannesburg: Jacana, 2018); Janet Hodgson and Theresa Edlmann, *Zonnebloem College and the Genesis of an African Intelligentsia, 1857–1933* (Cape Town: African Lives, 2018); and Catherine Burns, 'Louisa Mvemve: A Woman's Advice to the Public on the Cure of Various Diseases', *Kronos* 23 (1996): 108–34. For a set of essays looking at various aspects of Black experience in different parts of the British Empire see the contributions in Philip D. Morgan and Sean Hawkins (eds), *Black Experience and the Empire* (Oxford: Oxford University Press, 2004).
2. Anders Ingram, 'Black Lives in the Oxford DNB', *Oxford Dictionary of National Biography*, https://www.oxforddnb.com/view/10.1093/ref:odnb/9780198614128.001.0001/odnb-9780198614128-e-369302, accessed 8 January 2021.

3   There are exceptions, for example, Brian Willan's biography of Plaatje (see endnote 1) which had recourse to a rich body of primary material, much of it consisting of Plaatje's personal papers.
4   This is how Cole signed one of his pamphlets: *Reflections on the Zulu War and The Future of Africa* (London: Griffin and Farran; Sierra Leone: T. J. Sawyerr, 1883). Unless quoting directly from an historical source, I use 'African' for contemporary terms that are more obviously offensive today.
5   In recent years Cole has been recognized with a plaque at University College, Oxford, in film, and a student society at Oxford is called 'The Christian Cole Society for Classicists of Colour', whose aim is to decolonize Classics.
6   Thomas Richards, *The Imperial Archive: Knowledge and the Fantasy of Empire* (London: Verso, 1993), pp. 5–11.
7   The original plan for this chapter was to compare the archival documentations of the experience in Britain of Jonas Ntsiko, a Xhosa member of the Anglican missions in the Cape Colony, with Cole. Ntsiko studied in Britain at St Augustine's, Canterbury around the same time that Cole was at Oxford.
8   Grant Olwage, 'John Knox Bokwe, Colonial Composer: Tales about Race and Music', *Journal of the Royal Musical Association* 131. 1 (2006): 1–37.
9   For some reflections on how sound silence figure in archives see Erin Johnson-Williams' chapter above.
10 Brief surveys of Cole's life can be found in: Christopher Fyfe, *A Short History of Sierra Leone* (Oxford: Oxford University, Press, 1962); Pamela Roberts, *Black Oxford: The Untold Stories of Oxford University's Black Scholars* (Oxford: Signal Books, 2013); and Philip Burnett, 'Cole, Christian Frederick (1851/2–1885), Barrister and Author', *Oxford Dictionary of National Biography*, https://www.oxforddnb.com/view/10.1093/ref:odnb/9780198614128.001.0001/odnb-9780198614128-e-90000369317, accessed 5 August 2021. See also Robin Darwall-Smith, *A History of University College, Oxford* (Oxford: Oxford University Press, 2008), pp. 395–6. The letter, only recently rediscovered, is kept at St Catharine's College, Oxford: St Catherine's College Archives, IF.1 'Ledger Miscellaneous Record of the Delegacy, 1867–1884'.
11 Pamela Roberts' *Black Oxford* contains a very good outline of Cole's life and positions him in the context of the University of Oxford's Black History. Michele Mendelssohn's *Making Oscar Wilde* (Oxford: Oxford University Press, 2018) mentions Cole, but only as a means to support the narrative of Oscar Wilde, one of Cole's contemporaries at Oxford.
12 Church Missionary Society Archives, Cowley, Oxford: West Africa Mission O 74/2: 'Rev. Nicholas Jacob Cole: Account of Life and Application for Ordination 1874'.
13 Fyfe, *History of Sierra Leone*, p. 346, identifies G.A. Metzger as George Anthony Metzger, the Bendu trading agent for the Liverpool-based Company of African Merchants.
14 *Letters and Journals of Thomas Wentworth Higginson, 1846–1906* (Boston: Houghton Mifflin Company/The Riverside Press Cambridge, 1921), pp. 201–2.
15 Cole's name was recorded in various official account books now held in the University College Archives, and his matriculation slip which recorded his formal entry into the University of Oxford in 1874 is kept in the University of Oxford Archives.
16 Charles Mallet, *Herbert Gladstone: A Memoir* (London: Hutchinson & Co, 1932), 65–6.
17 Oxfordshire History Centre, Oxford Union Society Archives, O22/1/A1/11: 'Minute Book (volume XI) 1874–1880'.

18 See 'Charge Against a Barrister' (1883), *Manchester Courier and Lancashire General Advertiser*, 6 July, p. 6. The story also appeared in newspapers in Bristol, London and Derby.
19 For a collection of essays discussing the breadth of information the mission archive offers to nineteenth-century studies, see the contributions in Robert A. Bickers and Rosemary Seton (eds), *Mission Encounters: Sources and Issues* (Richmond, Surrey: Curzon Press, 1996).
20 Cecil S. Pollard (1886), 'Mr. Christian Cole', *Oxford Magazine*, 24 February, p. 82. The UMCA archive is held in the Bodleian Library, Oxford. I am grateful to Peter Gilliver who pointed out the obituary in *The Oxford Magazine*.
21 On the UMCA in Zanzibar and Christ Church Cathedral, Stonetown, see G. Alex Bremner, 'The Architecture of the Universities' Mission to Central Africa: Developing a Vernacular Tradition in the Anglican Mission Field, 1861–1909', *Journal of the Society of Architectural Historians* 68. 4 (2009): 514–39.
22 Bodleian Library, Oxford, Universities' Mission to Central Africa Archives, UMCA/A1/(VI)/A, f. 451: Letter, J. P. Farler (Zanzibar) to W. H. Penney (London), 21 December 1885. On the unattached students see Allan Bullock, '"A Scotch University Added to Oxford?": The Non-Collegiate Students', in M. G. Brock and M. C. Curthoys (eds), *The History of the University of Oxford, Volume 7: Nineteenth-Century Oxford, Part 2* (Oxford: Oxford University Press, 2011), pp. 193–208.
23 Bodleian Library, Oxford, Universities' Mission to Central Africa Archives, UMCA/A1/(VI)/A, ff. 1299–1303. Letter, Jones-Bateman (Kiungani) to Penney (London), 17 January 1885.
24 Oxfordshire History Centre, Oxford Union Society Archives, O22/8/A2/1: 'Index of Members, 1873–1890'.
25 On Pan-Africanism, see Hakim Adi, *Pan-Africanism: A History* (London: Bloomsbury Academic, 2019).
26 For a biography of Blyden see Hollis R. Lynch, *Edward Wilmot Blyden: Pan-Negro Patriot* (New York: Oxford University Press, 1967).
27 Blyden teaching Nicholas Cole: Letter dated 16 October 1871, Edward Blyden to Henry Venn (C.M.S.) in Hollis R. Lynch (ed.), *Selected letters of Edward Wilmot Blyden* (Millwood. NY: KTO Press, 1978). Cole signing Blyden into the Oxford Union: Oxfordshire History Centre, Oxford Union Society Archives, O22/12/A4/1: 'Stranger's Book, 1862–1880'.
28 University College Oxford Archives, UC:L1/A1/3: 'Library Borrowing Books'.
29 This was Samuel Ajayi Crowther, bishop of the Niger, who was awarded a Doctor of Divinity in 1864.
30 Fyfe, *History of Sierra Leone*, p. 77.
31 This chapter cannot provide a full consideration of where Cole's pamphlets are kept today. A glance at Table 11.1 shows that Cole's pamphlets are known to exist largely in major repositories in the global North, a circumstance that if investigated would reveal further linkages and insights into the circulation of information during and since the nineteenth century.
32 The 'Statement' was published in the 1877–8 Unattached Students' report, and a copy is kept in St Catherine's College, Oxford, Archives, IF.1 Ledger: 'Miscellaneous Record of the Delegacy 1867–1884'.
33 It is possible that a passage where the narrative contains a derogatory description of Africans is what Cole refers to. Frederic Edward Weatherly, *Oxford Days: Or, How Ross Got His Degree* (London: Sampson Low, Marston, Searle, & Rivington, 1879), p. 134.

34 'Works by A Negro B.A.', *Oxford and Cambridge Undergraduates' Journal* (23 October 1879), p. 32.
35 Cole, 'Mr. C.F. Cole's Works'; and J. Renner Maxwell 'Disclaimer', *Oxford and Cambridge Undergraduates' Journal* (30 October 1879), p. 49.
36 Maxwell also became a barrister, and returned to West Africa where he became chief magistrate for the colony of The Gambia. He also published a treatise entitled *The Negro Question: Or, Hints for the Physical Improvement of the Negro Race, with Special References to West Africa* (London: T. Fisher Unwin, 1892).
37 Achille Mbembe would explain this as a 'double consciousness' which arose from a knowledge of Africa while being disconnected from it. Black writing and thought, Mbembe continues, is characterized by a tradition of mutual concern and coidentification. See Achille Mbembe, *Critique of Black Reason*, translated by L. Dubois (Durham: Duke University Press, 2017), pp. 25–6.
38 'A Negro at the Parish Church', *Jackson's Oxford Journal* (23 June 1877); and 'Untitled news item' *Riverine Grazier* [New South Wales] (8 September 1877).
39 On Colenso see Jeff Guy, *The Heretic: A Study of the Life of John William Colenso* (Johannesburg: Raven Press, 1983).
40 Eccl. 12.13.
41 Vivian Bickford-Smith notes that the exchanges that resulted in the development and emergence of creole society were mostly at the level of the everyday or quotidian, such as dress, agricultural practices, objects and diet, to name a few. See Vivian Bickford-Smith, 'The Betrayal of the Creole Elites, 1880–1920', in Philip D. Morgan and Sean Hawkins (eds), *Black Experience and the Empire* (Oxford: Oxford University Press, 2006), pp. 194–227.
42 Olivette Otele, *African Europeans: An Untold Story* (London: Hurst and Company, 2020).
43 This is made no clearer than through the careful work found in Imtiaz Habib, *Black Lives in the English Archives, 1500–1677: Imprints of the Invisible* (Abingdon, Oxford: Routledge, 2008).
44 Exceptionalism and absence are not necessarily delimited along lines of race, but can be determined by other 'taboos' such as sexual embarrassment or immorality, as Judith Phillips' analysis in the previous chapter shows.
45 Tiziana Morosetti in her chapter (see above) suggests something similar in the ways that Sara Baartman's life story generated allegories that tell us not so much about the past as about our own present.
46 Kwezi Mkhize, '"To See Us As We See Ourselves": John Tengo Jabavu and the Politics of the Black Periodical', *Journal of Southern African Studies* 44. 3 (2018): 413–30. Mkhize's analysis of John Tengo Jabavu (1859–1921) provides an interesting comparison with Christian Cole.
47 [Christian Frederick Cole], *Reflections on the Zulu War* (1879 and 1883).

Bibliography

Adi, Hakim. *Pan-Africanism: A History*. London: Bloomsbury Academic, 2019.
Bickers Robert A., and Rosemary Seton (eds). *Mission Encounters: Sources and Issues*. Richmond, Surrey: Curzon Press, 1996.
Bickford-Smith, Vivian. 'The Betrayal of the Creole Elites, 1880–1920'. In *Black Experience and the Empire*, edited by Philip D. Morgan and Sean Hawkins, 194–227. Oxford: Oxford University Press, 2006.

Bremner, G. Alex. 'The Architecture of the Universities' Mission to Central Africa: Developing a Vernacular Tradition in the Anglican Mission Field, 1861-1909'. *Journal of the Society of Architectural Historians* 68, no. 4 (2009): 514-39.

Bullock, Allan. "'A Scotch University Added to Oxford?': The Non-Collegiate Students'. In *The History of the University of Oxford, Volume 7: Nineteenth-Century Oxford, Part 2*, edited by M. G. Brock and M. C. Curthoys, 193-208. Oxford: Oxford University Press, 2011.

Burnett, Philip. 'Cole, Christian Frederick (1851/2-1885), Barrister and Author'. *Oxford Dictionary of National Biography*. https://www.oxforddnb.com/view/10.1093/ref:odnb/9780198614128.001.0001/odnb-9780198614128-e-90000369317. Accessed 5 August 2021.

Burns, Catherine. 'Louisa Mvemve: A Woman's Advice to the Public on the Cure of Various Diseases'. *Kronos* 23 (1996): 108-34.

Cole, Christian Frederick. *Reflections on the Zulu War and the Future of Africa*. London: Griffin and Farran; Sierra Leone: T. J. Sawyerr, 1883.

Darwall-Smith, Robin. *A History of University College, Oxford*. Oxford: Oxford University Press, 2008.

Fryer, Peter. *Staying Power: The History of Black People in Britain*. London: Pluto Press, 2010.

Fyfe, Christopher. *A Short History of Sierra Leone*. Oxford: Oxford University, Press, 1962.

Guy, Jeff. *The Heretic: A Study of the Life of John William Colenso*. Johannesburg: Raven Press, 1983.

Habib, Imtiaz. *Black Lives in the English Archives, 1500-1677: Imprints of the Invisible*. Abingdon, Oxford: Routledge, 2008.

Higginson, Thomas Wentworth. *Letters and Journals of Thomas Wentworth Higginson, 1846-1906*. Boston: Houghton Mifflin Company/The Riverside Press Cambridge, 1921.

Hodgson, Janet, and Theresa Edlmann. *Zonnebloem College and the Genesis of an African Intelligentsia, 1857-1933*. Cape Town: African Lives, 2018.

Ingram, Anders. 'Black Lives in the Oxford DNB'. *Oxford Dictionary of National Biography*. https://www.oxforddnb.com/view/10.1093/ref:odnb/9780198614128.001.0001/odnb-9780198614128-e-369302. Accessed 5 August 2021.

Killingray, David. 'Significant Black South Africans in Britain Before 1912: Pan-African Organisations and the Emergence of South Africa's First Black Lawyers', *South African Historical Journal* 64, no. 3 (2012): 393-417.

Lynch, Hollis R. *Edward Wilmot Blyden: Pan-Negro Patriot*. New York: Oxford University Press, 1967.

Lynch, Hollis R. (ed.). *Selected letters of Edward Wilmot Blyden*. Millwood, NY: KTO Press, 1978.

Mallet, Charles. *Herbert Gladstone: A Memoir*. London: Hutchinson & Co, 1932.

Maxwell, R. Jenner. *The Negro Question: Or, Hints for the Physical Improvement of the Negro Race, with Special References to West Africa*. London: T. Fisher Unwin, 1892.

Mbembe, Achille. *Critique of Black Reason*, translated by L. Dubois. Durham: Duke University Press, 2017.

Mendelssohn, Michele. *Making Oscar Wilde*. Oxford: Oxford University Press, 2018.

Mkhize, Kwezi. '"To See Us As We See Ourselves": John Tengo Jabavu and the Politics of the Black Periodical'. *Journal of Southern African Studies* 44, no. 3 (2018): 413-30.

Morgan Philip D. and Sean Hawkins (eds). *Black Experience and the Empire*. Oxford: Oxford University Press, 2004.

Ngqulunqa, Bongani. *The Man Who Founded the ANC: A Biography of Pixley ka Isaka Seme*. Cape Town: Penguin, 2017.

Olwage, Grant. 'John Knox Bokwe, Colonial Composer: Tales about Race and Music'. *Journal of the Royal Musical Association* 131, no. 1 (2006): 1–37.

Otele, Olivette. *African Europeans: An Untold Story*. London: Hurst and Company, 2020.

Richards, Thomas. *The Imperial Archive: Knowledge and the Fantasy of Empire*. London: Verso, 1993.

Roberts, Pamela. *Black Oxford: The Untold Stories of Oxford University's Black Scholars*. Oxford: Signal Books, 2013.

Weatherly, Frederic Edward. *Oxford Days: or, How Ross Got His Degree*. London: Sampson Low, Marston, Searle, & Rivington, 1879.

Willan, Brian. *Sol Plaatje: A Life of Solomon Tshekisho Plaatje, 1876–1932*. Johannesburg: Jacana, 2018.

Part Four

Layered archives

12

The power of invisibility: Nursing nuns and archival gatekeeping

Jemima Short

A note on terminology: whilst Canon law distinguishes between the following terms, this chapter uses the terms 'nun', 'woman religious' and 'sister' interchangeably.[1]

France faced multiple health crises in the nineteenth century: epidemics of infectious diseases such as cholera and typhoid fever, and workplace injuries and alcoholism plagued many communities. Despite significant scientific advancements such as germ theory and a growing debate around public health, secular services remained patchy and insufficient. Congregations of Catholic women provided the majority of grassroots care work up until the early twentieth century, working with the poor and socially marginalized. Nursing congregations remained intrinsic to healthcare even after the 1902 Law of Associations, as the Republican state lacked both the resources and the personnel to replace them.[2] Working in a variety of public roles, the number of nuns in France grew tenfold over the course of the nineteenth century.[3] Regardless of the scale and importance of their work, the invisibility of nursing nuns in historical scholarship and in the historical archive of medicine and welfare has been a widely recognized problem for decades.[4]

As Trouillot has argued, 'any historical narrative is a particular bundle of silences, the result of a unique process, and the operation required to deconstruct these silences will vary accordingly'.[5] There are a whole variety of reasons why the labour of nursing nuns has fallen through the cracks. These women worked at the intersection between religion and science, negotiating republican anticlericalism, emerging professional boundaries and strict gender roles, and caring for the marginalized and 'unproductive'.[6] Capitalist hierarchies of labour tend to privilege profitable and productive work, meaning that care work – which is emotional, practical and often difficult to quantify – has, in the nineteenth-century archive of medicine and welfare, been systematically overlooked and undervalued.[7] These are issues which persist today: in light of the global coronavirus pandemic it is clear that questions of what care work is 'worth' remain a divisive political issue.[8]

The invisibility of nursing nuns stems also from archival processes and the narrativization of records. Here, religious congregations must be understood as both actors and narrators.[9] Most congregations retain private archives, carefully protected by the mother superior and individual sisters responsible for the records. This ownership over nineteenth-century records allows nuns to act as gatekeepers and 'editors' of these institutional histories. As Steedman has argued, we might see the process of record-keeping and of history writing as a writing of the self through the narrative of one's origins:

> "History" is one of the great narrative modes that are our legacy from the nineteenth century, and as a way of plotting and telling a life (of giving shape and meaning to the inchoate items of existence) it is useful to compare it with the modern idea of childhood, and the way in which the remembered childhood – the narrative of the self – has become the dominant way of telling the story of how one got to be the way one is.[10]

With this in mind, the problem of invisibility surrounding religious congregations must be understood – at least in part – as a result of the historiographical practices of the institutions themselves. These are family histories, in which the values of the community are prioritized. As O'Brien has argued, nuns have faced the historical invisibility common to many groups of women, but this invisibility is compounded by an institutional culture where self-abnegation and humility are understood as exemplary behaviour.[11]

Thus, congregational archives form the basis of a family history which is vital to identity-building in these groups, and which is closely aligned with institutional priorities regarding modesty and piety. Existing scholarship has established the ways in which congregational archives fulfil a role in shaping family histories, and a number of scholars have discussed the role of nuns as archival gatekeepers and the methodological challenges which such institutions present for external researchers.[12] I particularly draw upon the work of Sarah Curtis, whose analysis of congregational archive practices has shaped this chapter considerably.[13] There remains scope for further discussion of how congregational approaches to archives impact the methodologies of researchers and the narrative choices of academic historians. If religious congregations choose to perpetuate their own invisibility, seeking out self-abnegation, this presents significant political and ethical considerations for academic research which are further developed in this chapter.

Working with congregational archives, researchers must recognize the significance of these records to the identity and integrity of modern-day communities. However, it is also important to recognize the plurality of these histories, and to consider that institutional histories provide a very limited view of the activities of these groups. Many congregational archives fall somewhere between private community records and public records, because the work of these women involved many groups outside of the religious community. Nursing congregations worked predominantly in communities where people lived with poverty, isolation, sickness or disability. By and large, the nuns' patients left no written record and had no opportunity to participate in the construction of historical narratives: their life experiences were not generally considered worth recording. Thus, the narrative choices of congregations have a direct impact on our knowledge not only of nursing nuns, but also of their patients.

Two issues arise from this: as care givers, Catholic congregations had power over the groups they cared for. Whilst there is no evidence of abuse in the groups researched here, there is substantial evidence that power over the poor and socially marginalized was used in contentious ways. These groups preached a philosophy of acceptance in the face of suffering, which factored into wider forms of social control, as religious teachings protected existing social hierarchies. Moreover, nursing nuns used their authority to influence people's reading habits, social circles, living arrangements, drinking habits and use of language (e.g. not swearing), all in an attempt to fundamentally alter the religious practice and day-to-day lives of their patients.[14] The invisibility of nursing nuns means that the experiences of these patients are also absent from medical and welfare histories. Secondly, through the curation of historical narratives, religious congregations are able to employ the stories of their patients in histories which perpetuate the power dynamics of the past. In congregational archives, the patient appears as the object of charity, the 'Other' who is used to edify the congregation. Steedman has argued that through historical writing,

> Working-class people, their image, their appurtenances, were used to tell other people's stories: to tell some kind of story of the bourgeois self. Following the trajectory of this tradition, of representation and use of the working-class story, all that can be suggested for the moment, is that perhaps the working-class domestic is read and written out of the same obscure desire: that desire means you understand – and write – the self through others, who are not like you.[15]

Through my own experiences attempting to gain access to three archives owned by French congregations of nursing nuns, this chapter further explores these issues and the ethically complex nature of working with private religious archives.

Encounters in the congregational archive

This chapter deals with three French congregations founded in nineteenth-century France: Les Petites Sœurs des Pauvres (the Little Sisters of the Poor, 1839–), Les Auxiliatrices des Ames du Purgatoire (the Helpers of the Holy Souls of Purgatory, 1856–) and Les Sœurs de l'Espérance (the Sisters of Hope, 1836–). Each group rapidly expanded to other countries in Europe and beyond, and all three groups still exist in some form. The Little Sisters ran hospices caring for the elderly, whilst the Helpers of the Holy Souls and the Sisters of Hope provided domestic care to the poor and to the bourgeoisie, respectively.

When I began researching these congregations in 2016, I wrote to each group via post and email, in French, requesting access to their private archives. I provided information on my research background and my research interests and entered into a negotiation process which differed from congregation to congregation. The Sisters of Hope proved unforthcoming, and my research into this group stalled fairly quickly, as the congregation did not reply to repeated letters. I was eventually able to obtain a telephone number for this congregation, but the conversation was very brief. I was informed that the congregation had no archival holdings in France, at least for the nursing branch of the congregation, and that if there was anything of use it would be found in Rome. The congregation also proved very difficult to trace in French state and departmental archives, where records for this group are extremely fragmented. The Sisters of Hope are one branch of a larger congregation, the Holy Family of Bordeaux. The Holy Family have a website, but here too the Sisters of Hope are largely absent – their website includes an online digitized archive, yet virtually no information on the nursing branch. The archive focuses instead on the congregation's founder, a priest named Noailles, and mainly comprises his correspondence pertaining to spiritual matters.

The Helpers of the Holy Souls and the Little Sisters of the Poor were more forthcoming: both groups were quick to respond and I was able to arrange visits with them. But here, too, the archive visits differed considerably. The archive of the Little Sisters of the Poor is, I suspect, uncatalogued, and on my arrival I was not able to access any primary sources. It transpired that the archive I had come to visit was not a space to which I would be allowed access. Working instead from the room where I was staying at the motherhouse, I was offered secondary sources, mainly histories of the order and one or two religious texts. I had informal discussions with the Mother Superior and with a sister who I was told was responsible for the archive and with whom I stayed in touch after my visit. I was shown a *Positio*, a text prepared by the congregation as part of the process of canonization for their founder, Jeanne Jugan. The sisters were keen to show me the exhibition for Jugan at the motherhouse and took me to visit significant places from her lifetime – the house where she was born, her local Church, the house in which she worked as a servant and so on. The information I was given repeated and reproduced recent hagiographical histories of the congregation and the information available on their website. Emphasis was placed on the charism of the congregation: the unique spiritual gift which is believed to have been given to the community by God and which has come to be seen as their unique founding spirit, a cornerstone of a community's identity.[16] There was an expectation that, as a historian, my research would reproduce the carefully curated story of the order's foundation, in which the life story of a single woman, Jugan, has come to stand for an institution which has expanded across France and overseas.[17]

This approach to congregational history has become common following the Second Vatican Council which ran from 1962 to 1965. Called to address the position of the Church in the modern world, the Council initiated a shift in the way congregations approached their histories. Following the Council, an almost formulaic approach to congregational histories has emerged, in which carefully curated narratives of small groups of founding individuals have become the focal point for the histories of international institutions.[18] The 1964 encyclical – a letter sent by the Pope to the Roman Catholic clergy – entitled *Ecclesiam Suam* (His Church) called for self-reflection, self-examination and restoration of perfection within the Church through a return to origins and 'authoritative sources' known as *ressourcement*.[19] The 1965 Vatican decree on the Adaptation and Renewal of Religious Life, *Perfectae Caritatis*, highlighted the importance of a founders' spirit and personal aims, which were taken as key distinguishing features for each individual congregation.[20]

I attempted to move beyond the foundation story of the Little Sisters: using the bibliography of the texts available I was able to determine the types of records which the congregation may have pertaining to their work as nurses. Having made very specific requests, I was eventually given access to some copies of primary sources, all of which were typed out on computers or typewriters – never original manuscripts or even images of originals. A few more sources of this type were sent to me via post or email after my visit, again in response to specific requests. Thus, the congregation's archival sources were delivered one by one, the fruits of an ongoing dialogue with the Mother Superior and the sister responsible for the archive. This negotiation process shaped and constrained the research itself and cast an additional layer of doubt over how comprehensive or reliable the information might be. Moreover, I was told anecdotally that individual sisters had previously changed or destroyed records which no longer aligned with the desired historical narrative regarding their foundation.

The Little Sisters were welcoming and keen to help, but there was a clear assumption that my work should, and would, focus on the foundation story and on their saintly founder. This attitude shaped and limited the documents I was able to access. It was further exacerbated by the fact that I had to ask questions about what might be available rather than working from any sort of list or catalogue, interacting with sisters who no doubt had other duties within the congregation. Finally, there was an obvious reticence to show me primary documents, and certain sources, such as the minutes of general chapter meetings – meetings bringing together Superiors from communities in different locations – were considered to be too private and remained off-limits.

The archives of the Helpers of the Holy Souls were quite different. A member of this congregation reached out to me via an academic mailing list when I first started the project, demonstrating a genuine desire to engage with external researchers. The congregation employs a lay archivist who is responsible for the organization and cataloguing of documents. I was able to access any documents relating to the nursing work of the sisters, many of which the archivist had located for me in advance of my visit. These included rules for nursing nuns, training manuals, written commentary by nuns, patient registers and visit reports. This was an archive visit more comparable with a visit to the national or departmental archives with considerably fewer obstacles to access than I had experienced with the other congregations. The sources available for this congregation were by far the most rich and varied.

These three very different encounters with congregational archives demonstrate the power which modern-day groups retain as owners of nineteenth-century records. The historiographical practices of the congregations had a significant impact on my own research and what could be known about each of these groups and the people they cared for. Such experiences in the congregational archives align with those reported by other scholars, and similar issues of access, of simplistic foundational narratives and of the relationship between archivist and researcher are also subjects of discussion in the field of business and organizational archives.[21] In many cases, congregations appear to play a significant role in perpetuating their own invisibility in historical scholarship, choosing to restrict or limit access to their records. Even when congregations allow scholars conditional access to records, they retain significant power to shape the way these histories are told, often reducing their history to a formulaic origin story. By limiting access to archives, gatekeepers influence which events and people are considered important and decide which are edited out completely.[22]

Archival ownership and power

Schwartz and Cook argue that 'archives, ever since the mnemons of ancient Greece, have been about power – about maintaining power, about the power of the present to control what is, and will be, known about the past, about the power of remembering over forgetting'.[23] The constructed nature of the archive and the power of owners and archivists to gatekeep and mediate knowledge should not be underestimated.

The result of current processes of authorship and gatekeeping is that the 'neat' stories told by congregations are constantly reproduced at the expense of other narratives. As this chapter has established, congregational histories are histories of community, of family, and the actions of congregations must be understood in the context of priorities entirely different from those of academics. These are private records of closed communities. However, congregations are not only families, they are also institutions which played an important role in public life. In carefully curating a single version of their history, no room is left for divergent narratives, and no space is given to critical voices. Disenfranchised and marginalized groups appear in these records which can enrich our understanding of the past, beyond the narratives of the dominant classes, but these records remain carefully guarded.

Monteiro et al. have argued that congregations exercise a kind of historical monopoly over their records and how they are interpreted.[24] They argue that congregations write and curate their histories from a perspective of institutional singularity, with little to no room for dialogue or dissenting voices.[25] This means that members who critique the congregation, former members who choose to leave or members of the public who come into contact with the institution in schools or hospitals or their homes, are seldom heard from. Monteiro et al. contend that the silencing of dissenting voices has proven to be an endemic problem in the Catholic Church and has in its worst iterations facilitated abuse, and allowed that abuse to remain hidden. They write:

> Historians should take account of the fact that religious communities also are commemorative communities, which via processes of self-historicizing have been able to shape a collective memory that does not necessarily match their factual history ... Vatican II contributed to the chiefly spiritualized perceptions of the past and uncomplicated appraisal of one's own legacy ... The latter is in danger of being cleansed of what the new self-image perceives as undesired legacy or what could be marked as awkward and shameful episodes.

As the authors go on to argue, this selective interpretation of the past, focusing on spiritualized perceptions of events, often obscures the plurality of experience within and around these institutions:

> The religious cannot monopolize their own history. They share that history with many who form no part, or no longer form a part, of religious communities and whose memories of that shared past are different. They lay claim to what has been characterized by Marjet Derks as a shared, but essentially plural and contradictory memorial space, which surpasses individual orders and congregations and which historical research should be doing justice to (Derks 2011a).[26]

Abuse scandals have been rare in the context of French female congregations.[27] Curtis discounts child abuse scandals as one of the reasons French congregations act with caution when dealing with outside researchers, highlighting that only one French order, the Sisters of Bon Secours, has been implicated in child abuse. Moreover, the reticence of French congregations to share their archives long predates the emergence of such scandals. Having discounted abuse as a likely cause of their reticence to engage with outsiders, Curtis concludes that the privacy of congregations must be understood not as secrecy, but rather as a protection of the family history which serves an entirely different purpose to those within the congregation than it does to those without.[28] She goes on to highlight the importance of the French political and historical context, where religious congregations were part of the culture wars which dominated the late eighteenth, nineteenth and early twentieth centuries, as anticlericalism became a dominant force in French politics and was a key impetus for Republican policies. The wariness with which congregations continue to treat outsiders must be understood within the context of a state which has historically demonstrated hostility and even violence towards the Catholic Church and its personnel.[29]

Curtis's conclusions regarding the causes of congregational privacy and wariness towards outsiders are important. These groups – which have historically faced intense anticlericalism in France – act in protection of a family history, safeguarding their records from outsiders who may be hostile to the institution. There is no evidence that French congregations have remained private in order to cover up a scandal. As stated above, my own research into French nursing congregations indicates no evidence of child abuse in these groups. However, the issue of how power is used and misused remains highly pertinent as one of the consequences of congregational privacy. While congregations may not have acted with the intention of covering up a scandal, the result of their privacy is that the ways they used their social power largely remain unscrutinized. Moreover, the ownership which congregations retain over the historical narrative also confers power on them: they are able to produce and reproduce their authority over said narrative through the gatekeeping of records and the narration of their past from a single institutional perspective. This singular viewpoint is problematic because of the plurality of experiences in and around these groups. As Curtis writes: '[c]learly, the orders own the records, but the bigger issue of who owns the history of Catholic sisters – the orders that maintain the tradition and the records or the larger society in which they participate – required more reflection.'[30]

The answer to this question has ethical implications for researchers. Power can be misused in many ways, and with groups other than children, and in the records kept by nursing nuns I encountered a number of behaviours that would now be considered deeply problematic. While under the care of the Little Sisters and the Helpers of the Holy Souls, adult patients in severe economic difficulties were coerced into conversion, into confessing despite clear reticence and, in the case of the latter congregation, into moving house or cutting people out of their lives if the sisters deemed their neighbours or friends to be inappropriate company.[31] The Little Sisters of the Poor expected residents of their hospices to work for the congregation – work such as washing wool or tending farmland – and funds and produce from this labour went towards the congregation and the upkeep of hospices.[32] It is unclear how patients felt about this work, or to what extent it was voluntary. The Helpers of the Holy Souls would disguise the fact that they were nuns until they felt they had won the patients' trust and would then seek to convert them. The congregation had a policy of disguising their religious identity from patients who were anticlerical or distrustful of the Church until they had built a relationship with them. Mme de Mainville is one example among many: the visiting nun pretended to be a bourgeois lady on charitable visits in order to win over this hostile patient.[33] Thus, in myriad ways, nursing nuns were able to use their positions as carers to exercise remarkable influence over their patients. Whilst we might not categorize such examples as abuse, they belong to an area of congregational history where power over the poor and socially marginalized was used in contentious ways – an area which remains almost entirely unexplored.

Those who are suffering, ill, infirm or living in poverty are often in a position of subordinance in relation to their carers. To be a carer is to hold a position of power. Even outside of institutions such as hospitals and hospices, where carers decide the structure of most aspects of a patient's day-to-day activities, the practice of care work creates a relationship rooted in vulnerability and dependency. This may be repressive (certain behaviours may be forbidden) but also productive. Establishing norms and deviancy, prescribing appropriate behaviours, managing the emotional aspects of this relationship and shaping discourse all facilitate the carer's power in relation to the patient.[34] The practice of providing nursing care with the express purpose of changing people's religious practice therefore presents clear ethical problems. People in immediate need of physical or economic relief may feel significant pressure to comply with their carers. Feelings of gratitude to their religious carers may have led people to consent to confessions or conversions with which they were not comfortable.

It is possible to be overly cynical about the motivations of Catholic congregations. Most nuns were motivated by a desire to help people. The nursing nuns studied here believed that conversions, confessions and communions would improve people's lives and help to grant them salvation. The reports made by the Helpers of the Holy Souls show nuns weeping at the misery they observe and shouting for joy when a patient recovers.[35] Little Sisters of the Poor died whilst caring for others.[36] There is clear evidence that such women pursued their proselytizing missions with the view to please God and to help those in need. This help may have been paternalist or even patronizing, but it was not necessarily intended as such. In many cases the extent to which nursing nuns used their power consciously is virtually impossible to trace, as it is very difficult to trace agency in these archives and the decision-making processes can be opaque. Congregational superiors clearly exercise authority, but the agency of individual members, or the contributions of the external male Church hierarchy, are often more difficult to identify.

It is nevertheless clear that in their day-to-day practice, nuns used their social power to influence and shape the ways people behaved. These women benefited from social hierarchies in which members of the Church had religious and moral authority. They also benefitted from the fact that Catholic networks provided resources, wealth and connections which people living in poverty needed but often could not access without the help of the Church. The work of nursing congregations is therefore one of the means by which the social order was maintained. Religious congregations were often affiliated with social elites, albeit in different ways. The Sisters of Hope provided domestic nursing to the bourgeoisie. In a hagiographical history of the congregation from 1920, the author shows an awareness of the ways inequalities of class – specifically the need for support – facilitated the religious conversion of those living in poverty:

> Offering a little assistance, it is always possible to approach the poor, to enter the house and reach the bedside, to talk to them of heaven, to bring to him God's ministry which will fortify his soul for the final fight. It is not so for the rich: secluded in his apartments, he gives the order to receive no guests, and if the priest presents himself, hoping to accomplish his holy ministry, he is often ousted with a thousand false excuses.[37]

Congregations were linked to the dominant classes through both funding and recruitment. The Little Sisters of the Poor received a significant number of bequests from wealthy donors; the Empress Eugénie (wife of Emperor Louis-Napoléon III) donated multiple times to the lottery which the congregation organized to raise funds.[38] The Helpers of the Holy Souls recruited principally from the bourgeoisie – their founder Eugénie Smet was the niece of a former mayor of Lille – and affiliates and benefactors to the congregation came from rich and elite families, with a number of noble titles appearing in their records. Through these connections with the dominant classes and their position within the Catholic Church, the care work of nuns takes on a further political edge. The nuns' moralizing influence on the working classes was of value to both the Church and to these elite groups who had a vested interest in maintaining the existing hierarchical social order. Price has shown how the dominant classes encouraged Catholic practice, church-led education and private charity as a means of maintaining their power in France during the Second Empire (1852–70):

> Religion offered both a justification for poverty – providential – and encouraged resignation to their lot on the part of the poor. It enjoyed obedience to the representatives of the state and to social superiors. Even where members of the political elite remained indifferent to the day-to-day activities of the Church it was possible to share Voltaire's conviction that *un Dieu pour le peuple* was essential. The problem was how to win back the poor to religion. Thus, in town and country,

substantial sums were provided by the elites and state for the construction and renovation of churches and schools and the payment of priests and teachers.[39]

By reserving aid and welfare for those who were peaceful, compliant and obedient, social elites were able to regulate the behaviour of the poor. The very system of private religious charity perpetuated a transactional relationship between the elites, the Church and the poor, placing the working classes in a position of subordination laced with potential feelings of shame, dependence and gratitude on the part of recipients.[40] As nurses to the poor and socially marginalized, nuns must be understood as a workforce operating within this hierarchy.

There is a tendency to underestimate the power which nuns exercised within this hierarchy. Scholars often do not exploit congregational archives or recognize their value in relation to broader social histories.[41] The absence of nuns in histories of medicine and welfare in France stems in part from capitalist, patriarchal hierarchies of work which mean women's work, and particularly care work, are often overlooked and undervalued.[42] But there is also a tendency to underestimate nuns and religious congregations as institutions specifically, because nuns do not fit within dominant conceptions of power. Dolan, writing on nuns in the Stuart era, has argued that the combination of invisibility and triviality which typify the historical treatment of nuns may in fact lend them certain advantages. In a sense, nuns benefitted from this 'invisibility'. As Dolan states: 'The fact that no one took such women seriously may have actually helped them with such political involvement as they did undertake'.[43]

Numerous scholars have identified that nuns exercised remarkable agency in periods of limited opportunities for women.[44] But, as this chapter has established, the invisibility of nursing nuns is further exacerbated by the way these groups frame their own actions: there is a tendency to consistently downplay this agency. In the archives of the Helpers of the Holy Souls, there are many examples of nuns eschewing credit for their work. All agency is attributed not to the individual, but to God. For example, in the visit reports for Paris an unnamed nun cares for a sick woman who is accompanied by her cousin. The cousin is hostile to the unnamed nun, who she mistakes for a doctor. The nun's reply is quoted: 'No, Madame, replied the sister, laughing, but as my greatest joy is to help those who suffer, I know masses of remedies, very simple ones, to which God often gives the virtue of providing relief'.[45] In this account all the agency of curing people is given to God – a theme common to these nursing reports. The nun describes her remedies as simple, downplaying her own skill and experience. The sister considers her care work a joy, not a job, is careful to emphasize the simplicity of what she does and attributes her success to God rather than her own skill. At the individual level, nuns such as this one can be seen to actively seek abnegation and self-effacement.[46]

This attitude to nursing work appears to be replicated in the way congregations archive their institutional history. By focusing entirely on a formulaic foundation story, congregations perpetuate the invisibility of their labour. Even the names of these institutions evoke notions of modesty, littleness and helpfulness, reflecting the values which congregations wished to prioritize.[47] Crucially, these women are not presented as workers. However, when congregations resist any promotion of their nursing work, seeking abnegation and downplaying their social influence, it is not only the nuns who tend to disappear from history.

The social authority which nuns had in the homes of the poor, in hospices and in hospitals has no doubt declined dramatically in France since the 1800s. However, this past authority continues to have a significant impact on the historiography of their work. Those same social hierarchies which nuns used and reinforced in their day-to-day practice can also be seen at work in the way these histories have been recorded. The position of these groups within wider social hierarchies allowed them to establish their authority as the owners of this history. Having members who were educated and literate, having the resources to make and keep records, meant that congregations were able to construct their own historical narrative. Many of the people they worked with – the sick, the elderly, school children, Indigenous peoples in the French empire – would not have had this option.

The archives of religious congregations cannot redress this gap, but they do exacerbate the problem. If the work of nuns with the poorest members of society remains poorly understood and carefully downplayed, what little we might know about the experience of their patients tends to disappear as well. Thus, the sources themselves reproduce the power hierarchies of the nineteenth century between carer and patient, and confer authority on the congregations as the owners and narrators of this history. While this chapter concerns itself in particular with the example of nursing congregations, similar hierarchies of power can be observed in the actions of nuns working in other contexts such as education or on colonial missions.[48] Narratives of the past, created by the institutional processes of archiving, do not simply reflect established power structures; they also produce and reproduce them in the present.

Historical authority and the ethics of negotiation

While scholars of religious congregations have addressed questions of archival restrictions, methodological difficulties, institutional idiosyncrasies and the use and misuse of power, very little has been said on the subject of ethics. In reality, research in congregational archives presents scholars with a number of ethical challenges. This is particularly true when dealing with nineteenth-century nursing congregations whose archives may contain sensitive material which could even be considered personal medical records. In some congregational sources the most intimate details of people's lives are put on display, largely for the purpose of edifying and inspiring other sisters and congregational affiliates. This is the case for patient records and chronicles kept by both the Helpers of the Holy Souls and the Little Sisters of the Poor.

As we have seen, scholars such as Monteiro et al. frame this as an issue of historical justice, arguing that scholars should be doing justice to the plurality of experience and moving away from singular institutional narratives. But what are the implications of challenging historical narratives around which congregations have built and continue to build their identities? Could attempts to retell these stories in new ways have a negative impact on the integrity of these communities? What authority (if any) do academics have over these records? Is it possible to achieve the historical justice which scholars such as Monteiro et al. have called for? Researchers must be mindful of their role as an outsider entering into a community space where stories of the institution's past are treated as family history, as scholars such as Curtis and O'Brien have argued.[49] Nineteenth-century congregations provided women with a rare opportunity to exercise agency, to work in public roles, to create and manage records and to control how these records were used. To challenge congregational privacy is also to challenge this agency.

At the same time, it is worth recognizing that these archives are records kept by institutions directly tied to the Catholic Church: an affiliation from which they draw significant authority. The family metaphor does not adequately cover the more problematic aspects of congregational histories, and to leave the singular institutional narrative unchallenged is to ignore the plurality of these histories.

There is a tension between researchers and congregations when it comes to authority over the historical narrative built from congregational archives. Steedman argues:

> The historian's massive authority as a writer derives from two factors: the way archives *are*, and the conventional rhetoric of history-writing, which always asserts (through the footnotes, through the casual reference to PT S2/1/1 ...) that you *know* because you have been there ... it comes from *having been there* (the train to the distant city, the call number, the bundle opened, the dust ...) so that then, and only then, can you present yourself as moved and dictated to by those sources, telling a story the way it has to be told.[50]

In the congregational archives, researchers rarely benefit from the experience of *having been there*. In many archival settings scholarly status opens doors, granting access to restricted papers. In congregational archives, this is not necessarily the case, with institutions carefully mediating access. In my own experience, only one of the three congregations I researched for my thesis gave me full and physical access to their archive. This was also the only archive which had been catalogued and which was run by a professional archivist. Thus, research in and on congregational archives often boils down to a negotiation between individuals: the researcher, the Mother Superior, the sister responsible for the archive. Here, the processes of building relationships, of building trust, of asking the right questions to the right person, are just as important as any institutional policy. Aspects of one's own identity play into the negotiation process: my gender probably worked in my favour in gaining access to an all-female community.[51] Fluency in multiple languages was an asset, whilst my status as an 'outsider' to the Catholic Church was no doubt an additional barrier.

Further ethical challenges arise for individual scholars. When research hinges on relationships with a small number of individuals, this has a direct impact on the narratives we may choose to construct around archival sources. While those conducting research into religious congregations have acknowledged the limitations of access, there is an inevitable risk in critiquing these issues too openly. Possibilities for future access hinge on the ongoing relationship with modern-day congregations, meaning that scholars may feel compelled to modify or mitigate their analysis in order to preserve ongoing relationships. More needs to be done to explore the ethical implications of this relationship between nuns, as gatekeepers, and academic researchers. The dialogue between academics and Catholic congregations has proven to be positive and enriching for all concerned. But it is neither ethically nor politically neutral.

Notes

1 The women discussed here took simple vows, engaged in active missions outside of the cloister and were run by a superior general and accountable directly to Rome (as distinguished from diocesan congregations overseen by clergy at a local level).
2 For more on the difficulties of replacing nuns see Ralph Gibson, 'Female Religious Orders in Nineteenth-Century France', in Frank Tallett and Nicolas Atkin (eds), *Catholicism in Britain and France since 1789* (London: Hambledon Press, 1996), p. 109; and Gérard Cholvy, *Le XIXe: Grand siècle des religieuses françaises* (Perpignan: Editions Artège, 2012), pp. 110–11. For discussion of how nuns responded to secularization see Matthieu Brejon de Lavergnée, 'Les religieuses qui soignent. Naissance de l'infirmière moderne, 1900–1930', *Émulations* 38 (2021): 15–33.
3 Claude Langlois, 'Les Effectifs des Congrégations Féminines au XIXe Siècle. De l'Enquête Statistique à L'Histoire quantitative', *Revue d'Histoire de l'Eglise de France* 60. 164 (1974): 56.
4 Nursing is here broadly defined and includes care work in domestic settings and in private hospices. These women religiously worked to fulfil the physical and emotional needs of those living with illness, infirmity and the effects of poverty. Often this work was conducted with a view to renewing religious practice among those cared for, or converting those who were not Catholic. For further discussion of the problem of invisibility around this work see Colin Jones, 'Sisters of Charity and the Ailing Poor', *Social History of Medicine* 2. 3 (1989): 339–48; Evelyne Diebolt, 'Prémices de la profession infirmière: de la complémentarité entre soignantes laïques et religieuses hospitalières XVIIe–XVIIIe siècle en France', *Recherches en Soins Infirmières* 113 (2013): 6–18; and Olivier Faure, *Aux marges de la médecine: Santé et souci de soi* (Aix-en-Provence: Presses Universitaires de Provence, 2015).
5 Michel-Rolph Trouillot, *Silencing the Past: Power and the Production of History* (Boston, MA: Beacon, 1995), p. 26.
6 Sylvia Federici describes the 'unproductivity' of diverse forms of care work in *Revolution at Point Zero: Housework, Reproduction, and Feminist Struggle* (Oakland: PM Press, 2012).
7 For more on the lack of value attribute to care work see Silvia Federici, *Revolution at Point Zero: Housework, Reproduction, and Feminish Struggle* (Oakland: PM Press, 2020); Pat Armstrong, Hugh Armstrong, and Krista Scott-Dixon, *Critical to Care: The Invisible Women in Health Services* (Toronto: University of Toronto Press, 2016); Pamela Herd and Madonna Harrington Meyer, 'Care Work: Invisible Civic Engagement', *Gender and Society* 16. 5 (2002): 665–88; Rachel McIlroy, 'Nurses Have Been Invisible and Undervalued for Far Too Long', https://www.theguardian.com/society/2020/jan/29/nurses-invisible-devalued-women-inequality-change accessed 1 September 2020; Jean-Christophe Mino and France Lert, 'Le Travail Invisible des équipes de soutien et conseil en soins palliatifs au domicile', *Sciences Sociales et Santé* 21. 1 (2003): 35–64; and Deborah Rutman, 'Child Care as Women's Work: Workers' Experiences of Powerfulness and Powerlessness', *Gender & Society* 10. 5 (1996): 629–649.

8 The salaries and working conditions of nurses and carers have been the subject of debate, protest and reform throughout the pandemic in countries including France, Britain and India. See for example France Bleu, https://www.francebleu.fr/infos/sante-sciences/salaire-des-infirmiers-l-enorme-retard-de-la-france-1589776159, accessed 20 July 2021.
9 Trouillot discusses the dual role of humans as actors and narrators of history in *Silencing the Past*, p. 2.
10 Carolyn Steedman, *Dust: The Archive and Cultural History* (New Jersey: Rutgers University Press, 2002), pp. 75–6.
11 Susan O'Brien, '*Terra Incognita*: The Nun in Nineteenth-Century England', *Past & Present* 121. 1 (1988): 118.
12 See for example Carmen Mangion, *Contested Identities: Catholic Women Religious in Nineteenth-Century England and Wales* (Manchester: Manchester University Press, 2008); Anne Jusseaume, 'Dévoiler les sœurs, retrouver le soin. L'Histoire des congrégations hospitalières au XIXe siècle, entre archives privées et publiques', *Source(s). Arts, Civilisation et Histoire de l'Europe* 10 (2017): 31–46; Annelies van Heijst, 'The Disputed Charity of Catholic Nuns: Dualistic Spiritual Heritage as a Source of Affliction', *Feminist Theology* 21. 2 (2012): 155–72; Marit Monteiro, Marjet Derks, and Annelies van Heijst, 'Changing Narratives: The Stories the Religious Have Lived by Since the 1960's', in R. Ganzevoort, M. de Haardt, and M. Scherer-Rath (eds), *Religious Stories We Live By: Narrative Approaches in Theology and Religious Studies* (Leiden: Brill, 2014) pp. 221–40; and O'Brien, '*Terra Incognita*: The Nun in Nineteenth-Century England'.
13 Sarah A Curtis, 'Writing the Lives of Saints: Archives and the Ownership of History', *French Historical Studies* 40. 2 (2017): 241–66.
14 For more on this see Mathilde Rossigneux-Méheust, *Vies d'Hospice: Vieillir et mourir en institution au XIXe Siècle* (Ceyzérieu: Champ Vallon, 2018) and Jemima Short, *An Invisible Workforce: Nursing Nuns in France (1830–1905)* (Forthcoming, Liverpool University Press).
15 Steedman, *Dust*, p. 127.
16 For further discussion of Charism and how it shapes community identity see Margaret Susan Thompson, '"Charism" or "'Deep Story'"? Toward a Clearer Understanding of the Growth of Women's Religious Life in Nineteenth-Century America', *Review for Religious* 58. 3 (1999): 230–50.
17 See https://petitessoeursdespauvres.org/ou-sommes-nous/, accessed 21 January 2019.
18 For further discussion of the impacts of Vatican II see Thompson, '"Charism" or "Deep Story"?', pp. 230–50; and Monteiro, Derks, and van Heijst, 'Changing Narratives', pp. 221–40.
19 Pope Paul VI, 'Ecclesiam Suam (English Translation)', *The Pope Speaks* 10 (1965): 253–92.
20 'Perfectae Caritatis: Decree on the Adaptation and Renewal of Religious Life', http://www.vatican.va/archive/hist_councils/ii_vatican_council/documents/vat-ii_decree_19651028_perfectae-caritatis_en.html, accessed 23 July 2021.
21 On experiences in congregational archives see Curtis, 'Writing the Lives of Saints'; and Monteiro, Derks, and van Heijst, 'Changing Narratives'; Jusseaume, 'Dévoiler les sœurs'. For scholarship on business and organizational archives see, for example, Alix Green and Erin Lee, 'From Transaction to Collaboration: Redefining the Academic-Archivist Relationship in Business Collections', *Archives and Records* 41. 1 (2020): 32–51; and Nancy Cushing and Kevin Markwell, 'Balancing Biography and Institutional

History: Eric Worrell's Australian Reptile Park', *Public History Review* 16 (2009): 78–91.
22 For more on this see Monteiro, Derks, and van Heijst, 'Changing Narratives', p. 235.
23 Joan Schwartz and Terry Cook, 'Archives, Records, and Power: The Making of Modern Memory', *Archival Science* 2 (2002): 3.
24 Monteiro, Derks, and van Heijst, 'Changing Narratives', p. 237.
25 A similar point is made in Claude Langlois, *Le Catholicisme au féminin. Les congrégations françaises à supérieure générale au XIXe siècle* (Paris: Le Cerf, 1984), p. 28.
26 Monteiro, Derks, and van Heijst, 'Changing Narratives', pp. 236–7.
27 A commission investigating sexual abuse in the French Catholic Church is currently underway with a report due in autumn 2021. Initial findings suggest up to 10,000 victims across France since the 1950s. See CIASE, https://www.ciase.fr/, accessed 31 July 2021. Catholic congregations of French origin have recently been implicated in abuse scandals in Canada, where hundreds of unmarked and mass graves have been discovered at residential schools which enforced assimilation of Indigenous children. See for example, BBC News, 'Canada: 751 Unmarked Graves Found at Residential School', https://www.bbc.co.uk/news/world-us-canada-57592243, accessed 31 July 2021.
28 Curtis, 'Writing the Lives of Saints', pp. 256–62.
29 Ibid., p. 248.
30 Ibid., p. 242.
31 Rossigneux-Méheust, *Vies d'Hospice*, pp. 215–17.
32 Livres de fondation Saint Servan, 1847, p. 15; 1857, p. 24, Archives des Petites Sœurs des Pauvres, Saint Pern, France. For a discussion of similar findings in the archives of the Little Sisters, see Rossigneux-Méheust, *Vies d'Hospice*, pp. 215–17.
33 'Mme de Mainville', N.D. 'Rapports des Visites de Malades, Paris'. Archives des Auxiliatrices des Ames du Purgatoire.
34 B. Poland et al., 'How Place Matters: Unpacking Technology and Power in Health and Social Care', *Health and Social Care in the Community* 13. 2 (2005): 173–4.
35 Mme Désirée Lepetit, 1860, 'Rapports des Visites de Malades, Paris'. Archives des Auxiliatrices des Ames du Purgatoire; 'Famille H+++'; 'Famille Pellejot', N.D., 'Rapports des Visites de Malades, Nantes'. Archives des Auxiliatrices des Ames du Purgatoire.
36 See for example the death of Sister Felicity, 'Livres de Fondation Saint Servan'. Archives des Petites Sœurs des Pauvres, Saint Pern, France, 1876, p. 43.
37 My translation from French. Anonymous, *Vie Abrégée du Bon Père P.-B. Noailles, fondateur de la Congrégation de la Sainte-Famille* (Imprimerie Saint-Paul: Bar-le-duc, 1920), pp. 360–1.
38 'Livres de Fondation Saint Servan'. Archives des Petites Sœurs des Pauvres, Saint Pern, France, 1854, p. 21.
39 Roger Price, *People and Politics in France, 1848–1870* (Cambridge: Cambridge University Press, 2004), p. 45.
40 Ibid., p. 319.
41 This point has been made by multiple authors. See for example Colin Jones, 'Medicine in France on the Eve of the French Revolution: Sisters of Charity and the Ailing Poor', *The Society for the Social History of Medicine* 3 (1989): 339–48; O'Brien, '*Terra Incognita*'; Sarah A. Curtis, 'The Double Invisibility of Missionary Sisters', *Journal of Women's History* 28. 4 (2016): 134–43; and Curtis, 'Writing the Lives of Saints'.
42 Federici, *Revolution at Point Zero*, p. 116.

43 Frances E. Dolan, 'Why Are Nuns Funny?', *Huntington Library Quarterly* 70. 4 (2007): 511.
44 Olwen Hufton, 'Whatever Happened to the History of the Nursing Nun?' (Hayes Robinson Lecture Series No. 3, Royal Holloway, University of London, 2000); Jones, 'Medicine in France'; Curtis, 'Writing the Lives of Saints'.
45 My translation from French. 'Mme Rosalie Larose, N.D., 'Rapports des Visites de Malades, Paris'. Archives des Auxiliatrices du Ames du Purgatoire.
46 O'Brien, '*Terra Incognita*', p. 118.
47 For an extended discussion of the names of nineteenth-century congregations see Langlois, *Le Catholicisme au féminin*, pp. 177–80.
48 See for example Sarah A Curtis, *Civilising Habits: Women Missionaries and the Revival of the French Empire* (Oxford: Oxford University Press, 2000); and Curtis, 'The Double Invisibility of Missionary Sisters'.
49 Curtis, 'Writing the Lives of Saints'; and O'Brien, '*Terra Incognita*'.
50 Steedman, *Dust*, p. 145. Emphasis original.
51 This question of how gender shapes access to female congregational archives was the topic of a recent keynote given by Matthieu Brejon de Lavergnée entitled 'The Gown and The Veil: How a Male Scholar Made His Way In a Woman's World (2010-20s)'. History of Women Religious of Britain and Ireland Annual Research Showcase 2021.

Bibliography

Armstrong, Pat, Hugh Armstrong, and Krista Scott-Dixon. *Critical to Care: The Invisible Women in Health Services*. Toronto: University of Toronto Press, 2016.

BBC News. 'Canada: 751 Unmarked Graves Found at Residential School'. https://www.bbc.co.uk/news/world-us-canada-57592243. Accessed 31 July 2021.

Brejon de Lavergnée, Matthieu. 'Les religieuses qui soignent. Naissance de l'infirmière moderne, 1900-1930'. *Émulations* 38 (2021): 15–33.

Cholvy, Gérard. *Le XIXe: Grand siècle des religieuses françaises*. Perpignan: Editions Artège, 2012.

CIASE. https://www.ciase.fr/. Accessed 31 July 2021.

Curtis, Sarah A. *Civilising Habits: Women Missionaries and the Revival of the French Empire*. Oxford: Oxford University Press, 2000.

Curtis, Sarah A. 'The Double Invisibility of Missionary Sisters', *Journal of Women's History* 28, no. 4 (2016): 134–43.

Curtis, Sarah A. 'Writing the Lives of Saints: Archives and the Ownership of History'. *French Historical Studies* 40, no. 2 (2017): 241–66.

Cushing, Nancy, and Kevin Markwell. 'Balancing Biography and Institutional History: Eric Worrell's Australian Reptile Park'. *Public History Review* 16 (2009): 78–91.

Diebolt, Evelyne. 'Prémices de la profession infirmière: de la complémentarité entre soignantes laïques et religieuses hospitalières XVIIe–XVIIIe siècle en France'. *Recherches en Soins Infirmières* 113 (2013): 6–18.

Dolan, Frances E. 'Why Are Nuns Funny?', *Huntington Library Quarterly* 70, no. 4 (2007): 509–35.

Faure, Olivier. *Aux marges de la médecine: Santé et souci de soi*. Aix-en-Provence: Presses Universitaires de Provence, 2015.

Federici, Sylvia. *Revolution at Point Zero: Housework, Reproduction, and Feminish Struggle*. Oakland: PM Press, 2020.

France Bleu. https://www.francebleu.fr/infos/sante-sciences/salaire-des-infirmiers-l-enorme-retard-de-la-france-1589776159. Accessed 20 July 2021.

Gibson, Ralph. 'Female Religious Orders in Nineteenth-Century France'. In *Catholicism in Britain and France since 1789*, edited by Frank Tallett and Nicolas Atkin, 115–34. Hambledon Press: London, 1996.

Green, Alix, and Erin Lee. 'From Transaction to Collaboration: Redefining the Academic-Archivist Relationship in Business Collections'. *Archives and Records* 41, no. 1 (2020): 32–51.

van Heijst, Annelies. 'The Disputed Charity of Catholic Nuns: Dualistic Spiritual Heritage as a Source of Affliction'. *Feminist Theology* 21, no. 2 (2012): 155–72.

Herd, Pamela, and Madonna Harrington Meyer. 'Care Work: Invisible Civic Engagement'. *Gender and Society* 16, no. 5 (2002): 665–88.

Hufton, Olwen. 'Whatever Happened to the History of the Nursing Nun?' Hayes Robinson Lecture Series No. 3, Royal Holloway, University of London, 2000.

Jones, Colin. 'Sisters of Charity and the Ailing Poor'. *Social History of Medicine* 2, no. 3 (1989): 339–48.

Jones, Colin. 'Medicine in France on the Eve of the French Revolution: Sisters of Charity and the Ailing Poor'. *The Society for the Social History of Medicine* 3 (1989): 339–48.

Jusseaume, Anne. 'Dévoiler les sœurs, retrouver le soin. L'Histoire des congrégations hospitalières au XIXe siècle, entre archives privées et publiques'. *Source(s). Arts, Civilisation et Histoire de l'Europe* 10 (2017): 31–46.

Langlois, Claude. *Le Catholicisme au féminin. Les congrégations françaises à supérieure générale au XIXe siècle*. Paris: Le Cerf, 1984.

Langlois, Claude. 'Les Effectifs des Congrégations Féminines au XIXe Siècle. De l'Enquête Statistique à L'Histoire quantitative'. *Revue d'Histoire de l'Eglise de France* 60, no. 164 (1974): 39–64.

Mangion, Carmen. *Contested Identities: Catholic Women Religious in Nineteenth-Century England and Wales*. Manchester: Manchester University Press, 2008.

McIlroy, Rachel. 'Nurses Have Been Invisible and Undervalued for Far Too Long'. https://www.theguardian.com/society/2020/jan/29/nurses-invisible-devalued-women-inequality-change. Accessed 1 September 2020.

Mino, Jean-Christophe, and France Lert. 'Le Travail Invisible des équipes de soutien et conseil en soins palliatifs au domicile'. *Sciences Sociales et Santé* 21, no. 1 (2003): 35–64.

Monteiro, Marit, Marjet Derks, and Annelies van Heijst. 'Changing Narratives: The Stories the Religious Have Lived by since the 1960's'. In *Religious Stories We Live By: Narrative Approaches in Theology and Religious Studies*, edited by R. Ganzevoort, M. de Haardt, and M. Scherer-Rath, 221–40. Leiden: Brill, 2014.

O'Brien, Susan. '*Terra Incognita*: The Nun in Nineteenth-Century England'. *Past & Present* 121, no. 1 (1988): 110–40.

Petites Sœurs des Pauvres. https://petitessoeursdespauvres.org/ou-sommes-nous/. Accessed 21 January 2019.

Poland, B. et. al. 'How Place Matters: Unpacking Technology and Power in Health and Social Care'. *Health and Social Care in the Community* 13, no. 2 (2005): 173–4.

Pope Paul VI. 'Ecclesiam Suam (English Translation)'. *The Pope Speaks* 10 (1965): 253–92.

Pope Paul VI. 'Perfectae Caritatis: Decree on the Adaptation and Renewal of Religious Life'. http://www.vatican.va/archive/hist_councils/ii_vatican_council/documents/vat-ii_decree_19651028_perfectae-caritatis_en.html. Accessed 23 July 2021.

Price, Roger. *People and Politics in France, 1848–1870*. Cambridge: Cambridge University Press, 2004.

Rossigneux-Méheust, Mathilde. *Vies d'Hospice: Vieillir et mourir en institution au XIXe Siècle*. Ceyzérieu: Champ Vallon, 2018.

Deborah Rutman, 'Child Care as Women's Work: Workers' Experiences of Powerfulness and Powerlessness', *Gender & Society* 10. 5 (1996): 629–649.

Schwartz, Joan, and Terry Cook. 'Archives, Records, and Power: The Making of Modern Memory', *Archival Science* 2 (2002): 1–19.

Short, Jemima. *An Invisible Workforce: Nursing Nuns in France (1830–1905)*. Forthcoming, Liverpool University Press.

Steedman, Carolyn. *Dust: The Archive and Cultural History*. New Jersey: Rutgers University Press, 2002.

Thompson, Margaret Susan. '"Charism" or 'Deep Story'? Toward a Clearer Understanding of the Growth of Women's Religious Life in Nineteenth-Century America'. *Review for Religious* 58, no. 3 (1999): 230–50.

Trouillot, Michel-Rolph. *Silencing the Past: Power and the Production of History*. Boston, MA: Beacon, 1995.

Vie Abrégée du Bon Père P.-B. Noailles, fondateur de la Congrégation de la Sainte-Famille. Imprimerie Saint-Paul: Bar-le-duc, 1920.

13

The instability and ideology of the archive
Archival evidence and nineteenth-century British theatre

Jim Davis

The archives and its discontents

The archive is an unstable phenomenon, and its meaning and value are open to multiple interpretations. On face value scholars often perceive it as a receptacle for documents and objects through which the past may be researched. Yet the archive's composition and the decisions that have been made about what should constitute it mean that scholars need to understand and interpret the intentions, policies and belief systems behind its formation and its subsequent acquisitions before drawing on the evidence that it offers.[1] There is now a considerable body of work drawing attention to the limitations, political implications and lack of neutrality of the archive.[2]

Yet, despite the ambivalence with which scholars rightly regard archives, most scholars working on the nineteenth century still have to use them. This is certainly the case for historians of nineteenth-century British theatre, whether exploring the commercial theatre of London's West End, the neighbourhood theatres to the south and east of London or provincial theatre. This chapter will consider some of the problems faced by theatre historians using archival resources for this period. Each of us has a personal history of archive use and our relationship with the archives may, in some cases, be akin to a love affair, a love-hate relationship or even a nightmare, factors explored in Carolyn Steedman's *Dust*. Often, any pleasure to be gained from the archive is offset by myriad frustrations. Inaccessibility, erasure, disappearance, exclusions and/or incompetence may well sour our engagement with the archive, although its pleasures (which may include accidental and even life-changing discoveries) can be equally seductive. Given the instability of the archive, we ourselves as researchers become both archivist and curator through the ways in which we assemble documents and objects in the research process and deal with ethical dilemmas and choices raised by our use of archives, the way we have been trained to use them and their proximity.

Archives and their usage have generated a considerable discursive literature. While Jacques Derrida (from a distinctly Freudian perspective) and Michel Foucault have alerted us to the impact of the archive on memory and forgetting, political control and public order, hierarchy and thought processes, the performance scholar Diana Taylor has defined the archive in relation to embodied memory, which she defines as 'repertoire', a physical transference from the past similar to Joseph Roach's concept of 'surrogation'.[3] For Taylor, the value, relevance and meaning of the archive inevitably change over time, while there are also

> several myths attending the archive. One is that it is unmediated, that objects located there might mean something outside the framing of the archival impetus itself. What makes an object archival is the process by which it is selected, classified, and presented for analysis. Another myth is that the archive resists change, corruptibility, and political manipulation. Individual things ... might mysteriously appear in or disappear from the archive.[4]

Taylor's points are both obvious and valid. However, her interest is in the somatic transmission of past performance, an approach not applicable to the recovery of many other aspects of theatre history, much of which still depends on the exertions of individual researchers in the archive. Carolyn Steedman, discussing the specificity of the individual's experience of the archive, refers to the disappointment of commentators on Derrida who:

> have been brought face to face with the *ordinariness*, the unremarkable nature of archives, and the everyday disappointments that historians know they will find there. There is a surprise in some of these reactions, at encountering something far less portentous, difficult, meaningful than Derrida's archive would seem to promise ...
>
> No one historian's archive is ever like another's (let alone Jacques Derrida's). Each account of his or her experience within them will always produce counter narratives, of different kinds of discomfort.[5]

The uniqueness of archival experience, the search for accidental discoveries, the painstaking progression from one document/object/artefact to another, may be open to generalization, but the experience also remains deeply personal.

However, while we can all draw upon personal anecdotes relating to our use of archives, there may be little value in a shared history of individual frustrations and discoveries. Our experience of the archive is normally a solitary one (as Derrida realized) and forms a significant part of our personal research histories. Steedman, drawing on Bachelard, talks of the loneliness of the Archive and its function as 'the counting house of dreams' and as

> a place to do with longing and appropriation. It is to do with wanting things that are put together, collected, collated, named in lists and indices; a place where a whole world, a social order, may be imagined by the recurrence of a name in a register, through a scrap of paper, or some other little piece of flotsam.[6]

The archive, according to Steedman, is also 'a place where people can be alone with the past; historians who work in the archives are taking part in minority activity which is part of the way of being in the world which is often called play'.[7] For Steedman this is not exactly the same as children's play, but reflects the capacity to be alone and concentrate, which can in itself also be a facet of child play. Consequently, absorption in the archive as a form of play also predicates a creative experience in which the imagination is allowed free rein. As Rebecca Schneider suggests, all kinds of things, immaterial or material, may drag the present into the past or the past into the present.[8] Yet our engagement with the past is not authentic: it is shaped by our imagination and by the connections we make between objects and documents. Authenticity, then, can only be attributed to our personal, imaginative, speculative relationship with the past. It is a playful and unique relationship, sometimes stimulated by accidental discoveries, at other times tightly controlled by the limits and boundaries that shaped the archive's origins and purpose.

In the following section my discussion of the archive will be based on specific examples relating to British theatre history, theatre regulation and audiences in the nineteenth century.

Theatre history and the archive

The case for archives devoted specifically to British theatre history was not an easy one to make. The most significant British collection is hosted by the Victoria and Albert Museum (V&A) and is now referred to as the Theatre and Performance Collections. Originally known as the Enthoven Collection, it was established between 1924 and 1925 by Gabrielle Enthoven (1868–1950), who had lobbied for such a collection to be established for many years. Enthoven, whose acquaintances had included Oscar Wilde and Edward Gordon Craig, was a playwright and a founder member and President of the Pioneer Players, a feminist theatre group. In 1911 she proposed:

> a comprehensive theatrical section in an existing museum to comprise specimens of all the different branches necessary to the workings of a play from the construction of the theatre, the designing of the scenery and costumes, to the smallest workings necessary in the house.
> Also a library and a collection of playbills, prints, pictures and relics etc. I want the section to be the place where the producer, actor, author and critic will naturally go for information, both on what is being done in this and other countries at present, and what has been done before.[9]

Initially, neither the British Museum nor the V&A showed much interest in her proposal, although the London Museum was more positive. After the First World War Enthoven continued her campaign and the V&A eventually agreed to accept Enthoven's own theatre collection, which was transferred to the Museum the following year. Enthoven managed the collection unpaid and financed the assistants who worked with her. The collection was London-focused and particularly strong in materials relating to the West End and commercial theatre. Over the years the collection has expanded rapidly, partly as the result of bequests, placing heavy demands on storage space and on cataloguing newly acquired material. Thus, in 2010, when the Theatre and Performance Collections mounted an exhibition celebrating the work of Diaghilev at the V&A, a central feature was *Picasso*'s backdrop for the 1924 Ballets Russes' production of *Le Train Bleu*, measuring 10.4 × 11.7 metres. In principle, it is perhaps laudable that such objects are being preserved, although questions of space, storage and funding often hang over these sorts of acquisitions, not to mention their perceived value as artefacts that need to be preserved.[10]

Another of the problems continually faced by the collection is the lack of financial resources to maintain an up-to-date catalogue of the collection's holdings. Overall, this collection reminds us that, firstly, areas such as theatre history need to be taken seriously enough for a public archive to be established and empowered. Secondly, its focus is very much likely to reflect the priorities of its instigators and curators. Thirdly, its value as an archive depends on its accessibility through up-to-date indexing and cataloguing, which often means digitizing both older records and information on new acquisitions. Thus, power is in the hands of those who determine an archive is worthwhile in the first place, those who decide what it should contain and those who determine the financial support available to maintain it. The Theatre and Performance Collections at the V&A are an Aladdin's cave of documents, objects and ephemera, but so long as so many of the contents remain uncatalogued, their value as an archive is clearly diminished. Moreover, archives are often heavily secured, and access may be limited.

Even when archives are established and regulated as depositories for government records, they do not always yield what one might expect to find. Omission, disappearance, exclusion, absence – all are contributory factors to the shortcomings of the archive. When I undertook some research on Ernest Boulton and Frederick Park, who used to attend theatres in London cross-dressed and who were eventually arrested while so attired at London's Surrey Theatre in 1870, I expected to find copious references, letters and police reports concerning these events in the Lord Chamberlain's Papers in the Public Record office in London. Censorship and the licensing and conduct of theatres were overseen by the Examiner of Plays, a functionary based in the Lord Chamberlain's Office in this period. It might seem reasonable to assume that the Examiner would have been disturbed by the fact that men dressed as women had attended the theatre (and the possible connotations of male prostitution this might have implied). However, the Examiner (W. B. Donne) was mainly concerned that Boulton and Park had been allowed behind the scenes and requested an explanation from the manager, a Mr Shelley. Shelley replied that he was not in the habit of admitting strangers behind the scenes, only 'a few privileged friends ... to take a view of the scenes'. Donne noted that Shelley had not really given a satisfactory explanation, adding 'Mr Shelley is not particular about his "private friends" if these hermaphrodites be among them'.[11] And there the matter rested. Unless a whole cache of material was surreptitiously removed from the files, this incident, one of several which eventually resulted in a trial at the Old Bailey generating massive press coverage, was not significant enough to warrant further reports or correspondence from the Lord Chamberlain's Office. Sometimes the archive can be silent when we least expect it.

The Public Record Office, which holds the Lord Chamberlain's papers, containing police reports on theatres as well as correspondence and memoranda on such matters as licensing, censorship and the annual inspection of theatres, is a major archive for anyone with an interest in nineteenth-century British theatre, although most of its holdings relate to London and its immediate vicinity. Organized chronologically, it is a vital resource for the exploration of how the power of the state functioned in regulating both the organization of theatres and what was performed inside them. This becomes manifest in the paternalistic attitude taken by the Lord Chamberlain's Office not only towards the representation of political and religious issues and figures on stage, but also towards the control of crowd behaviour and protecting the public from moral contamination – through references to prostitution, adultery or the display of too much flesh, for example – and inducements to criminality. Public order (or a fear of a potentially disorderly public) partly informs this concern, but public safety is also a contingent factor in the state's interventions. Propriety and respectability, both in terms of audience composition and behaviour and in the content of the drama, are also frequently referenced, with a strong emphasis on the class and social status of the spectators. The state's concern is to protect the public from itself, from what it might see performed and from potential accidents. In a letter to the Lord Chamberlain's Office from architect Edward Hall, concerning theatre planning and accidents, the author maintains that accidents are less frequent in Paris because the theatres there are better regulated and 'because the demeanour of the people themselves, being orderly, is less calculated than that of the British public, to create or exaggerate alarm and entail accident'.[12] This comparison between British and Parisian audiences is taken further the following year in an article in the *Saturday Review*, which refers to 'the natural English jealousy of too much control':

> In Paris, paternal government manages things differently, the control of the Prefect of Police extends generally to the minutest points ... of course the public are well ruled, they are neither to take umbrellas into the pit, nor wear their hats, nor demand any song not set down in the programme. Any attempt to regulate English theatres or audiences after this fashion would fail through public revolt.[13]

This is part of a clipping related to discussions around the respective regulating of theatre and music halls, but archived among the Lord Chamberlain's Papers, as is a clipping from *The Times* of 5 January 1865 suggesting that, despite the difficulty of making 'English people submit habitually to the system of the *queue*', some means needs to be found to avoid fatalities, accidents and injuries in the crushes sometimes occurring at the entrances to places of entertainment. Almost ten years later a memorandum implied that the Lord Chamberlain wanted 'public feeling' rather than 'official authority' to direct the course of public events.[14] Nevertheless, despite this seemingly hegemonic approach, 'official authority' was exercised as and when the Lord Chamberlain's Office considered it necessary.

By the mid-1860s W. B. Donne tended towards self-congratulation in statements regarding the improvements effected in theatres through state control and regulation. Reporting on the annual inspection of the theatres in 1866, he commented that theatre managers now generally acknowledged the benefits accrued from the Lord Chamberlain's supervision and that, on account of the annual inspection, not only had the security and safety of the public been enhanced, but the character of the performances had also been raised.[15] A year later Donne set down his ideas on the extent to which the material performed on stage could be freely permitted:

> The freedom of the stage cannot be under any conceivable circumstances co-extensive with the freedom of the press ... Yet it would be absurd ... entirely to exclude from the stage political and social topics. The only possible or rather reasonable restrictions are such as a very large majority of the play-going public would themselves demand if they did not exist ... viz. that nothing be said or sung on the stage that is likely to bring into contempt the crown, the estates of the Realm, spiritual or temporal, the Ministries of religion or law, to set one class of society against another, or to tamper with the grounds of public or family morals.[16]

Given the literate public's access to books and more especially to newspapers, Donne was willing to 'allow some freedom in the political and moral sentiments [uttered on stage], taking care however that there shall be no allusions to party-politics and no attempt to touch the foundations of social or individual morality'.[17] Thus the archive reveals how, under the guise of a benevolent paternalism, power over the content of theatrical offerings is still very much determined and controlled by the state.

The desire of the Lord Chamberlain's Office to protect public morality,[18] especially if threatened by the inadequate costuming of female performers, was a constant concern. In 1864, W. B. Donne attended Astley's Theatre at the request of the Lord Chamberlain to ascertain whether or not Ida Isaacs Menken's costume in the scene in *Mazeppa* where her character is stripped naked and tied to the back of a horse, was indecent. His subsequent report to the Lord Chamberlain details just how extensive his scrutiny of Menken's costume had been on behalf of public morality:

> Certainly, the attire of Miss Ida Isaacs Menken is of the scantiest, consisting of a tunic or shirt which would be improved by being drawn a little more over her breast and shoulders, and a pair of drawers which would be better if less close-fitting and a little longer. She has ... a minor covering of web, that although I cannot call her appearance decorous, neither can I term it positively indecent.
>
> On the other hand Miss Menken is so immensely masculine in her structure and appearance that it requires some effort to fancy her not a robust boy ... and so her <u>androgyne</u> aspect detracts considerably from her female attractions. I paid the closest attention to her several gestures and poses after she was divested of all but the tunic and drawers and sandals, but the impression on me was, not so much the indecorum, as the absurdity of the performance.[19]

In Donne's view there was often greater indecency in Opera Ballets and the Spanish Dancers. At Astley's, as on other occasions, he carefully observed the audience's reaction to Menken, having seated himself 'in a front place in the stalls that I might be a competent eyewitness'.[20] From the conversations he overheard, his fellow spectators were more impressed by Menken's fighting and riding skills than her costume. Additionally,

> Next to me (by chance) in the stalls sat an elderly gentleman and his daughter and next to the lady a very clerical looking person, none of them, I inferred from their abundant approbation, habitués of Theatres. But neither lay nor clerical expressed any disapprobation of Miss Menken.[21]

Donne suggested to the Lord Chamberlain that Astley's be sent a caution rather than a prohibition, recommending in the report that extra material might be added to the costume. In 1869, Donne visited the Gaiety Theatre where he found the Ballet 'not particularly objectionable, as times go', even if 'the young females do wriggle more than they need'. Since he was accompanied by 'a beneficed clergyman's wife (very orthodox) and she saw nothing to be shocked at', he concluded that there was nothing to worry about.[22] Once again, respectability and a clerical association form the basis of a judgement based on spectator reaction. In these instances, Donne's evidence appears to be self-fulfillingly circular, using audience reactions to decide on audience reactions.

Protecting the theatre-going public from indecency reached its apotheosis in responses to the can-can, which was eventually banned in October 1874. Early in 1868, when asked to respond to a complaint published in the *Pall Mall Gazette* about performances of the can-can at the Lyceum Theatre, E. T. Smith, the Lyceum manager, claimed:

> I have watched the dance and have had Clergymen, Professionals, Bankers, Merchants, Counsel, Solicitors, Managers and officers from the highest to the lowest rank who have seen the dance and are ready and willing to sign a paper, that the attack on it is disgraceful. We have had noblemen with their wives and families applaud it. The Duke of Cambridge has been twice ...[23]

In 1870, W. B. Donne expressed his disquiet at the Surrey Theatre's advertising performance of the can-can in large capitals in its playbills, adding that, as it had been 'very properly stopped at the King's Cross Theatre, it may be as well to make some enquiries about the Surrey proclamation'. Many of the neighbouring music halls were also advertising the can-can and 'though very unlike the real thing, I dare say, whatever they do under the name, may be sufficiently indecent to draw'.[24] Four years later, a letter to the Lord Chamberlain's Office complaining about 'indecent cancan' dancing at the St James's Theatre after a performance of the melodrama *East Lynne*, added that the author was obliged to take the ladies accompanying him out of the theatre during the dance and was told by the theatre's officials that 'any respectable females were supposed to leave when the cancan dance was performed'.[25]

We might expect public records to provide reasonably accurate records of theatre audiences, their behaviour and composition. However, when the Theatre Regulation Act came into being in 1843, bringing many new theatrical venues under the Lord Chamberlain's control, police reports solicited by the Lord Chamberlain's Office on newly licensed theatres were sometimes quite sensational or even exaggerated. In 1845, a police report on the City of London Theatre, situated in East London, stated:

> Four hundred and sixty-six persons had been admitted to the gallery, which was crammed almost to suffocation. At the moment of my arrival a female with an infant in her arms begged that I would allow her to pass as she feared something had happened to the infant from the intense heat – *Jack Sheppard* was the piece performing, and the uproar was tremendous.[26]

The gallery capacity was around 400,[27] so an estimate of 466 patrons suggests it was certainly overcrowded. Gallery audiences tended to be young, given the lower prices charged for access, although there was also a tendency to stereotype such audiences:

> The audience in this part of the house was composed of the youth of both sexes, whose ages varied from 11 to 18, and chiefly of the lowest classes of society, the majority of the males being without coats or jackets – I, and the officers who were with me, saw several males the associates of thieves. There were between 40 and 50 young prostitutes, some apparently not more than 14 or 15 years old, and the language going forward among them was bad in the extreme. Among those described above there were (on rough calculation) from 70 to 100 children of both sexes apparently of a superior class from their manner and dress. I saw more than 20 little girls decently dressed intermixed with the Prostitutes, some of whom from their gestures and manners towards the boys they were with, were apparently making use of rude observations, but it was almost impossible to get near them to ascertain.[28]

This report was coloured further by a description of the staircase to the gallery, which was 'one mass of filth, and the smell intolerable, and on several of the stairs the contents of the stomach had been cast'.[29] The assumption that many of the youthful audience were thieves and prostitutes was common in many police reports on working-class theatres in this period.

Police reports of this nature could have serious consequences for the theatres involved since they were instigated by the very institution – the Lord Chamberlain's Office – that had the power to revoke or refuse licenses. The reports were often contingent on complaints from local inhabitants, in this case a local tradesman, or individuals or groups with a moral aversion to the theatre. Sometimes rival managements engineered the grounds for such complaints. The fact that *Jack Sheppard* was the play being performed may also have provoked both the tone of the report and even the visit, since the staging of adaptations from the so-called Newgate novels, such as *Jack Sheppard* and *Oliver Twist*, was eventually banned on the presumption of their adverse moral impact on the behaviour of young people in general.[30] Another factor that may have led to complaints in the first place and accentuated the problem was the fact that the theatre was undercutting other theatres in the neighbourhood and admitting three for the price of one to the gallery and boxes. Subsequent police reports on gallery spectators, even when *Jack Sheppard* was playing, were generally more favourable. Yet the presence of thieves and prostitutes in the audience was regularly noted in police reports on East End theatres in this period: one report on the Britannia Saloon in 1844 stated that prostitutes and juvenile thieves comprised half of its entire audience, although this is unlikely and was certainly disputed by the Britannia's proprietor, Samuel Lane.[31]

There is no way of establishing the veracity or objectivity of such reports or the extent to which they are works of observation, imagination or a mixture of both: the authors may be perfectly reliable, highly prejudiced or merely reporting to the Lord Chamberlain's Office what they felt the Office wanted to hear. While references to neighbourhood theatres, especially in police reports from the mid-1840s, often highlighted the presence of juvenile thieves and prostitutes in the gallery, the tone could also be more positive. A police report of July 1847 responded to a letter sent to the Lord Chamberlain's Office complaining that the respectability of the drama and the well-being of society were under threat. This was on account of the presence of shoeless boys from six to twelve years of age smoking pipes and getting intoxicated, while accompanied by the most low-life girls, on Saturday and Monday evenings at the Effingham in Whitechapel and Britannia in Hoxton, both catering for a local working-class audience.[32] The ensuing report based on a visit to the Britannia Saloon indicated that, since the institution of monthly visits by the police, its conduct had much improved, there was no evidence of boys smoking pipes or getting intoxicated and that, while the gallery audience consisted of 'the lower classes of both sexes from the age of 12 years and upwards', audience members under twelve were generally accompanied by parents.[33] Since the Lord Chamberlain's Office had instigated more frequent visits to venues such as the Britannia, the police report may also be coloured by a desire to demonstrate that the police were doing their job effectively. Overall, what the reports and letters archived among the Lord Chamberlain's Papers expose is the operation of state power (and the police) in the regulation of theatres and the extent to which unmediated evidence in the archives has the power to impact on our own interpretations of the past. In its dealings with East End theatres, as represented through police reports, occasional correspondence and notes on annual inspections, this archive also provides access to an aspect of theatre history that remained under-explored for several generations.

In the nineteenth century the East End of London was predominantly a working-class area serviced by local neighbourhood theatres, information on which can sometimes be hard to come by. National newspapers such as *The Times* only began to review East End productions, such as the Britannia Theatre's annual pantomime, in 1868. The V&A Theatre and Performance Collections have a relatively small (but substantial) series of holdings on East End theatres, while the British Library and some local collections extend this archive slightly, especially through playbill collections. Material relevant to the history of East End theatres can sometimes be submerged through misleading cataloguing. It was only by accident that I discovered the diaries of F. C. Wilton, stage manager of the Britannia Theatre, Hoxton, in the Mitchell Library in Sydney, Australia. The Mitchell Library specializes in Australian history and had described the content of the diaries in its catalogue as merely containing 'some Australian interest', with no reference at all to its comprehensive overview of the day-to-day life of the Britannia Theatre over a period of twelve and a half years.[34] In 1876 Wilton had retired to Australia, where several of his children were already living, at the age of seventy-five. His diaries also cover his life in Australia from his arrival early in 1877 until his death in 1889. This was the material of interest to the Mitchell Library.

In 2009 access to material on East End theatres was enhanced by the launch of a digital project entitled the 'East London Theatre Archive' (ELTA) under the auspices of the University of East London. This brought together a range of archived material from East London theatre venues and companies as well as 10,000 items from the V&A Theatre and Performance Collections. According to Claire Hudson, the then-Director of the collection, this project opened up new research opportunities for scholars and the necessity of creating 'an authoritative and scholarly resource for use by the research community while at the same time presenting the content in an accessible style' for the more general user. A grant of £200,000 of the project funding enabled the Theatre and Performance Collections:

> To catalogue and digitize material that had been severely under-exploited in the past. Some of the C19th playbills we digitized had been inaccessible for years because of the fragility of the paper on which they were printed.[35]

This initiative was an extremely valuable online presence, but it was decommissioned in 2018 and, at the time of writing, it no longer has an online presence, although options are being pursued by the University of East London to restore its availability.[36] As a result, even today the history of nineteenth-century working-class theatre in the East End of London is still being marginalized. This raises several questions about online archives, most obviously the danger of such archives disappearing. Since this archive included materials too fragile to make available in their original state, the removal of the digitized sources also represents a loss of access to archived documents. There is also a broader question around the power invested in whoever controls the archive when it comes to making decisions about what should or should not be digitized in the first place. However well-intentioned the provision of online access to objects and images, many collections can only afford to provide partial access to their archives and, in whatever decisions are made about what is to be foregrounded and emphasized, fail to represent the full scope of what the archive can offer. Unless archives are fully digitized, online access may be a limited and disempowering experience for the user, one that has been accentuated by the limited access to such resources during the Covid pandemic.

These examples indicate that some of the problems associated with the use of archives are much more basic than the broader (and important) ethical issues raised by Derrida, Foucault, Diana Taylor and others. More generally it is very unlikely today that any researcher would engage with detailed research in an archive without considering the premises on which it was established and recognizing the distance between what an archive contains and what it means. An excellent example of this type of exploration, again relating to archives throwing light on the relationship of the state to theatre in the nineteenth century, is Jan Lazardig's essay 'Performing *Ruhe*: Police, Prevention and the Archive', in which he reveals that in the German-speaking world:

> [t]he continually surprising combinations of pedanticism, effort, and painstaking care with which the police's administrative observation of the theatre was carried out in the nineteenth century, under the imperatives of Ruhe, security and order, however, allows something else to become visible in the Ruhe of the archives: the inexhaustible fantasies of Unruhe, of insecurity and disorder that lie at the origin of the archive's order.[37]

Thomas Postlewait and Charlotte M. Canning provide a theoretical basis for recognizing the archive's complexity by suggesting that it is not merely something we use:

> It is a category of thought, a way of conceiving and reconceiving the identities and meanings of past events. It is a kind of mind game – a hermeneutics of historical consciousness – that puts in play the rules and procedures for historical research, analysis, argument and reporting.[38]

However regulated or accidental, these days the archive and its contents are equally targets for careful investigation and require responsible usage.

Back to the future: Performing the nineteenth-century archive

While my focus on archival resources in this chapter has been grounded in sources for British theatre history in the nineteenth century, some of the more contemporary issues raised by the archive have recently been explored in a 2018 publication entitled *Artists in the Archive: Creative and Curatorial Engagements with Documents of Art and Performance*. The focus of this work is on contemporary performance and performance art and its aim is to explore 'the agency and materiality of the archival document' and to examine 'the politics and philosophy behind re-using remains, historicizing the artistic practice and considering the breadth of ways in which archival materials inform, inflect and influence new works'.[39] *To archive*, this publication maintains, is

> to give place, order and future to the remainder; to consider *things*, including documents, as reiterations to be acted upon; as potential evidence for histories yet to be completed ... [T]he archive is never static nor simply pertains to the past. Archives are comprised in their continuing and future enactment and use; in layers of performance.[40]

The emphasis is very much on performance itself rather than the context of performance, and the book approaches 'archival acts as performative in their aesthetic social and political staging of the remainder and the document'.⁴¹ The editors of this collection then proceed to argue that:

> Whereas traditional scholarship invariably appraises archives in relation to historical and art-historical narratives, positioning its documents as *evidence* of past events, this book explores models for the future use of documents in practice-as-research, and the potentialities, effects and implications of such processes.⁴²

Three keywords here, in relation to the archive, are 'performative', 'agency' and 'potentialities'.

The notion that the archives can support subsequent performances in ways that go beyond mere reconstructions or quotation seems to fly in the face of Peggy Phelan's view that:

> Performance's only life is in the present. Performance cannot be saved, recorded, documented, or otherwise participate in the circulation of representations; once it does so, it becomes something other than performance ... Performance's being ... becomes itself through disappearance.⁴³

This claim also tallies with Diana Taylor's view that the archive cannot capture and store the live event.⁴⁴ However, Nick Kaye suggests that the re-enactment of past performances is an implicitly archival act and uses the word 'entanglement' rather than 'engagement' to describe 'an analogous and dynamic process, in which the interdependence and meanings of things and their associated narratives remain in transition; and in which objects are lent agency'.⁴⁵ While accepting the ephemerality of live performance, there is the potential for new creative work both to be based on and to be in dialogue with work that has been archived. The archive, for Kaye, his co-editors and his contributors, is something that relates to the past, present and the future. Admittedly, the immediate context for these deliberations is the place of the archive in relation to contemporary performance research and practice, but there are also implications for the theatre historian, not least in relation to the archive's own performance of power.

No archive is purely accidental although each archive is unique. And the expectations aroused by an archive, as well as the uses we make of it, can be variable. Agency, performativity and potentialities are among the keywords highlighted in *Artists in the Archive*, to which we might add Steedman's notion of 'play'. In conclusion, I want to ask whether we can learn anything or even extend the possibilities of our own archival work through an interrogation of the uses to which an archive might be put. I am not advocating a theatre history equivalency of performance reconstruction, since I do not believe that past performance can ever be reconstructed effectively as a live event. On the other hand, entanglement via an archive with the past and creative interactions with that past may be more than possible. As an example, I would cite theatre historian Janice Norwood's sharing of her research on nineteenth-century actresses with contemporary dancers in order to stimulate creative, somatic responses to the material she has unearthed for her recent monograph on the subject.⁴⁶ The notion that an archived object or document can stimulate creativity is not exactly new, but it demonstrates possibilities beyond more conventional scholarly outputs and more diverse forms of empowerment. Norwood writes:

> My first surprise came when I discovered that one of the practitioners who had expressed an interest in the project was a dancer, Julia Cheng of House of Absolute and Kolesk Dance. I had anticipated an end result that would be largely text-based, so contemplating how it might be interpreted into movement and sound offered a new but exciting challenge. Collaborating with Julia, who specialises in contemporary and street dance, could attract a younger and very different audience to my research.[47]

Norwood also charts the initial stages of her research:

> After spending several years painstakingly researching minor details, it is a salutary lesson to jettison much of it to focus on the key points. It quickly became obvious that both Julia and I found visual images of the actresses and theatrical ephemera (playbills, posters and adverts) could be useful as prompts to energise ideas.[48]

Written texts and images gathered from the archive were translated into gesture and movement, culminating in a public performance entitled *Ghost Papers*.

The overarching question, as to the multiple uses to which an archive can be put, still remains and offers plenty of scope for future debate. Perhaps we need to cease talking about 'the' archive and think of archives in the plural and of our own specific relationships with individual archives. And, finally, in an age in which the words 'historic' and 'historical' are applied *ad nauseam* to current events, perhaps we should take heed of Terry O'Connor's caveat that,

> Written into the idea of every archive, is the sense that what may be important to a future researcher, maker or thinker cannot be predicted, that the nugatory and the crucial are categories we cannot determine for future sensibilities.[49]

For theatre historians archives are just as significant as they are for any other historian, raising shared questions around ideological and interpretative issues. Inevitably, significant archives for the theatre historian include not only written documents, but also visual resources and material objects, not to mention those traces of past performance handed down and located somatically. They provide an interdisciplinary basis for the study of theatre history, while in their interplay with the performing and creative arts they offer exciting possibilities for new and innovative forms of intersection.

Notes

1   Theatre archives often depend on curatorial notions as to what constitutes appropriate content. This has sometimes meant that records of more popular forms of theatre and the ephemera related to them have not been deemed worth preserving.

2   For instance, see Jacques Derrida, *Archive Fever: A Freudian Impression* (Chicago and London: The University of Chicago Press, 1995); Michel Foucault, *The Archaeology of Knowledge* (London: Tavistock Publications Ltd., 1972); Carolyn Steedman, *Dust* (Manchester: Manchester University Press, 2001); and Diana Taylor, *The Archive and the Repertoire: Performing Cultural Memory in the Americas* (Durham and London: Duke University Press, 2003).
3   Joseph Roach, *Cities of the Dead: Circum-Atlantic Performance* (New York: Columbia University Press, 1996).
4   Taylor, *The Archive and the Repertoire*, p. 19. Taylor claims that 'repertoire' 'enacts embodied memory: performances, gestures, orality, movement, dance, singing – in short, all those acts thought of as ephemeral, nonreproducible knowledge', p. 20.
5   Steedman, *Dust*, p. 9.
6   Carolyn Steedman, 'The Space of Memory: In an Archive', *History of the Human Sciences*, II. 4 (1998), p. 76.
7   Ibid., p. 77.
8   Rebecca Schneider, *Theatre & History* (Basingstoke: Palgrave Macmillan, 2014), 44–5.
9   Letter to the *Observer*, 12 November 1911, Enthoven Scrapbook PN1620.L7, Theatre Collection, Victoria and Albert Museum quoted in Kate Dorney, 'Excavating Enthoven: Investigating a Life of Stuff', *Studies in Theatre and Performance* 34. 2 (2014), p. 117.
10 Scenery has not been traditionally preserved in theatre collections. Although the best nineteenth-century British scenery and act drops were greatly admired as works of art at the time, they were invariably painted over or destroyed.
11 Letters, 13, 14 & 16 May 1870, LC1/232, Lord Chamberlain's Papers, Public Record Office (Henceforth LCP, PRO).
12 Letter, 9 February 1864, LC1/141, LCP, PRO.
13 *Saturday Review* 19, no. 490 (18 March 1865): 312. LC1/142, 1865, LCP, PRO.
14 Memorandum, 29 December 1874, LC1/287, LCP, PRO.
15 Report on annual inspection, 1866, LC1/167.
16 Memorandum, 30 July 1867, LC1/186, LCP/PRO.
17 Ibid.
18 For a fuller discussion of the Lord Chamberlain's Office and its approach to morality in the theatre see John Russell Stephens, *The Censorship of English Drama 1824-1901* (Cambridge: Cambridge University Press, 1980), pp. 78–91.
19 Report to the Lord Chamberlain, LC1/128, 3 November 1864, LCP, PRO. Emphasis original.
20 Ibid.
21 Ibid.
22 Report, 10 July 1869, LC1/221, LCP, PRO.
23 Letter, 6 February 1868, LC1/200, LCP, PRO.
24 9 May 1870, LCI/232, LCP, PRO.
25 Letter 13 June 1874, LCI/285, LCP, PRO.
26 Police Report, 22 July 1845, LC7/6, LCP, PRO.
27 A. E. Wilson, *East End Entertainment* (London: Arthur Barker Ltd., 1954), p. 142.
28 Police Report, 22 July 1845, LC7/6, LCP, PRO.
29 Ibid.
30 In 1858, W. B. Donne, the Examiner of plays, wrote that this class of drama – 'in which highway robbery, burglary and larceny form the staple interest of the action' –

was now almost extinct. In Donne's opinion, 'such Dramas are extremely prejudicial to the younger portions of the Pit and Gallery audiences at the minor theatre'. Letter, 20 July 1858, LC1/58, LCP, PRO. See also Stephens, *The Censorship of English Drama*, 61–77.

31 Police Report, 22 July 1844, LC7/6, LCP, PRO.
32 Letter, 7 July 1847, LC7,7, LCP, PRO.
33 Police Report 12 July 1847, LC7/7, LCP, PRO.
34 See Jim Davis (ed.), *The Britannia Diaries 1863–1875: Selections from the Diaries of Frederick C. Wilton* (London: Society for Theatre Research, 1992).
35 Claire Hudson, 'The Digital Museum', in Lorna M. Hughes (ed.), *Evaluating and Measuring the Value, Use and Impact of Digital Collections* (London: Facet Publishing, 2012), p. 39.
36 No reason has been given publicly for why this resource was decommissioned.
37 Jan Lazardzig, 'Performing *Ruhe*: Police Prevention and the Archive', in Rosemarie K. Bank and Michal Kobialka (eds), *Theatre/Performance Historiography: Time Space, Matter* (New York: Palgrave Macmillan, 2015), p. 140. 'Ruhe' is not easily translatable into English, but broadly implies peace, security and public order.
38 Charlotte M. Canning and Thomas Postlewait, 'Representing the Past: An Introduction on Five Themes', in Charlotte M. Canning and Thomas Postewait (eds), *Representing the Past: Essays in Performance Historiography* (Iowa City: University of Iowa Press, 2010), p. 21.
39 Paul Clarke, Simon Jones, Nick Kaye and Johanna Linsley, 'Introduction', in Paul Clarke, Simon Jones, Nick Kaye and Johanna Linsley (eds), *Artists in the Archive: Creative and Curatorial Engagements with Documents of Art and Performance* (Abingdon: Routledge, 2018), p. 5.
40 Clarke, Jones, and Linsley Kaye, 'Introduction', *Artists in the Archive*, p. 11. Emphasis original.
41 Ibid.
42 Ibid., p. 13. Emphasis original.
43 Peggy Phelan, *Unmarked: The Politics of Performance* (London and New York: Routledge, 1993), p. 146.
44 Taylor, *The Archive and the Repertoire*, p. xvi.
45 Nick Kaye, 'Liveness and the Entanglement with Things', in Paul Clarke, Simon Jones, Nick Kaye and Johanna Linsley (eds), *Artists in the Archive: Creative and Curatorial Engagements with Documents of Art and Performance* (Abingdon: Routledge, 2018), p. 49.
46 Janice Norwood, *Victorian Actresses: Crossing Boundaries and Negotiating the Cultural Landscape* (Manchester: Manchester University Press, 2020).
47 University of Hertfordshire Heritage Hub, www.herts.ac.uk/heritage-hub/heritage-and-history-projects/creative-arts-and-literature/sparks-might-fly-theatre-commission/dr-janice-norwood, accessed 19 January 2021.
48 Ibid.
49 Terry O'Connor, 'Nothing Goes to Waste', in Paul Clarke, Simon Jones, Nick Kaye and Johanna Linsley (eds), *Artists in the Archive: Creative and Curatorial Engagements with Documents of Art and Performance* (Abingdon: Routledge, 2018), p. 283. See also Taylor, *The Archive and the Repertoire*, p. 19. Taylor argues that 'What changes over time is the value, relevance or meaning of the archive, how the items it contains get interpreted, even embodied'.

Bibliography

Canning, Charlotte M. and Thomas Postlewait. 'Representing the Past: An Introduction on Five Themes'. In *Representing the Past: Essays in Performance Historiography*, edited by Charlotte M. Canning and Thomas Postewait, 1–33. Iowa City: University of Iowa Press, 2010.
Clarke, Paul, Simon Jones, Nick Kaye and Johanna Linsley (eds). *Artists in the Archive: Creative and Curatorial Engagements with Documents of Art and Performance*. Abingdon: Routledge, 2018.
Davis, Jim. *The Britannia Diaries 1863–1875: Selections from the Diaries of Frederick C. Wilton*. London: Society for Theatre Research, 1992.
Dorney, Kate. 'Excavating Enthoven: Investigating a Life of Stuff'. *Studies in Theatre and Performance* 34, no. 2 (2014): 115–25.
Hudson, Claire. 'The Digital Museum'. In *Evaluating and Measuring the Value, Use and Impact of Digital Collections*, edited by Lorna M. Hughes, 35–48. London: Facet Publishing, 2012.
Kaye, Nick. 'Liveness and the Entanglement with Things'. In *Artists in the Archive: Creative and Curatorial Engagements with Documents of Art and Performance*, edited by Paul Clark, Simon Jones, Nick Kaye and Johanna Linsley, 25–51. Abingdon: Routledge, 2018.
Lazardzig, Jan. 'Performing *Ruhe*: Police Prevention and the Archive'. In *Theatre/Performance Historiography: Time Space, Matter*, edited by Rosemarie K. Bank and Michal Kobialka, 55–73. New York: Palgrave Macmillan, 2015.
Norwood, Janice. *Victorian Actresses: Crossing Boundaries and Negotiating the Cultural Landscape*. Manchester: Manchester University Press, 2020.
O'Connor, Terry. 'Nothing Goes to Waste'. In *Artists in the Archive: Creative and Curatorial Engagements with Documents of Art and Performance*, edited by Paul Clark, Simon Jones, Nick Kaye and Johanna Linsley, 278–83. Abingdon: Routledge, 2018.
Phelan, Peggy. *Unmarked: The Politics of Performance*. London and New York: Routledge, 1993.
Roach, Joseph. *Cities of the Dead: Circum-Atlantic Performance*. New York: Columbia University Press, 1996.
Schneider, Rebecca. *Theatre & History*. Basingstoke: Palgrave Macmillan, 2014.
Steedman, Carolyn. 'The Space of Memory: In an Archive'. *History of the Human Sciences* 11, no. 4 (1988): 65–83.
Steedman, Carolyn. *Dust*. Manchester: Manchester University Press, 2001.
Stephens, John Russell. *The Censorship of English Drama 1824–1901*. Cambridge: Cambridge University Press, 1980.
Taylor, Diana. *The Archive and the Repertoire: Performing Cultural Memory in the Americas*. Durham and London: Duke University Press, 2003.
Wilson, A. E. *East End Entertainment*. London: Arthur Barker Ltd., 1954.
University of Hertfordshire Heritage Hub. www.herts.ac.uk/heritage-hub/heritage-and-history-projects/creative-arts-and-literature/sparks-might-fly-theatre-commission/dr-janice-norwood. Accessed 19 January 2021.

14

'Our mind strives to restore the mutilated forms': Nineteenth-century virtual museum tours in children's periodicals

Rachel Bryant Davies

In 2018 Cambridge University Library held an exhibition, 'Tall Tales: The Secrets of the Tower', curated by Liam Sims to showcase recently catalogued copyright accession holdings.[1] Almost a million items deemed 'non-scholarly' had been relegated to the Tower. This 'performance' of archival hierarchies reinforced pre-existing perceptions of children's literature and periodicals as not only unimportant, but even worth hiding, in order to maintain the prestige of the visible research collection. These informally censored holdings, however, are now recognized as vital for a wide range of academic research, including classical reception and nineteenth-century popular culture, areas central to my own work. I was asked to advise on the selection of fourteen items for 'Tall Tales': a display-case of 'Everyday Antiquity', to convey the range of Classics in popular nineteenth-century publishing. Among my selection was an illustrated spread in *The Girl's Own Paper* from 1885 (Figure 14.4), a virtual tour of the Elgin room at the British Museum explaining the displays of fragmented marble sculptures. 'Greek and Roman Art at the British Museum', contributed by painter and feminist activist Eliza Bridell-Fox, commented on the 'archival' aspects of understanding antiquity, confiding how 'our mind strives to restore the mutilated forms ... broken and damaged ... many without heads, or hands, or feet'.[2] Bridell-Fox's combination of academic details and poetic fancy aimed to fill in these gaps, 'fragmented by time and exposure'.[3]

This chapter is a story of how Victorian British children were taught to view museum displays of ancient artefacts. The archive of how people have accessed the past illumines how material display can construct narratives from artefacts, issues which resonate today. As the essays in our volume's first section have shown, researchers are increasingly examining the ethics of museum display, provenance and repatriation in light of wider societal movements, while institutions rethink how to use overwhelmingly extensive holdings, balancing preservation of material objects with increasing demands for digitization, and making collections accessible for researchers and wider publics.[4]

My analysis of ephemeral publications, such as the once-silenced cheaper print and children's culture catalogued through the Cambridge University Library Tower

Project, is crucial to my monograph examining children's encounters with Greco-Roman Antiquity through home-schooling and leisure activities.[5] Encountering this archival material also encouraged me to think about non-academic nineteenth-century holdings as silenced, rediscovered archives – and to approach instances of historical encounters in children's culture as carefully curated, frequently conflicting archives of the past. At the same time, using the Gale Cengage database *Nineteenth-Century Periodicals UK* has led me to examine how children's periodicals offer a remarkable perspective on nineteenth-century forms of archiving through virtual tours, both of ancient sites and contemporary museums.

Here, I examine nineteenth-century 'virtual tours' of Parthenon sculptures at the British Museum, then known as the 'Elgin room', as a record of the complex ways in which the past was archived for the future.[6] Written using a range of nineteenth-century archives and collections, this essay explores nineteenth-century perceptions of how children could (and should) interact with the British Museum's holdings. Focusing on how children encountered these sculptures in affordable but self-consciously respectable Victorian magazines, I consider how the nineteenth-century British Museum collection was itself framed through children's literature as a form of archiving antiquity, and how these forms of preservation were mediated through curated displays of a wider collection, which included what is now the Natural History Museum and the British Library. These collections were further mediated through explanations and virtual tours, which fulfilled a dual purpose for readers: to perform ideal modes of visiting, and to initiate future visitors.

The middle-class periodicals discussed here include titles such as *The Girl's Own Paper* (1880–1956; one penny weekly in 1885), *Kind Words for Boys and Girls* (1866–80; one-half penny per month in 1867) and its successor *Young England* (1880–92; one penny weekly). Victorian children's literature, which often clearly draws didactic links between content and overarching agendas, shaped perceptions of the museum displays. The children's periodical literature analysed here addressed, in varying ways, wider debates about how the purpose and intended audiences of nineteenth-century museums could be negotiated through a deliberate archiving of the past.

Nineteenth-century British Museum displays and official guidebooks, by contrast, were not oriented for child visitors:[7] many consisted of essays citing multilingual scholarship and simply catalogued sculptures, including lists of 'marble fragments'.[8] Furthermore, practical access, for non-leisured visitors, was challenging: working people could not visit on the selected weekdays. Approaching engagement with museum displays through a case study of how children's culture mediated the many sculptural fragments displayed in the Elgin room illumines Victorian perceptions of the purpose and function of 'archiving' in, and about, nineteenth-century museums. The archive of children's encounters with antiquities, through virtual site and museum tours, offers an invaluable insight into how ancient artefacts were seen to be preserved and communicated by museums, interpreted and explained by successive authors and illustrators, and experienced by visitors and readers.[9]

Nineteenth-century children's magazines, many of which have been digitized relatively recently, provide an insight into contemporary normative opinions. Perhaps the closest historical equivalent to feedback from community focus groups, these adult-contributed 'virtual tours', however, provide didactic rather than interactive or child-authored content.[10] Lessons in how to become ideal museum spectators (through interpreting sculpture fragments and appreciating their cultural significance) are bound up with justifying the social function of museums and magazines. Articles explaining the Parthenon marbles to nineteenth-century child consumers illustrate perceptions of museums and their antiquities collections: magazines often promoted Romantic philhellenic narratives about the British 'rescue' of the ancient marbles.

As Aishwarya Subramanian has noted, children's literature is only now beginning to engage with museum debates.[11] In contrast, discussions about viewing and preserving the marbles in some of the nineteenth-century children's literature analysed here are, at times, astonishingly frank – even if, for restitution arguments, one must look to magazines targeting adult readers, or children's books written by radical, religious dissenters. At the same time, these articles suppress much of the vocal ethical debate contended in literary and adult-oriented titles, about the marbles' removal and potential repatriation.[12] The narration of the past for nineteenth-century children appears designed to encourage adults of the future to uphold Victorian archival curations. Descriptions of the Elgin room and Parthenon marbles in children's periodicals therefore embody intersections between archival theorizing around silences, excess, and agency,[13] and the value of modern archives for digitizing historical 'ephemera'. Such meta-archival layering encapsulates how sculptural fragments facilitated acculturation into ideal spectating and the gatekeeping of museum displays, and how ancient artefacts were mediated through ephemeral print, now experienced as fragmentary evidence.

Bridell-Fox's articles in *Girl's Own* promoted imaginative restoration as ideal viewing. The accumulation of articles, across several magazine titles, which described the Parthenon and its marbles, inducted child consumers into the art of museum visiting – and introduced Classics (and Romantic Hellenism) as cultural currency which intertwined contemporary politics and art. Bridell-Fox encourages readers to 'take our stand in this room and gaze round us at these grand fragments ... the finest work of the best masters at the time of the highest development of Greek art'.[14] The ability to perceive this cultural significance is what such articles aim to inculcate: readers would avoid being caricatured by other visitors as 'incompetent spectators',[15] or, the 'uninitiated', as described by *Young England*, to whom 'broken parts and fragments ... the most precious legacies of antiquity' were 'scarcely intelligible'.[16] Both Bridell-Fox in *Girl's Own* and Clarke in *Young England* link ideal spectating with wider acculturation. Bridell-Fox's imaginative restoration can itself be framed as a form of curation: virtual museum and site tours create and negotiate an archive of explanations of collections or ruins. Descriptions of the Elgin room displays emphasize the museum's role in archiving antiquity: virtual tours play out conflict between the completeness of a collection *versus* the fragmentation of its constituent parts, and the reunification of fragments through display and reconstructions.

The fragmentation of the marbles, the 'gather[ing] together' and 'set[ing] up' of which was outlined in Victorian British Museum guides,[17] also offers useful metaphors for child viewership, education and (now) digitization. The archive of children's magazines is now simultaneously experienced as whole, collected in bound annuals and title runs, and fragmentary: keyword searches of entire publications encourage skimming individual articles, sometimes without dates or issue numbers. This seems a churlish criticism, a fetishization of paper copies – and it is true that bound annuals can miss out individual issues (as I found when purchasing *Girl's Own* for illustrative purposes!), but it does underline how tantalizingly elusive such ephemeral archives continue to be, even once digitized.

Children's periodicals: Patchwork fragments

The nature of magazines enabled children to encounter ancient sites and museum objects unintentionally, and in passing. The Parthenon and its sculptures frequently appear in fiction,[18] as well as the accounts of visiting the British Museum and Crystal Palace, and descriptions of travelling to the Acropolis examined here. Often these topics were not indicated by titles, but are now identifiable through keyword searches: this research process resembles the reconstruction of a 'lost whole', an alluring illusion that probably 'never existed in reality', as few readers might subscribe to multiple titles over several years.[19] For example, an article on horse-riding in *Our Young Folk's Weekly Budget* used 'the Elgin marbles ... so well known to every visitor to the British Museum' as proof of the 'safety of riding without stirrups'.[20] In contrast, virtual tours dramatize the incompleteness of a museum visit: for example, a Sunday-school outing ended, realistically, by postponing the Elgin room (until the next instalment) in favour of refreshments.[21]

The experience of chance encounter (both for nineteenth-century readers and present-day researchers) and the fragmented nature of information synthesized within an educational framework is exemplified in one periodical by an unlikely sounding article: 'The Chalk Family'.[22] Ostensibly about geology, an image of 'The Parthenon at Athens' prefaces this section of 'Uncle James' Sketch-Book'. The artistic merit 'of the richly sculptured figures' establishes their significance as 'the admiration of every artist and traveller', 'the wonder ... of the world', while Romantic descriptions of their 'ruinous condition', illustrated by giant fragments looming over visitors, justifies why 'the "*Elgin marbles*", are in our British Museum'.[23]

The Parthenon's 'whitest marble ... deposited for thousands of years', here illustrates Christian doctrine: 'God ... never does anything in vain ... these chalk families have been ... transformed into the most glorious temples and figures'.[24] This moral is applied to the spiritual instruction of individual readers: '*you* will be pillars in *another* temple'.[25] Such an interrelationship between religious and classical knowledge exemplifies how these piecemeal, 'fragmented' articles, as mediations of the marble fragments and museum displays, construct 'whole' specific narratives.

The co-option of Greco-Roman antiquity and scientific details about 'fossil remains' for religious education was not uncommon.[26] Many Victorian children's magazines were published by groups such as the Religious Tract Society (*Girl's Own Paper*). Evangelizing editorial priorities often justified learning about the Greco-Roman context of early Christianity. Museums were therefore closely linked to religious pedagogy. Charlotte Yonge extolled the benefits to her target readers, 'Younger Members of the

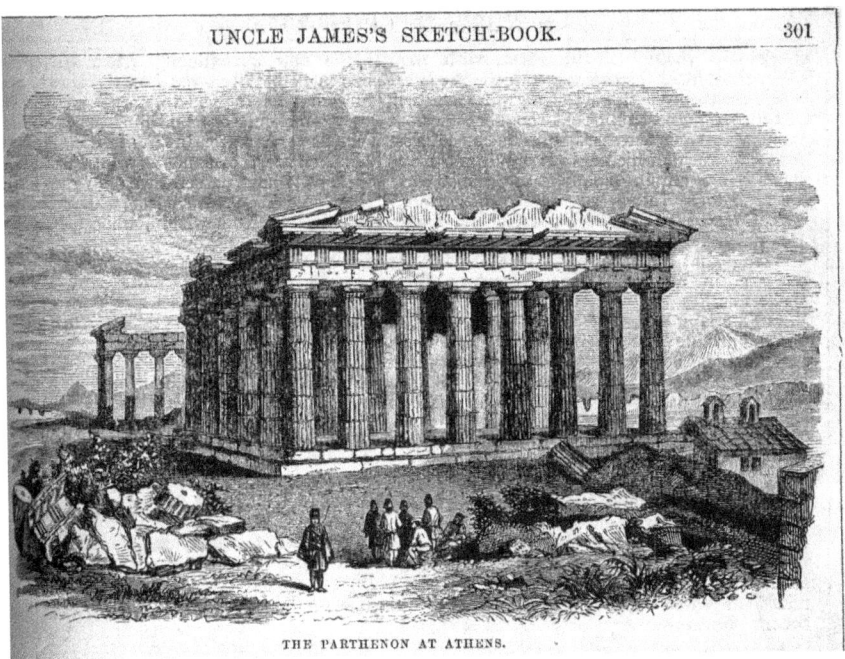

Figure 14.1 'Uncle James's Sketch-Book. The Chalk Family', *Kind Words: A Weekly Magazine for Boys and Girls* (19 September 1867): 301–4, p. 302. Scan from author's collection.

English Church', of studying 'Grecian history … and the Elgin marbles'.[27] *The Children's Friend*, aimed at Sunday-school readers, serialized visits to the British Museum: the Elgin room is framed as an immersive guide to 'where Paul stood when he preached to the Areopagus … (Acts xvii. 24)'.[28]

Victorian children's periodicals, where information is more often provided than assumed, therefore highlight recurrent – even if submerged – trends in how the marbles were presented to nineteenth-century audiences. Children's periodicals also highlight how frequently readers encountered fragmentary information. Articles which pieced together the Elgin room displays assembled discrete strands of moral, cultural and political education to be extracted from the marbles, modelling the ability to compose discrete parcels of knowledge into a coherent whole.

'Broken old stone dolls':[29] Viewing fragments

Assembling fragmented information into a coherent whole was an overriding educational concern, a deliberate cultural negotiation of the museum archive. Virtual tours of the Elgin room modelled interpretation of the physical fragments. Their ostensible aim was the creation of ideal viewers, whose aesthetic and cultural appreciation could 'restore' marble fragments. In 1857, *The Friendly Companion* celebrated the British Museum's holdings as public property, of which visitors, imagined as a singular group, should feel proud:

> Of the tens of thousands of persons who visit the British Museum in the year, there are none who may not consistently feel proud ... that the invaluable collection there deposited is the property of one and all of us; that it is *ours*.[30]

This rhetoric elides pride, property, and purchase: the museum is presented as founded for the public 'benefit', and 'given' into public possession.[31]

Peter Parley's Annual likewise hailed the public benefit of museums, claiming astonishment 'on Easter Monday at the numbers of persons thronging into the British Museum'. The author describes 'pushing my way in with hundreds of well-dressed Artisans'.[32] This account emphasizes benefits to the 'working people of London ... instead of sitting in public houses'. Patronizing benevolence segues into pedagogical didacticism designed to 'impress[ing] on my young readers ... the advantage it would be to them, to visit it frequently'.[33] *Peter Parley's* illustrations also convey the holiday crowds, including child visitors, in the entrance hall and at glass cabinets. Children are even more evident in the illustrations to 'Half-holiday rambles' in *Young England*, published, like Bridell-Fox's first *Girl's Own* article, in November 1885.[34] Drawn by Henry Edward Tidmarsh, the collage captioned 'Inside the Museum' shows views of stairway, galleries and individual objects in clockwise order:[35] 'No. 2 represents some of the most important of the Elgin marbles from the Parthenon'.[36]

Despite its title, 'Half-holiday Rambles' celebrates the museum's potential for 'instruction ... in an interesting form'.[37] Clarke presents the museum as 'a mine of information, whose treasures need not be searched for ... but are brought to the surface for us'. Yet the illustration, which privileges whole displays over fine details, itself mines 'prominent' galleries, including 'the Elgin and Phigaleian marbles'.[38] This collage, 'an inkling of what may be seen in the museum', illustrates the challenge of interpreting fragments within wider collections. Clarke's text emphasizes the role of illustrations such as Tidmarsh's in widening accessibility: the marbles' 'marvellous beauty ... has been long familiar to all the world from numerous illustrated descriptions'.[39]

Another collage, in *The Children's Friend*, depicts the Elgin, Phigalian, Lycian and Mausoleum galleries, with three Greek busts: Athene and Asclepius, in the Elgin room, and Pericles, under whose leadership the Parthenon was built, in the Phigaleian room.[40] These views are surprisingly empty: rather than modelling tours, *The Children's Friend* pictured pristine exhibitions; perhaps suggesting clear illustrations surpass a crowded visit. The layout reinforces this suggestion: a sterile, symmetrical and geometric arrangement, rather than Tidmarsh's informal, organically overlapped abundance of artefacts and visitors. In performing the very treasure-hunt that Clarke claims the museum's displays render unnecessary (an over-optimistic claim given the proliferation of guide-books and virtual tours), these two collages further curate the display for virtual visitors: Tidmarsh's in *Young England* conveying visitor engagement, and *The Children's Friend* focused on displayed artefacts.

In 1881, a description in *Kind Words* of visiting Athens diverted into lambasting 'benighted' visitors to the Crystal Palace at Sydenham, where the Greek Court included

'Our Mind Strives to Restore the Mutilated Forms' 261

Figure 14.2 Collage by Henry Edward Tidmarsh, 'Inside the Museum', in Courtenay Clarke, 'Half-Holiday Rambles in London', *Kind Words* (1 November 1885): 487–9, p. 488. Scan from author's collection.

a model Parthenon: 'Hundreds of season-ticket holders … remained grossly ignorant of the unrivalled collection'.[41] This indignant author, purporting to be 'ashamed', shares the same aim as *Peter Parley's*: not to describe displays in detail, but to educate readers into ideal viewers who 'will be able to visit that portion of the museum intelligently, and may study the descriptive catalogue with very different interest from that of the multitude'.[42] The dismissively caricatured visitors 'stroll and stare in blind wonderment at what appears to them merely a ruinous collection of broken old stone dolls'.[43] This disconcerting image, likening the sculptures to inappropriately heavy playthings, seems calculated to communicate the enormity of these 'ignorant' misinterpretations, which reduce the sculptures to children's toys.

The author, a Fellow of the Chemical Society and Royal Astronomical Society, had funded a two-year walking tour of Europe by working as an artisan *en route*, following an apprenticeship.[44] His apparently snobbish judgement, in this biographical context, appears intended to encourage children to emulate his self-motivated education and social advancement into learned societies. Such descriptions underscore several tensions inherent in inducting children to idealized viewing through virtual tours: periodicals reached more children than the more expensive formal guidebooks, and further afield beyond those who could (afford to) travel to London; yet they both enable social mobility and police its limitations, distinguishing their readers from the 'multitude' of uninformed visitors, who are otherwise praised for undertaking museum tours 'calculated to improve them'.[45]

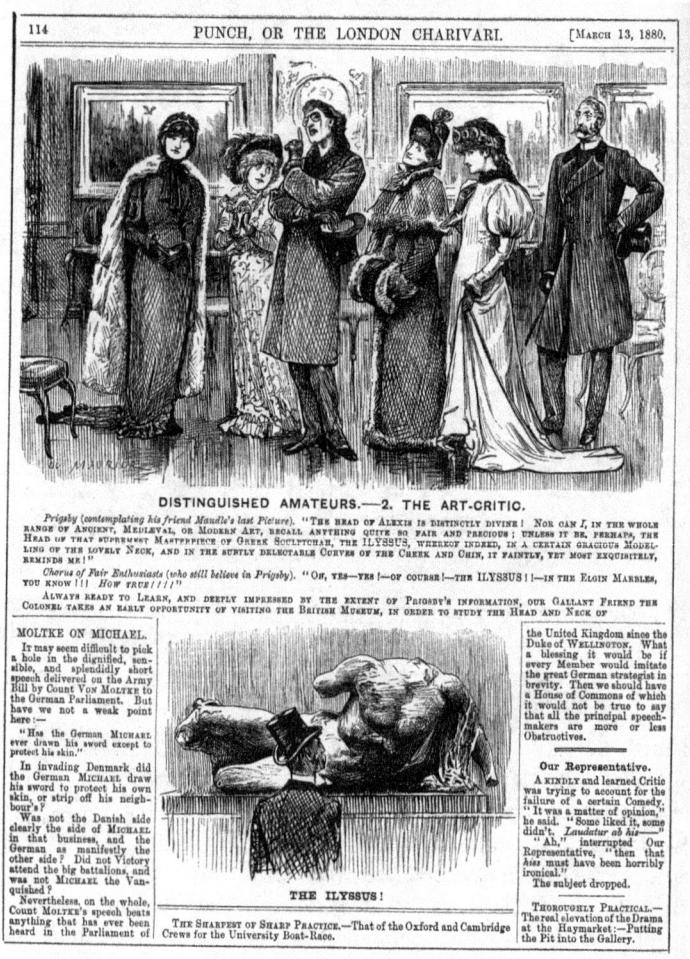

Figure 14.3 Cartoon by George du Maurier: 'Distinguished Amateurs 2 – The Art Critic', *Punch* (1880): 114. Scan from author's collection.

Similar tensions were played out in the adult, satirical milieu, such as in a series of drawings by George du Maurier satirizing the Aesthetic Movement.[46] One, published as a cartoon in *Punch*, mocks pretentious viewers of highbrow modern art.[47] A pompous art critic, 'Prigsby' (a satire on Oscar Wilde), presents himself as ideal viewer but, mis-remembering the Elgin room display, promotes a mistaken imaginative reconstruction. His hapless interlocutor finds that the 'head and neck' to which he had been directed 'in the Elgin Marbles, you know', was of a notoriously headless figure.[48] This erroneous completion of a famous fragment satirizes the snobbery often involved in policing others' claims of classical authority and spectating the institutionalized classical archive of the museum. The cartoon enacts the consequences of not learning to view antiquities correctly, both reinforcing the benefits of education for social mobility and satirizing the very judgement of visitor competencies it perpetuates.[49] In an added twist, du Maurier's original drawing did not contain the Ilyssus sculpture:[50] it seems additional explanation made the joke accessible for publication in *Punch*.

Viewing the Elgin room in the manner each author considered 'correct' is shown, in these articles, as both a key to cultural literacy, and a test-case of the social gatekeeping evident in virtual museum tours. The archive of displays, as mediated through children's magazines, is important evidence not only of how a 'classical archive' in the museum was perceived, but also of how such displays and guides constructed wider narratives from the ancient objects.

Relics: The significance of assembling fragments

As Clarke's description of 'relics ... the most precious legacies of antiquity' suggests,[51] learning to view the sculptures was bound up with wider acculturation, via religious education, artistic training and romantic philhellenism, of the children who would become the next generation of archival curators. The fifth-century BCE milieu of the Parthenon's creation was crucial: for example, one article illustrated Phidias sculpting the marbles, but emphasized the role of Pericles, the Athenian leader who adorned *The Children's Friend*'s collage.[52]

Such articles archive contemporary art education. When *Routledge's Every Girls Annual* explained 'Sculpture Modelling', it claimed the Parthenon Sculptures supplanted 'the beautiful works in Rome' and cited Goethe's advice that 'all students of sculpture' visit 'London to study ... the Elgin marbles'.[53] The illustration of three young women shifts the focus to present-day hobbies inspired by antiquities. Likewise, exemplary biographies of the artist Sir Edwin Landseer illustrate the marbles' educational potential across a wider publication range than features virtual museum tours. *The Child's Companion* reported that, aged thirteen, Landseer 'made a study of the Elgin marbles'.[54] *Every Boy's Magazine* also reported that Landseer studied 'with the painter Haydon ... first to recognise the beauties' of the sculptures.[55]

Williams and Clarke in *Young England* both endorsed the potential of this 'most perfect specimen of Greek architecture ... the final climax of Greek art, and ... the highest excellence that human handiwork has ever reached' to inspire Victorian artists.[56] While Williams noted the Parthenon's perpendicular columns, Clarke praised the marbles as 'delightful sources of instruction and interest': Clarke asked, 'who would not like to attend classes and lectures in these various galleries?', and credited 'the museum' with 'every facility ... for such classes'.[57]

The artist Bridell-Fox's twin articles for *Girl's Own* provide the most meticulous description of the Parthenon and its sculptures.[58] Her articles exemplify a Victorian Romantic idealization of the marbles' ability to revivify Athenian democracy: 'the vast relief ... must carry us to Athens, and, with them to lead us, we must travel back through the long ages to the world's golden youth in Greece'.[59] This virtual time machine bears witness to 'that great war when the Greeks, with Athens at their head, beat back the invading army of Persians, and preserved civilisation for Europe ... when the brave little nation had stemmed the tide of Asiatics under Xerxes'.[60] Written from a philhellenic perspective, the xenophobic language here, indicative of everyday racism, seems intended to glorify Athenian democracy. Rees's biography of Phidias also praises this 'period most favourable for the development and encouragement of genius, when Greece was triumphant over external enemies'.[61]

Bridell-Fox is not alone in endowing museum displays with weighty transtemporal emotion: where she labels the 'interesting prize vases ... in the British Museum – links with the dead past', Clarke describes the sculptures as 'The means of restoring ... history ... buried and kept safe from the all-devouring effects of time, to be brought to light for the information of the later ages'.[62] The sculptures are not only an ancient archive for nineteenth-century artistic education, but their display creates a nineteenth-century archive for future inspiration. Regardless of any reservations about the marbles' removal from Athens, possibly indicated by her Byronic quotations, Bridell-Fox approves that 'they are now placed where they can be seen of all sightseers, and studied by all lovers of art'.[63] This, of course, understands 'all' as those within reach of the London museums: geographically, financially and practically able to visit during opening hours.

Fragmented opinions and archival agency

Bridell-Fox remains silent about Elgin, perhaps separating artistic study from the ethics of collection and display; others, such as Williams, present forceful arguments. These authors are active participants in debates about museum accessibility and acquisitions: while mediating the artefacts, institutions and debates for child readers, they also shape the formation of Victorian archives about classical history. Archival theory is a helpful way to negotiate these complexities: Ann Laura Stoler describes colonial document production as a 'force field' and archives as 'unquiet movements'.[64] Children's magazines, which – on the surface at least – appear to support the status quo of institutions such as museums, tend to elide disputes about ethics, acquisition and ownership of museum objects: relatively neutral verbs such as 'brought', 'bought' and 'carried' describe the marbles' movements.[65] The ethical debate is apparently not perceived as germane to children's education.

This gap is, itself, a statement that the ethics of provenance was not deemed relevant to appreciate the marbles' artistic, cultural or political significance. Such 'archival silences' are apparent in minimal descriptions, quotations or slippery choices of verbs.[66] The archival fragments discussed here can be constructed into a bigger picture, with the caveat that it is impossible to tell whether the author intended such interpretation, or whether it reflects their, or the magazine's editorial, opinion.

Three articles explicitly mention the sculptures' removal and acquisition in the context of the Elgin room's display.[67] The only apparently boastful instance is 'the museum obtained possession of … the Elgin marbles', in *The Friendly Companion*'s survey of British Museum acquisitions.[68] Williams' support of Elgin challenges the apparent neutrality of 'collected'.[69] Clarke, also in *Young England*, explains how the sculptures were 'collected by the Earl of Elgin during his embassy at Constantinople'.[70] Shifting the blame for 'allowing' Elgin's removal onto Greek officials (although Athens was under Turkish control), Clarke presents a patronizing lesson: 'neither the Greek and Roman governments will now allow any of the [remaining] monuments … to be sold or taken away to other lands'.[71]

Accounts of the Parthenon's prior ruin that explain fragmentation of the sculptures often justify the museum's preservative role. Bridell-Fox 'pause[s] a moment' in her virtual tour 'to account for the shattered condition' of the 'fragments'.[72] Her museum visit merges into a virtual tour of 'the Parthenon … the centre of attraction for visitors to Greece': the description of 'a shattered wreck' again suggests she was torn between disapproving of Elgin's removal and appreciating easier access.[73] Bridell-Fox mentions the Parthenon's transformation into a Christian church, to explain why some sculptures were damaged. However, she does not discuss any subsequent damage, so often used (retrospectively) to justify the removal of the marbles to London. Even shorter articles present Elgin in the context of previous 'incredible damage'; as *Little Folks* explained: 'To save some of the figures from further injury, Lord Elgin brought many of them to England in 1816'.[74]

Williams's travel narrative is the article most explicitly in favour of Elgin. Yet it is the only acknowledgement I have found in children's magazines that 'Lord Elgin and our government have been accused of barbaric Vandalism'.[75] Williams changed his opinion while travelling, as he discovered the extent of the ancient artistic archive lost to posterity, in his view, 'For want of an early Elgin'. Emphasizing his eyewitness account of 'the wreck of battles and barbaric builders', with the 'ruins … shown in the illustration' (repeated from the *Kind Words* article on chalk fourteen years earlier), Williams details more modern damage to explain his change of opinion about Elgin, acknowledging that 'Much has been said and written' about the controversy.[76]

Admitting that 'Before visiting the Acropolis I was inclined to join in this chorus of reprobation', Williams establishes himself as an authority with whom most readers could not disagree: 'what I saw there and have since learned convince me that this purchase and this conveyance to London was the best thing that could have been done'. His primary reason is hardship in Turkish-occupied Athens: 'nobody living there … was capable of … preserving these precious relics', but 'destroyed what remains standing' to build pigsties'. Although Williams notes that metallic decorations were 'stolen … long before the Turks appeared', his descriptions seem conditioned by national caricatures: the artistic and 'market value' of the sculptures, he claims, 'mattered little or nothing … until the payment of 35,000 in hard cash by mercantile people like the English'.[77]

Most articles, and museum guidebooks, catalogue damage occasioned by the Parthenon's successive transformations into church, mosque and munitions store for Turkish gunpowder which, as Erskine explains, 'exploded' and 'completely destroyed the centre' of the temple.[78] Moreover, 'unskilful Venetians' were blamed for 'carry[ing] off' sculptures, in contrast to Elgin's crew which, Erskine implied, were more skilful in avoiding breakages.[79] As Bridell-Fox notes, 'Athens was again bombarded and the Parthenon still further destroyed', after Elgin's removals, 'in the Greek struggle for independence and freedom in 1827'.[80] Williams also adds: 'the whole Acropolis was shelled so severely that when I was there sixteen years afterwards, fragments of solid human bones were lying about amid the heaps of splintered marble'.[81] These gruesome fragments underpin his moral: 'But for Lord Elgin we should have had little else than tradition to tell us of the … masterpieces that anybody now may study in the British Museum'.[82]

When a child assumes the marbles predate Egyptian sculptures because 'they look so battered', his Sunday-school leader blames 'inclement weather' in Greece.[83] Bridell-Fox details how bas-reliefs 'under the colonnade' were 'protected'[84] but other sculptures were 'damaged … by time and exposure'.[85] The British Museum's display was often presented as preservation: this justified Elgin's removal and sidestepped the issue of repatriation.

Reconstruction

The imaginative restoration, advocated by Bridell-Fox as ideal spectating, comprised three elements which recur in descriptions of the displayed marbles: the completeness of the collection of fragments (and casts), their display in 'authentic' arrangements and the aid of models. The perceived success of these reconstructive, reunifying elements effectively recentred the classical archive to nineteenth-century Britain, endowing the British Museum's Elgin Room with archival authority.

Representing and filling the gaps between fragments also fulfilled what Sophie Thomas terms 'fantasies of retrieval'.[86] Where 'Only a few figures remain', Clarke's 'view' demonstrates that 'nearly all the subordinate figures are here preserved'.[87] Erskine also drew attention to how 'The British Museum now contains very nearly all that is left', while Williams provided figures: '249 feet of the originals are preserved, to which is added 76 feet more of plaster copies'.[88] As Clarke explained, 'the entire series has been completed by casts'.[89] This enabled fragments to be 'placed in their original order'; that 'in which they occurred on the Parthenon itself', which was widely praised as a measure of authenticity.[90] In addition, *Peter Parley* appreciated how 'fragments removed from other public buildings in Athens complete the whole' in the Elgin room.[91] However, Bridell-Fox explains the challenges of viewing the frieze in a 'reconstructed' indoor display. Recent scholars note that the inversion from its external architectural placement conveys 'a semblance of the original order' but is 'undercut by the unreal juxtapositions forced on the objects'.[92]

The casts are unlikely to have been obvious to many visitors, or those viewing images of displays which appear 'whole'. Museum guidebooks detail casts and their provenance, but buried within an inaccessible mass of scholarly, rather than explanatory, information. Guides for the full Elgin room alone cost eight pence, equivalent to eight issues of *Girl's Own*.[93] Bridell-Fox encouraged imaginative reconstruction from 'all that now remain to the world' in which these 'grand broken fragments' were correctly interpreted as 'majestic figures'[94] rather than, as Williams supposed uninitiated spectators to imagine, 'broken old stone dolls'.[95] Museum display could, as Bridell-Fox suggests, transcend fragmentation.

The striking variety of images in these sources underscores that Victorian museum spectating was experienced both as loss and gain. Bridell-Fox's illustrations emphasize reconstruction. Her first illustration, captioned simply as 'The Parthenon', is a widely circulated image by E. Thiersch, 'The Temple of Athené Parthenos, Restored', while the bas-reliefs depicted opposite show few signs of damage (Figure 14.4). Her second article ends with 'A conjectural arrangement' of 'The Interior of the Parthenon'. Bridell-Fox's articles are unique in depicting neither museum displays nor Greek ruins. Rather, British Museum displays launch her virtual tour of the Parthenon as imagined in antiquity. It is this sort of imaginative reconstruction – of both architectural setting and historical context – which Bridell-Fox idealizes: the best way to view a museum display is to see beyond the display itself.

Models facilitating this process were considered the most compelling aspect of the Elgin room display for child readers/visitors. Montague's Sunday-school leader was able to show his party, 'by means of the model of the Parthenon at the northern end of the room, the places which the sculptures occupied in the building'.[96] He also 'showed them, by means of a German model at that end of the room, where Paul stood when he preached'.[97] Model reconstructions also enabled the sort of time travel with which Bridell-Fox had credited the sculptures.[98]

An 1851 museum guidebook located two models in the Phigaleian room: 'Model of the Parthenon at Athens, after the Venetian Bombardment, AD 1687. Restored Model of the Parthenon, by R. C. Lucas'.[99] The single listing, including another gallery, might explain why some authors, whose titles do not specify the Elgin room, appear to disagree: Williams described 'two models representing the original building in perfect condition',[100] whereas Bridell-Fox praised 'a colourful model of the Parthenon in its present condition', which enabled viewers to 'identify the fragments on the pediments, and … the position of the various sculptures'.[101] As Bridell-Fox explained, 'The sculptured figures on [the model] are copied from drawings made from the Parthenon itself in Athens in 1674 … when many of the figures were far less damaged'.[102] This earlier artistic archive enabled the model to appear more authentic than the marbles themselves: *Peter Parley's* 'Walks around London' misleadingly pointed out 'a fine model of the Parthenon, well situated among its remains'.[103]

The models are not depicted in these articles, perhaps so as not to upstage a trip to the museum: they are tools to aid ideal viewing in person, whereas a reconstructed view, such as Bridell-Fox chose, made a more compelling magazine illustration. Just as empty views of galleries might trump a crowded visitor experience, so artistic reconstructions and copies apparently held more appeal than the remaining originals: imaginative restorations and pre-destruction records could be as educationally superior to the actual preserved marble as virtual tours to a real-life museum visit. Virtual tours,

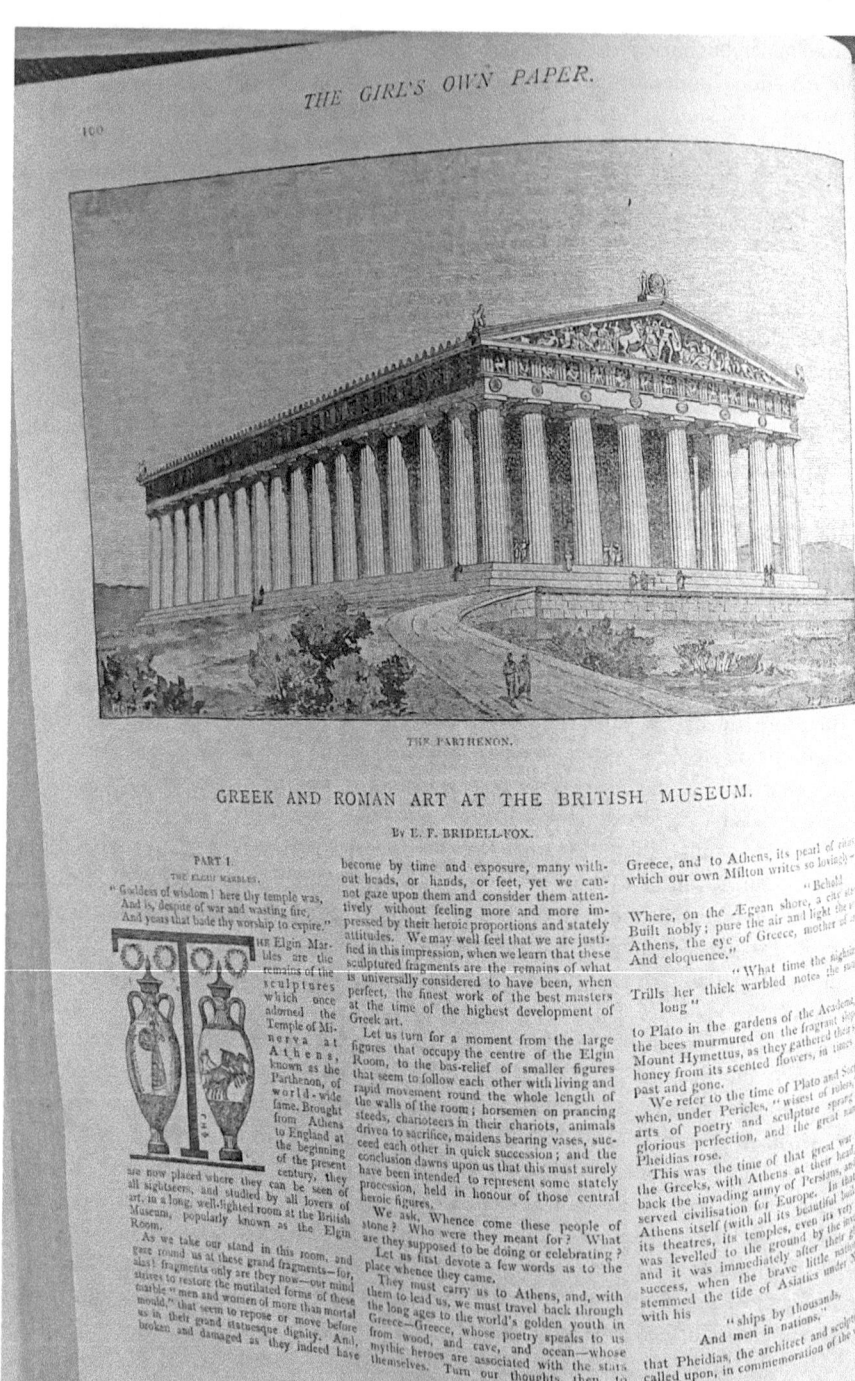

Figure 14.4 Double-page spread of illustrated article by E. F. Bridell-Fox, 'Greek and Roman Art at the British Museum', *The Girls' Own Paper* (13 November 1886): 100–3, pp. 100–2. Scan from author's collection.

to build a temple to the patron goddess of Athens, and to adorn it with sculpture which should be worthy alike of the occasion and the divinity.

THE TEMPLE.—In the centre of the city of Athens rises the bold rocky eminence known as the Acropolis, in earliest prehistoric days the citadel and stronghold of her kings, but long since given up exclusively to her temples. From this commanding height might be seen the city stretched below, the fertile plain beyond, enclosed by the two winding streams, the Ilissus and the Cyphissus, which spread verdure and abundance as they flowed on into the blue Ægean sea. The view was bounded on the south by the dark waters of that sea, while the distant mountains skirted the plain on the north, and varied the beauty of the scene.

On this rocky height, and on the highest part thereof, was erected the new temple, built entirely of white marble. It was called the Parthenon, and was dedicated to Pallas-Athéné, the patron goddess of Athens. The same divinity was worshipped by the Romans under the name of Minerva. For, just as Ephesus is known to have worshipped especially the great goddess Diana, so Athens devoted herself to the worship of Pallas-Athéné, the goddess of wisdom, the virgin daughter of Jove. She was one of twelve chief gods who were worshipped throughout Greece, but was held as more peculiarly the protecting deity of ancient Athens. A temple to this goddess had stood on the self-same spot before the war, which the Persians had destroyed. The former one was called the Hecatompedon, referring to its size.* The new one, the Parthenon, was the house (or chamber) of the virgin.† It was to be used for festivities and ceremonies in honour of the goddess, rather than for worship. It was of the same size as its predecessor, and was for that reason occasionally, but very rarely, called by the older name. The building of this temple was commenced 445 B.C., soon after the happy termination of the Persian war, while peace and prosperity ruled in the land. It took ten years to complete, and was accordingly finished in 435 before the Christian era. The times were therefore pagan times; but a great wave of civilisation passed over the favoured land of Greece, to which all modern art and literature owes so much; and the worship of Athéné, the goddess of wisdom and activity, takes its place amongst the purest and most elevating of the heathen religions.

It is, then, with Athéné and her worship that we have now to do.

ATHÉNÉ.—We must pause to devote a few words to the description of the qualities and attributes of this goddess who inspired these works of art, once so perfect. Athéné (or Pallas-Athéné, as she is frequently called) was the fair daughter of Zeus or Jupiter.‡ In her,

* Hecaton—Greek for hundred; pedon, feet.
† Parthenos—Greek for virgin.
‡ The Greek Zeus is the Jupiter of the Roman mythology.

"power and wisdom were harmoniously blended; she appears as the preserver of the State, and of everything which gives to the State strength and prosperity. She was the protectress of agriculture." With the Greeks, those most superstitious people, every fresh invention that led the way for the arts of civilisation was at once attributed to the inspiration of a god, thus "Athéné was said to have invented the plough and the rake, and to have created the olive tree"—that tree of so much importance in all Eastern countries, where the fruit is often an article of daily food, and the oil extracted from the olives is also serviceable for domestic purposes. As Apollo is associated with the sun, so Athéné is associated with the dawn, which wakes men from their slumbers when there is work to be done. She is therefore the goddess of industry and work, which daylight brings to all mortals. Athéné was thus the goddess of industry in every form. Besides agriculture, she was the patroness of arts and artificers, of embroidery and spinning, and all kinds of women's needlework. Also of intelligent and scientific warfare, as opposed to Ares (or Mars), the other Greek god of war, who was the god of "blind brute force," while she is called the "preventer of war," "the defender of towns." She protected the State from outward enemies, and, as the patron divinity, she maintained the authority of law and order in the courts of the assembly of the people. It was she who was believed to have instituted the Court of the Areopagus, the Court of Justice, at Athens. She was, moreover,

which appreciated models as tools of visitor accessibility and engagement, reveal how institutional power and discourse was played out in the nineteenth century through these modes of archival authority. Models which could display antiquity 'in perfect condition' also imply that the nineteenth-century museum archive creates, curates and maintains the past for future generations. This was not only a way to make sense of the fragments, for wider aims such as religious education, but also justified their removal to, and continued location in, the British Museum.

Archival silence and the nature of evidence

The issue of acquisition, so central to any discussion for adult readers, is markedly absent from children's magazines. Opinions are most often implied or omitted. It is also impossible to be certain of an author's opinion. Controversy was often avoided in favour of teaching artistic and historical details in the available column-space; this silence also suggests emerging undercurrents of contemporary conflict of opinion.

Bridell-Fox nowhere provides details about how 'Lord Elgin had removed' the sculptures and 'brought [them] from Athens to England'.[104] Her silence is surprising since she campaigned for the Married Woman's Property Bill and female admission to the Royal Academy of Art,[105] while her friend Elizabeth Barrett Browning labelled Elgin's removal a 'profanation'.[106] Both Bridell-Fox's articles begin by quoting Byron.[107] *Childe Harold's Pilgrimage* (1812–18) romanticizes how travellers could find inspiration in antiquity: Bridell-Fox imagines the Parthenon sculptures enabling museum visitors to travel imaginatively through space and time.

Childe Harold condemns Elgin's removal of the marbles: quoting Byron in this context usually indicates disapproval of Elgin: Bridell-Fox may be embedding this as code.[108] An article in the *Ladies' Treasury* explained:

> The poet's eyes wandered to the Parthenon, ... stripped of its masterpieces ... and asks, "who was the last, the worst stole spoiler? To rive what Goth and Turk and Time had spared." It was by the influence of Lord Elgin that these friezes and entablatures were brought to England.[109]

This juxtaposed quotation and explanation exemplify how British constructions of the classical archive are fraught with contradiction: contact with the past is romanticized, but acquisitions which enable that very contact were as controversial then as now.

The only example of 'Restitution' I have found for nineteenth-century children is the conclusion of Maria Hack's *Grecian Stories* (1819; revised 1840).[110] Hack is equally concerned with educating children as idealized spectators. However, in her context of 'guarded' religious education, shaped by the Society of Friends (Quakers), her agenda is radical social change. Hack also does not criticize Elgin. Rather, she details changes since her first edition: by 1840, Athens was no longer a war zone.

Within her dialogue between fictional mother and children, Hack's opinion is clear: the running header of 'Restitution' becomes 'Lucy settles it'.[111] Mother suggests visiting the British Museum to 'see with your own eyes some of the ornaments of the Parthenon, while they remain': international travel is unaffordable for this middle-class family.¹¹² When Lucy asks: 'why do you speak as if those beautiful things were not going to remain in the Museum?' Mother argues: 'it would be much for the honour of the British nation to restore them'. King Otho, she explained, was restoring ruins, such as the temple of Victory on the Acropolis, her final illustration. Its sculptures were 'replaced, except four, which are in the British Museum'. In answer to her direct question, 'should they be sent to Athens?', Lucy 'instantly exclaimed "Oh they should go back"'; her brother Harry's comparison to 'how disagreeable it would be ... to give up one of the best specimens in my little cabinet' makes the question relatable for child readers.¹¹³

Lucy, ultimately, has the last word: 'you would do it, Harry ... if you knew that it had once belonged to a person who valued it, and was deprived of it by misfortune'. Hack is clear: 'There is no longer the same excuse to plea for retaining them'.¹¹⁴ She appreciates the sculptures 'were rescued from the destruction which seemed to await them, and ... carefully preserved'.¹¹⁵ Nonetheless, since 'Greece was delivered from the power of the Turks', applying the social justice taught through *Grecian Stories* requires their repatriation.¹¹⁶ Her focus on the future, only eight years after Greece had regained independence from the Turks, contrasts with articles which only mention or omit changed circumstances. Accessibility for Hack's (British) children does not trump ethics, but neither does she consider travel essential for an informed opinion, as Williams implies. Hack's emphasis on 'restitution', following preservation from specific dangers, presents a dynamic conception of the museum: a temporary holding bay rather than a collection for posterity.

The closest comparison to Hack's call for 'restitution' is not in a children's magazine, but in the cheap satirical publication *Funny Folks* which takes the form of spoof archaeological reports.¹¹⁷ This publication imagined twentieth-century Greek archaeologists 'Bring[ing] us back our buried treasures!'.¹¹⁸ Subtitled as if quoting three London newspapers in 1985, this three-act fantasy described Greek archaeologists taking 'a ship of war' to retrieve artefacts from 'the home of the barbarian; England, where the priceless art treasures of our national past lie buried'. London is characterized as a 'dreary prison-house', a 'colossal grave'.¹¹⁹ *Funny Folks* concludes its spoof report by declaring: 'the Greeks are sending off all the treasures to their ship'. Since it imagines twentieth-century Britain without fleet or army, 'the government is powerless ... and we Londoners today can thus enter into the bitterness of heart of the Athenians who lived in the time of the removal of the Elgin marbles to London'.¹²⁰ *Funny Folks* carefully avoids criticizing the British Museum itself. Nonetheless, it characterizes acquisition and collection as violence – especially when stored and excerpted, rather than fully displayed.

Hack's children's history and *Funny Folks'* futuristic archaeology, juxtaposed with the children's periodical archive, clarify how the writers' aims to mediate antiquity through museum acquisitions and displays were, in turn, mediated to child readers. Virtual tours and their ideal spectating, a metaphorical fragment of wider contemporary debates surrounding museums, shaped how the marble fragments were perceived at the time, and curated for future generations.

Conclusion

The archive of how children's magazines mediated the Parthenon sculptures reveals how nineteenth-century writers, readers and museum visitors engaged with museums, and, through them, the past and the future. The 'meta-archival' layers through which we can glimpse fragments of these encounters display a range of opinions about accessibility and the ethics of acquisition, exhibition and gatekeeping. They also underline the 'inherent ambivalence' of archival fragments, both tangible and metaphorical.[121] Virtual museum tours, considered in this way, constitute a distinctive, hidden archive about how Victorians were curating the past, both for present visitors and for posterity.

Nineteenth-century accounts of the British Museum's Elgin room revealed a notable divergence between adult debates and children's archives, as well as the challenges of engaging with antiquity through fragmentary remains. Journalism for adults reflects a wider range of ethical stances, while the imaginative leaps required for successful virtual tours exemplify the promise and limitations of both museum display and the periodical medium. The fact that repatriation controversies tend not to surface in children's literature shows how such debates can function silently, possibly revealed in linguistic, illustrative or quotation choices, and often in surprising contexts. Hack argued in *Grecian Stories* that educating children is the fastest way to effect societal change.[122] Her radical conviction suggests that, in contrast, the ostensible promotion of the *status quo* represented by the Elgin room displays in children's magazines, and their concomitant silence surrounding repatriation debates, ensures the future of the classical archive within the museum.

Magazine articles are revealing ephemeral evidence for how nineteenth-century children interacted with Greco-Roman antiquity through museum displays: ironically, in reaching more readers through virtual tours, periodicals both replaced and enabled engagement with the object. For readers who, unlike Hack's middle-class family or the *Children's Friend* Sunday School day-trippers, were not able to visit, these tours brought museum displays and art classes into their homes. They also perpetuated popular perceptions of institutional gatekeeping by modelling ideal viewing and dictating interpretation, which inform current disputes over display of the sculptures in the British and Acropolis museums.

In contrast to guides that simply listed hundreds of items, 'virtual tours' curate coherence as well as completeness: narrative and illustration interpret selected artefacts or rooms.[123] Bridell-Fox, promoting imaginative reconstruction of fragmentary displays and ancient ruins, was more positive than Erskine and Williams: 'in spite of the terrible gap, enough of the building is still left for us to admire ... more than enough to recognise the general plan and places of most of the sculptures'.[124] She is optimistic that models, virtual narratives and illustrations, as well as the original fragments, can foster competent spectating, and thereby facilitate engagement with the past.

Even while inducting children into idealized modes of engagement, these articles avoided issues of acquisition by romanticizing the cultural significance of ancient artefacts. Their didactic purpose apparently precludes criticism of the museum's collections: virtual tours justify the museum's function, showing the significance of different sources for debates *about* museums, which in turn create mediated 'archives' of the past, amidst twenty-first-century decisions about cataloguing and digitization. The archive of nineteenth-century children's and popular printing that was segregated into the Tower of Cambridge University Library, for example, included periodicals which, if digitized, are now more often accessed online: two layers of archival selection and access to articles which themselves archive the British Museum's 'archiving' of Greek antiquity through acquisition, cataloguing and display.

Moreover, virtual outreach has produced modern ephemeral children's engagement with this space that historically enabled segregation of such material from the research library: a video demonstrates how children can craft their own 'tower'.[125] Viewers can curate their own library (comparable to the child-size 'cabinet' which helps Harry process ideas about repatriation in Hack's *Grecian Stories*). A miniature accordion book captures the allure of archival fantasies, even as it reifies the concept of meta-archival layers: the accretions of mediation through which we can glimpse how nineteenth-century magazines transmitted museum archives of classical antiquity for children.

Acknowledgements

I am grateful to Liam Sims for inviting me to be involved with 'Tall Tales', and to Ruby Punt for her assistance with preparing the bibliography and endnotes. My thanks to Tim Barringer, Erin Johnson-Williams and Kiera Vaclavik for their suggestions on draft versions: all errors remain mine.

Notes

E. F. Bridell-Fox, 'Greek and Roman Art at the British Museum I', *The Girls' Own Paper* 8, no. 359 (13 November 1886): 100–3, p. 100. Gale ID: DX1901223190. Periodical citations throughout this essay include digitization document numbers for the Gale Cengange database Nineteenth-Century Periodicals Online.

1 Stuart Roberts, 'Tall Tales: Secrets of the Tower', *University of Cambridge*, 2018, https://www.cam.ac.uk/TallTales, accessed 30 July 2021. During this exhibition, the Tower was opened for public tours. The Tower Project, funded by the Andrew W. Mellon Foundation, catalogued the collection, finding large numbers of popular and ephemeral material from the nineteenth century.

2 Bridell-Fox, 'Greek and Roman Art I', p. 100.

3 Ibid.

4 For example, Cambridge University Library's display of its censored 'Arcana' collection (2020): 'Erotica Comes to Cambridge – Cambridge University Library Special Collections', https://specialcollections-blog.lib.cam.ac.uk/?p=19711, accessed 30 July 2021; and the Bodleian's 'Story of Phi' (2018–19), curated by Jennifer Ingleheart: 'Bodleian Libraries' "'Obscene' Books Go on Display", *BBC News* (8 November 2018).

5 Rachel Bryant Davies, *Classics at Play: Greco-Roman Antiquity in British Children's Culture, 1750–1914* (Oxford: Oxford University Press, forthcoming).

6   The Parthenon sculptures have, since their arrival at the British Museum in 1816, been at the centre of controversies over preservation and repatriation. For analysis of Elgin's papers, see William St Clair, *Lord Elgin and the Marbles* (Oxford: Oxford University Press, 1998). For recent interventions, see Geoffrey Robertson, *Who Owns History?: The Case of Elgin's Loot* (London: Biteback Publishing, 2019); and Tiffany Jenkins, *Keeping Their Marbles: How the Treasures of the Past Ended up in Museums* (Oxford: Oxford University Press, 2016).

7   For example, Barbara J. Black, *On Exhibit: Victorians and Their Museums* (Charlottesville: University Press of Virginia, 2000), pp. 148–66; and Virginia Zimmerman, 'Bringing Egypt Home: Children's Encounters with Ancient Egypt in the Long Nineteenth Century', in Rachel Bryant Davies and Barbara Gribling (eds), *Pasts at Play: Childhood Encounters with History in British Culture, 1750–1914* (Manchester: Manchester University Press, 2020), pp. 48–68.

8   British Museum Department of Greek and Roman Antiquities, *Synopsis of the Contents of the British Museum: The Sculptures of the Parthenon. Elgin Room. Pt. I.* (London: William Clowes & Sons, 1882), pp. 83–107.

9   The Parthenon sculptures at the British museum were often presented as part of the wider collection. For example, the prior 'acquisition' of 'antiquities … from Abercromby's campaign in Egypt' was also praised ('The British Museum', p. 268). Nor were such descriptions restricted to Britain: *St Nicholas* noted that 'some fine pieces of sculptured marble were obtained' from Egina; 'they are now in the Glypothek, or Museum of sculpture, at Munich'. Clara Erskine Clement, 'Stories of Art and Artists – Fourth Paper', *St. Nicholas Scribner's Illustrated Magazine for Girls and Boys* 8. 7 (1 July 1881): 676–85. DX1901783607. p. 554.

10 Such as puzzles: see Rachel Bryant Davies, '"Fun from the Classics": Puzzling Antiquity in *The Boys Own Paper*', in Rachel Bryant Davies and Barbara Gribling (eds), *Pasts at Play: Childhood Encounters with History in British Culture, 1750–1914* (Manchester: Manchester University Press, 2020), pp. 96–122.

11 Aishwarya Subramanian, '"This Was a Great, Big Room Full of Dead Things": British Children's Literature and the Museums Debate', *The Lion and the Unicorn* 44. 2 (2020): 153–63; p. 154.

12 See Kate Nichols, 'Marble for the Masses. The Elgin Marbles at the Crystal Palace, Sydenham', in Viccy Coltman (ed.), *Making Sense of Greek Art* (Exeter: University of Exeter Press, 2012), pp. 179–201; Eric Gidal, *Poetic Exhibitions: Romantic Aesthetics and the Pleasures of the British Museum* (Lewisburg, [PA]: London; Cranbury, NJ: Bucknell University Press; Associated University Presses, 2001); and Emma Peacocke, *Romanticism and the Museum* (New York: Palgrave Macmillan, 2014), pp. 112–49.

13 William St. Clair, *The Elgin Marbles: Questions of Stewardship and Accountability* (Oxford: University Press, 1999), cf. the alleged cover-up of cleaning damage in 1930s: https://www.theguardian.com/uk/1999/nov/29/jamiewilson.davidhencke, accessed 3 August 2021. See also Michael Moss and David Thomas (eds), *Archival Silences: Missing, Lost and Uncreated Archives* (London: Routledge, 2021); Peter McMurray, 'Archival Excess: Sensational Histories Beyond the Audiovisual', *Fontes Artis Musicae* 62. 3 (2015): 262–75; and Ann Laura Stoler, *Along the Archival Grain: Epistemic Anxieties and Colonial Common Sense* (Princeton, NJ: Princeton University Press, 2010).

14 Bridell-Fox, 'Greek and Roman Art I', p. 100.

15 On the terminology used of Victorian burlesque spectators, see: Richard Schoch, *Victorian Theatrical Burlesques* (Burlington: Ashgate Publishing, 2003), p. xix; and Rachel Bryant Davies, *Troy, Carthage and the Victorians: The Drama of Classical Ruins in the Nineteenth-Century Imagination* (Cambridge: Cambridge University Press, 2018), pp. 213–16.
16 Courtney Clarke, 'Half-Holiday Rambles in London', *Young England* 50. 1 (1885): 487–9. DX1901530949.
17 British Museum, 'Elgin Marbles – No. 199. Statue of Icarus', in *Guide Cards to the British Museum* (British Museum, 1840). British Library digital store 1044.a.7, pp. 143–4.
18 Thompson Sharp, 'Mythic Lore and Tales of Yore', *Kind Words for Boys and Girls* (1 February 1879): 54–5. DX1901498967; and Lizzie W. Champney, 'Myrto's Festival', *St. Nicholas* 8. 2 (1880): 83–8. DX1901783412.
19 William Tronzo, *The Fragment: An Incomplete History* (Los Angeles: Getty Publications, 2009), p. 18.
20 'How the Ancients Rode Horses', *Our Young Folk's Weekly Budget* 26. 742 (21 February 1885): 160. DX1901064601.
21 C. J. Montague, 'Visits to the British Museum No. 2', *The Children's Friend* (n.d.): 43–6. DX1901499298.
22 'Uncle James's Sketch-Book. The Chalk Family', *Kind Words: A Weekly Magazine for Boys and Girls* (19 September 1867): 301–4. DX1901499298.
23 'Uncle James's Sketch-Book', pp. 301–4.
24 Ibid., p. 302.
25 Ibid.: emphasis original.
26 Ibid., p. 301.
27 Charlotte M. Yonge, 'Womankind', *The Monthly Packet* 18. 4 (1 August 1874): 186–93, p. 189. DX1902022388.
28 C. J. Montague, 'Visits to the British Museum No. 3', *The Children's Friend* (n.d.): 129–44. DX1902015305.
29 W. Mattieu Williams, 'My Wanderings in Greece', *Young England* 2. 74 (1881): 468–70. DX1901530282.
30 'The British Museum', *The Friendly Companion and Illustrated Instructor* 1. 10 (1857): 267–70. DX1901671024.
31 Ibid.
32 'Walks about London', *Peter Parley's Annual: A Christmas and New Year's Present for Young People* (n.d.): 137–44. DX1901717293.
33 Ibid.
34 Clarke, 'Half-Holiday Rambles', 487–9; Bridell-Fox, 'Greek and Roman Art I'.
35 'Tidmarsh, Henry Edward', *DMBI: A Dictionary of Methodism in Britain and Ireland*, https://dmbi.online/index.php?do=app.entry&id=2736, accessed 2 August 2021.
36 Clarke, 'Half-Holiday Rambles', p. 487.
37 Ibid.
38 Ibid.
39 Ibid., p. 488.
40 Montague, 'Visits to the British Museum No. 3', 139–43.
41 Williams, 'Wanderings', p. 468.
42 Ibid., p. 469.
43 Ibid.

44 B. Woodward and Frank A. J. L. James, 'Williams, William Mattieu (1820–1892), Science Teacher and Industrial Chemist', *Oxford Dictionary of National Biography*.
45 'Walks about London II'.
46 Anne Anderson, 'The Mutual Admiration Society, or Mr Punch Against the Aesthetes', *Popular Narrative Media* 2. 1 (2009): 69–89; and 'The Colonel: Shams, Charlatans and Oscar Wilde', *The Wildean* 25 (2004): 34–53.
47 'Distinguished Amateurs 2 – The Art Critic', *Punch* 78 (1880): 114. DX1901942589.
48 Ibid.
49 Ibid.
50 https://www.nga.gov/collection/art-object-page.93681.html, accessed 6 August 2021.
51 Clarke, 'Half-Holiday Rambles', p. 487.
52 N. O. Rees, 'Great Men of Greece', *Good Things: A Picturesque Magazine for the Young of All Ages* 31 (1875): 492–4. DX1901053164; and Montague, 'Visits No. 3'.
53 'Busy Brains and Useful Fingers', *Routledge's Every Girls Annual* 51 (n.d.): 240–6. DX1901656717.
54 Edwin Landseer, 'The Boy Artist', *The Child's Companion; or Sunday Scholar's Reward* (n.d.): 20–1, p. 20. DX1902148725.
55 'Famous Artists', *Every Boy's Magazine (UKP)* 71 (n.d.): 524–8, p. 526. DX1901729887.
56 Williams, 'Wanderings', p. 468.
57 Ibid; and Clarke, 'Half-Holiday Rambles', p. 487.
58 Bridell-Fox, 'Greek and Roman Art I'; E. F. Bridell-Fox, 'Greek and Roman Art at the British Museum', *The Girls' Own Paper* 8. 363 (11 December 1886): 161–4. DX1901223227.
59 Bridell-Fox, 'Greek and Roman Art I', p. 101.
60 Ibid., p. 102.
61 Rees, 'Great Men of Greece'.
62 Bridell-Fox, 'Greek and Roman Art II', p. 102; and Clarke, 'Half-Holiday Rambles', p. 487.
63 Bridell-Fox, 'Greek and Roman Art I', p. 100.
64 Stoler, *Along the Archival Grain*, pp. 14, 32.
65 See Rees, 'Great Men of Greece', p. 494; 'Famous Artists', p. 526; Champney, 'Myrto's Festival'; Montague, 'British Museum III', p. 139; Erskine, 'Fourth Paper', p. 555; and Clara Erskine Clement, 'Stories of Art and Artists – First Paper', *St. Nicholas Scribner's Illustrated Magazine for Girls and Boys* 8. 3 (1 January 1881): 187–92, pp. 191, 192. DX1901783456.
66 Cf. Erin Johnson-Williams's discussion of 'archival silences' in Chapter 6.
67 'Walks about London II', p. 143; Bridell-Fox, 'Greek and Roman Art II', p. 163.
68 'The British Museum', p. 268.
69 Williams, 'Wanderings', p. 469.
70 Clarke, 'Half-Holiday Rambles', p. 488.
71 Ibid.
72 Bridell-Fox, 'Greek and Roman Art II', p. 161.
73 Ibid., p. 161.
74 The Editor's Pocket Book', *Little Folks: The Magazine for Boys and Girls; A Magazine for the Young*, n.d., pp. 58–61. DX1901514086; ibid., p. 59.
75 Williams, 'Wanderings', p. 469.
76 Ibid., pp. 468–9; 'Uncle James's Sketch-Book'.
77 Ibid.

78 Erskine, 'Fourth Paper', p. 555.
79 Ibid.
80 Bridell-Fox, 'Greek and Roman Art II', p. 163.
81 Williams, 'Wanderings', p. 469.
82 Ibid.
83 Montague, 'Visits to the British Museum III', p. 142.
84 Bridell-Fox, 'Greek and Roman Art I', p. 102.
85 Ibid., p. 100.
86 Sophie Thomas, 'Assembling History: Fragments and Ruins', *European Romantic Review* 14. 2 (2003): 177–86, p. 180.
87 Clarke, 'Half-Holiday Rambles', p. 489.
88 Erskine, 'Fourth Paper', p. 555; and Williams, 'Wanderings', p. 469.
89 Clarke, 'Half-Holiday Rambles', p. 489.
90 Williams, 'Wanderings', p. 469; and 'Walks about London II', p. 143.
91 'Walks about London II', p. 143.
92 Tronzo, *Fragment*, p. 40.
93 Elgin Room. Part I. 2nd edn. London: William Clowes & Sons. 1882.
94 Bridell-Fox, 'Greek and Roman Art I', p. 102.
95 Ibid., p. 102; and Williams, 'Wanderings', p. 469.
96 Montague, 'Visits to the British Museum III', p. 139.
97 Ibid., p. 142.
98 Bridell-Fox, 'Greek and Roman Art I', p. 101.
99 Henry Green Clarke, *The British Museum; Its Antiquities and Natural History. A Hand-Book Guide for Visitors* (London: H. G. Clarke & Co., 1851), p. 12.
100 Williams, 'Wanderings', p. 469.
101 Bridell-Fox, 'Greek and Roman Art II', p. 163.
102 Ibid.
103 'Walks about London II', p. 143.
104 Bridell-Fox, 'Greek and Roman Art II', p. 163, 100.
105 Brenda Colloms, 'Fox, Eliza Florance Bridell- [Née Eliza Florance Fox] (1823/4–1903), Painter', *Oxford Dictionary of National Biography*, https://doi.org/10.1093/ref:odnb/48583, accessed 30 July 2021.
106 Clara Drummond, 'A "Grand Possible": Elizabeth Barrett Browning's Translations of Aeschylus's "Prometheus Bound"', *International Journal of the Classical Tradition* 12. 4 (2006): 507–62; 513–14.
107 Bridell-Fox, 'Greek and Roman Art I', p. 100; Byron, *Childe Harold's Pilgrimage*, II.1.3-5; Bridell-Fox, 'Greek and Roman Art II', p. 161: *Childe Harold*, II.3.4.
108 E.g. 'Pug's Tour through Europe, or, The Travell'd Monkey: Containing His Wonderful Adventures in the Principal Capitals of the Greatest Empires, Kingdoms, and States'. *Harris's Cabinet of Amusement and Instruction* (London: John Harris, 1824), p. 44.
109 E. W. Francis, 'Short Notes on Lord Byron's "Pilgrimage of Childe Harold"', *The Ladies' Treasury* (1886): 150–2, p. 151. DX1902003152.
110 Maria Hack, *Grecian Stories* (London: Harvey & Darton, 1840). The first edition (1819) was bequeathed, and the 1824 edition was a copyright accession, but this third edition does not appear in the Cambridge University Library's catalogues.
111 Ibid., p. 349.
112 Ibid., p. 347.
113 Ibid., p. 348.

114 Ibid., p. 347.
115 Ibid., p. 331.
116 Ibid., p. 293.
117 On *Funny Folks* and classical archaeology, see further Bryant Davies, *Troy, Carthage, and the Victorians*, pp. 110–12.
118 'A Romance of Buried Treasure', In *Funny Folks: A Weekly Budget of Funny Pictures, Funny Notes, Funny Jokes, and Funny Stories* 12. 591 (20 March 1886): 90. DX1901776361.
119 Ibid. C.f. Chapter 15 by Tim Barringer on Albertopolis.
120 Ibid., p. 90.
121 Tronzo, *The Fragment*, p. 1.
122 Hack, *Grecian Stories*, p. 64.
123 E.g. British Museum, *Guide Cards to the British Museum*, 1840.
124 Bridell-Fox, 'Greek and Roman Art II'.
125 https://www.museums.cam.ac.uk/school-sessions/watch-and-learn-how-make-your-own-tiny-tower-book, uploaded to Youtube July 2020.

Bibliography

'A Romance of Buried Treasure'. In *Funny Folks: A Weekly Budget of Funny Pictures, Funny Notes, Funny Jokes, and Funny Stories* 12, no. 591 (20 March 1886): 90. DX1901776361.

Anderson, Anne. 'The Colonel: Shams, Charlatans and Oscar Wilde'. *The Wildean* 25 (2004): 34–53.

Anderson, Anne. 'The Mutual Admiration Society, or Mr Punch against the Aesthetes'. *Popular Narrative Media* 2, no. 1 (2009): 69–89.

British Museum Department of Greek and Roman Antiquities. *Synopsis of the Contents of the British Museum: The Sculptures of the Parthenon. Elgin Room. Pt. I*. London: William Clowes & Sons, 1882.

'Bodleian Libraries' '"Obscene" Books Go on Display'. *BBC News* (8 November 2018), section Oxford. https://www.bbc.com/news/uk-england-oxfordshire-46131472. Accessed 30 July 2021.

Bridell-Fox, E. F. 'Greek and Roman Art at the British Museum'. *The Girls' Own Paper* 8, no. 359 (13 November 1886): 100–3. DX1901223190.

Bridell-Fox, E. F. 'Greek and Roman Art at the British Museum'. *The Girls' Own Paper* 8, no. 363 (11 December 1886): 161–4. DX1901223227.

British Museum, 'Elgin Marbles – No. 199. Statue of Icarus'. In *Guide Cards to the British Museum*, 143–4. London: British Museum, 1840. British Library digital store 1044.a.7, pp. 143–4.

British Museum. *Guide Cards to the British Museum*. London: British Museum, 1840.

Bryant Davies, Rachel. *Troy, Carthage and the Victorians: The Drama of Classical Ruins in the Nineteenth-Century Imagination*. Cambridge and New York: Cambridge University Press, 2018.

Bryant Davies, Rachel. '"Fun from the Classics": Puzzling Antiquity in The Boys Own Paper'. In *Pasts at Play: Childhood Encounters with History in British Culture, 1750–1914*, edited by Rachel Bryant Davies and Barbara Gribling, 96–122. Manchester: Manchester University Press, 2020.

Bryant Davies, Rachel. *Classics at Play: Greco-Roman Antiquity in British Children's Culture, 1750–1914*. Oxford: Oxford University Press, forthcoming.

'Busy Brains and Useful Fingers'. *Routledge's Every Girls Annual* 51 (n.d.): 240–6. DX1901656717.

Champney, Lizzie W. 'Myrto's Festival'. *St. Nicholas Scribner's Illustrated Magazine for Girls and Boys* 8, no. 2 (1880): 83–8. DX1901783412.

Clarke, Courtney. 'Half-Holiday Rambles in London'. *Young England* 50, no. 1 (1885): 487–9. DX1901530949.

Clarke, Henry Green. *The British Museum; Its Antiquities and Natural History. A Hand-Book Guide for Visitors*. London: H.G. Clarke & Co., 1851.

Clement, Clara Erskine. 'Stories of Art and Artists: First Paper'. *St. Nicholas Scribner's Illustrated Magazine for Girls and Boys* 8, no. 3 (1 January 1881): 187–92. DX1901783456.

Clement, Clara Erskine. 'Stories of Art and Artists: Fourth Paper'. *St. Nicholas Scribner's Illustrated Magazine for Girls and Boys* 8, no. 7 (1 July 1881): 676–85. DX1901783607.

Colloms, Brenda. 'Fox, Eliza Florance Bridell – [Née Eliza Florance Fox] (1823/4–1903), Painter'. *Oxford Dictionary of National Biography*. https://doi.org/10.1093/ref:odnb/48583.

Coltman, Viccy. *Making Sense of Greek Art*. Exeter: University of Exeter Press, 2012.

'Distinguished Amateurs, 2: The Art Critic'. *Punch, or the London Charivari* (1880): 114.

Drummond, Clara. 'A "Grand Possible": Elizabeth Barrett Browning's Translations of Aeschylus's "Prometheus Bound"'. *International Journal of the Classical Tradition* 12, no. 4 (2006): 507–62.

'Edwin Landseer, 'The Boy Artist'. *The Child's Companion; or Sunday Scholar's Reward* (n.d): 20–1, p. 20. DX1902148725.

'Famous Artists'. *Every Boy's Magazine (UKP)* 71 (n.d): 524–8. DX1901729887.

Francis, E. W. 'Short Notes on Lord Byron's "Pilgrimage of Childe Harold"'. *The Ladies' Treasury: An Illustrated Magazine of Entertaining Literature* (1886): 150–2. DX1902003152.

Gidal, Eric. *Poetic Exhibitions: Romantic Aesthetics and the Pleasures of the British Museum/Eric Gidal*. Lewisburg, [PA.]: London; Cranbury, NJ: Bucknell University Press; Associated University Presses, 2001.

Hack, Maria. *Grecian Stories ... With Thirty-Nine Illustrations by Gilbert, Etc.* London: Harvey & Darton, 1840.

'How the Ancients Rode Horses'. *Our Young Folk's Weekly Budget* 26, no. 742 (21 February 1885): 160. DX1901064601.

Jenkins, Tiffany. *Keeping Their Marbles: How the Treasures of the Past Ended up in Museums ... and Why They Should Stay There*. Oxford and New York: Oxford University Press, 2016.

McMurray, Peter. 'Archival Excess: Sensational Histories beyond the Audiovisual'. *Fontes Artis Musicae*, 62, no. 3 (2015): 262–75.

Montague, C. J. 'Visits to the British Museum No. 2'. *The Children's Friend (UKP)* (n.d): 43–6. DX1901499298.

Montague, C. J. 'Visits to the British Museum No. 3'. *The Children's Friend [UKP]* (n.d): 129–44. DX1902015305.

Nichols, Kate. *Greece and Rome at the Crystal Palace: Classical Sculpture and Modern Britain, 1854–1936*. Oxford: Oxford University Press, 2015.

Peacocke, Emma. *Romanticism and the Museum*. New York: Palgrave Macmillan, 2014.

'Pug's Tour through Europe, or, The Travell'd Monkey: Containing His Wonderful Adventures in the Principal Capitals of the Greatest Empires, Kingdoms, and States'. *Harris's Cabinet of Amusement and Instruction*, 44. London: John Harris, 1824.

Rees, N. O. 'Great Men of Greece'. *Good Things: A Picturesque Magazine for the Young of All Ages* 31 (1875): 492–4. DX1901053164.

Roberts, Stuart. 'Tall Tales: Secrets of the Tower'. *University of Cambridge*, 2018 https://www.cam.ac.uk/TallTales. Accessed 30 July 2021.

Robertson, Geoffrey. *Who Owns History?: The Case of Elgin's Loot*. London: Biteback Publishing, 2019.

Schoch, Richard. *Victorian Theatrical Burlesques*. Burlington: Ashgate Publishing, 2003.

Sharp, Thompson. 'Mythic Lore and Tales of Yore'. *Kind Words for Boys and Girls* (1 February 1879): 54–5. DX1901498967.

Sims, Liam. 'Erotica Comes to Cambridge – Cambridge University Library Special Collections'. https://specialcollections-blog.lib.cam.ac.uk/?p=19711. Accessed 30 July 2021.

Stoler, Ann Laura. *Along the Archival Grain: Epistemic Anxieties and Colonial Common Sense*. Princeton, NJ: Princeton University Press, 2010.

Subramanian, Aishwarya. '"This Was a Great, Big Room Full of Dead Things": British Children's Literature and the Museums Debate'. *The Lion and the Unicorn* 44, no. 2 (2020): 153–63.

'The British Museum'. *The Friendly Companion and Illustrated Instructor* 1, no. 2 (1857): 267–70. DX1901671024.

'The Editor's Pocket Book'. *Little Folks: The Magazine for Boys and Girls; A Magazine for the Young* (n.d): 58–61. DX1901514086.

'The Girl's Own Paper Index'. *The Girl's Own Paper Index*. https://www.lutterworth.com/gop/all-authors/https%3A%2F%2Fwww.lutterworth.com%2Fgop%2Fall-authors%2Fef-bridell-fox-1. Accessed 8 July 2021.

Thomas, Sophie. 'Assembling History: Fragments and Ruins'. *European Romantic Review* 14, no. 2 (2003): 177–86.

'Tidmarsh, Henry Edward'. *DMBI: A Dictionary of Methodism in Britain and Ireland*. https://dmbi.online/index.php?do=app.entry&id=2736. Accessed 2 August 2021.

Tronzo, William. *The Fragment: An Incomplete History*. Los Angeles: Getty Publications, 2009.

'Uncle James's Sketch-Book. The Chalk Family'. *Kind Words: A Weekly Magazine for Boys and Girls* 90 (19 September 1867): 301–4. DX1901499298.

Vernon, Richard. *Historical Redress: Must We Pay for the Past?*. London and New York: Continuum, 2012.

'Walks About London'. *Peter Parley's Annual: A Christmas and New Year's Present for Young People*. (n.d.): 137–44. DX1901717293.

Williams, W. Mattieu. 'My Wanderings in Greece'. *Young England* 2, no. 74 (1881): 468–70. DX1901530282.

Woodward, B., and Frank A. J. L. James. 'Williams, William Mattieu (1820–1892), Science Teacher and Industrial Chemist', *Oxford Dictionary of National Biography*. https://doi.org/10.1093/ref:odnb/29563.

Yonge, Charlotte M., 'Womankind'. *The Monthly Packet* 18, no. 4 (1 August 1874): 186–93, p. 189. DX1902022388.

Zimmerman, Virginia. 'Bringing Egypt Home: Children's Encounters with Ancient Egypt in the Long Nineteenth Century'. In *Pasts at Play: Childhood Encounters with History in British Culture, 1750–1914*, edited by Rachel Bryant Davies and Barbara Gribling, 48–68. Manchester: Manchester University Press, 2020.

15

Afterword: Intersectional Albertopolis

Tim Barringer

The essays in this volume explore a spectrum of approaches to the politics and poetics of the archive, acknowledging the potentialities and pitfalls implicit in the historian's engagement with archival hierarchies, lacunae and silences. Chapter after chapter, in different ways, has revealed the oppressive taxonomies that structure collections and libraries – systems of value that silently import racial and social hierarchies of empire into the present. The critical study of archives and empire has focused on a re-reading of texts to reveal what Ann Laura Stoler evocatively describes as 'lettered governance and written traces of colonial lives'.[1] The essays collected here confirm that the collections held in imperial museums and galleries, too, substantially derive from colonialism's inexorable work of extracting value and transferring it from one part of the globe to another. Objects were collected at the peripheries of empire and gathered at its centre, where they were ordered to form material archives and to generate meaning – processes that recent decolonial thinking seeks to reverse.[2] The challenge for contemporary thought, and for curators working in museums and archives today, is to formulate a critical practice that interrogates collections, identifies areas of silence or invisibility and actively works to redress historical imbalances and inequalities in archival formation. This book gathers accounts of important initiatives that model possibilities for the future, at the Tropenmuseum, Amsterdam (Adiva Lawrence), the 'Oriental Museum' at Durham University (Rachel Barclay, Lauren Barnes, Gillian Ramsay, Craig Barclay, Helen Armstrong) and the V&A itself (Alexandra Watson Jones). In each case the founding logics of a collection are subjected to a fundamental decolonial critique, which in turn generates new possibilities for research, interpretation and display.

As part of her compelling insistence that we should 'unlearn imperialism', Ariella Aïsha Azoulay argues that we must disavow 'the dissociation that unleashed an unstoppable movement of (forced) migration of objects and people in different circuits and the destruction of the worlds of which they were part'.[3] She makes a powerful move in linking the forced movement of people – as in slavery and the Middle Passage, but also the population flows determined by racial capitalism – with the forced movement of objects through looting, or trade between partners with differing levels of power and wealth. The museum becomes a place of captivity for a diaspora of objects deprived of connection to their 'home communities'.

The processes and principles of categorization and taxonomy by which these objects of empire were ordered in the imperial archives were proposed with supreme self-confidence. They remained nonetheless constantly inadequate to exert mastery over a field of impossible magnitude and variety. The 'grids of intelligibility', imposed by curators on the imperial collections, were, to adapt Stoler, 'fashioned from uncertain knowledge', constantly threatened with collapse.[4]

I write this critique from within the discipline of art history, aware that, as currently constituted, the field has been slow to acknowledge that its methods and categories are steeped in imperial ideologies and associated racial taxonomies and hierarchies that took shape in the eighteenth and nineteenth centuries.[5] The editors of *Relational Formations of Race* remind us that 'Colonialism and white supremacy have always been relational projects. They rely on logics of sorting, ranking, and comparison that produce and naturalize categories of racial difference necessary for the legitimation of slavery, settler colonialism, and imperial expansion'.[6] Sorting, ranking, comparing: these acts are the stock-in-trade of art history, applied to images and objects from around the world. Concepts once embedded in file cards and slide labels have seamlessly transferred to databases and PowerPoints. Questions of value, of 'quality', of beauty, naturalized within the frameworks of our discipline, can be seen to enshrine the racial hierarchies of an age of empire. At this moment, a reckoning with art history's assumptions, institutions and practices is overdue. Implicit in the study of empires, as in the study of a 'global' art history, is the danger of a reinscription of long-established norms. In histories of 'world art', the western imperium, formal or informal – be it Rome, Madrid, London, Paris or New York – has often continued to insist upon itself as the center, rendering all other parts of the world, notably those once or still under European colonial dominion – to the status of a periphery. A first step is to make empire visible as a formational strategy of the archive and the museum: to engage with its processes and practices, and to square up to its tangible remains is to begin a process of reckoning, and one of restitution.[7]

In this Afterword, I propose that 'Albertopolis', the complex of institutions created at South Kensington in London initiated in 1851 and named after Queen Victoria's Prince Consort, embodies many of the themes discussed in this book, constituting an 'intersectional archive'. It does so both as metaphoric structure, and in a more direct sense as a meta-collection of ordered material data in two and three dimensions – millions of texts, images and objects. The Victoria and Albert Museum, Natural History Museum, Science Museum, Imperial College, Royal Albert Hall, Royal College of Music, Royal Geographical Society and other, smaller, units; each has collections, libraries and archives of its own. Together, however, I suggest that the complex be understood as a totalizing entity.[8] I propose, furthermore, that South Kensington as a collective is a fulcrum of collections and practices that constitute a residue of the British Empire. These bear the indelible imprint of imperial ideology even in our post-colonial era. They were moreover reflective and formative of dominant bourgeois constructions of class and gender in British society. Intersectional analysis insists that race, class and gender cannot be treated as separate categories. Racial capitalism has had a profound, determining impact on modern, normative constructions of all three.[9] An imperial archive and a liberal educational mechanism, Albertopolis stood at the meeting point – the intersection – of national state and colonial empire: it articulated and enacted the activist responses of a governing elite aiming to impose specific hierarchies of race, class and gender. The South Kensington campus was an ideological engine designed to address and redress the class tensions generated by a century of industrial development, to proselytize for normative constructions of gender and to naturalize hierarchies of race within an imperial framework. Today the 'museums district' is an imperial archive without an empire, positioned within a multicultural city at a major node of a globalized world. It stands now in need of a strategy for decolonizing its collections and epistemologies. The effective pursuit of a decolonial strategy effectively, however, cannot be achieved by addressing questions of race and empire alone, overdue though those issues are for a reckoning. Rather, work is needed to understand the ways in which race and empire intersect with, and are interpellated by, issues of class, gender, region and religion. Only then can we confront our collective inheritance from the age of empires and the archives it produced. For South Kensington's very project was the initiation of an intersectional archive, in terms both of ideology and media: just as it operated at the fulcrum of issues of race, class and gender, it was most effective where text and object, word and image, sight and sound came together.

At the core of Albertopolis lay the South Kensington Museum, founded in 1857 and renamed in 1899 the Victoria and Albert Museum (V&A), which will be the main focus of this chapter. The aim of its founders was to create a three-dimensional archive which would include 'not only works of art selected as fine examples of design or art workmanship, but others chosen with a view to an historical series of manufactures'.[10] It aimed at 'the illustration, by actual monuments, of all art which is materially embodied or expressed in objects of utility'.[11] The museum effectively aspired to offer a taxonomy of every object made by mankind – a complete historical sequence of manufactured goods, a total archive in three dimensions. Within it would be a multitude of further archives. At its core would stand a library, containing every book ever written on the subjects of art and design. The entire project, moreover, would itself be subject to a paper archive, its collections meticulously catalogued, the registrars maintaining precise actuarial control over the vast endeavour. The new technology of photography, furthermore, would be used for the first time to maintain a visual meta-archive of the material collection.[12]

Racial taxonomies and material culture

The genesis of the Albertopolis can, undoubtedly, be located in the popular success of the Great Exhibition of the Industry of All Nations in 1851, which was housed in Joseph Paxton's Crystal Palace in Hyde Park. Like many triumphs of Victorian liberal imperialism it was rooted in a tense alliance of classes, emblematized in the collaboration between the patron, Prince Albert, the administrator and ideologue, Henry Cole, a career bureaucrat from a relatively humble background, and the 'respectable working classes' who formed a significant proportion of the Exhibition's six million visitors. What did they experience? In Chapter 13, Jim Davis offers possibilities for reading the archive against the grain to reconstruct the responses of British theatre audiences of the same period. Although the archive of the Great Exhibition is vast, its contents reflect the aims and actions of the organizers rather than the experience of the visitor. More work is needed, in the vein Davis proposes, to disinter fragments of evidence that might illuminate the ways particular people encountered the archive – such as the group of Blackburn metalworkers who paid a day trip to the Exhibition in 1851.[13]

A euphoric commodity spectacle, the Exhibition gathered manufactured objects from all over the world in an event widely ascribed world-historical importance. 'The activity of the present day', Cole announced in his portentous introduction to the *Official Descriptive and Illustrative Catalogue*, 'chiefly develops itself in commercial industry, and it is in accordance with the spirit of the age that the nations of the world have now collected together their choicest productions'.[14] Every form of commodity, every manufactured object – from musical instruments to textile looms, umbrella stands to jewellery – was represented. Indeed, the sheer extent of the exhibition, with 100,000 works on show from almost every nation on earth, raised the spectre of material confusion, archival and epistemological chaos – an anarchy of the commodity, a mutinous empire of things. Countering this, the exhibition's organizers made Herculean, if ultimately doomed, efforts to give order and meaning to the material world under industrialization, to order the imperial archive (albeit a temporary one).[15] To this end, they developed a theory of the 'arts of industry', a founding taxonomic gesture – a founding of archival principles – that was articulated through a range of publications including the massive catalogue.[16] It would have implications for the rest of the century. Led by Cole, this monumental endeavour in epistemology divided British objects into a four-part hierarchical classification: 'Raw Materials', 'Machines', 'Manufactures' and 'Fine Arts'. The last category was defined by the specific materials used for the production of an object – 'the taste and skill displayed in such applications of human industry'.[17] Art stood within, not beyond, the commodity culture of the era, and could be put to commercial use.

This ordering, crucially, was implicitly mapped onto an imperial racial hierarchy, with the upper echelons of commodity and fine-art production associated only with European cultures; 'machinery', 'manufactures' and 'whiteness' were implicitly linked. The spectacular displays of machines, and elsewhere of their products, would represent the future and the transformative powers of modernity. India and, more still, Africa, the Caribbean and large parts of the Americas, would appear merely as the origin point of resources whose potential could be realized only through colonization and mechanization. The injection of British energy and direction, so the exhibition proposed, was necessary to 'awaken' Africa and Asia. India, already largely under the control of the East India Company and local leaders under its control, was presented as a rich source of raw materials (themselves subject to a regime of colonial taxonomy), ripe for colonial expropriation. Thus hemp, flax, coal, oil, precious stones, saltpetre and spices, a cornucopia of metals and minerals headed by the great Indian diamonds, were identified as the true objects of value in the Indian sub-continent. 'Taste' and 'skill' were sought in the products of European industry and not in the allegedly barbarous products of the colonial periphery.

A surplus of £186,000 from the Great Exhibition made possible the construction of more permanent institutions devoted to the promotion of Science and Art. In this way (so Albert declared) 'man' could 'conquer nature to his use; himself a divine instrument'.[18] In a Memorandum which indicates the grandiosity of his ambitions, Albert advocated the purchase of a land on which to build institutions based on the classification of objects adopted in the catalogue to the Great Exhibition: Raw Materials, Machinery, Manufactures and Plastic Art.[19] Each of these would contain a library and study rooms, lecture rooms, exhibition space and rooms for 'conversazioni' and commercial meetings. He also imagined that all the learned societies, formed by specialist groups of scientists and other scholars, at present self-governing, independent and scattered throughout London, would be prevailed upon to move to the new complex and submit themselves to the overall control (in a revealing gesture revealing a fantasy of empirical precision) of the Statistical Society. Although none of these plans – which Cole instantly recognized as being impractical – were to come directly to fruition, some elements of Albert's blueprint were eventually realized at South Kensington.

Cole's more mundane priority was 'the Application of the Principles of Technical Art to the improvement of manufactures, together with the establishment of Museums, by which all classes may be induced to investigate those common principles of taste, which may be traced in the works of excellence of all ages'.[20] This vision of a museum was quite different from those other national institutions: Enlightenment concepts of knowledge production lay at the heart of the British Museum, founded in 1753, whereas the National Gallery was founded in 1824 after the government purchased the Angerstein collection of Old Masters, a connoisseur's picture gallery. These institutions would yield their secrets only to those with education and privilege: Cole's museum was itself concerned to educate, a free-acting mechanism of the liberal state with a primary concern for the education of artisans (as he put it) in their 'fustian jackets'.[21] In order to draw in the working class, the museum developed innovative facilities, including the installation of gas lamps in new permanent buildings, and late openings to facilitate visits after work. With such 'arrangements' in place, the museum, Cole felt, could now 'furnish an antidote to the gin palace'.[22] Many of the museum's pathbreaking features such as a lecture theatre, library and public refreshment rooms were directed towards working-class visitors. Above all it communicated through texts – labels, plans, guides, pamphlets, catalogues. Journalistic accounts of museum visits like Moncure Conway's *Travels in South Kensington* drew extensively on these documents, reaching out to distant audiences unable to visit the museum. Conway's text also suggests the impact of the displays from the point of view of a privileged visitor: 'Vista upon vista! The eye never reaches the farthest end in the past from which humanity has toiled upwards, its steps traced in victories over chaos, nor does it alight on any historical epoch not related to himself'.[23] As Rachel Bryant Davies notes in her perceptive analysis of the range of texts generated by the Parthenon Sculptures: 'Virtual tour explanations, scattered across a representative range of publication titles and article types, form an invaluable historical archive of perceptions of museums: their purpose, function, and usage'.

South Kensington aimed to ensure a revival of design innovation – with a newly expert class of designers generating improved profits for investors. The larger aim was to ensure the conformity of a key, potentially revolutionary, class fraction – the skilled artisans – to the national project. Crucially, the institution would also serve an intersectional function, educating a British public deeply divided along class lines about the value of empire, implicitly asserting the existence of a unified, white community, united across lines of class difference, standing in superiority to a larger non-white population of colonial subjects in territorially distant spaces. Through the careful policing of its spaces and a multi-layered practice of modelling particular behaviours, the museum aimed to promote 'respectability', itself an intersectional construct with wide-ranging social and ideological implications, all of them centring on the concept of conformity to social norms.[24]

The interior in the 1850s (Figure 15.1) looked more like a schoolroom than an art museum. The educational collection included geographical materials and scientific apparatus. Unimpressed, the *Saturday Review* described the Museum as 'that universal receptacle of humbugs, home and mother of all shams', claiming that 'we may just as well collect all our national nonsense into one heap, and for this purpose South Kensington is admirably suited'.[25] The sheer excess of South Kensington's collections epitomizes Theodor Adorno's description of the modern museum as 'a metaphor … for the anarchical production of commodities in fully developed bourgeois society', though Adorno could have added that this excess also characterizes imperialism's

Figure 15.1 Interior view of the Educational Museum, South Kensington Museum, ('the Brompton Boilers') *c.* 1859. Photograph: V&A Accession number 32055.

relentless extraction of value from colonies.[26] It was this 'heap' to which the imperial archive aimed to give order and meaning.

'Imperial rather than Metropolitan'[27]

The taxonomies of the Great Exhibition presupposed that exhibits from the colonial peripheries of empire would signify historical stasis and degeneracy while the products of Britain's advanced, mechanized economy would point to progress and the future. However, a very different picture soon emerged. Although a stark dichotomy did indeed appear between British machine-made and hand-crafted manufactures, notably those from the Indian colonies, the conclusions it suggested were as uncomfortable as they were unexpected for the exhibition's organizers – one of the many moments of taxonomic crisis and epistemic rupture encountered in South Kensington's history. The design theorist and historian Gustav Waagen, Director of the Berlin Museum, noted in November 1851 that

> The Indian stuffs in the Exhibition ... are remarkable for the rich invention shown in the patterns, in which the beauty, distinctness, and variety of the forms, and the harmonious blending of severe colours, called forth the admiration of all true judges of art. What a lesson such designs afford to manufacturers, even in those nations of Europe which have made the greatest progress in industry![28]

This revelation was corrosive of mid-Victorian assumptions about national and racial superiority, progress and mechanization, that were enshrined in the exhibition's catalogue. Hand-made Indian objects shown in 1851, such as the golden sari from Benares (now Varanasi) later purchased as a foundational object in the South Kensington Museum's collection, displayed higher qualities of design than the ingenious but generally vulgar products of mechanized industry. Like every object in the imperial archive, it bears an accession number, 769-1852, the last four digits recording the year of purchase. An institution – a new form of archive that would reinforce the authority of empire's centre over its peripheries – was needed to respond to this crisis. Later, the Museum's collections of objects from South Asia would be massively enhanced by the transfer of the collections of the East India Company to South Kensington in 1875. The Company's India Museum, originally established in 1801, included a range of objects including many acquired as loot and displayed as triumphant spoils of war. Among the collection were the natural history paintings commissioned by Raja Serfoji II of Tanjore, products of the complex hybrid culture of early-nineteenth century Tanjore, in South India, that are the subject of a meticulous and revealing study in this volume by David Lowther. His essay demonstrates the inadequacy of the European conceptual frameworks within which such appropriated works were understood. Transferred to the British Museum's library in 1879, Lowther reveals that they 'incorporated European scientific methodologies into South Indian traditions of seeing and understanding the natural world', in ways that diminished their status within imperial hierarchies but which render them fascinating subjects for analysis today.

'Albertopolis', which grew up at South Kensington from 1856, was a campus of bureaucracies rather than merely a museum. It did not aim merely to represent the world, but rather to change it. The imperial archive was militant. Among the Commissioners of the Great Exhibition, the distinguished scientist, Lyon Playfair, urged action to remedy the inadequacy of British technical education, while Cole advocated changes in and design education through the study of historical and colonial examples. An early presence among the permanent institutions at South Kensington were a large art school (later the Royal College of Art) and the offices of the Department of Science and Art (Figure 15.2). These institutions regulated government art and design education though a centralized network of art schools with standardized methods of teaching and examination which extended throughout Britain, Ireland and the British Empire. In 1858 John Charles Robinson, the first curator of the museum drew attention to 'the Art-Library, Schools, and general Departmental Machinery, at Kensington, the action of which, be it remembered, is emphatically *Imperial* rather than Metropolitan'.[29] There are many analogies between the early administration of the South Kensington Museum and the methods of colonial authorities. Tight central control was exerted

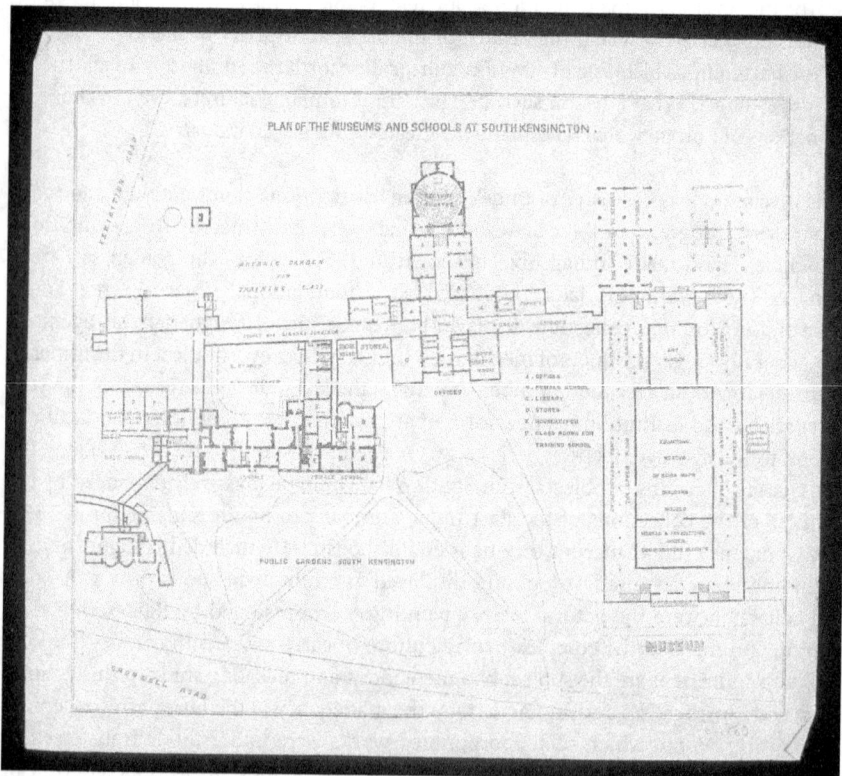

Figure 15.2 Plan of Museums and Schools at South Kensington *c.* 1860. Lithograph: V&A Accession number E.1515-1913.

over local art education with regular inspection by officers from the centre, strategies which underscored the authority of the 'home' institution, the imperial archive.

Cole was anxious to erect permanent buildings on the site which would put into practice the principles of design reform promoted through his writings and exhibitions: fine historical and colonial examples of the decorative arts shown in the collection would be 'applied' to the fabric of the museum. Its centrepiece was the South Court, opened in 1862. On the walls, large mosaics represented eminent figures in the history of the fine and decorative arts, soon earning the nickname the 'Kensington Valhalla', a reference to Leo von Klenze's 'hall of fame' at Regensburg near Munich, completed in 1842. An early exercise in canon formation, and a visual means of signalling hierarchies within the imperial archive, the series of mosaics included no person of colour, despite the high significance the South Kensington authorities attached to non-western objects.

To the sides of the main galleries stood a cloister-like space developed in 1863–4 for the display of the so-called Oriental collections – Indian, Chinese, Japanese and Persian objects being subsumed under this rubric.[30] Here the fabric of the building, rather than a mere housing for the objects – a filing cabinet for the archive – took on the status of an ideological intervention. The commission for polychrome wall and ceiling decorations and tile pavements went to Owen Jones, who had installed elaborate decorative schemes evoking historic styles of ornament – Greek, Egyptian and Indian – at the Crystal Palace after its re-erection as a profit-making concern at Sydenham in South London.[31] Jones created a series of richly coloured designs for a decorative paint scheme, inspired variously by Chinese, Japanese and Islamic objects to demonstrate their value as source materials for contemporary British commercial design.[32] By appropriating 'Oriental' design for this 'British' institution, the decorative scheme re-enacted the process of extraction and imbrication that structured the imperial archive. South Kensington's ideology was manifest on its walls. The Oriental courts, through their very separateness, served the function, described by Edward Said, of asserting an absolute difference between the Orient and the Occident, while collapsing differences within each category.[33]

A subsequent addition to the South Kensington buildings, in the early 1870s, represented a new tendency in the imperial archive, one subjected to derision by modernist critics of the twentieth century, but more congenial in our age of virtual realities. The Architectural Courts designed by Henry Scott were intended to house the museum's collection of plaster casts of great monuments of western art, notably Trajan's column – significantly, one of the principal monuments of Imperial Rome, often seen as a parallel to the British Empire.[34] Still today the visitor is overwhelmed by the sheer physical size, the cultural scope and technological prowess of the museum, which functions as a metonym of the state itself. But from the raised viewing platform separating the gallery's two lengthy glazed arcades, the viewer saw more than a panorama of western sculpture. For here too were exhibited casts of Indian ancient monuments and sculpture, largely as a result of the work of Lt. Henry H. Cole, son of the Museum's Superintendent, who as a Royal Engineer was himself Superintendent of the Archaeological Survey of India's North Western Provinces.

Figure 15.3 Isabel Agnes Cowper, *South Kensington Museum, Eastern Cast Court, c.* 1872. Photograph: Albumen print. V&A Accession number. 72507.

In a photograph of the court in 1872 with decorative work in hand, taken by the museum's official photographer Isabel Agnes Cowper, can be seen a cast of the Eastern Gateway of the Great Stupa at Sanchi in India, thirty-three feet high (Figure 15.3). The Sanchi site, stumbled upon in 1818 by a British officer, Gen. Henry Taylor, had been partly excavated by various military expeditions and published by James Fergusson in *Tree and Serpent Worship* in 1868.[35] The cast was made by the Royal Engineers in 1869, at a cost of £900. Copies of the cast were made at South Kensington and were exhibited in Berlin and Paris. Their political significance was unmistakable: the monument was situated in British India, rediscovered, excavated, photographed and published by officers of the British Army: the South Kensington cast was proudly displayed in the imperial archive as a symbol of responsible British treatment of, and authority over, Indian history and culture. By such means, the British authorities claimed custodianship over the cultural terrain of Britain's Asiatic empire as well as the history of western art and design. The Sanchi cast was destroyed after the Second World War, after India and Pakistan won independence.

Whatever the claims to power and knowledge implicit in an imperial archive of facsimiles, however, such a display of simulacra does not exhibit the raw lust for colonial appropriation visible elsewhere at South Kensington; indeed it implicitly critiques the wholesale removal of antiquities from colonial settings when cast copies could produce such an effective reproduction leaving the original in situ. By contrast, the history of the treasures of Emperor Tewodros II, laid out in exemplary detail by Alexandra Watson Jones in Chapter 2, relates directly to British imperial violence, as does the exhibition of some objects seized during a bloody campaign in 1873-4 in response to Asante efforts to protect a coastal trading outlet. British forces invaded Kumasi on 4 February 1874 in what imperial historians Robinson and Gallagher describe as 'a sharp act of supremacy'[36] and the Asantehene, Kofi Karikari, fled. The precious royal regalia looted by British forces was later sold at auction at Garrard's in London, where the South Kensington Museum purchased several pieces. Greatest attention was paid to a *kyinië*, a huge canopy or parasol that was part of the royal regalia. It was given to Queen Victoria and placed on display in the cast court at South Kensington, incongruously juxtaposed with the full-size plaster cast of Donatello's St George, where it gained the derogatory nickname 'King Koffee's Umbrella. Such triumphalist displays were by no means universally admired. As Moncure Conway remarked in 1882, 'These African trophies are unpleasantly reminiscent of the worst phase of British policy'.[37]

Figure 15.4 Maw & Co., *Albertopolis Tile Panel c.* 1871–1888. Lead-glazed earthenware with underglaze blue and relief decoration. Inscribed MUSIC SCHOOL/ROYAL ALBERT HALL/SCIENCE SCHOOL/N. ARCADE HORTICULTURAL GARDENS & CONSERVATORY/FACADE INNER COURT KENSINGTON MUSEUM/MEMORIAL OF INTERNATIONAL EXHIBITION 1851. V&AC.158-1979.

Audio-visual intersections

Henry Cole was profoundly concerned to extend South Kensington's reach beyond the visual and material and into the aural sphere – that of music. One aspect of this was to fulfil Albert's vision of a large concert hall that might engineer a meeting of art and music under the auspices of the imperial-industrial state. After an extended wrangle over the proposed form and style of the building, on 20 May 1867 Victoria laid the foundation stone of 'The Royal Albert Hall of Arts and Sciences', a building created by Henry Scott in the neo-Renaissance style of South Kensington, but on a massive scale. The *Pall Mall Gazette* in 1872 felt that the Hall was 'more of an engineer's than an architect's building', but 'being at bottom a simple, genuine and effective piece of construction, on a big scale' it gave a 'sense of vastness with dignity'.[38] It looms large in a decorative tile panel made by Maw & Co to commemorate the institutions of Albertopolis (Figure 15.4).

The Albert Hall served as the site for massed choral events and musical competitions of a type already heralded by the Handel Festivals held at the Crystal Palace from 1857 and the brass band contests mounted there by Enderby Jackson. These provided visible and audible performances of class solidarity under the aegis of a benign liberal state. The tonic sol-fa movement offered the 'respectable artisan' the opportunity to assume bourgeois comportment.[39] Yet we may seek other valencies for the voices joined in choral singing, an activity that could be repressive as easily as it could be celebratory. On the one hand, as expressions of working-class solidarity, the great Chartist meetings were characterized by the collective singing, on a massive scale. A favoured item was the 'Hymn of the Unions:'

> Over mountain, over plain,
> Echoing wide, from sea to sea,
> Peals, and shall not peal in vain,
> The trumpet call of liberty.

'There were nine stanzas containing fifty-four lines in all,' recalled Chartist organizer George Holyoake: 'Never did political meeting so large sing a song so long, before or since in this world'.[40] Yet original research by Erin Johnson-Williams produces a quite different reading of choral singing in Chapter 6. Hymn singing, she notes, could also serve as an agent of colonial power, operating as 'a mandatory form of religious and pedagogical discipline' in the residential reform schools and concentration camps where imperial power revealed its full harshness.

At South Kensington, Cole believed that, as with the education of the 'respectable' working classes, education in music could yield social benefits:

> drawing is encouraged by the state because it is useful to individuals in industrial occupations; manufactures are improved by the artisan having a knowledge of drawing; but I think music is to be encouraged in order not that any special class, but that the country at large may derive benefit from it. It seems to me that it is the

business of some central institution – say the government – to take care that the musical talent of the country is not wasted and lost.⁴¹

These comments indicate that Cole was more interested in participatory music-making as a social good – formative of conformity and respectability – than he was in promoting concert going or canonizing the Austro-German classical tradition. In 1874, ground was broken for a new institution, the National Training School for Music, intended to 'take care' of the nation's music, largely by preparing music teachers for the schoolroom. Cole surely imagined that it would create a national bureaucracy to develop curricula and implement the teaching and examining of musical skills in the way that the South Kensington Schools had done for art and design. Cole's son, Henry Hardy Cole, returning from India, provided his services as architect free of charge, creating (again in South Kensington style) an eclectic neo-Renaissance palazzo with a plasterwork facade bearing decorative panels in *sgraffito*. The iconography and style all made preparation for a renaissance of English music to rival that of the arts in fifteenth-century Italy. Rather than by Mediciean patronage, this would be brought about through the institutional machinery of Albertopolis in conjunction with the free market. The facade was a euphoric declaration of faith in the effectiveness of government institutions to bring about cultural and economic improvement – of the imperial archive to reshape the world around it.

The National Training School for Music opened in the spring of 1876 with no less a luminary than Arthur Sullivan as principal. Eighty-two free scholarships had been established by donation, though the aim had been to fund 300. But Sullivan's heart was elsewhere and a series of Examiners' Reports, signed by some of London's leading musical figures, were highly critical of the lacklustre management of the School. The NTSM was then absorbed into a new, larger and more prestigious institution. The Royal College of Music was founded in 1883 and directed by a formidable administrator and scholar, George Grove, formerly secretary of the Crystal Palace at Sydenham. A new, vastly larger premises was designed by Arthur Blomfield. The aims of the RCM were substantially different from those of the NTSM. It was to transform standards in orchestral playing, and, by adding an opera school, to encourage British composers to create ambitious stage works. This was a Renaissance of sorts, but one that barely extended beyond the middle class, committed to a particular vision of classical music and uninterested in contemporary working-class culture.⁴² Lavish financial support for Blomfield's building, amounting to £45,000, was offered by Samson Fox, an industrialist who had patented at his Leeds works the use of corrugated steel in boilers and pressed steel undercarriages for railway cars. A foundation stone was laid in 1890, to musical accompaniment from Fox's Leeds Forge brass band which 'nearly blew the marquee away' – more a collision than an intersection of music as a manifestation of class.⁴³ While Cole's vision of a regulatory system of examinations did indeed come to fruition, it was in the form of another body, the Associated Board of the Royal Schools of Music (ABRSM), established in 1889 jointly by the Royal Academy of Music and the Royal College of Music. Whereas the standardized examinations in art and design were long ago abandoned, ABRSM examinations remain significant to this day, with more than half a million examinations per year, in UK and the countries of the Commonwealth, especially New Zealand, South Africa, Hong Kong, Malaysia and Singapore.[44]

Cole's successor, Philip Cunliffe-Owen, organized an event cementing South Kensington's commitment to popular imperialism, the Colonial and Indian Exhibition of 1886, which was attended by 5.5 million people.[45] This event was the very embodiment of the intersectionality of Albertopolis. Reaching across the entire campus, its plan offered visitors a simulacrum of the entirely of the British Empire with every territory represented by displays. It was a multimedia extravaganza, dedicated to persuading the mass of the British population to embrace imperial ideology. The exhibition opened in a blaze of ceremonial glory with a musical event at the new Albert Hall on 4 May 1886, one of the culminating pageants of empire.[46] Victoria was invited to be seated upon the golden throne of Ranjit Singh, captured during the annexation of the Punjab in 1849 and by 1886 a celebrated object in the South Kensington Museum's collection. It remains in the V&A today but was subject to an unsuccessful restitution claim in 1983.[47] For the 1886 opening event an Ode was specially written by Alfred, Lord Tennyson, and set to music by Sullivan:[48]

> Welcome, welcome with one voice!
> In your welfare we rejoice,
> Sons and brothers that have sent,
> From isle and cape and continent,
> Produce of your field and flood,
> Mount and mine, and primal wood;
> Works of subtle brain and hand,
> And splendors of the morning land,
> Gifts from every British zone;
> Britons, hold your own![49]

The opening of Sullivan's score opens with a magnificent orchestral flourish, followed by a hushed choral passage whose arching melody is taken by the chorus. Tennyson's first paragraph derives conceptually from the episteme of the 1851 Exhibition, which was reasserted with garish overemphasis in 1886. Its primary insistence on the extraction of raw materials and agricultural produce – 'Produce of your field and flood/Mount and mine, and primal wood' – is followed by consideration of the manual, but not machine, labour: 'Works of subtle brain and hand'. This took on a literal dimension in 1886, when visitors to the exhibition were able to watch a group of thirty-four living Indian craftsmen – 'native artisans ... at work as they would be in India'.[50] A draughtsman for the *Illustrated London News* depicted the 'Gold Brocade Weavers' at work in an informal, picturesque composition, suggesting that we have chanced upon this timeless scene in some remote Indian marketplace. Indeed, the catalogue featured colour-coded maps of the exhibition and of the world, with British possessions in pink, offering the visitor the chance to process through the empire in miniature. The exhibition was a massive exercise in publicity for the imperial ideal and a bonanza of national self-aggrandizement, the imperial archive as performative spectacle:

No alien, of whatever race he may be – Teuton, Gaul, Tartar or Mongol – can walk through the marvellous collection at South Kensington and look at the innumerable variations of our national Union Jack, without feeling the enormous influence that England has had, and still has, over every part of the globe.[51]

1886 by no means marked the last of the great imperial pageants; the British Empire Exhibition at Wembley in 1924 can claim that mantle. But it was certainly the most exuberant.[52]

The imperial jamboree had been such a success that, as after 1851, a permanent building was proposed, to create a 'an Institute which should represent the Arts, Manufacture and Commerce of the Queen's Colonial and Indian Empire. Such an institution would ... illustrate the progress already made during Her Majesty's reign in the Colonial and Indian Dominions, while it would record year by year the development of the Empire in the arts of civilization'.[53] The task and identity of the imperial archive now became far more explicit and legible. The financiers of the City of London, conceiving of it as primarily a commercial centre, argued against South Kensington as the site. However, Albertopolis had become so embedded in the symbolic geography of London, Britain and the British Empire as a point of intersection between empire and scholarship, between learning and display, education and entertainment, that the new Institute was indeed erected there, to a grandiose design by T. E. Colcutt. The foundation stone of granite from the Cape, on a pedestal of Indian bricks, was laid by Queen Victoria in 1887. The Institute's functions were to display Imperial produce, to illustrate the Empire's economic growth, to collect and disseminate commercial and other information; to hold special exhibitions, promote commercial and industrial education in the colonies and 'to advance systematic colonization'. Happily, it failed in each of these respects. The demolition of the Institute between 1957 and 1965 was a tangible sign that not only the empire, but its most visible architectural avatar, was gone.[54] Imperial College, renowned for science and engineering, now occupies the site. The tower is the sole survivor of Colcutt's building, a melancholy, phallic presence in today's post-colonial Albertopolis.

Envoi

The imperial archive is not the sole remnant of an empire that has vanished as a political entity. Racial capitalism and the resulting environmental crisis and political instability are also parts of its unsavoury legacy. While this essay has fully acknowledged the repressive functioning of such a grandiose institutional machine as Albertopolis in historical context, however, it dares to suggest in conclusion that, if subjected to rigorous critique and following the restitution of key looted or appropriated objects to communities of origin (a process we may call decolonization), that potential value remains in such institutions as those gathered at South Kensington for the present and future.[55] If the imperial archive was a powerful tool in the white supremacist project of the British Empire, in the settlement of class under industrialization and in the regulation of constructions of gender, that same archive can also, if subjected to an effective process of decolonization and epistemological challenge, contest the imperial endeavour and provide a generous space for a spectrum of alternatives.

Recent work at the former Tropenmuseum in Amsterdam, described and interrogated by Adiva Lawrence in Chapter 3, offers a powerful model for making visible the continuities between historical materials in the archived and lived experience in the present. A key aim of the 'Afterlives of Slavery' display at the Tropenmuseum was, in Lawrence's paraphrase, to make clear to visitors that 'the historical archive of slavery is still active in struggles for equality in the contemporary world, and that it continues to produce material culture'. The team at Durham University's Oriental Museum describe in Chapter 2 their creative response to the display of 'difficult objects', responses sensitive to contemporary local and global audiences. Such interpretative approaches could be applied with profit across the V&A's collections, thinking intersectionally about questions of class and gender as well as race. Indeed, a beginning has been made with the Museum's important self-reflexive account by Alexandra Watson Jones. The V&A's Research Department already shares with the Dutch Research Center for Material Culture (RCMC; as discussed by Lawrence) the aim of fostering interdisciplinary research; but by turning the imperial archive inside out South Kensington could also share the RCMCs aim 'to shed new lights on societal questions around issues of heritage, cultural identity and belonging that these objects raise'. This is all the more important given the diversity of London's present multicultural demography.

Given the range of collections, programs and archives it comprises, Albertopolis has unique potential for intersectional programming and outreach. If managed and presented self-reflexively, against the grain of its founders' intentions, the once-imperial museum can again serve a significant educational and social function in the present. It is necessary to put the machinery into reverse, generating positive change through intersectional engagements with multiple publics and communities, across media. The potential for a creative, decolonial restructuring of the archive is formidable.

Notes

1. Ann Laura Stoler, *Along the Archival Grain: Epistemic Anxieties and Colonial Common Sense* (Princeton: Princeton University Press, 2010), p. 1.
2. Felwine Sarr and Bénédicte Savoy, *Restitution of African Cultural Heritage: Toward a New Relational Ethics*, translated by Drew S. Burk (Paris, 2018), http://restitutionreport2018.com/sarr_savoy_en.pdf.
3. Ariella Aïsha Azoulay, *Potential History: Unlearning Imperialism* (London: Verso, 2019), p. x.
4. Stoler, *Along the Archival Grain*, p. 1.
5. Such concerns are entirely ignored, for example, in Christopher Wood, A History of Art History (Princeton: Princeton University Press, 2019).
6. Natalia Molina, Daniel Martinez Hosang, and Ramón A. Gutiérrez (eds), Relational Formations of Race: Theory, Method, and Practice (Berkeley CA: University of California Press, 2019), p. 3.

7   For a full exposition of this argument see Charlene Villaseñor Black and Tim Barringer, 'Decolonizing Art and Empire', *Art Bulletin*, forthcoming spring 2022. I am grateful to Charlene Villaseñor Black for productive discussion of these issues.
8   On the history of Durham's Memorial to the Great Exhibition and statue of Albert, erected in 1863, see 'The Memorial to the Exhibition of 1851', in F. H. W. Sheppard (ed.), *Survey of London*, Vol. 38, *South Kensington Museums Area* (London: Athlone Press, 1975), pp. 133–6.
9   The term 'racial capitalism' originated in Cedric Robinson, *Black Marxism: The Making of the Black Radical Tradition* (Chapel Hill: University of North Carolina Press [1983], 2000).
10 'Catalogue of the Museum of Manufactures', published as Appendix V of *First Report of the Department of Practical Art* (London: H. M. S. O., 1853), p. 233.
11 John Charles Robinson, *On the Museum of Art* in Introductory Addresses on the Science and Art Department and the South Kensington Museum, No. 5. (London: Chapman and Hall, 1858), p. 16.
12 Charles Thurston Thompson was the museum's official photographer. See Anthony J. Hamber, *'A Higher Branch of the Art': Photographing the Fine Arts in England, 1839–1880* (Amsterdam: Gordon and Breach, 1996).
13 See Tim Barringer, 'Blacksmith and Artist', in *Men at Work: Art and Labour in Victorian Britain* (New Haven: Yale University Press, 2005), pp. 133–86.
14 Henry Cole, 'Introduction', in *Official Descriptive and Illustrated Catalogue*, 3 vols. (London: Spicer Bros, 1851), Vol. 1: p. 1, quoted in Jeffrey A. Auerbach, *The Great Exhibition of 1851: A Nation on Display* (New Haven: Yale University Press, 1999), p. 96.
15 The Great Exhibition closed on 15 October 1851, but the Crystal Palace was re-erected, much enlarged, at Sydenham in South London, where it opened on 10 June 1854, and remained until destroyed by fire in 1936. A for-profit enterprise, the Crystal Palace at Sydenham was used for a variety of educational and commercial purposes, among them musical performances. See Kate Nichols and Sarah Victoria Turner (eds), *After 1851: The Material and Visual Cultures of the Crystal Palace at Sydenham* (Manchester: Manchester University Press, 2017).
16 *Great Exhibition of the Works of Industry of All Nations, 1851: Official Descriptive and Illustrated Catalogue*, 3 vols. (London: Spicer Brothers, 1851).
17 'Classification of Exhibits', quoted Auerbach, *The Great Exhibition of 1851*, p. 93.
18 [Prince Albert] 'Speech given at a Banquet given by the Right Hon. the Lord Mayor [of London], Thomas Farncombe, to Her Majesty's Ministers, Foreign Ambassadors, Royal Commissioners of the Exhibition of 1851 and the Mayors of one hundred and eighty towns, at the Mansion House', reprinted in *Principal Speeches and Addresses of His Royal Highness the Prince Consort* (London: John Murray, 1862), p. 112.
19 Prince Albert, 'Memorandum', in Martin Theodore, *The Life of HRH The Prince Consort*, Vol. 2 (London: Smith Elder, 1876), pp. 569–73.
20 *First Report of the Department of Practical Art* (London: H. M. S. O., 1853), p. 2.
21 Henry Cole, *Fifty Years of Public Work* (London: G. Bell, 1884), p. 292. See also Louise Purbrick, 'The South Kensington Museum: The Building of the House of Henry Cole', in M. Pointon (ed.), *Art Apart: Art Institutions and Ideology across England and North America* (Manchester: Manchester University Press, 1994), p. 83.
22 Henry Cole, *The Functions of the Science and Art Department* (London: Chapman and Hall, 1857), pp. 23–4.

23 Moncure Daniel Conway, *Travels in South Kensington, with Notes on Decorative Art and Architecture in England* (London: Trübner and Co, 1882), p. 25.
24 On 'respectability' see Mike Savage and Andrew Miles, *The Remaking of the British Working Class* (London: Routledge, 1994).
25 *Saturday Review*, 20 May 1865.
26 Theodore Adorno, 'Valery Proust Museum', in Samuel and Sherry Weber (trans.), *Prisms* (Cambridge, MA: MIT Press, 1983), pp. 175–77. See also Daniel J. Sherman, 'Quatremère/Benjamin/Marx: Art Museums, Aura and Commodity Fetishism', in Daniel J. Sherman and Irit Rogoff (eds), *Museum Culture: Histories, Discourses, Spectacles* (London: Routledge, 1994), pp. 123–43.
27 John Charles Robinson, 'Our National Collections', *Athenaeum* 27. 3 (1587): 403–4.
28 C [sic]. Waagen, 'Class XXX: Supplementary Report', in *The Great Exhibition of the Industry of All Nations: Reports by the Juries on Subjects in the Thirty Classes into which the Exhibition was Divided* (London: Spicer Brothers, 1852), Vol. 2, p. 1558.
29 John Charles Robinson, 'Our National Collections', *Athenaeum* 27. 3 (1587): 403–4.
30 Sheppard, *Survey of London*, p. 110.
31 S. Phillips, *Guide to the Crystal Palace* (London: Bradbury and Evans, 1857), pp. 141–3. I am grateful to Christine Olson for discussion of Owen Jones.
32 Julius Bryant, *Designing the V&A: The Museum as a Work of Art* (London: Lund Humphries, 2019), pp. 108–11.
33 Edward Said, *Orientalism* (New York: Vintage Books, 1979).
34 John Physick, *The Victoria and Albert Museum: The History of Its Building* (London: V&A, 1982), pp. 156–60.
35 James Fergusson, *Tree and Serpent Worship: Or, Illustrations of Mythology and Art in India in the First and Fourth Centuries after Christ* (London: India Museum, 1868); and Tapati Guha-Thakurta, *Monuments, Objects, Histories: Institutions of Art in Colonial and Postcolonial India* (New York: Columbia University Press, 2004), pp. 38–9.
36 Ronald Robinson and John Gallagher, *Africa and the Victorians: The Climax of Imperialism* (Garden City, New York: Doubleday, 1981), p. 31.
37 Conway, *Travels*, p. 71.
38 Sidney Colvin, 'The Albert Memorial', *Pall Mall Gazette* 2306 (5 July 1872), p. 74.
39 See Charles McGuire, *Music and Victorian Philanthropy: The Tonic Sol-Fa Movement* (Cambridge: Cambridge University Press, 2009).
40 George Jacob Holyoake, *Sixty Years of an Agitator's Life* (London: T. Fisher Unwin, 1893), Vol. 1, p. 30. See also Kate Bowan and Paul A. Pickering, '"Songs for the Millions": Chartist Music and Popular Aural Tradition', *Labour History Review* 74. 1 (2009), p. 48.
41 Society for the Encouragement of Arts, Manufacturers and Commerce, *First Report of the Committee ... on the State of Musical Education at Home and Abroad* (1866), quoted David Wright, 'The South Kensington Music Schools and the Development of the British Conservatoire in the Late Nineteenth Century', *Journal of the Royal Musical Association* 130. 2 (2005): 240.
42 Meirion Hughes and Robert Stradling, *The English Musical Renaissance, 1840–1940: Constructing a National Music* (Manchester: Manchester University Press, 2001).
43 Quoted in Sheppard, *Survey of London*, p. 229.
44 For a related case study, see Erin Johnson-Williams, 'The Examiner and the Evangelist: Authorities of Music and Empire, c. 1894', *Journal of the Royal Musical Association* 145. 2 (2020): 317–50.

45 John Mackenzie, *Propaganda and Empire: The Manipulation of British Public Opinion, 1880-1960* (Manchester: Manchester University Press, 1984), pp. 101-2.
46 'The Queen Opening the Colonial and Indian Exhibition', *Graphic* (8 May 1886), p. 487.
47 Richard Davis, *Lives of Indian Images* (Princeton: Princeton University Press, 1997), pp. 174-6; 181.
48 *Graphic*, 8 May 1886, p. 487; Tim Barringer, 'The South Kensington Museum and the Colonial Project', in Tim Barringer and Tom Flynn (eds), *Colonialism and the Object: Empire, Material Culture and the Museum* (London: Routledge, 1998), pp. 23-5; Saloni Mathur, 'Living Ethnological Exhibits: The Case of 1886', *Cultural Anthropology* 15. 4 (2000): 494-5; and Frank Cundall (ed.), *Reminiscences of the Colonial and Indian Exhibition* (London: Clowes and Sons, 1886).
49 Alfred Tennyson, *The Poetic and Dramatic Works of Alfred Lord Tennyson* (Boston: Houghton Mifflin, 1899), p. 657. See also Emily A. Haddad, 'Tennyson, Arnold, and the Wealth of the East', *Victorian Literature and Culture* 32. 2 (2004): 373-91, discussion on, pp. 385-6.
50 Cundall, *Reminiscences of the Colonial and Indian Exhibition*, p. 29. For a sophisticated analysis, see Mathur, 'Living Ethnological Exhibits', pp. 492-524.
51 *Graphic*, 8 May 1886.
52 Jiyi Ryu, 'Visualising and Experiencing the British Imperial World: The British Empire Exhibition at Wembley (1924/25)' (PhD: University of York, 2018).
53 *Times*, 20 September 1886.
54 Mackenzie, *Propaganda and Empire*, pp. 122-46.
55 For concerns about the use of this term in relation to practices that are the product of empires, see Tim Barringer, 'Decolonization', in Catherine Grant and Dorothy Price, 'Decolonizing Art History', *Art History* 43 (2020): 8-66; see pp. 11-14.

Bibliography

Adorno, Theodore. 'Valery Proust Museum'. In *Prisms*, translated by Samuel and Sherry Weber, 175-7. Cambridge, MA: MIT Press, 1983.

Albert, Prince Consort. *Principal Speeches and Addresses of His Royal Highness the Prince Consort*. London: John Murray, 1862.

Albert, Prince Consort. 'Memorandum'. In *The Life of HRH the Prince Consort*, edited by Martin Theodore, Vol. 2, 569-73. London: Smith Elder, 1876.

Auerbach, Jeffrey A. *The Great Exhibition of 1851: A Nation on Display*. New Haven: Yale University Press, 1999.

Azoulay, Ariella Aïsha. *Potential History: Unlearning Imperialism*. London: Verso, 2019.

Barringer, Tim. 'The South Kensington Museum and the Colonial Project'. In *Colonialism and the Object: Empire, Material Culture and the Museum*, edited by Tim Barringer and Tom Flynn, 11-27. London: Routledge, 1998.

Barringer, Tim. *Men at Work: Art and Labour in Victorian Britain*. New Haven: Yale University Press, 2005.

Barringer, Tim. 'Decolonization'. In Catherine Grant and Dorothy Price, 'Decolonizing Art History'. *Art History* 43 (2020): 8-66.

Black, Charlene Villaseñor, and Tim Barringer. 'Decolonizing Art and Empire', *Art Bulletin* 104, no. 1 (2022): 6-20.

Bowan, Kate, and Paul A. Pickering. '"Songs for the Millions": Chartist Music and Popular Aural Tradition'. *Labour History Review* 74, no. 1 (2009): 44–63.

Bryant, Julius. *Designing the V&A: The Museum as a Work of Art*. London: Lund Humphries, 2019.

'Catalogue of the Museum of Manufactures'. Published as Appendix V of *First Report of the Department of Practical Art*. London: H. M. S. O., 1853.

Cole, Henry. 'Introduction'. In *Official Descriptive and Illustrated Catalogue*, 3 vols. 1–35. London: Spicer Bros, 1851.

Cole, Henry. *Fifty Years of Public Work*. London: G. Bell, 1884.

Cole, Henry. *The Functions of the Science and Art Department*. London: Chapman and Hall, 1857.

Colvin, Sidney. 'The Albert Memorial'. *Pall Mall Gazette* 2306 (5 July 1872): 74.

Conway, Moncure Daniel. *Travels in South Kensington, with Notes on Decorative Art and Architecture in England*. London: Trübner and Co, 1882.

Cundall, Frank (ed.). *Reminiscences of the Colonial and Indian Exhibition*. London: Clowes and Sons, 1886.

Davis, Richard. *Lives of Indian Images*. Princeton: Princeton University Press, 1997.

Fergusson, James. *Tree and Serpent Worship: or, Illustrations of Mythology and Art in India in the First and Fourth Centuries After Christ*. London: India Museum, 1868.

Guha-Thakurta, Tapati. *Monuments, Objects, Histories: Institutions of Art in Colonial and Postcolonial India*. New York: Columbia University Press, 2004.

Haddad, Emily A. 'Tennyson, Arnold, and the Wealth of the East'. *Victorian Literature and Culture* 32, no. 2 (2004): 373–91.

Hamber, Anthony J. *'A Higher Branch of the Art': Photographing the Fine Arts in England, 1839–1880*. Amsterdam: Gordon and Breach, 1996.

Henry Cole. *Great Exhibition of the Works of Industry of All Nations, 1851: Official Descriptive and Illustrated Catalogue*, 3 vols. London: Spicer Brothers, 1851.

Holyoake, George Jacob. *Sixty Years of an Agitator's Life*, Vol. 1. London: T. Fisher Unwin, 1893.

Hughes, Meirion, and Robert Stradling. *The English Musical Renaissance, 1840–1940: Constructing a National Music*. Manchester: Manchester University Press, 2001.

Johnson-Williams, Erin. 'The Examiner and the Evangelist: Authorities of Music and Empire, c. 1894', *Journal of the Royal Musical Association* 145, no. 2 (2020): 317–50.

Mackenzie, John. *Propaganda and Empire: The Manipulation of British Public Opinion, 1880–1960*. Manchester: Manchester University Press, 1984.

Mathur, Saloni. 'Living Ethnological Exhibits: The Case of 1886'. *Cultural Anthropology* 15, no. 4 (2000): 492–524.

McGuire, Charles. *Music and Victorian Philanthropy: The Tonic Sol-Fa Movement*. Cambridge: Cambridge University Press, 2009.

Molina, Natalia, Daniel Martinez Hosang, and Ramón A. Gutiérrez (eds). *Relational Formations of Race: Theory, Method, and Practice*. Berkeley, CA: University of California Press, 2019.

Nichols Kate, and Sarah Victoria Turner (eds). *After 1851: The Material and Visual Cultures of the Crystal Palace at Sydenham*. Manchester: Manchester University Press, 2017.

Phillips, S. *Guide to the Crystal Palace*. London: Bradbury and Evans, 1857.

Physick, John. *The Victoria and Albert Museum: The History of Its Building*. London: V&A, 1982.

Purbrick, Louise. 'The South Kensington Museum: The Building of the House of Henry Cole'. In *Art Apart: Art Institutions and Ideology across England and North America*, edited by M. Pointon, 69–86. Manchester: Manchester University Press, 1994.
'The Queen Opening the Colonial and Indian Exhibition'. *Graphic* (8 May 1886): 487.
Robinson, Cedric. *Black Marxism: The Making of the Black Radical Tradition*. Chapel Hill: University of North Carolina Press, [1983] 2000.
Robinson, John Charles. 'Our National Collections'. *Athenaeum* 27, no. 3 (1857): 403–4.
Robinson, John Charles. On the Museum of Art in *Introductory Addresses on the Science and Art Department and the South Kensington Museum*, No. 5. London: Chapman and Hall, 1858.
Robinson, Ronald, and John Gallagher. *Africa and the Victorians: The Climax of Imperialism*. Garden City, New York: Doubleday, 1981.
Ryu, Jiyi. 'Visualising and Experiencing the British Imperial World: The British Empire Exhibition at Wembley (1924/25)'. PhD: University of York, 2018.
Said, Edward. *Orientalism*. New York: Vintage Books, 1979.
Sarr, Felwine, and Bénédicte Savoy. *Restitution of African Cultural Heritage: Toward a New Relational Ethics*, translated by Drew S. Burk (Paris, 2018). http://restitutionreport2018.com/sarr_savoy_en.pdf.
Savage, Mike, and Andrew Miles. *The Remaking of the British Working Class*. London: Routledge, 1994.
Sheppard, F. H. W. (ed.), *Survey of London*, Vol. 38, *South Kensington Museums Area*, London: Athlone Press, 1975.
Sherman, Daniel J. 'Quatremère/Benjamin/Marx: Art Museums, Aura and Commodity Fetishism'. In *Museum Culture: Histories, Discourses, Spectacles*, edited by Daniel J. Sherman and Irit Rogoff, 123–43. London: Routledge, 1994.
Stoler, Ann Laura. *Along the Archival Grain: Epistemic Anxieties and Colonial Common Sense*. Princeton: Princeton University Press, 2010.
Tennyson, Alfred. *The Poetic and Dramatic Works of Alfred Lord Tennyson*. Boston: Houghton Mifflin, 1899.
Waagen, C [sic]. 'Class XXX: Supplementary Report'. In *The Great Exhibition of the Industry of All Nations: Reports by the Juries on Subjects in the Thirty Classes into which the Exhibition was Divided*, Vol. 2, 1547–87. London: Spicer Brothers, 1852.
Wright, David. 'The South Kensington Music Schools and the Development of the British Conservatoire in the Late Nineteenth Century'. *Journal of the Royal Musical Association*, 130, no. 2 (2005): 236–82.

Index

Aboriginal
  in Australia 142, 144–5, 148
  in Canada 116–17, 126
Aborigines' Friend 142, 147
Aborigines Protection Society (APS) 142–4
Abrahams, Yvette 175–7
Abyssinia. *See* Ethiopia
Acropolis 258, 265–6, 271, 272
Adorno, Theodore 286–7
Africa/African 57, 61, 72, 74–6, 143, 173, 208–9
African Institution 172–3, 178
Afrikaner. *See* Boer
Afterlives of Slavery exhibition 10, 51–3, 55–63, 76, 296
Albertopolis 282–3, 288, 292–6
Albert, Prince Consort 284–5
Alemayehu, Prince 72, 74, 80
Amsterdam 9, 51, 54, 57, 63
Anglican missions 12, 204, 206
animals, paintings of 98–106
Anne With an E 117–19
anticlericalism 221, 227–8
antiquity, Greco-Roman 8, 256, 258, 272
Apartheid 124–6
archaeology 6, 8, 52, 61, 271
Archer, Mildred 95–6, 103
archives 2, 7–8, 116, 119, 126, 231, 256–7, 272–273. *See also* digitisation; ephemera; ownership
  access 2, 16 n.12, 273
  activism 6, 9–13, 18 n.29
  authority 3–4, 266, 270
  debris 1–2
  defined 53
  ethics 231–3, 264
  evidence 12–13, 172, 177
  excess 97
  fetishization 3–4, 12, 15, 172, 258
  gaps 9, 11, 41, 117, 119
  museum 43, 53, 61, 189, 259, 270, 272
  'new archival turn' 3–4, 6, 9–14
  re-archiving 11, 63, 116, 124–6
  relational 2–4, 7, 9
  relics 263–4
  silences 6–7, 14, 116–17, 121, 124–6
  theory 257, 264
art. *See also* collecting
  Company 91, 103, 106, 107 n.2
  European 104–5
  Greek 257
  history 282
  Indian 103
  objects 193
  performance 249
artefacts 8, 13, 33, 39, 42–4, 56–7, 92, 242, 255–7, 260, 264, 272
Arthur, Walter George 144–5
Arts Council England (ACE) 36, 47 n.15
Asia
  South Asia 10, 36, 38–41, 46, 91–2, 104, 106
  Southeast Asia 36, 38–9, 45
Asiatic Society of Bengal 104–5
assimilation 119–20
Assmann, Aleida 138, 142, 147
Associated Board of the Royal Schools of Music (ABRSM) 293–4
Athens 211, 258, 260, 263–7, 270–1
audiences 13–14, 35–6, 38, 46, 140, 146, 175, 177–9, 243, 245–7, 251
audio-visual, intersections between 292–5
Australia
  literature 137–42, 144–5, 147–8
  theatre archives 148
Auxiliatrices des Ames du Purgatoire, Les (the Helpers of the Holy Souls of Purgatory) 223–5, 228–31

Baartman, Sara (Saartje) 12, 171–3, 179–81, 183 n.46
  European exotic 173–6
  ventriloquizing for 176–9
Barnard Castle 187–8
Barrackpore 95–6, 100, 104
Baxi, Pratiksha 159–60
belonging 8, 55, 76, 121, 206, 296
Berhanu, Samuel 78–9
Bett-Bett 138, 140–1
Bible 145, 210–11, 213
bilingual 45–6
biography 11–12, 14, 74, 194, 204, 206, 209, 262–4
biopolitics 60, 115–16, 119, 121–2
birds, paintings of 95, 97–8, 100, 102, 106
Black Archives, The 57–8
Black Lives Matter 2, 62, 81, 115
Black Pete (Zwarte Piet) 58, 62
Black women 5, 62, 164
de Blainville, Henri 174, 182 n.17
Blyth, Edward 104–5
Boer 124–5
Bowes, John 12, 187, 190–1, 194
Bowes, Joséphine 12, 187–94
Bowes Museum, The 6, 9, 12, 187–9, 194
Bradford, Clare 139–41, 152 n.63
Brahman, Darshan 158–9
brass band contests 292–3
Bridell-Fox, Eliza 255, 257, 260, 264–7, 268, 270, 272
Britain 6, 11, 13–14, 38, 71–5, 77, 79, 124–5, 147, 171–2, 179, 203, 207, 209, 211–13, 271, 288, 291, 295
Britannia Theatre, Hoxton 247–8
British Army 45, 72, 77, 290
British Library 10, 91, 96, 98, 102–3, 247, 256
British Museum 9, 13, 74, 81, 103, 241, 255–60, 264–72, 285, 287
  Elgin Room 13, 255–60, 263, 265–7, 272
  Parthenon sculptures 13, 256–8, 263, 265, 270, 272, 274 n.6, 274 n.9, 285
Brune, Thomas 144–8
Buchanan-Hamilton, Francis 95, 98, 106

Caesars, Hendrick 172, 176–7, 179–80, 184 n.69
Calcutta 93–5, 104

Cambridge University Library 255–6, 273, 273 n.1
Canada 11, 63, 116–17, 119, 121–6, 129 n.18
cancan 192, 245, 250–1
canon 2, 7–8, 11, 115, 137–9, 142, 144, 147–8, 224, 289, 293
capitalism, racial 117, 281, 283, 295, 297 n.9
caracal, paintings of 98–9
carceral 63, 115–17, 120–6, 127 n.3
Carey, Daniel 171–2
Caribbean, the 56–7, 212, 284
Castañeda, Claudia 141–2
Catholic congregations 223, 228, 233, 235 n.27
Catholicism 13, 221, 223–4, 226–9, 232–3, 235 n.27
censorship 6, 12, 14, 145, 187–8, 194, 242–3
Chapman, Caroline 188, 190
childhood 141–2, 222
childlessness 12, 187–8, 193–4
children
  culture 5, 255–6
  literature 10, 14, 139–41, 255–7, 272
  magazines 13, 256–8, 263–5, 270, 271–2
  periodicals 255–9, 262, 271–2
Children's Friend, The 259–60, 263, 272
China 33, 45–6, 289
Christian Cole Society for Classicists of Colour, the 214 n.5
Christianity 72, 74, 122–3, 144, 146, 211–12, 258, 265
church 72–4, 76–8, 123, 206, 208, 211, 224, 226–30, 232, 259, 265–6
Clarke, Courtney 257, 260–1, 263–6
classical
  history 264
  reception 4, 8, 19 n.43, 255
Classics 2, 7–8, 255, 257
classification 6–7, 101–2, 106–7, 284–5
class, social inequalities 3, 5, 51, 61, 187, 191–2, 229, 281
coercion 116–18, 122, 145
Coffin Chevallier, Joséphine 191–2
Cole, Christian Frederick 12, 203–13

Cole, Henry 284–5, 288–9, 292–3
Colenso, John 209, 211–12
collecting 74
    archival 32–4
    art 106, 187–8
    and health 193
collections
    Chinese 33
    Enthoven 241
    online 36–7
    Oriental Museum 41, 289
    Serfoji 92
    South Kensington Museum (*See* South Kensington Museum)
    V&A's Ethiopian 10, 71–6, 296
colonial/colonialism 10–11, 31, 63, 74, 91–2, 126, 139–40, 147–8, 159, 161–3, 171, 281–2
    British 33, 45, 162
    Dutch 51, 55
    European 61, 91
    incarceration 7, 11, 117–18, 120–1, 126, 128 n.11, 148
    India 159–62
    legacies 10, 40, 52, 60, 71–2, 81–2, 115, 160
    logics 52
    settler 115–17, 120–3, 126, 146, 282
    site 54–5
community
    engagement 9, 32, 39
    home 281
    imagined 140
    Sikh 41
    source 36
concentration camps 115, 117, 121–2, 124–6, 127 n.3, 145, 292
confession (Catholicism) 157, 159–60, 162, 228
conflict 32, 42, 74, 102, 256–7, 270
congregational archives 222–6, 230–2. *See also* nursing, nuns, mission stations, hymns
consent 53, 117, 228
control 120, 204, 243
conversion, religious 115, 229
Conway, Moncure Daniel 285, 291
courts of law, India 160–2
Covid-19 2, 5, 14, 37, 46

Crais, Clifton 173, 179–81
Crenshaw, Kimberlé 5, 17 n.23
Crystal Palace
    Greek Court in 260–1
    in Hyde Park 283–4
    in Sydenham 260–1, 289, 293, 297 n.15
curation 6, 10, 13, 115, 119, 188, 210, 223, 257
Curtis, Sarah A. 222, 227, 232
Cuvier, Georges 172–4

dance. *See* cancan
deaccessioning 31, 33–4, 44
dealers, art 188, 190
death 1, 43, 52, 76, 94, 104, 125, 142–3, 145–6, 163, 187, 190, 192, 206, 248
debris, archival 1–2
decolonial 2, 4, 6–8, 14–15, 36, 115–17, 119–20, 124–6, 130 n.32, 283, 295–6
Derrida, Jacques 1–2, 239–40, 248
Diamond, Beverley 119, 122
digitization 15, 81, 138, 255, 257, 273. *See also* archives
discipline 2, 7, 11, 58, 94, 106, 116–17, 122, 125, 207, 282, 292
display 8–10, 12–13, 33–5, 37–43, 58–60, 71, 73–82, 172, 175–7, 188, 255–61, 263–8, 271–2, 291, 295–6
dolls 259–63, 267
Donne, W. B. 242, 244–5, 252–3 n.30
donor(s) 9, 33, 41, 229
drums 57. *See also* music
du Maurier, George 262–3
Dunlop, Alexander 172, 176, 179
Durham, County 9, 36, 188
Durham University 2, 9, 31–6, 42–4, 76, 281, 296
Dutch
    in the Netherlands 51–4, 56, 58–9, 63
    in South Africa 124–6
Dutch National Museum of World Cultures, NMW 10, 51–2

East End, London 247–8
East India Company 10, 54, 91–5, 102, 107 n.1, 108 n.7, 284, 287
education 11, 14, 32, 212–13, 231, 258–9, 262–4, 285–6, 288–9, 292, 295

Elgin, Lord 265–6, 270
Elgin Room. *See* British Museum, Elgin Room
empire 8, 31, 40, 116–17, 119, 122, 126, 211, 281–4, 286–9, 294–5
enclosure 11, 115–22, 126, 127 n.3
England 9, 32, 36, 72, 189–93, 203–4, 206, 209–12, 265, 270–1
English, language 40, 77, 96, 116–18, 121–4, 126
Enthoven Collection 241. *See also* Theatre and Performance Collections
envoi 295–6
ephemera 1, 6–8, 13–14, 242, 250–1, 251 n.1, 255, 257–8, 272. *See also* archives
ethics, archival 231–3, 264, 271
Ethiopia 10, 71–81
    Embassy in London 10, 75
    Ethiopian Orthodox Church 74, 78
Europe 6, 43, 59–60, 94, 172, 175, 177, 180–1, 191, 223, 262, 264, 287
evidence, archival 12–13, 162, 172, 174, 177, 181, 206, 223, 227–8, 245, 247, 250, 257, 270–71, 284
Exell, Karen 78–9

faith 32, 36, 39–42, 45–6, 105, 124, 293
fertility. *See* infertility
fetishization 3, 12, 15, 172, 258
Flinders Island Chronicle (1836–7) 138, 144–7
Foucault, Michel 6–7, 52–3, 60–1, 116, 120, 128 n.8, 160, 239–40
Freetown 205–6, 209
French congregations 223–7
Friendly Companion, The (1857) 259–60, 265
funding 32, 40, 45, 55, 94, 181, 229, 242, 248

gallery 10, 31, 33, 35, 37–42, 47 n.12, 63, 76, 81, 207, 246–7, 267, 285, 289
gatekeeping 13–14, 226–7, 257, 263, 272
gender 6, 160, 163, 178, 232, 236 n.51, 283, 295–6
Girl's Own Paper, The (1885) 255–8, 260, 264, 267
gonorrhoea 190–1, 193
good luck flag 42–5

Gordon-Chipembere, Natasha 173, 176, 180
graves, unmarked 116–17
Great Exhibition of the Industry of All Nations (1851) 283–4, 297 n.15
Grecian Stories (1840) 270–2
Greek 257, 260, 263–7, 271, 272
Guardian, The 14, 116
guidebooks, in museums 194, 256, 262, 266–7
Gunn, Jeannie 11, 137, 140–1, 147–8

Hack, Maria 270–2
Hale, Mathew 142–4, 147–8, 150 n.33
harmony
    musical 118–22, 124–6, 284, 292–4
    musical instruments 57–8, 284
    social 122
Hartman, Saidiya 1, 52–3, 58, 130 n.31
hierarchies, institutional 3–4, 61, 78, 115, 118–21, 139, 282–3
Higher Education (HE) 5, 32–3
Himalayas 10, 35, 38–9
Hindu 39, 97, 105, 158
historiography 2, 6, 8, 11–12, 15, 78, 92, 138, 188, 190, 222, 225, 231
history, of archives 2, 4–8, 10, 38, 53, 56, 58–9, 72–4, 92, 94–6, 222, 224, 226–32, 241–9, 282, 291
Hodgson, Brian Houghton 102–4
Holmes, Rachel 174, 184 n.69
Hottentot Venus 12, 171, 173, 175–6, 178, 181
Hoxton 247–8
Hoxworth, Kellen 172–3
hymnic coloniality 121–3
hymns 11, 63, 115–26, 129 n.22, 131 n.52, 204

ideology 11, 14, 122, 138–9, 145–7, 282–4, 286, 289
imperialism 1–2, 4, 6, 10–11, 13, 71, 116–17, 119, 122, 125, 143, 147–8, 281–4, 287–96
incarceration 7, 11, 116–18, 120–2, 124–6, 145, 148
India
    art 92, 103, 106
    Independence 40

Indigenous Canadians 117
  natural history in 94–6
  Office 95, 107
  Partition 41
Indigenous/Indigeneity 11, 74, 92, 116–18, 120–3, 125–6, 138–48, 173, 204, 231
Indonesia 52, 54, 56
industrialization 61, 284, 295
infantilization
  Indigenous archive 144–7
  literary classic 139–42
  settler archive 142–4
infertility 187–8. *See also* childlessness
institutions
  ability 115
  abuse 118
  and collectors 33
  histories 222, 230
  power 2, 11, 116, 270
  racism 117
intersectionality 5–6, 8–9, 14, 17 n.23, 294
invisibility 13–14, 203–4, 209, 221–3, 230, 281
Itwaria, Mussamat 157–60, 162–3, 165 n.19

Jahangir, Shah 103, 109 n.18, 110 n.45
Japan 42–5, 48 n.33, 289
jewellery 73, 76, 80, 284

Ka'kwet 117–18
Kemble, Philip 178–9
Kind Words for Boys and Girls (1881) 260–1, 265
knowledge, sharing 39–40
Kunstkammer 93–4

language 7, 32, 37–8, 40, 57, 59, 61, 63, 79, 81, 116–18, 121–4, 126, 177, 179
Lazreg, Marnia 161–2
Lemke, Thomas 60–1
liberation 116, 126
Links Japan 44, 48 n.33
Linnean Society of London 94, 104
listening 8, 124–5
literature, children's. *See* children, literature

Little Black Princess, The (1905) 11, 137–42, 144, 148
lockdowns. *See* Covid-19
London. *See* East End; West End
looted 10, 14, 21 n.55, 42, 72–9, 281, 287, 291, 295
Lord Chamberlain's Office 13, 242–7
Lose Your Mother (2006) 52–3

Macaulay, Zachary 172, 176–8, 180, 184 n.69, 209
Madras 92–3, 96, 103
magazines. *See* children, magazines
Magubane, Zine 172–4
Mandela, Nelson 124–6
Maqdala 10, 59, 71–5, 82
  curating 75–9
  legacy of 81
  responses to 79–81
marble fragments 256, 258–9, 271. *See also* British Museum, Elgin Room; British Museum, Parthenon sculptures
Mathews, Anne 173, 175, 179
Mathews, Mrs Charles 178–9
Maxwell, J. Renner 210, 216 n.36
Mbembe, Achille 137, 163, 211, 216 n.37
mechanization 284, 287
Memoirs of Charles Mathews, Comedian (1839) 175, 178–9
methodologies, intersectional 3–8
Miller, Benjamin 144–5, 147–8, 149 n.1, 151 n.48
mission stations 12, 72, 91, 93, 103, 117, 122, 124–5, 162, 204, 206, 210–12
Modest, Wayne 52, 54–6, 72, 81
Monteiro, Marit 226, 231–2
Moojen, John George 176, 178, 180
Mughal 41, 95, 102–3
Mullick, Rajendra 104–5
museums
  archive 43, 53, 61, 189, 259, 270, 273
  British 9, 74, 81, 103, 241, 255–60, 264–72, 287
  colonial 54–5
  Oriental 32–6, 41, 45
  small 37
music 7–8, 10–11, 115, 117–21, 292–4

musicology 2, 4, 7–8, 115, 126 n.1, 130 n.32
Mysore 95–6

Nair, Savithri Preetha 92–4, 96
Nana 192, 197 n.54
Nanavutty, E. M. 157–9
National Museum of World Cultures (NMW) 51–2, 55, 62
Natural History Museum 103, 256, 282
naturalists 93, 101–6
Ndlovu, Siphiwe Gloria 180–1
Nemser, Daniel 121–2
Nepal 102, 104
Netflix 117–18
Nettlebeck, Amanda 145–6
neutrality 59, 239, 265
Newcastle 39, 41
nineteenth century 1–15, 31–2, 43, 52–3, 57, 60–1, 71, 91–2, 95, 101, 115–16, 119–22, 124–6, 138–41, 144, 148, 158, 160–2, 173–6, 187–90, 194, 203–4, 206, 209, 221–3, 225, 231–2, 239, 241, 243, 247–51, 255–9, 270, 272–273
North East of England 9, 32, 36
nuns 13, 221–3, 225, 228–32
nursing 221–5, 227–31, 233 n.4

O'Brien, Susan 222, 232
online, collections 36–7
oppression 61, 116, 125, 158, 211
Oriental Museum, Durham University 6, 9, 31–7, 41–6, 59, 76, 281, 296
Osborne, Thomas 71, 78
Oscar Wilde 241, 263
otherness 172, 212, 223
ownership 2, 5, 9, 15, 80–1, 222, 226–31, 264. *See also* archives
Oxford Union 205–7, 209

Pacific 43, 71
Pakistan 46, 291
Paris 172, 178, 191–3, 230, 243
Parks, Suzan-Lori 173–4
Parthenon sculptures. *See* British Museum, Parthenon sculptures
pedagogy 2, 34, 117, 258, 260, 292
performance 6, 58–9, 249, 255

Pericles 260, 263
periodicals. *See* children, periodicals
permanent galleries 10, 34, 37–41, 74
Peter Parley's 260–1, 266–7
Peterson, Indira 92–4
Petites Sœurs des Pauvres, Les (the Little Sisters of the Poor) 223–5, 228–9, 231
Phidias 263–4
Phigaleian room, British Museum 260, 267
police 11, 157–62, 243, 246–7, 249. *See also* torture
postcolonialism 4, 7, 35, 51, 62, 91, 120, 123–6, 282, 295
power 1–14, 53–4, 60–2, 71–2, 91, 115–22, 125–6, 146, 163
  dynamics 9, 160, 163, 180, 223
Prichard, James Cowles 143–4, 151 n.37
priest 76, 118, 206, 224, 229–30
Prigsby. *See* Wilde, Oscar
prisons 115–17, 119–22, 124–6
prostitution 191, 242–3
Public Record Office 13, 242–3
Punch 262–3

race (racism) 5–7, 11, 32, 36, 51, 56, 58–9, 61–3, 74, 117, 123, 140–4, 146, 171–6, 180–1, 209–12, 264, 283, 295
  capitalism 117, 281, 283, 295
  taxonomies and material culture 283–7
rape 11, 159–63
reconstruction 250, 257–8, 263, 266–9, 272
records 37, 44, 53, 77, 81, 96, 106–7, 118–19, 121–2, 124, 139, 142, 189, 206, 210, 212, 225–9, 231–2, 246
Reflections on the Zulu War (1879) 204, 207–8, 210–11
relics, archival 241, 263–5
religious conversion 115, 229
repatriation 6, 9–10, 13–14, 34, 75, 81, 255, 257, 266, 271–2
Research Centre for Material Culture (RCMC) 52, 55–7, 59, 62–4, 296
residential schools, in Canada 116–19, 121–3, 125–6

resistance 6–7, 11, 58, 63, 115–16, 119–21, 123–5, 138, 145–8
restoration, of objects 224, 257, 266–7
Robinson Crusoe 171, 177
Robinson, George 144–6
Romanticism 142, 144, 174, 257–8, 263–4, 270, 272
Rome 224, 263, 282, 289
Royal College of Music 13, 282, 293
Royal Tropical Institute. *See* Koninklijk Instituut voor de Tropen (KIT)

Said, Edward 147, 181, 289
Sanchi 290–1
School of Oriental Studies, Durham University 31–2, 38
schools. *See also* Training Schools
  in Britain 288
  in Canada 126
Schwartz, Charles Friedrich 93–4
science 94, 174–5, 221. *See also* zoology
Scott, Henry 289, 292
Scully, Pamela 173, 179–81
sculptures 13, 255–6, 258, 261, 263–7, 270–2
sea-bathing 191, 193
Second Vatican Council 224–5
Second World War 32, 43, 291
Serfoji, Raja II Bhonsie 91–106, 287
Seven Little Australians (1894) 147–8, 152 n.63
sexual health 11–12, 187, 194
sexually transmitted infections 187–8, 190–3
sexual violence 11, 157, 159–64, 174. *See also* violence
Sibpur Botanic Garden 93, 104
Sierra Leone 12, 203–4, 206–12
Sikh 39, 41–2
silence
  archival 7, 13–14, 116–17, 120–1, 124–5, 270–71
  musical 118–22, 124–6, 293–4
  sonic 11, 116, 118–19, 121–2, 124, 126
Singh, Amar 92–3
singing 11, 115, 118–19, 125–6, 128 n.16. *See also* hymns
  congregational 115, 129 n.22, 222–32

slavery 10, 51–63, 143, 163, 171, 177–8, 282, 296
Smithsonian Museum for African American History and Culture 63
Sœurs de l'Espérance, Les (the Sisters of Hope) 223–4, 229
Solly, Samuel 176, 178, 180
songs. *See* hymns
sonic discipline 11, 116, 118–19, 121–2, 124, 126
sound 7–8, 115–26, 258
South Africa 11, 63, 116–17, 124–6, 173, 179–81
South African War 124, 126, 145
South Kensington, London 13, 74, 282–3, 285–96
South Kensington Museum 10, 13, 74, 287–91, 294. *See also* Victoria and Albert Museum (V&A)
spectating 13, 257, 263, 266–7, 271–2. *See also* museums
Spivak, Gayatri Chakravorty 7, 91, 162–3
stakeholder communities 31–2, 36, 39–42, 45
stakeholders, museum sector 10, 35–6, 41, 79
Steedman, Carolyn 1, 7, 15, 189, 222–3, 232, 239–41, 250
Stevens, Leonie 139, 144, 146
Stoler, Ann Laura 71, 137–9, 160, 188, 264, 281–2
storage 31, 33–4, 41, 46, 73, 242
subaltern 7, 11, 126, 148, 163–4
Sunday School 211, 258–9, 266–7, 272
Suriname 52, 54, 57–8
Sydenham 260, 289, 293, 297 n.15

Tamboli, Medai 157–8
Tanjore 10, 91–8, 103, 287
taxonomies, racial 282–7
Taylor, Diana 240, 248, 250, 252 n.4, 253 n.49
theatre
  archives 251 n.1
  East End 247–8
  history 240–51
Theatre and Performance Collections 241–2, 247–8. *See also* Victoria and Albert Museum (V&A)

Torin, Benjamin 91, 95–7, 103, 106
torture 57, 118, 120, 125–6, 158–9, 161–3
Tower Project. *See* Cambridge University Library
Training Schools 142–4, 293
trauma 117, 119, 124, 126, 129 n.18
Tropenmuseum 9–10, 51–7, 61, 63, 281, 296
Trouillot, Michel-Rolph 120–1, 221, 234 n.9
Truth and Reconciliation Commission (TRC) 116–17, 123–5

United Kingdom (UK) 10, 32, 37–8, 48 n.33, 63, 71–3, 116, 294
United States of America 38, 122
Universities' Mission to Central Africa (UMCA) 206, 211
University of Oxford, archives in 12, 14, 32, 203–4, 206, 209–11

Venus (1996) 173–4
Victoria and Albert Museum (V&A) 9–10, 71–6, 78–9, 81, 241–2, 247–8, 281–3, 294, 296
Victorian 13, 74, 116, 118, 120–2, 125–6, 173–5, 209, 256–9, 263–4, 267, 272, 283, 287
Victoria, Queen 72, 80, 241, 282, 291, 294–5

violence 91, 145
  colonial 71, 74, 80, 144–5
  imperial 11, 138, 291
  sexual 11, 157, 159–64, 174
virtual tours 13, 255–60, 262, 265, 267, 271–2, 285
visibility 11, 58, 116, 160, 163. *See also* invisibility
visual art and culture 4, 6, 10–11, 14, 58, 91–2, 107
voice 12, 14, 35–6, 79–81, 92, 106, 115, 120, 139–41, 173, 176–9, 226

weapons 41, 43, 72–3
West End, London 239, 242
Whitla, Becca 121–2, 126
Williams, W. Mattieu 263–7, 271–2
World War II 32, 43, 291
Wybalenna 144–6

yosegaki hinomaru. *See* good luck flag
Young, Bryanne 121, 131 n.46
Young England 256–7, 260, 263, 265
Young, Hershini Bhana 176–7, 180

Zanzibar 203, 206, 209
Zola, Emile 192, 197 n.54
Zoological Society of London 94, 103–4
zoology 93–5, 103, 106

www.ingramcontent.com/pod-product-compliance
Lightning Source LLC
Chambersburg PA
CBHW052149300426
44115CB00011B/1578